Integrity *in the* Spotlight

Audit Committees

in a High Risk World

Library and Archives Canada Cataloguing in Publication

Sabia, Maureen J.
    Integrity in the spotlight : audit committees in a high risk world/
Maureen J. Sabia, James L. Goodfellow. — 2nd ed.

ISBN 1-55385-145-5

    1. Audit committees. I. Goodfellow, James L. II. Canadian Institute of
Chartered Accountants. III. Title.

HF5667.15.S22 2005   658.15'1   C2005-900069-4

Integrity *in the* Spotlight

Audit Committees in

a High Risk World

SECOND EDITION

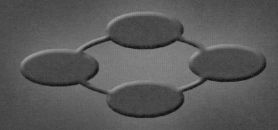

 The Canadian Institute of Chartered Accountants

Maureen J. Sabia, LLB
James L. Goodfellow, FCA

This book is dedicated to those audit committees and the auditors who advise them for whom integrity, transparency, discipline of oversight and accountability are sacred obligations.

Foreword

Again it is a pleasure to provide an introduction to the second edition of this book. I wrote in 2002 that this book should be read by everyone who is a member of an audit committee. After the scandals of the last two years, this text continues to be a timely and useful reference guide.

The lesson from these scandals is that the work of the audit committee is crucial. Unfortunately there are no organizations giving in-depth training specifically to members of audit committees. *Integrity in the Spotlight* is an excellent place for board members to start the quest to improve their knowledge.

The authors deserve credit for updating this book. They offer experience and insight from two different perspectives.

Maureen takes the view of share owners, focusing on the responsibility of board members to ask questions of auditors and accountants, and probe to ascertain that the books are well-kept. The audit committee, which represents the owners, must know everything that an owner should know and has a duty to communicate this knowledge to them.

Jim comes from the auditing profession — those hired by the owners and their representatives, the members of audit committees. During his career, he has answered questions from audit committees and has felt that many times the wrong questions were asked. His focus here is clear and simple: it is the auditor's job to make sure that the financial results are accurate and fairly represent the affairs of the corporation. He reminds us that the role of the external auditor is essential to make our financial system work.

The audit committee has to make sure that management communicates results in a clear and concise way in annual reports as well as news releases. As representatives of the owners, they have to ask the questions that every owner would. Completing financial statements by satisfying Generally Accepted Accounting Principles is a minimum. Management has to go beyond this. Management has to make sure that owners understand where there are grey areas.

This is a great how-to book. It is a very important tool for audit committee members. Owners are grateful for this effort and board members will find solid advice based on years of experience.

Claude Lamoureux

Authors' Foreword

We have been gratified by the reception the first edition of this book has received since it was published in the fall of 2002. Five thousand copies have found their way into the hands of people curious about and committed to ways of enhancing the effectiveness of audit committees! But events have moved quickly since that time. The regulatory environment has become clearer, governance issues have evolved rapidly and the responsibilities of the audit committee have continued to grow. Audit committees have become more powerful, but with that power has come a far more onerous workload and more onerous responsibilities. The frequency with which the committee meets has increased substantially, and rules dictating its composition and independence have emerged. Questions are being raised about the potential for audit committees to evolve into mini boards and the problems that may pose.

In these circumstances, we were asked to undertake a second edition of the book. It follows the same format as the first edition, but reflects the updated regulatory environment, deals with issues arising from that changed environment and provides an enhanced focus on the critical necessity of establishing, managing and nurturing effective relationships among the board of directors, the audit committee, management and the external auditors. We continue in our belief that rules alone will not be enough. We recognize, however, that they can provide the foundation on which to build the kind of relationships that will ensure a more effective audit committee and the integrity of a company's financial information.

We believe that the fundamental principles of the first edition have weathered the recent regulatory storm of initiatives extremely well, but our real learning from the reception accorded the first edition is the importance of maintaining our focus on the critical issues of relationships, leadership and behaviours. These are the issues that, in the future, will assume greater importance than those around mere compliance with the rules, although there can be no doubt that the compliance agenda is huge. In this second edition we have increased our emphasis on these issues, and focused more emphatically on the need for the chairman of the audit committee to provide leadership on them.

Moreover, in recognition of the publicity surrounding some recent failures in the integrity of financial information, and some other corporate scandals, we have added a chapter, which provides some guidance to audit committees that find themselves in crisis situations.

On October 29, 2004, just as this second edition was about to go to print, the Canadian Securities Administrators published a *Notice of Request for Comment on Proposed National Policy 58-201 Corporate Governance Guidelines* and *Proposed National Instrument 58-101 Disclosure of Corporate Governance Practices, Form 58-101F1 and Form 58-101F2 and Proposed Amendments to Multilateral Instrument 52-110 Audit Committees, Form 52-110F1, Form 52-110F2 and Companion Policy 52-110*. The comment period for the proposed amendments to MI 52-110, "Audit Committees" ends on January 27, 2005. As a result of this late breaking news, we have added Chapter 17, in which we discuss the impact on audit committee practices of the proposed National Policy on Corporate Governance, the proposed National Instrument on the Disclosure of Corporate Governance Practices, and the proposed amendments to MI 52-110. We have also included the full text of the proposals in Appendices O and P. We urge readers to refer to this new chapter.

It is our hope that readers of the second edition will find in it some guideposts on the continuing journey to enhanced effectiveness of their audit committees.

JLG *and* MJS

About the Authors

Maureen J. Sabia, B.A., J.D., is a lawyer and director of several major Canadian companies. Since 1986, she has served on the audit committees of several corporations and chaired three of them. She is the current chairman of the audit committee of Canadian Tire Corporation, Limited.

Maureen Sabia's reputation as both a member and chairman of audit committees is characterized by her insistence on adopting and implementing leading edge practices, on rigorous standards of accountability, on high standards of disclosure, and by demanding much of audit committee members, auditors and management.

She believes that an audit committee's effectiveness is, in large part, determined by how well the relationships among the board, the audit committee, management and the external auditor are managed. She also believes that the responsibility for managing these relationships lies with the chairman of the audit committee, and therefore, for her, the choice of the right chairman is critical to the committee's effectiveness.

Maureen Sabia has served and continues to serve on the boards of several companies including Canadian Tire Corporation Limited, Canadian Tire Bank Limited, O&Y Properties Corporation, O&Y First Place Tower Inc., Hollinger Inc., Medway Capital Corporation, Gulf Canada Resources Limited, Laurential General Insurance Company, and Skyjack Inc. She has also been the chairman of the Export Development Corporation.

James L. Goodfellow, FCA, is a partner and vice chairman of Deloitte who advises boards of directors, audit committees, corporate executives and securities regulators in Canada and internationally on corporate reporting and governance related issues.

He served as research director for the Joint Committee on Corporate Governance, is a past chairman of the CICA Accounting Standards Board, and has served on the CICA's Emerging Issues Committee. He currently chairs the CICA Canadian Performance Reporting Board and is a member of the Board of Directors of the Canadian Institute of Corporate Directors.

Jim Goodfellow is a frequent speaker on issues related to financial reporting, corporate governance and audit committees. He believes strongly that the external auditor should be accountable to the board of directors and the audit committee as representatives of the shareholders, and that this repositioning of the auditor/client relationship can produce significant benefits to the effectiveness of the audit.

Jim Goodfellow has served on the board of directors of Deloitte and, in the past, served as the firm's National Director of Accounting & Auditing. He is a senior partner responsible for providing services to some of his firm's largest clients including Chrysler Canada Ltd., Nortel Networks, Canadian Tire Corporation, Limited, the Greater Toronto Airport Authority, and Mitel Networks.

Acknowledgements

We owe many debts.

The partners and staff at Deloitte not only provided us with the benefit of their wisdom and experience, many of them generously read individual chapters of this second edition of the book and made valuable suggestions. They also made it possible, once again, for JLG to spend many hours on this project.

The board and management of Canadian Tire Corporation have a history of seeking to improve continually the company's governance practices and, as such, have provided a "laboratory" in which many of the ideas in both editions of this book have been tested. Thank you for striving always to make things better.

A special word of appreciation to Claude Lamoureux who generously agreed, for a second time, to write the Foreword. Thank you, Claude, for continuing to allow some of your enormous credibility, experience, insight and wisdom to devolve on us and on this book.

Carol Hansell of Davies, Ward, Phillips & Vineberg contributed the legal overview for a second time. Thank you, Carol, for lending us your considerable stature.

Gillian Wyett of Deloitte contributed enormously to this second edition by taking on the task of updating and organizing the appendices to this book. We are very grateful to Gillian for the many ideas she contributed to the appendix material.

Hugh Miller, our editor, continued to display enormous good grace in dealing with his testy and protective authors. We thank Hugh for staying with us for the second edition.

Cheryl Saunders, who works with JLG at Deloitte, supported us once again with her generous spirit, her calm efficiency and her unfailing good humour. She is a truly courageous woman!

Our publisher, the CICA, who commissioned both the first and second edition of this book, continued to be truly professional, forgiving of some delay on our part (once again!) in producing the manuscript and providing us with continued encouragement when our creativity and energy waned. Thank you for putting up with us for a second round.

There are many others who supported us throughout this project. You know who you are. To all of you, we say a heartfelt thank you.

A last word. Collaborating on a book is not always easy. Our collaboration continues to be challenging, rewarding and fun.

JLG *and* MJS

Table of Contents

Chapters

Appendices

In the Spotlight

Beginning with the Enron debacle, the last few years have witnessed dramatic business failures and a sufficient number of significant examples of corporate malfeasance to cause investors to lose confidence in the capital markets. More particularly, they have caused investors to question the integrity of the financial information disclosed by public corporations.

These events have thrust boards of directors and audit committees into the spotlight, where they have faced, and continue to face, substantial and increasing pressure to improve significantly their oversight responsibilities. The role of both has come under intense scrutiny by securities regulators and institutional investors who, quite properly, are demanding greater integrity of financial information, greater clarity in reporting and greater transparency in disclosure. As a result, new rules governing the way in which the board and the audit committee should conduct themselves are being promulgated at a furious rate.

While it is understandable that the regulators should place their reliance on rules, and while well thought out rules can form a foundation on which to build improvements in the ways that public companies are governed, no set of rules or other legislated imperatives can guarantee that there will never be any business failures or that there will never be any egregious examples of corporate wrong doing. Investors, however, do have the right to expect our system of publicly traded equities to weather the inevitable "feast or famine" business cycles without major companies collapsing as a result of the failure of diligence, ethics, integrity, controls and transparency.

Nor are rules alone sufficient to ensure either the effectiveness of board and audit committee oversight or the integrity of financial information. Rules are just the first step. What is needed is to go beyond compliance and to embrace a fundamental change in behaviour.

We are fearful that reliance on rules alone can, in fact, be counterproductive. There are dangers inherent in a rules-only based regime. It can lead to the triumph of form over substance. For example, we believe that independence is an attitude of mind, rather than a list of business credentials. What price independence if the individual has no knowledge of the business or the industry or is incompetent? And how do you legislate judgment or leadership? Moreover, we are beginning to see a "tick the box" mentality emerging and that kind of response will do little to cause a company to invest properly in the rules themselves in order to create value for the business, to say nothing about having the incentive to invest heavily in establishing the appropriate relationships.

Audit committees have come to be recognized as the cornerstone of a successful and credible financial reporting system. As a result, the demands being placed on them and the expectations of them continue to increase exponentially.

Most audit committees have responded quickly and positively to the increasing expectations of investors and regulators. While some audit committees have had their shortcomings in the past, it is clear that there can no longer be any expectation that these weaknesses will be regarded benignly. Indeed, the climate has changed even for the many audit committees that have been discharging their duties and responsibilities diligently. More is demanded of all audit committees and there is no longer a tolerance for anything less than the highest degree of diligence.

As a public policy matter, sufficient attention has been paid to the rules that should govern boards and audit committees. Insufficient attention, however, has been paid to the behaviours that must go hand in hand with these rules if the rules are to have the desired effect. Key among these behaviours is leadership, courage and relationship building. Boards and audit committees should view making the investment in new behaviours as a significant opportunity to improve the credibility of their company's financial information and disclosure, and, hence, the company's credibility among investors. Quite simply, the risks of not doing so are just too significant.

In the rush to rules, some other critical issues have been overlooked. One is the importance of having the right corporate culture and values embedded in a company and in its CEO. Statements of corporate values abound these days, but the mere articulating of them is not enough. What counts is the actual practice, reinforced each and every day by the actions of the CEO and the management team. Senior management, particularly the CEO, lead by example and inappropriate actions by leaders in the organization, tolerance of such behaviour by the CEO, senior management and other employees, lack of accountability for such behaviour and reward systems that reinforce these behaviours will inevitably lead to a dysfunctional organization and to the kinds of problems we have all recently witnessed. Directors must not only approve values statements, they must hold management accountable for living by them. All the governance rules in the world will be inadequate to protect the company and its directors and shareholders if the company's real culture is inappropriate or dysfunctional.

Another and related issue is the information challenge. Directors need to know what is really going on in the company. Often, when information comes to them primarily through the CEO or the CFO, it is filtered. There may not be any malice in this; it may simply arise out of a positive bias on the part of the senior management. But problems can result if this bias is excessive and the true picture of the company's results, prospects, potential problems or risks is concealed from the board until it is too late. The challenge facing directors is how to assess the quality of the information given to them. In the case of the audit committee, the existence of internal audit and the external auditor provide valuable assistance, but this may not be enough. Both the audit committee and the board need to know what is going on both at and below the CEO and CFO levels. This is not easy, but it becomes virtually impossible without the right relationships in place and without the right values in place. In an organization that embraces an accountability culture, there will be a bias towards telling the truth, towards open, direct and shared communications; there will be much less fear of reprisal if employees and management do speak out if they see major problems and risks that are being inadequately addressed or disclosed; and the chances of the board getting an early warning increase exponentially.

The challenge for directors is to be proactive, even nosy, while respecting management. Time invested in relationship-building, relationship-nurturing and in getting to know the people in decision-making roles in the organization will pay huge dividends in solving the information challenge. This takes time, energy and commitment.

We strongly urge boards and audit committees to select directors prepared to commit the time, energy, courage and persistence to do the job. The "we are here to support management" philosophy so rampant a few short years ago must give way to the philosophy of "we are here to hold management accountable, and while we will not manage the company, we will forge the relationships with management that will permit us to more effectively fulfill our responsibilities to the shareholders and that will provide us with an effective platform on which to build the necessary checks and balances that will encourage the appropriate corporate behaviour".

This is a "how to" book. Its objective is to provide readers with practical suggestions for making the transition from the more traditional audit committee to the new audit committee demanded today. It is important to make a real transition — one of substance and not merely of form. A transition that only addresses the form will result in an audit committee that provides investors, and itself, with a false sense of security.

This book will deal with both the rules governing audit committees and the behaviours that should be expected of them. It will provide tools and techniques for improving the performance of the audit committee similar to those that were provided in the first edition of this book, but these have been updated and refined in order to reflect the current regulatory environment. Many of the best practices that we described in the first edition have now been codified into minimum requirements.

While events in the marketplace have put audit committees into the spotlight, the onus is on boards of directors and on audit committees to seize the opportunities that have been presented to them to enhance the quality and the effectiveness of their oversight. Investing in real (as opposed to "tick the box") compliance with the rules, making a commitment to go beyond compliance and making a substantial investment in enhancing the relationships among the board, the audit committee, management and the external auditor will pay enormous dividends.

A Perspective on Audit Committee Evolution

Recent high profile corporate scandals have undermined investors' confidence in the capital markets and, in particular, in the integrity of the financial information disclosed by public corporations. While the financial, employment and wider economic damage caused by these events is far reaching, some good will arise out of these unfortunate occurrences if they serve as a stimulus to reinforce the integrity of financial reporting and protect against similar events occurring in the future.

Quality of earnings, transparency of disclosure and integrity of reporting can no longer be considered as mere compliance issues. These are factors that can significantly affect investor confidence, share values and ultimately the enterprise's cost of capital. Today, no company can afford any suspicions about the quality of its financial reporting or any hint of accounting irregularities or rumours of investigation by securities regulators. An increased focus on the integrity of information is not an optional exercise, it is an essential one. Moreover, there is another compelling reason for management to ensure integrity and rigour in their accounting practices. Bad accounting leads to bad decision-making, and can impact the allocation of capital and resources within the company.

While we continue to believe that the majority of companies' financial reporting adheres to high standards of quality and integrity, there is clearly room for enhanced oversight on the part of directors, audit committees and auditors. By the same token, there is an increased need for CEOs and CFOs to set very high standards of integrity in their organizations. Zero tolerance should be their standard. We believe that the existing and future certification requirements will provide the catalyst for both the CEO and the CFO to insist on the highest degree of integrity, rigour and discipline in their organizations.

With respect to the role of management in the governance equation, we feel compelled to sound a cautionary note. Governance is now seen as the key to eradicating management malfeasance and to maximizing value. We question that point of view. Boards do not manage. The focus on the board of directors has obscured the fact that boards are only one part of the equation. Management is the other critical player. At least as much emphasis must be put on the expectations of management as is put on those of the board. And while the board must play a role in setting those expectations, no board can ensure that their expectations will be met without the full co-operation and commitment of management.

In addition to the board of directors, corporate reporting involves three players — the audit committee, management and the external auditor. Concerns about the quality of such reporting are being played out against a backdrop of changing business conditions, a plethora of new accounting standards, investor anxiety, media paranoia and an ever-increasing pressure to "meet your numbers" and "street expectations".

Figure 1 | **The Financial Reporting Environment**

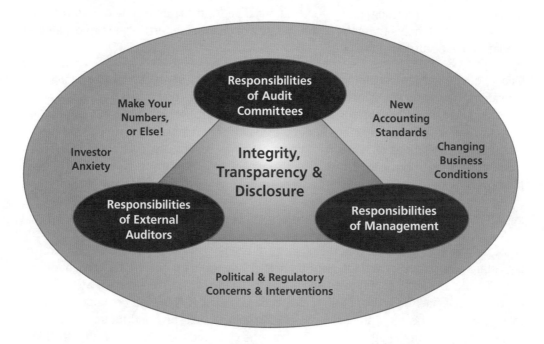

Unfortunately, the public has been treated to a continuous parade of financial reporting irregularities, executive greed, fraud, conflicts of interest, losses caused by management self-interest, and directors and auditors who appear to have been ineffective in protecting shareholders' interests. There are some who suggest this has generated a crisis of confidence in our capital markets, which results in part from increasing skepticism about the integrity of business in general. Irrespective of the perception of the problem — or whether this crisis is real or not — key components of any solution to strengthen confidence in business and the capital markets will be the integrity of management and the enhanced effectiveness of audit committees and external auditors.

The time has come for a significant shift in audit committee behaviour. The new rules that govern audit committee practices have made it certain that traditional or "old" audit committee practices must give way to the new practices. But the new practices will be greatly enhanced in terms of their efficacy if the audit committee also embraces new behaviours, which go beyond compliance with the new requirements. The audit committee's shift in behaviour will also require substantial behavioural changes for both management and the external auditor, resulting in a very different dynamic among all these players. The board of directors will also be affected, since the audit committee is a creature of the board.

The Evolution of Audit Committees

For nearly two decades, we have watched with interest the evolution of audit committees, how the expectations of audit committees and external auditors have changed and how each have or have not responded to evolving standards and changing business conditions.

When we began to serve on and advise audit committees, we were dismayed by the narrowness of the audit committee's focus and how perfunctory was the agenda for meetings and, as a consequence, how perfunctory was the review of issues. We recall a time when some chairmen worked to keep audit committee meetings as brief as possible, and spent little time with senior financial and operational management to gain an understanding of the issues affecting the financial statements and the accompanying disclosure. We remember when little attention was paid to the role of internal audit and to risk management.

We also recall how little time and effort was spent establishing (to say nothing of enhancing) the relationships between the external auditor and the audit committee, between the external auditor and management, and between management and the audit committee. Some audit committee chairmen made superficial and perfunctory reports to the full board (indeed some chairmen consistently asked management to write their reports to the board). Little time was spent by audit committee chairmen in meeting privately with the external auditor and rarely, if at all, did audit committees hold *in camera* meetings with the external auditor, with management and with their members.

> ### The Old Audit Committee
>
> - Underutilized
> - Not empowered
> - Dominated by management
> - Reactive
> - Focused on compliance with minimum legal requirements
> - Uncertain as to role beyond minimum legal requirements
> - Little attention paid to relationships
> - Dealt with the external auditor principally through management
> - Minimum involvement in the selection of members and chairman
> - Undemanding
> - Superficial
> - Lacking in courage

We remember how little attention was given to educating audit committee members about the operational or financial initiatives that might have the potential to affect financial reporting and disclosure. Many audit committee members were remarkably undemanding of the material presented to them and of the timeliness of its presentation. If the audit committee had a written mandate at all, it was a superficial one.

In short, we were amazed and disappointed at how mechanically and narrowly many audit committees operated and how little was expected of them.

Gradually, greater demands were made of audit committees and, indeed, changes were made for the better. But it was not until a few years ago, beginning with the New York Stock Exchange and National Association of Securities Dealers' Blue Ribbon Committee on Improving the Effectiveness of Corporate Audit Committees (and in Canada with the Joint Committee on Corporate Governance), that the spotlight was focused more brightly on the role and functioning of audit committees. These initiatives were followed by the *Sarbanes-Oxley Act* of 2002 that was enacted in the United States and more recently by Multilateral Instrument 52-110, "Audit Committees" issued by the Canadian Securities Administrators (CSA), which is based on the requirements that had been adopted in the United States.

We applaud this continued evolution. For too long, audit committees have been underutilized and expectations of them have been woefully insufficient. For too long, those of us who called for more effective use of audit committees and higher expectations for their performance have been in a small and often derided minority.

The Corporate Governance System

Today, the audit committee is widely recognized as a senior board committee that has "front line" governance responsibilities related not merely to financial reporting, but also to the oversight of continuous disclosure, corporate reporting and soon, internal controls and risk management.

It is important to consider the audit committee's role in the context of the governance process of the corporation as a whole. As a committee of the board, the audit committee must carry out its duties within the framework of the governance principles and practices established by the board of directors. Good governance promotes accountability of the key players, and ensures that management works in the best interests of the company and its shareholders to enhance shareholder value, while taking into account the legitimate interests of other stakeholders. The audit committee's role, and its commensurate accountability to the board, is directly related to how the board chooses to discharge its oversight function. The audit committee's effectiveness is directly linked to that of the board, and therefore many of the issues that impact the audit committee's effectiveness are also likely to impact the effectiveness of the board.

There are four key players in the financial governance process: the board of directors, the audit committee, the external auditor and management. Management includes financial executives, such as the CFO, treasurer, controller and head of internal audit, and non-financial executives, such as the CEO, CIO, and COO.

These players must consider both their own roles and responsibilities and also how they interact with each other and work together. Indeed, the quality of financial and corporate reporting is ultimately determined by the players' effectiveness in working together as a system.

We believe that corporate governance should be viewed as a "system", and the interaction and interdependency among the players is key. Most studies of governance focus on structure and many of the rules promulgated by the CSA's multilateral instruments are related to structural issues. While structure is important, we believe a critical factor in determining how well an audit committee fulfills its responsibilities is the relationships the committee forges with management, the external auditor and board of directors. Equally important is the quality of communications among them. These factors will determine the integrity of financial information and the clarity with which it is disclosed. Without effective and productive relationships, and direct and unequivocal communication, the audit committee will never be an effective cornerstone of a successful financial reporting system.

Figure 2 | **The Traditional Model of Corporate Governance**

When audit committees were first introduced the relationships among the parties were often very hierarchical and linear (see Figure 2).

The audit committee's focus was usually restricted to reviewing the annual financial statements, the external auditor's report and the audit fee. While the auditor was appointed at the annual general meeting, the firm was for all practical purposes retained by management and the auditor's fees and scope of services were negotiated with management. The audit committee was a legislative creature that was inserted between management and the board. The auditor often appeared to be little more than an extension of management at the audit committee meetings.

Changes occurred over the years. In more progressive companies, the working relationship among the board, management and the audit committee evolved and matured. This evolution was often dictated by the expansion of the audit committee's role to include oversight of internal control, the management of financial risks and, more recently, quarterly reporting. With this expanded responsibility, audit committees have required greater assurances from both management and the external auditors over a much broader range of issues.

In 2001, the Joint Committee on Corporate Governance (JCCG) examined this issue and in its Report made the following observation:[1]

> *We believe that the relationship between audit committees and the external auditors could be improved in most companies. Fundamental to such improvement is a mutual recognition that the external auditors are accountable to shareholders, and to the board and audit committee as their representatives. The external auditors are not accountable to management. Both audit committees and auditors need to work hard to improve this relationship, and management needs to understand and support their efforts.*

[1] *Beyond Compliance: Building a Governance Culture.* Final Report, Joint Committee on Corporate Governance, November 2001, page 30.

In 2004, MI 52-110 codified the view that the external auditor is accountable to the board of directors and the audit committee, as representatives of the shareholders, and that these shareholder representatives have the ultimate authority and responsibility to select, evaluate and, where appropriate, recommend replacement of the external auditor.

In the United States, the *Sarbanes-Oxley Act* embraces a similar model. That Act, however, provides more specificity to the concept.

Figure 3 | **The New Model of Corporate Governance**

In the new model of corporate governance (see Figure 3), the auditor is accountable to shareholders through the audit committee and the board. We believe, however, that the auditor should also be in continuous dialogue with and have much stronger working relationships with the audit committee and, where required, with the board itself. This results in a much more dynamic and stronger working relationship.

In this model, all parties understand their roles and what is expected of them and each other. They must be prepared to take action when other parties do not fulfill their obligations because — in a system that is only as strong as its weakest link — all players must work co-operatively to ensure that the system as a whole operates effectively and efficiently.

The task of forging productive and effective relationships is not one that lends itself to simple, mechanical, "one size fits all" solutions or to regulated solutions. Rather, it is up to the key players themselves to develop such relationships in their organizations — something that can be done if each player possesses the necessary commitment to doing so.

The New Audit Committee

- Increasing expectations
- More onerous responsibilities
- More accountable
- Empowered
- Prepared
- Pro-active
- Not dominated by management
- Focused on appropriate, not minimum requirements
- Focused on relationships
- Educated and current with developments (inside and outside the corporation)
- Insistent on high quality and timely materials and presentations
- Willing to commit the time required
- Insistent on candid and direct communication
- Independent
- Financially literate
- Demanding
- Courageous

Audit committees must have leadership, vision, discipline and, very importantly, the courage to ask tough questions and expect informative answers. In addition, to be effective, audit committees must acquire sufficient information about the business to understand the critical issues that impact financial reporting. For these reasons, audit committees must be made up of the right people — those who have the right knowledge, skills and commitment, and are willing to devote the time necessary to understand the business, prepare for meetings and attend more frequent and longer meetings. In addition, audit committees should foster an environment of open and direct communication. This is essential to the committee's effectiveness.

The chairman of the audit committee must be committed, hard-working, persistent and willing and able to devote sufficient time to his or her duties. Because we believe the chairman has the key task of championing the relationship-building process, his or her selection is a very important part of ensuring the integrity of financial reporting.

Management must be an integral part of the relationship-building process. The CEO and CFO must adopt new attitudes, be willing to relinquish, even a little, the ever-present territorial games in favour of building relationships, and be committed to direct and candid dialogue with the audit committee, its chairman and the external auditor.

The external auditor must also have courage and skills. The external auditor is nominated by, works for, and is accountable to the audit committee and the board of directors. Auditors, therefore, need to understand the changing expectations that audit committees have for their performance. Conflicts or tensions may arise between what the audit committee expects, what management desires, and the auditor's professional responsibilities. The auditor must be able to work in this environment and build the requisite levels of trust with both management and the audit committee.

Making the transition from the "old" to the "new" is function of both compliance and going beyond compliance. This is not an easy task. It starts with the right people and requires effective leadership. Over the next few chapters, we will present ideas and suggestions to help guide audit committees in making this important transition.

We wish, however, to emphasize that even the most committed, disciplined, rigorous, courageous, qualified and hard-working audit committee will never be a substitute for a management that is not committed to acting with integrity in all matters and at all times. Nor can the external auditor be such a substitute.

Managing the Transition

- Start with the right people
- Choose the right chairman
- Have a clear understanding of what the audit committee will and will not do
- Forge the right relationships with:
  - Management
  - External auditor
  - Board of Directors
- Hold management and the external auditors accountable
- Encourage a culture of candid, open, direct communication
- Understand the value of an educated committee
- Hold regular, separate *in camera* meetings to assess progress

---

If management has a laissez-faire attitude towards integrity, the audit committee and the external auditor have a responsibility to inform the board, and to urge the board to take appropriate action. Boards should not retain a CEO or CFO who does not insist upon and foster an environment of the highest integrity. There should be no tolerance for management behaviour of the type that appears to have been tolerated at Enron or in other situations where public lapses of good corporate conduct have occurred.

Audit committees find themselves in the spotlight to provide more rigorous oversight — which is clearly necessary. But the spotlight should also be turned on both management and the board in ensuring that the CEO adheres to the highest standards of corporate good conduct, both personally and in his or her executive team.

Key Messages

- The imperative for change cannot be ignored. Changes must be changes of substance, not merely of form.
- Rules are just the first step. There is a need to go beyond compliance and to embrace new behaviours.
- Corporate governance is a system. The interaction and interdependence of the board, audit committee, external auditor and management is of primary importance.
- The shift from old-style audit committees to new-style audit committees will provide opportunities for enhanced quality of oversight and added value.

3

A Roadmap for Transition

The transition from "old" to "new" is always challenging, but the process can be made easier with a framework to guide it. Our framework is built on five key factors that determine the audit committee's effectiveness.

This chapter briefly describes each factor and how all of them interact to contribute to the audit committee's effectiveness. More detailed discussions of each factor are the subjects of the following chapters.

In its June 24, 2002 issue, *Fortune* magazine published a feature article, which described the challenges facing corporate America:[1]

> *Phony earnings, inflated revenues, conflicted Wall Street analysts, directors asleep at the switch — this isn't just a few bad apples we're talking about here. This, my friends, is a systemic breakdown. Nearly every known check on corporate behavior — moral, regulatory, you name it — fell by the wayside, replaced by the stupendous greed that marked the end of the bubble. And that has created a crisis of investor confidence the likes of which hasn't been seen since — well, since the Great Depression.*

The loss of confidence in the capital markets and in the financial information reported by companies is not confined to the United States but has extended throughout the world. This has created an undeniable "imperative for change" in how business everywhere is conducted and in its accountability, including the transparency and integrity of financial reporting. As a result, the public and regulatory pressure on management, boards of directors, audit committees and auditors has become very intense, and relief is not likely anytime soon.

---

[1] "System Failure; Corporate America has lost its way. Here's a road map for restoring confidence", Joseph Nocera, *Fortune*, June 24, 2002.

With audit committees squarely in the public and regulatory spotlight, expectations of their performance have exploded exponentially. To meet these expectations, audit committees must not only set themselves much higher standards of rigour and discipline, they must also ensure that they deploy their resources wisely and efficiently, concentrating on the areas of highest priority.

Elements of Effectiveness

The fundamental basis of audit committee effectiveness is, in our view, the relationship between the audit committee and the board of directors. The audit committee operates in the context of the board's corporate governance principles and structure; therefore its effectiveness is related directly to the effectiveness of the board as a whole. It is difficult to imagine a situation where a corporation could have an effective audit committee in the context of an ineffective or dysfunctional board.

The factors that ensure an audit committee's effectiveness are its ability to:

- *Do the right things.* Audit committees need to understand clearly what they will do and what they will not do. A charter helps audit committees keep a sharp focus on the most important corporate reporting issues and business risks, set their priorities clearly and know what they want to accomplish.
- *Have the right people.* Audit committees comprise a chairman and group of directors with the requisite commitment, business experience, knowledge and financial expertise that are commensurate with the critical issues facing the company's business and corporate reporting. The audit committee must also be supported by competent people from management and the external audit firm.
- *Manage critical relationships.* Audit committees, led by their chairmen, need to manage a complex set of relationships, including those with the board of directors, the external auditor, management (including internal audit) and other advisors, such as outside corporate counsel and investment bankers.
- *Do the right things right.* It takes more than a well thought out mandate, good people and the ability to build and manage key relationships to make an audit committee effective. Audit committees also need to establish the right processes to guide their meetings and discussions. The chairman must be a strong leader who knows what information and assurances the committee needs to discharge its responsibilities — and ensures this information is provided on a timely basis and in appropriate detail.
- *Strive for continuous improvement.* Audit committees must be accountable for their actions, and should report regularly though the chairman to the board of directors and externally to shareholders and the investment community. They must also continually assess their performance and improve their effectiveness.

Figure 4 | **Elements of Audit Committee Effectiveness**

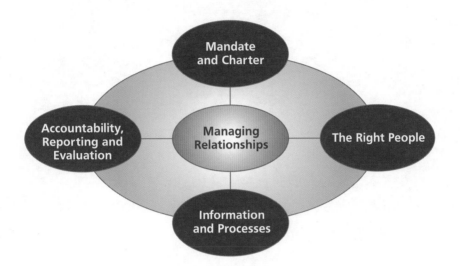

Figure 4 illustrates the components of audit committee effectiveness, and how all of them must work together and be integrated in a manner that contributes towards enhancing the integrity of the information. In other words, addressing the individual components alone is not sufficient to ensure effectiveness — a comprehensive approach must be adopted.

Such an approach requires leadership. It falls to the audit committee chairman to play a critical role in leading and managing the committee. The other parties — including other committee members, management and the external auditor — must also do their part to ensure that each component is addressed and that all work together towards a common objective.

Key Messages
- *The imperative for change requires a comprehensive response, not an ad hoc one.*
- *Changes to the audit committee can only take place in the context of a board governance structure that supports and encourages it.*
- *The audit committee must address all elements of audit committee effectiveness.*

An Overview of Capital Market Reform

Financial reporting scandals such as Enron, Worldcom and others have produced the most comprehensive reform of securities legislation in the United States since the introduction of the Securities Acts of 1933 and 1934. In response, legislators and regulators around the globe, recognizing that capital moves across geographical boundaries at the speed of light, had little appetite for having their domestic markets viewed as less attractive. As a result, the U.S. capital market reforms are having a direct, albeit uneven, impact on the regulation of capital markets around the world.

The efficiency of capital markets depends on well-developed securities laws, stock exchange regulations and enforcement mechanisms that ensure that all issuers and investors are treated fairly and equitably. It also depends on companies providing timely, accurate and reliable information to investors, especially financial reports, to help them assess the performance and financial condition of listed companies and make investment decisions. When investors lose confidence in the integrity of financial reporting, the public loses confidence in the integrity of the markets themselves posing a serious threat to one of the fundamental underpinnings of our free enterprise system.

While Canada has a well-developed and highly respected set of securities laws and regulations, it is not immune to financial reporting and other corporate scandals. The reform of its securities legislation and regulation, however, must take into account the unique characteristics of the Canadian economy. Effective market regulation that encompasses the needs of both large and small public companies is particularly challenging for Canada, a relatively small market that is highly integrated with that of the United States and one in which many large companies go outside the country for capital.

Currently, 177 Canadian public companies are listed on both Canadian and U.S. stock exchanges. These companies must comply with the *Sarbanes-Oxley Act* and the requirements of the SEC and are, therefore, operating at "North American" if not "world class" standards. While they include some of Canada's most prominent companies and account for approximately 70% of the market capitalization of the TSX, they represent just 5% of the listed companies in Canada. Of the remaining 95% of Canadian public companies, many are very small and approximately 40% have a market capitalization of less than $50 million. The policy question now bedeviling Canadian regulators is: should the new standards being imposed on the inter-listed 5% also be applied to the 95%?

Some argue that being a public company brings with it certain fundamental obligations that all such companies must meet — irrespective of their size, industry, geographical location etc. They suggest that the credibility of Canada's markets is critical to economic growth and requires harmonization with the United States, our largest trading partner, to ensure a free flow of capital across the border. Others argue that this approach would impose an undue burden on smaller public companies, which would restrict the flow of capital to them, stifling economic growth. This debate is further complicated by the lack of a national securities regulator, which raises questions as to "who speaks for Canada" — a subject to which we will return later in this chapter.

Capital Market Reforms

The Government of Ontario and the Ontario Securities Commission have been catalysts for capital market reform in Canada. A recent milestone in this reform was contained in amendments to the *Ontario Securities Act*, which were included in what is commonly referred to as "Bill 198" or the *Budget Measures Act of* 2002.

Two key components of this legislation, which came into force in April, 2003, gave the OSC the authority to issue regulations with respect to audit committees and CEO/CFO certification, and to impose tougher penalties under Ontario securities laws.

Three further amendments, which relate to the civil liability for secondary market disclosure, fraud and market manipulation, and misleading or untrue statements offences, have yet to be proclaimed but are expected to be in the near future.

The New CSA Instruments

Another milestone in capital market reform in Canada was reached on January 16, 2004. On that date, the Canadian Securities Administrators released three significant instruments: Multilateral Instrument 52-110, "Audit Committees" contained the final rules for audit committees; Multilateral Instrument 52-109, "Certification of Disclosure in Issuer's Annual and Interim Filings" set out the rules for CEO and CFO certification; and National Instrument 52-108, "Auditor Oversight" addressed the rules around auditor oversight.

While the new requirements of these instruments are based on those that have been implemented in the United States, specifically as a result of the *Sarbanes-Oxley Act* and the SEC regulations, the CSA modified a small number of them to be more responsive to the needs of the Canadian market. Some amendments to certain *Sarbanes-Oxley* requirements have been made, for example the U.S. requires the audit committee to have a financial expert on the committee, while Canada requires only financial literacy for membership on the audit committee, and provides an exemption for Venture Exchange-listed companies from some of the criteria mandated for qualification for membership on the audit committee. In addition, the CSA continues to study both the substance and timing of certain other potential requirements, for example, management reporting on internal control.

While any differences between the requirements in the United States and Canada may create some challenges for inter-listed companies, every effort has been made to ensure that compliance with the more stringent U.S. requirements will satisfy the Canadian rules.

The new rules, with certain exceptions, apply to "reporting issuers". The term "reporting issuers" includes listed public companies but is not restricted to them. For example, income trusts are reporting issuers but not public companies as they are not incorporated entities. As a result of the new rules, income trusts are now subject to the new requirements for audit committees, whereas previously they had not been subject to the TSX rules for listed companies. The significance of the application of the newly mandated audit committee rules becomes apparent when one considers that there are approximately 8,000 reporting issuers in Canada compared with approximately 3,600 listed public companies.[1]

The new instruments will have a significant and pervasive impact on audit committees, external auditors and on management. These instruments, together with the penalties contained in the enabling legislation, the accounting standards that govern financial reporting and the various disclosure requirements released by the CSA, may be organized in four key dimensions as illustrated in Figure 5.

---

[1] In this book we use the term "company" to include all reporting issuers.

Figure 5 | **Four Dimensions of Capital Market Reform**

Audit Committees
• Director Independence
• Financial Literacy
• Relationship with External Auditors

Regulation of Auditors
• Canadian Public Accountability Board
• Auditor Independence

Financial Reporting (Management)
• Accounting Standards
• Continuous Disclosure Requirements
• Management Discussion and Analysis
• CEO and CFO Certification
   • Presents Fairly
   • Disclosure Control
   • Internal Control

Penalties
• Fines and Sanctions
• Disgorgement
• Civil Liability for Disclosures in Secondary Markets

The new instruments are discussed in detail in the following chapters:

• The impact of MI 52-110 on the audit committee's role and responsibilities is addressed in Chapter 5, Doing the Right Things.

• The impact of MI 52-110 on the independence and other qualifications of audit committee members is addressed in Chapter 7, The Right People.

• The impact of MI 52-110 and NI 52-108 on the external auditor, as well as the Canadian Public Accountability Board and the Canadian Institute of Chartered Accountants' new independence standards for auditors are addressed in Chapter 6, Audit Committees and the External Auditor.

• A summary of the CEO and CFO certification requirements of MI 52-109, together with our assessment of the implications for audit committees, is addressed in Chapter 12, CEO and CFO Certification.

• The new rules contained in the instruments complement the CSA's National Instruments on Continuous Disclosure and Acceptable Accounting Principles, which are discussed in Chapter 11, Corporate Reporting.

• The new penalties and proposed civil liability for continuous disclosure in the secondary markets is discussed later in this chapter.

Further material is provided for reference in the appendices:
- The text of MI 52-110 is provided in Appendix B.
- The executive summary of the CICA discussion brief, CEO *and* CFO *Certification —* *Improving Transparency and Accountability*, is presented in Appendix L. The required certificates for the CEO and CFO certification are included in Appendix M, and the text of MI 52-109 is provided in Appendix N.

The multilateral instruments were adopted by 12 of the 13 Canadian Securities Administrators. British Columbia was the sole exception. It was because there was one exception that these instruments were entitled "Multilateral Instruments" and not "National Policies", which is what the CSA normally entitles their pronouncements.

Implementation of the instruments has been effected in different ways across the country. They have been implemented as a rule in each of Quebec, Alberta, Manitoba, Ontario, Nova Scotia, and Newfoundland and Labrador. In Saskatchewan and Nunavut they have been implemented as a commission regulation. In each of New Brunswick, Prince Edward Island and the Yukon, they have been implemented as a policy, and in the Northwest Territories, they have been implemented as a code.

Notwithstanding the different nomenclatures of the implementing vehicles, the requirements of the instruments are imperatives, and are not mere guidelines.

Both MI 52-110 and MI 52-109 contain companion policies, which expand on the requirements of the instruments themselves.

When the new Canadian regulatory regime is fully implemented, its requirements will be similar to those in the United States. It is important to note, however, that the instruments dealing with financial reporting are being introduced in three phases. Figure 6 illustrates the effective dates for a company with a December 31 year-end. Companies with year-ends other than December 31 should consult the instrument for guidance.

Figure 6 | **Effectiveness Schedule for Multilateral Instruments**

| | Audit Committee Requirements | CEO and CFO Certification | | Management Report on Internal Control |
		Fairly Present Certification	Certification of Disclosure Controls	
2004 Interim	■	✓	■	■
2004 Annual	■	✓	■	■
2005 Interim	✓	✓	■	■
2005 Annual	✓	✓	✓	TBA
2006 Interim	✓	✓	✓	■
2006 Annual	✓	✓	✓	TBA

NOTES: 1) Issuers listed on the TSX Venture Exchange are exempted from certain audit committee requirements.
2) Audit committee requirements become effective on the earlier of the first annual meeting of the issuer after July 1, 2004, and July 1, 2005.
3) The management reporting on internal control requirements have, at time of writing, not been finalized.

Audit committees and management should not lose sight of the fact that the full implementation of the requirements of these multilateral instruments (especially the management report on internal control) will place a further burden on the CFO and on the finance function and, indeed, on the audit committee, compounding their current struggle to deal with enhanced disclosure requirements, new accounting standards and shorter filing deadlines. Audit committees must take steps to ensure that management has a comprehensive and practical plan to enable the company to meet the compliance deadlines. The committee should review the CFO's implementation plan, assess its reasonableness, including the allocation of resources to this task, and monitor its implementation.

Penalties, Sanctions and Civil Liability

As part of capital market reform, securities regulators in Canada and abroad continue to revise the various penalties and sanctions and to strengthen their enforcement activities and resources. While the following overview focuses on the proposals and actions in Ontario, other Canadian jurisdictions have also taken own steps to strengthen their penalties and sanctions.

The amendments to the Ontario Securities Act of 2002:

- increased the maximum court fines for general offences to $5 million from $1 million and maximum prison terms from two years to five years less a day; and
- provided the OSC with the authority to impose administrative fines of up to $1 million for securities law violations and to order disgorgements, which would require offenders give up the profits they gained from violations of the Securities Act. The OSC can use the amounts it receives from "disgorged profits" to assist any third parties approved by the Minister of Finance.

When the amendments contained in the Ontario legislation are fully implemented, it will be an offence to commit fraud and market manipulation through omissions or misrepresentations made in public disclosures, including those required by continuous disclosure regulations. The legislation will also enable the OSC to seek quasi-criminal sanctions against those engaged in such activities, including management and audit committees.

It is interesting that, while legislators have strengthened the powers of the securities regulators to impose penalties and sanctions, the courts have indicated a willingness to review the penalties and sanctions imposed by securities regulators. A recent decision by the Ontario Divisional Court appears to suggest that, while the courts will continue to defer to decisions made by securities regulators, they are not opposed to providing judicial scrutiny of regulatory imposed penalties and sanctions and may, therefore, provide a check on the enhanced powers of the securities regulators.

The Ontario government's stated intention to implement civil liability for secondary market disclosure has important implications for all officers and directors. Institutional investors have argued for years that Canadian investors face significant hurdles and obstacles in suing corporations and their officers and directors for false and misleading disclosure, especially when compared with the rights of investors in the United States. The proposed civil remedies put forward in the Ontario legislation, while less onerous than those in the United States, will provide Canadian investors with a means to seek redress when they have suffered damages as a result of misleading disclosure. This type of legislation will, of course, increase the risks for the audit committee should the financial disclosures made by the company be found to be materially incomplete or misleading. It should, therefore, motivate companies to comply with their continuous disclosure and financial reporting obligations, and motivate audit committees to be vigilant in their oversight of these activities and related controls.

Finally, the securities regulators have been trying to develop more effective working relationships with the law enforcement groups who have the responsibilities for criminal prosecutions. The OSC has entered into a strategic alliance with the RCMP, and formed a joint Securities Fraud Unit to detect and disrupt criminal activity in the capital markets, with a particular focus on detecting organized crime activity in the stock market.

Canada's Response to Initiatives in the United States: The Rationale

The response of the CSA to the initiatives taken in the U.S. has not been without controversy. There are many who believe that, rather than following the American lead, a uniquely "made in Canada solution" should have been sought. We disagree. The fact of the matter is that there is only one market: the North American market. And there is another fact: the attributes of the Canadian market in terms of size and dependency make it essential that there be no significant differences between Canada and the United States in terms of each country's securities regulation.

Given Canada's dependence on the larger U.S. market, it is not surprising that many of the initiatives taken in the United States should have found their way to Canada, whether in the same or somewhat altered form. Moreover, the smaller size of the Canadian market and the significant requirements of our markets for capital make it essential that Canada render its capital markets as attractive as possible to both domestic and foreign investors.

A distinguishing feature of the North American economy is the close relationship between the Canadian and American economies, with their highly integrated trading and capital markets. This close inter-relation makes it imperative that Canadian and U.S. responses to the lack of confidence in the integrity of corporate information do not diverge significantly, and that investors and business people on both sides of the border understand the initiatives each country is taking to restore and maintain confidence in the capital markets.

The objective in both countries is a common one: to create an environment that is more successful in holding management, directors and their advisors accountable to shareholders, thereby restoring credibility to and confidence in their capital markets. For regulators in Canada, ensuring that Canadian standards are not too dissimilar to those in the United States is important, since they have a responsibility to maintain the attractiveness of the Canadian capital markets.

As Canadian companies look increasingly to the larger U.S. markets for growth opportunities and for capital, they transform themselves from purely Canadian businesses to North American and global businesses. Thus, the impact of American regulatory initiatives and American corporate governance practices has become more and more important to them. The result of this transformation has been to create greater awareness in Canada of U.S. regulatory initiatives and best practices and to encourage their adoption, where appropriate, by Canadian companies. Cross-border directorships have also contributed to the adoption of these initiatives and practices.

Maintaining the attractiveness of Canadian capital markets for investors whether institutional or otherwise, whether domestic or foreign, is an absolute necessity. Canadian governance and financial reporting standards and practices, including an enhanced and more rigorous role for audit committees, must be part of the strategy for maintaining competitive advantage and as such, must be of a comparable quality to those existing in other jurisdictions, specifically those in the United States.

Not all provinces in Canada, however, agree with the desirability of harmonizing our securities laws and regulations with those in the United States. British Columbia has been the most vocal critic, having recently passed new legislation focused on reducing the number of rules and fundamentally changing the structure of many existing requirements.

Issues, Challenges and Questions

The issues currently being debated by the business community, regulators and investors revolve around the role of securities laws, improving the efficiency of the regulatory systems and harmonizing rules, practices and standards.

The Role of Securities Law in Regulating Corporate Governance Practices

Prior to the introduction of the *Sarbanes-Oxley Act* as part of U.S. securities legislation, corporate governance standards and practices in the United States were part of the corporate law and the corporate legislative framework. In Canada, with the CSA's introduction of its new instruments, specifically MI 52-110 and MI 52-109, Canadian governance standards and practices have become much more the subject of securities laws, and much less the subject of corporate law. This is still a matter of some controversy. There are those who do not believe governance practices are an appropriate subject for securities laws. In their opinion, securities laws should be reserved for disclosure and market regulation, while governance should be left to the corporate law.

Sarbanes-Oxley and MI 52-109 and MI 52-110 provide the SEC and Canadian securities commissions, respectively, with regulatory influence and a measure of control over audit committees. Therefore, we have included relevant portions of all three, not only throughout this book, but also in Appendices B, H, I, L, M and N. We have also included Appendix K, which contains an audit committee checklist for *Sarbanes-Oxley*, and the NYSE and NASDAQ listing requirements.

The message for audit committees is that their composition and many aspects of their behaviour are now the subject of securities regulation. This is both a more specific and more invasive measure of control.

Federal Securities Regulation

In Canada, securities law is the exclusive responsibility of the provinces. As a result, each of the 10 provinces and the three federally administered territories sets and enforces its own rules. Companies that wish to sell their securities to investors across the country must obtain the approval of all 13 jurisdictions.

In the United States, while state securities commissions do exist, the national securities regulator, the Securities and Exchange Commission, is by far the most important body and has the responsibility for regulating U.S. capital markets.

The existence of national securities laws and the SEC is the most striking and important difference in securities regulation between the United States and Canada. For many years, there have been attempts in Canada to create a national securities commission, similar to the SEC. To date, these attempts have failed. This is unfortunate, because this failure has impeded the efficiency and effectiveness of Canada's regulatory system.

There have, however, been attempts to compensate for the lack of a national securities commission in Canada.

While the co-ordination of the provincial securities regulations and regulators is an ongoing challenge, the Canadian Securities Administrators has been established to facilitate this process. The CSA is an informal organization made up of the 13 provincial and territorial securities regulators, and is funded and supported by them on a voluntary basis. It operates through regular meetings of the chairmen, vice-chairmen, and staff of each of the securities commissions, through special purpose committees that deal with common regulatory issues, and through informal interaction among the staffs of the commissions. The CSA's commitment to harmonize Canadian securities regulation is articulated in its Notice 11-303, "The Uniform Securities Legislation Project", which announced a senior level committee to develop uniform securities legislation for adoption across Canada.

To date, the CSA has issued over 40 instruments and policies, which contain rules and regulations developed by it and subsequently adopted by the provinces and territories. The CSA, however, has no enforcement powers *per se* and no authority to compel companies to adhere to its instruments. For the instruments to be rendered enforceable, they must be adopted and then enforced by the various provincial and territorial securities commissions, a time-consuming process.

The CSA has also implemented a mutual reliance system that enables a regulator in one jurisdiction to rely on the review of the regulators in another jurisdiction. This permits a company to deal with one principal regulator, usually the securities commission in the jurisdiction in which the company's head office is located. The principle behind this is that the principal regulator acts on behalf of the other provincial and territorial securities commissions. British Columbia has taken this one step further and has proposed that the CSA adopt a "passport" system which would permit issuers to deal with one regulator, but would not restrict them to observing only one set of securities regulations as does the mutual reliance system. Recently, all provinces except Ontario signed a Memorandum of Understanding, indicating their agreement to move ahead with a passport system for an improved securities regulatory framework, to harmonize and simplify their securities laws, and explore further opportunities to consolidate or strengthen the co-ordination and consistency of securities laws among provinces and territories.

While the CSA has taken steps to harmonize securities regulation in Canada, the process remains too cumbersome and too slow for today's global, real-time, 24/7, electronically supported capital markets.

The current multi-jurisdictional system also leaves unanswered the question of who speaks for Canada in matters of international securities regulation.

There is very little question that there is a need for Canada to succeed in overcoming the constitutional impediments and to create a national securities commission. This is a concept that we have advocated for over 30 years.

The Canada-U.S. Multi Jurisdictional Disclosure System

The Canada-U.S. Multi Jurisdictional Disclosure System is an initiative designed to reduce the duplication of regulation in cross-border transactions such as public offerings, issuer bids, take-over bids and business combinations, and in cross-border continuous disclosure and other filings.

The MJDS attempts to streamline regulatory reviews of offering documents and establishes a mutual reliance process for such reviews by the SEC and the Canadian securities commissions. The SEC is responsible for regulatory reviews of disclosure documents for offerings made by a U.S. issuer both in Canada and in the United States. The process for the review of documents for offerings made by Canadian issuers in the Untied States is not as simple. While a Canadian securities regulator is responsible for reviewing such documents, the process of selecting the appropriate reviewer can be cumbersome.

The MJDS does not change the liability provisions of Canadian securities legislation, neither does it change the authority of Canadian securities regulators to halt distribution, remove an exemption, issue a cease-trading order or refuse to issue a receipt for a preliminary MJDS prospectus or a MJDS prospectus.

For Canadian companies that wish to raise capital in the United States, the MJDS has become very important. The protection of the MJDS system is one of the key reasons why the OSC and other securities regulators have advocated harmonizing Canadian securities regulations with those in the United States.

Corporate Governance: The Next Wave of Reform

The CSA has recently issued proposals that go beyond financial reporting to address the broader issues of corporate governance. On October 29, 2004 the CSA released Proposed National Policy 58-201, "Corporate Governance Guidelines" and Proposed National Instrument 58-101, "Disclosure of Corporate Governance Practices" for comment.

The proposed National Policy 58-201 contains 18 best practices that have been derived from the TSX governance guidelines and other regulatory standards. The CSA is proposing to retain the "comply or explain" approach set forth in the existing TSX guidelines, with the following provision: if a company does not comply, it will be required to explain how it achieves the underlying objective.

These recent proposals, including proposed amendments to MI 52-110, which were released at the same time, are discussed further in Chapter 17, Capital Market Reform: Late Breaking News. In addition, NP 58-201 and NI 58-101 are presented in Appendix O, and the proposed amendments to MI 52-110 are presented in Appendix P.

It should be noted that as each of the requirements in the multilateral instruments and NP 58-201 is implemented, it will supersede the existing TSX governance guidelines and governance-related listing requirements.

The significance of the securities administrators' move into the field of pure governance should not be overlooked. Through this new initiative, securities regulators are becoming more actively involved in the oversight of boards of directors and of board committees. In other words, they are now promulgating governance standards. This invasion of the boardroom by securities regulators, coupled with their new and broader investigation and enforcement powers, has important implications for all boards and their committees.

In Summary

In summary, it is our opinion that one of the principal objectives of capital market reform must be that governance standards, securities regulations and accounting standards should facilitate the flow of capital across Canada, across the Canada-U.S. border, and globally. It is very important that regulatory regimes do not become barriers.

In a world of inter-linked business and uncertain and jittery capital markets, where the small size of the Canadian capital market and Canada's dependence on trade with the United States render Canada uniquely vulnerable, it is especially important that Canada's regulatory and governance framework not be too dissimilar to that of the United States.

The critical issue for Canada is to make every effort to see to it that our markets are healthy, vibrant, attractive and open. If they are, Canadian and foreign investors will choose Canada. If our markets do not measure up to international standards (especially, American standards), investors will look elsewhere.

The initiatives introduced by the CSA in pursuit of harmonization are to be applauded. Their introduction of the multilateral instruments, which impose on Canadian public companies requirements similar to those imposed in the United States on U.S. companies, is a step in the right direction, as is the MJDS system and the mutual reliance system. However, the exemptions granted by the CSA to venture issuers from the independence requirement and from the financial literacy requirement for membership on audit committees, may not be a step in the same direction.

We feel the need to emphasize once again the importance of a single securities regulator. While we recognize that the constitutional issues are thorny ones, and create a real impediment to timely action, the need for a single securities regulator in Canada is self-evident. We urge the federal government and the 13 provincial and territorial governments to find a solution that will truly reform the capital market environment in Canada.

While we firmly believe that more effective regulatory imperatives were and are needed, we also observe that it should not be forgotten that the most powerful weapon against the occurrence of egregious corporate behaviour is the existence of effective, informed, courageous and independent directors and effective, courageous and independent auditors.

The best corporate governance and securities regulation should be based on the fundamental premise that most managements are honest, most directors are vigilant, and most advisors to both boards and management carry out their professional responsibilities in an exemplary manner. We believe, justifiably, that these groups can and do play an effective role in preventing abuses of power and misleading corporate reporting. Therefore, it behooves both the pundits and the regulators to encourage the recruitment of the best possible directors who, in turn, have a responsibility to recruit management of the highest integrity. The pundits and regulators should be wary of creating an environment in which this becomes more difficult, or of relying solely on the existence of rules to prevent another corporate disaster.

We cannot emphasize too strongly the importance to both the United States and Canada of not only focusing on appropriate governance and securities rules, but also of focusing on how best to create a healthy governance culture. Such a governance culture is heavily dependent on the right people and heavily dependent on the development of interdependent relationships among them.

Key Messages

- Capital market reform is very much a "work in process". The first phase dealt almost exclusively with improving the timeliness, accuracy and reliability of financial reporting. The second phase deals with the broader issues of the board of directors and corporate governance. This will be followed by new legislation relating to civil liability for disclosure in the secondary markets.

- These capital market reforms impose additional substantial costs on all public companies. Companies that embrace the spirit of the reforms and use them to improve the effectiveness of their business operations and governance processes will derive greater benefits than those that treat the reforms as merely a compliance exercise.

- Multinational and multi-jurisdictional companies must understand the capital market reforms being implemented in the various jurisdictions in which they must report, and assess the differences and impact upon them.

- The provincial and territorial system of securities regulation is costly, cumbersome and in urgent need of fundamental reform. Canada cannot keep pace globally if it continues to be the only G7 country without a national securities regulator. We support the Committee to Review the Structure of Securities Regulation in Canada recommendation that "Canada must adopt a fundamentally new structure — a single regulator administering a single code". It's time.

5

Doing the Right Things

Audit Committee Role and Responsibilities

Until recently, the statutory duties of audit committees changed little, if at all. Today, audit committees are reeling from a regulatory onslaught that has expanded the responsibilities of the audit committee and the external auditor. The public's expectations of audit committees are also changing quickly — and some unrealistic ones are emerging. The danger of unrealistic expectations is that they may actually provide false assurance to the investing public.

It is critical that audit committees understand and comply with the new requirements and clearly articulate them and any additional responsibilities they will undertake in the audit committee charter.

To be effective, audit committees must focus on doing not only the required things, but also the right things. By the "right things", we mean a combination of the requirements and those additional responsibilities that an audit committee may wish to assume. Since there are real and practical constraints on the committee's resources, particularly in terms of the time committee members have to commit to the committee's work, it is important that the audit committee clearly determine its priorities. A well-written charter will ensure that the audit committee focuses on its priorities and enables the committee to communicate its expectations both to management and the external auditor. The process of developing and updating the charter builds commitment on the part of all those who are involved in supporting the work of the committee. Since it is prudent for the board of directors to approve the audit committee's charter, it must agree on the specific responsibilities (in addition to the requirements) that will be undertaken by the committee.

A well-articulated charter is key to ensuring that the relationship among the audit committee, management and the external auditor works effectively. A charter also provides the foundation for the development of a work plan and the committee's evaluation of its performance, an exercise that is essential to ensure continuous improvement.

This chapter provides a framework for addressing the issues to be included in the charter, and a process for boards of directors, audit committees and management to follow in developing or updating the committee's mandate or charter.

The Requirements for a Charter

MI 52-110, "Audit Committees" requires audit committees to have a charter. It also requires that the full text of the audit committee's charter — not just a summary of it — be disclosed in the Annual Information Form (AIF). Audit committees, of course, are free to also disclose their charter in the proxy material or annual report should they so choose.

The disclosure of the charter will help to ensure that the regulators and the investing public clearly understand the audit committee's duties and may minimize the risk that investors will harbour unrealistic expectations of the committee.

MI 52-110 prescribes certain minimum responsibilities for which the audit committee is accountable. These responsibilities form the basis for the audit committee's charter:

- reviewing the issuer's financial statements, Management's Discussion & Analysis (MD&A), and annual and quarterly earnings news releases before they are publicly disclosed by the issuer;
- recommending to the board of directors the external auditor to be nominated for approval at the annual meeting of the shareholders, as well as the compensation to be paid to the external auditor;
- overseeing the work of the external auditor;
- pre-approving all non-audit services to be provided to the issuer or its subsidiary entities by the issuer's external auditor;
- satisfying itself that adequate procedures are in place for the review of the issuer's public disclosure of financial information extracted or derived from the issuer's financial statements, other than the disclosures in the MD&A, earnings news releases and AIF, and periodically assessing the adequacy of those procedures;
- establishing procedures for the confidential, anonymous submission and treatment of complaints received by the issuer from employees and others regarding accounting, internal accounting controls, or auditing matters; and
- reviewing and approving the issuer's hiring policies regarding partners, employees and former partners and employees of the present and former external auditor of the issuer.

In this book, we do not attempt to prescribe what audit committees should or should not include in their specific responsibilities and duties, recognizing, however, that audit committees must comply with the requirements set forth in MI 52-110. We believe the articulation of those duties assumed by the audit committee beyond those prescribed is a task that is best undertaken by individual boards of directors and audit committees. We do, however, believe very strongly that every audit committee should clearly define the responsibilities it wishes to undertake beyond mere compliance, and that the charter should form the foundation for the committee's expectations of both management and the external auditor. The audit committee charter is a living document that should be reviewed and reassessed in terms of its adequacy annually.

In developing a charter, audit committees must understand and differentiate between the minimum legal and regulatory requirements, and activities that would be considered to be "best practices" and those that would be considered "leading edge" practices. We note that many of the "best practices" described in the first edition of this book have now been included in MI 52-110 and are, therefore, now minimum requirements. This illustrates how, over time, "best practices" become codified as minimum requirements.

It has been suggested that expanding the audit committee's duties beyond the minimum requirements will attract increased liability. We believe that expanding the audit committee's role will not, of itself, attract additional legal liability exposure for audit committee members. Rather, it is the failure to effectively discharge the responsibilities the committee has decided to undertake that could impact the members' liability.

Dimensions of the Charter

In developing a charter, audit committees should be aware of the following four major dimensions, as illustrated in Figure 7.
1) The committee's role in the oversight of the company's financial reporting and disclosures.
2) The committee's oversight of the appointment of the external auditor, the auditor's accountability and the audit activities to be performed.
3) The committee's oversight of risk management and control, including disclosure controls, internal control over financial reporting.
4) Other oversight responsibilities that may be assigned to the audit committee by the board of directors.

For each dimension, there is an increasing set of responsibilities that begins with the minimum legal and regulatory requirements, and expands to include "best practices" and even "leading edge practices", which an audit committee may or may not choose to assume.

Figure 7 | **Four Dimensions of Audit Committee Oversight**

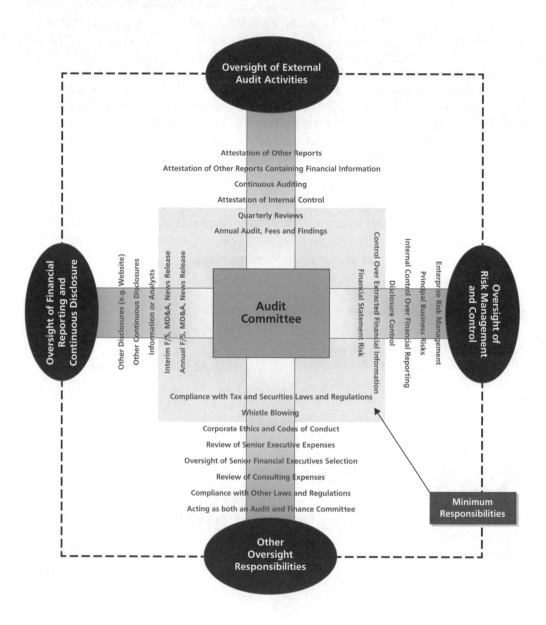

Dimension One: *Oversight of Financial Reporting and Continuous Disclosure*

The first dimension of an audit committee's role is its governance responsibilities for financial and MD&A reporting, which includes annual reporting, quarterly reporting and periodic reporting such as prospectuses, special reports containing information extracted from the financial statements, etc.

Financial Statements, MD&A and Earnings News Releases

When audit committees were first prescribed in Canada, their only statutory requirement was to review the annual financial statements for submission to the board and to review the annual audit performed by the external auditor. The only other requirement was for audit committees to review financial statements that were included in a prospectus. As a result, audit committees faced many choices in deciding what other financial information they should review.

MI 52-110 has significantly clarified the choices audit committees might make by expanding the audit committee's oversight responsibilities for financial reporting to include quarterly financial statements, the MD&A, and certain other continuous disclosure documents. As a result, the audit committee has fewer choices to make with respect to the information it should review because the requirements have been expanded. More specifically, MI 52-110 states:[1]

> 5) *An audit committee must review the issuer's financial statements, MD&A and annual and interim earnings press releases before the issuer publicly discloses this information.*
>
> 6) *An audit committee must be satisfied that adequate procedures are in place for the review of the issuer's public disclosure of financial information extracted or derived from the issuer's financial statements, other than the public disclosure referred to in subsection (5), and must periodically assess the adequacy of those procedures.*

MI 52-110 has swept a great many, if not most, of the "best practices" relating to the oversight of financial reporting that we discussed in the first edition of this book, into the "minimum legal and regulatory requirements" category.

The four minimum requirements with respect to financial reporting and disclosure are:
1) Review of the quarterly and annual financial statements;
2) Review of the quarterly and annual MD&A;
3) Review of the quarterly and annual earnings news releases;
4) Review of the procedures management has put in place for the review of public disclosure of financial information extracted or derived from the issuer's financial statements.

It should be noted that the first three requirements refer to the audit committee's review of documents, whereas the fourth refers to a review management's procedures, but not necessarily the documents themselves.

[1] Canadian Securities Administrators Multilateral Instrument 52-110, "Audit Committees", Section 2.3.

In many companies, the AIF is prepared by management and filed with the appropriate securities regulators with a limited review, if any, by either the board or the audit committee. Although it is not mandated, we believe that the AIF should be reviewed by the audit committee. Moreover, the CEO and CFO must include the AIF in their annual certification. One further point should be noted. Many AIFs are prepared after the financial statements and MD&A have been released. Since the review of the AIF by the audit committee may create a timing and logistical issue if this practice continues, we recommend that the AIF be prepared and reviewed concurrently with the annual financial statements and MD&A. The decision by the audit committee in this regard should be reflected in the charter.

The Auditors' Review of Quarterly Information

While MI 52-110 has expanded the audit committee's responsibilities for the review of financial information, a commensurate expansion of the auditor's responsibilities has not been mandated, although an expansion of their role to include quarterly reviews is, in fact, occurring. In these circumstances, the audit committee must decide whether to have the external auditor involved in the review of the quarterly financial statements, MD&A and earnings news release, and on the extent of the assurance it requires from the external auditor. These decisions should be reflected in the committee's charter.

At present, the minimum legal requirement is for the external auditor to conduct an audit and express an opinion on the annual financial statements. While it is becoming more common, there is, as yet, no requirement in Canada for the external auditor to perform a "review" of the quarterly financial statements, MD&A or earnings news release. However, subsection 4.3(3) and section 6.5 of the CSA National Instrument 51-102, "Continuous Disclosure Obligations", require that, if an auditor has not performed a review of the quarterly financial statements, a reporting issuer must disclose that fact. This instrument also requires that, if the auditor has performed a review and expressed a qualified or adverse report or denied any assurance, then the reporting issuer is required to include a written review report from the auditor, which must accompany the quarterly financial statements. No positive statement, however, is required when an auditor has performed a review and has provided an unqualified report to the audit committee.

In our view, it is prudent for audit committees to require that the external auditor perform a review of the quarterly financial statements, MD&A and earnings news releases.

It is, therefore, important for the audit committee to understand the objectives of an auditors' "review" of quarterly financial statements as contrasted with an "audit". The CICA *Handbook* provides an overview of the differences between a review and an audit:[2]

---

[2] CICA *Handbook*, Section 7050, "Auditor Review of Interim Financial Statements".

23. *The objective of a review of interim financial statements is to provide the entity's auditor with a basis for reporting whether he or she is aware of any material modification that needs to be made for such statements to be in accordance with Canadian generally accepted accounting principles. The auditor's assessment is based on applying the auditor's knowledge of accounting and financial reporting practices to significant accounting matters of which the auditor has become aware through enquiry, analytical procedures and discussion. An interim review does not normally contemplate the auditor's performing certain other procedures carried out during an audit, such as:*

    a) tests of accounting records through inspection, observation or confirmation;

    b) tests of controls to evaluate their effectiveness; or

    c) obtaining corroborative evidence of management's responses to the auditor's enquiries.

24. *The objective of a review of interim financial statements differs significantly from the objective of an audit of financial statements in accordance with generally accepted auditing standards. The objective of an audit is to enable the auditor to express an opinion on whether the financial statements are presented fairly, in all material respects, in accordance with Canadian generally accepted accounting principles. A review of interim financial statements does not provide a basis for the expression of such an opinion.*

At present, the external auditor's review of quarterly statements does not typically include an evaluation of controls or detailed testing of documentary evidence, although this may change when the rules dealing with management reporting on internal control are finalized and issued. Auditors will only perform an in-depth examination of documents and controls if the results of their inquiries, analytical procedures and discussions cause them to have concerns about the plausibility of the quarterly financial statements.

It is important for audit committees to clearly understand the nature of the work the auditor performs in reviewing the quarterly financial statements, which can best be accomplished through an in-depth review and discussion of the engagement letter. The audit committee should understand that while professional standards for such reviews do not include the MD&A and earnings news release, the audit committee is required to review both of these documents. It, therefore, should agree with the external auditor on the extent to which the auditor's quarterly review will cover those documents. In our view, the audit committee should require the external auditor to perform a review of the quarterly financial statements and to include the MD&A and earnings news release in this review.

It is also important for the audit committee and the external auditor to agree on the nature of the auditor's communication to the committee on the review. The auditor's communication may be a written or an oral report, either to the chairman of the audit committee or to the full committee. We believe, however, that the auditor's communication on the review of the quarterly financial statements should be in writing and presented to the full audit committee.

The auditor's report to the audit committee should describe the nature and extent of the quarterly review procedures performed, the results of the quarterly review, and whether the auditor is aware of any material modification necessary to bring the quarterly financial statements into accord with Canadian generally accepted accounting principles (GAAP). This is "negative assurance", as contrasted with the positive assurance report provided in the auditors' report on the annual financial statements. The auditor's report to the audit committee should include the details of any known or potential departures from Canadian GAAP and, if readily determinable, the effect of any departures on the quarterly financial statements. In addition, the auditor should bring to the attention of the audit committee any changes that should be made to the MD&A or earnings news release.

The external auditor is permitted to issue a public report on their quarterly review for distribution to third parties but, with the exception of reporting on quarterly information in prospectuses, this is very rare both in Canada and the United States.

While the professional standards for quarterly reviews performed by the auditor have been harmonized with those in the United States, the Canadian requirements regarding the audit committee's oversight of quarterly reporting and the requirements for the external auditor's involvement in this process differs from that in the United States. The SEC requires the external auditor to perform a quarterly review, but does not require either the board of directors or the audit committee to review the quarterly reports. The NYSE, however, does require the audit committee to "discuss" the quarterly financial statements, including the MD&A, with management and the external auditor.

In our opinion, audit committees should formally engage the external auditor to review the quarterly financial statements, MD&A and earnings news release, not only for their own protection but, more importantly, to enhance the quality and reliability of quarterly reporting. The committee's charter should be explicit on this point.

The Audit Committee's Review of Other Information

The "beyond the minimum requirements" choices and decisions related to this dimension centre around the extent to which the audit committee should review materials presented to analysts, institutional investors, credit rating agencies, etc. While the audit committee must review the procedures for the disclosure of financial information extracted or derived from the issuer's financial statements, the audit committee must decide whether it should also review the materials themselves. It should be noted that materials presented to analysts, credit rating agencies, etc., often contain significant amounts of non-financial information, which may present an additional challenge to audit committees with respect to the scope and depth of their review. Moreover, a few audit committees have chosen to review all continuous disclosure documents, including all news releases.

There are several factors that audit committees should take into account when considering the extent to which they wish to review documents as contrasted with their review of procedures. These include the impact of the information, the additional time and effort required to review the information, the timeliness of that review, and the audit committee's assessment of management's review procedures.

For example, an audit committee might decide that it should review all materials presented to analysts, investors and credit rating agencies because of the critical nature of the impact of the information on the company but, with respect to other information, such as speeches, promotional materials etc., it will rely on management's review procedures. When an effective disclosure committee exists within the company, that committee should provide the audit committee with a measure of comfort in making a decision not to review such "other" information.

We believe that the extent to which the audit committee should review information beyond the financial statements (and the depth of that review) is an important matter for all audit committees to consider. The charter should reflect the audit committee's position on this matter.

Dimension Two: *Oversight of the External Audit Activities*

A second dimension of audit committee activity is its responsibility for oversight of the appointment of the external auditor, the auditor's accountability, and the audit work to be performed. This activity is significant and, in our opinion, warrants a more detailed discussion, which we provide in Chapter 6, Audit Committees and the External Auditor.

Dimension Three: *Oversight of Control and Risk Management*

While the audit committee's responsibilities for the oversight of financial information have been both expanded and clarified since the first edition of this book, the audit committee's involvement in control and risk management is still evolving. The respective responsibilities of the CEO, CFO, audit committee, board, and external auditor for the oversight of control and risk management have not yet been finalized by the CSA. In our view, dimension three has replaced dimension one as the most challenging one in developing the audit committee's charter.

While the role of the audit committee is still evolving, we believe it has a substantive responsibility with respect to the oversight of control and risk management. In determining the audit committee's role in the oversight of the company's control and risk management activities, there must be a clear understanding of the responsibilities in this area to be undertaken by the board as a whole and by other committees of the board.

An additional element that needs to be considered is the oversight that the audit committee and/or the board should assume with respect to information systems, because control and risk management is inextricably bound up with the effectiveness of information systems.

The existing TSX guidelines and the CSA's National Policy 58-201, "Corporate Governance Guidelines", both prescribe that the board of directors should state in the board's charter that it explicitly acknowledges responsibility for the company's internal control and management information systems, and for identifying the principal risks of the company's business and ensuring the implementation of appropriate systems to manage these risks. The board may, however, delegate these responsibilities to one of its committees. In many companies, the board delegates the governance responsibilities for internal controls over financial reporting and part or all of its risk management responsibilities to the audit committee.

Information systems are critical to the effectiveness of control and risk management. The governance of information systems, however, is a more challenging matter for the board and the audit committee. There are a number of reasons for this. First, the accounting systems in most companies are highly integrated with other information systems, and often with those of suppliers, outsourcing service providers, and business partners. Thus, the boundary between the accounting systems and other information systems is no longer clear or discernable. Second, systems integration brings with it a level of interdependency and risk in which the entire system, or significant parts thereof, can be affected if one element fails — irrespective of whether this element is an accounting function, business support function or whether it exists within the company or within a supplier or business partner. The TSX guidelines and NP 58-201, however, clearly state that the board should be responsible for ensuring the integrity of both the internal control and management information systems. As a result, the board and the audit committee need to reach a common understanding of their respective governance responsibilities, not just for internal control (which is normally delegated to the audit committee) but also for information systems (which is broader than the responsibilities usually assigned to the audit committee).

In our view, it is important that both the board and the audit committee charters clearly define "who is responsible for what" with respect to the governance of control, risk management and information systems. The material that follows is provided to offer guidance to both boards and audit committees as they allocate and agree on their respective oversight responsibilities.

What is Control?

In creating its charter, it is important that the audit committee view control in its broad context, and not restrict itself only to those internal controls that ensure the accuracy of the company's accounting books and records. It should also consider the extent to which it wishes to include processes related to the identification and mitigation of risks — including strategic, operational and financial risks in its definition of control for purposes of its charter.

The CICA provides a broad definition of control:[3]

> *Control comprises those elements of an organization (including its resources, systems, processes, culture, structure and tasks) that, taken together, support people in the achievement of the organization's objectives. These objectives may fall into one or more of the following general categories.*
>
> - **Effectiveness and efficiency of operations** *includes objectives related to an organization's goals, such as customer service, the safeguarding and efficient use of resources, profitability and meeting social obligations. This includes the safeguarding of the organization's resources from inappropriate use or loss and ensuring that liabilities are identified and managed.*
> - **Reliability of internal and external reporting** *includes objectives related to matters such as the maintenance of proper accounting records, the reliability of information used within the organization and of information published for third parties. This includes the protection of records against two main types of fraud: the concealment of theft and the distortion of results.*
> - **Compliance with applicable laws and regulations and internal policies** *includes objectives related to ensuring that the organization's affairs are conducted in accordance with legal and regulatory obligations and internal policies.*

Audit committees should not lose sight of the fact that effective control is as much a function of the corporate culture and the integrity and ethical values of the company's people, as it is of rules, regulations and compliance processes. As a result, the tone at the top set by the CEO, together with his or her direct reports, has a significant impact on control processes and procedures. We believe the audit committee should encourage the board to hold the CEO accountable for setting the correct tone at the top.

The ongoing challenge for the board and the audit committee is to obtain timely, relevant and reliable information on which to make an informed assessment of the control environment, cultural values and tone at the top. The work and observations of the external and internal auditors can help the audit committee in understanding and assessing the control environment that actually exists throughout the company. We believe that the audit committee should keep the board informed of its observations on the control environment, which it can do through its regular reports to the board.

Figure 8 illustrates the broad control environment.

---

[3] The Canadian Institute of Chartered Accountants, Guidance of the Criteria of Control Board, *Guidance on Control: The Nature of Control*, paragraph 6.

Figure 8 | **The Control Environment**

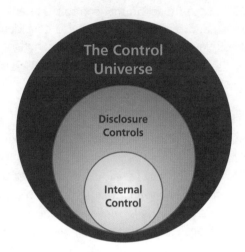

The control universe includes a great many control systems, for example operational controls, controls to ensure compliance with work place safety and privacy legislation, or monitoring systems to ensure that human resource policies are effectively implemented. It also includes the values, attitudes and the "tone at the top" that define the company's approach to its control environment. All of these are represented within the outer circle.

Certain elements of the control universe, however, are directly relevant to the responsibilities of the audit committee. These are, in addition to the "tone at the top", disclosure controls and internal control over financial reporting. The second circle represents the disclosure controls, which include all reports and information required to be filed under securities legislation and regulation. The third circle represents internal control over financial reporting, which includes the information contained in the annual and quarterly financial statements.

In defining its responsibilities, we believe that it is important for the audit committee to take a broad view of control and place emphasis on the control environment in its entirety.

Disclosure Controls

MI 52-109 introduces the concept of "disclosure controls" which it defines as:[4]

> *controls and other procedures of an issuer that are designed to provide reasonable assurance that information required to be disclosed by the issuer in its annual filings, interim filings or other reports filed or submitted by it under provincial and territorial securities legislation is recorded, processed, summarized and reported within the time periods specified in the provincial and terri-*

---

[4] Canadian Securities Administrators' Multilateral Instrument 52-109, "Certification of Disclosure in Issuers' Annual and Interim Filings", Section 1.1.

torial securities legislation and include, without limitation controls and procedures designed to ensure that information required to be disclosed by an issuer in its annual filings, interim filings or other reports filed or submitted under provincial and territorial securities legislation is accumulated and communicated to the issuers management, including its chief executive officers and chief financial officers (or persons who perform similar functions to a chief executive officer or a chief financial officer), as appropriate to allow timely decisions regarding required disclosure.

This definition of disclosure controls is very broad, and encompasses all reports and documents that are required to be filed by securities legislation.

It should be noted that the CEO and CFO certification process will require these executives to certify both the design and operating effectiveness of "disclosure controls" beginning in 2005. This will likely increase management's focus on disclosure controls and provide the board and audit committee with important information and input on the effectiveness of disclosure controls. The CEO and CFO certification process is more fully discussed in Chapter 12, CEO and CFO Certification.

Disclosure Policy

We believe an effective disclosure policy is the foundation for effective disclosure controls, and that ensuring such a policy exists is the responsibility of the audit committee.

The concept of a disclosure policy was introduced in National Policy 51-201, "Disclosure Standards," wherein the CSA recommends, but does not require, that companies establish a written corporate disclosure policy. NP 51-201 states that the disclosure policy should be practical to implement, be approved by the board of directors and widely distributed to officers and employees. It further recommends that directors, officers and those employees who are, or may be, involved in making disclosure decisions should receive appropriate education and training so they can effectively apply the disclosure policy. In addition, the disclosure policy should be periodically reviewed and updated, as necessary, and responsibility for these functions (i.e., review and update of the policy and education of appropriate employees and company officials) should be clearly assigned within the company.

With respect to content, the CSA recommends:[5]

Every disclosure policy should generally include the following:
a) *how to decide what information is material;*
b) *policy on reviewing analyst reports;*
c) *how to release earnings announcements and conduct related analyst calls and meetings;*
d) *how to conduct meetings with investors and the media;*
e) *what to say or not to say at industry conferences;*
f) *how to use electronic media and the corporate Web site;*

---

[5] Canadian Securities Administrators' National Policy 51-201, "Disclosure Standards", Section 6.2 (3).

g) *policy on the use of forecasts and other forward-looking information (including a policy regarding issuing updates);*

h) *procedures for reviewing briefings and discussions with analysts, institutional investors and other market professionals;*

i) *how to deal with unintentional selective disclosures;*

j) *how to respond to market rumours;*

k) *policy on trading restrictions; and*

l) *policy on "quiet periods".*

We believe audit committees should review, at least annually, the company's disclosure policy in order to be satisfied that it includes the appropriate principles and policies. The board, through the audit committee, should also be satisfied that management has put in place appropriate procedures for implementing the disclosure policy and monitoring compliance.

Disclosure Committee

A key factor in effectively implementing the disclosure policy is management's establishment of a disclosure committee. The terms of reference and the membership of the disclosure committee should be reviewed by the audit committee. The CICA has recommended that the disclosure committee's responsibilities should be:[6]

1) *To review, on an ongoing basis, the issuer's continuous disclosure policy to ensure that it addresses the issuer's principal business risks, changes in operations or structure, and facilitates compliance with applicable legislative and regulatory reporting requirements.*

2) *To design a set of "disclosure controls" to provide reasonable assurance that:*
   a) *the continuous disclosure policy is effectively implemented across all business units and corporate functions; and*
   b) *information of a material nature is accumulated and communicated to senior management, including the CEO and CFO, to allow timely decisions on required disclosures.*

3) *To review prior to issuance or submission to the audit committee or board of directors:*
   a) *annual and interim filings, management information circulars, material change reports, annual information forms, and any other information filed with securities regulators;*
   b) *news releases containing financial information, earnings guidance, information about material acquisitions or dispositions, or other information material to investors; and*
   c) *presentations and reports containing financial information broadly disseminated to analysts, creditors and investors, including financial information displayed on the issuer's website.*

---

[6] Canadian Institute of Chartered Accountants, *CEO and CFO Certification: Improving Transparency and Accountability*, Appendix C.

4) To direct and supervise an annual or interim evaluation of the effectiveness of the issuer's disclosure controls, unless this evaluation is performed by another group such as the internal audit department. (It should be noted that the U.S. requirements call for a quarterly evaluation of disclosure controls, whereas the Canadian requirements will require, after the prescribed transition period, the CEO and CFO to certify that they have performed an annual evaluation of disclosure controls.)

5) To ensure that policies and guidance related to corporate disclosure and financial reporting are developed and issued, and that communication of matters affecting disclosure and financial reporting efficiently flows down, across and up the organization.

6) To assist the CEO and CFO in monitoring and evaluating the integrity, ethical values and competence of the company's officers and employees in accordance with the policies and direction provided by the issuer's board of directors and its audit committee.

7) To bring to the attention of the CEO and CFO, all relevant information with respect to the committee's activities, the annual or interim filing, and the evaluation of the effectiveness of the issuer's disclosure controls.

MD&A and Earnings Releases

Two other areas affect the audit committee's role and responsibilities. First, and most important, MI 52-110 requires the audit committee to review the company's MD&A and annual and quarterly earnings news releases before the company publicly discloses this information. As a result, the audit committee should be satisfied that management has in place effective controls over the financial and non-financial information contained in the MD&A and earnings news release to ensure that the disclosures in these documents are complete, accurate and reliable. This should be included as part of the quarterly reports that the CEO and CFO provide to the audit committee on their certification process.

Second, disclosure controls include the procedures management has put in place for the review of the public disclosure of financial information extracted or derived from the company's financial statements, which was discussed earlier in this chapter. MI 52-110 requires audit committees to periodically assess the adequacy of those procedures. We suggest this be done annually, and that the assessment of the adequacy of these procedures be included as part of the reports that the CEO and CFO provide to the audit committee on their certification process.

In summary, the audit committee's minimum level of involvement with respect to disclosure controls is to satisfy itself that:

1) Management has developed and implemented an appropriate disclosure policy and has created a disclosure committee;

2) Management has implemented appropriate controls to ensure that the disclosures in the MD&A and earnings news releases are complete, accurate and reliable; and

3) Management has put in place appropriate procedures for the review of financial information extracted or derived from the financial statements for presentation to analysts, credit rating agencies or other parties.

The audit committee should carefully consider the extent to which it should take on oversight responsibilities for other elements of disclosure controls — for example, controls over material change reports, the risks of selective disclosure, news releases that do not contain financial information, etc. As with other elements of the audit committee's charter, the decisions the audit committee makes on these matters should be approved by the board. We believe most boards will prefer the audit committee to confine its review of documents to the financial statements, MD&A and earnings news releases, but will ask the audit committee to ensure that management has designed and implemented an effective set of disclosure controls that includes documents that contain non-financial information.

Internal Control Over Financial Reporting (ICFR)

MI 52-109 introduces another new control concept called "internal control over financial reporting" (ICFR), which it defines as:[7]

> ...*a process designed by, or under the supervision of, the issuer's chief executive officers and chief financial officers, or persons performing similar functions, and effected by the issuer's board of directors, management and other personnel, to provide reasonable assurance regarding the reliability of financial reporting and the preparation of financial statements for external purposes in accordance with the issuer's GAAP and includes those policies and procedures that:*
>
> a) *pertain to the maintenance of records that in reasonable detail accurately and fairly reflect the transactions and dispositions of the assets of the issuer,*
>
> b) *provide reasonable assurance that transactions are recorded as necessary to permit preparation of financial statements in accordance with the issuer's GAAP, and that receipts and expenditures of the issuer are being made only in accordance with authorizations of management and directors of the issuer, and*
>
> c) *provide reasonable assurance regarding prevention or timely detection of unauthorized acquisition, use or disposition of the issuer's assets that could have a material effect on the annual financial statements or interim financial statements.*

Since "internal control over financial reporting" relates to the preparation and filing of financial statements in accordance with the requirements of the securities laws and regulations, it is a subset of disclosure controls.

Figure 9 illustrates the way in which internal control over financial reporting relates to the way management controls its operations (operational control) and ensures compliance with applicable laws and regulations, which includes securities laws and regulations.

---

[7] Canadian Securities Administrators' Multilateral Instrument 52-109, "Certificate of Disclosure in Issuers' Annual and Interim Filings", Section 1.1.

Since MI 52-110 requires the audit committee to review the company's financial statements, the audit committee has a direct interest in the effectiveness of internal controls over financial reporting. As illustrated in Figure 9, the financial statements are entirely within the domain of ICFR. However, the MD&A, news releases and maintenance of records are all matters that are mandated and which, while they contain financial information, are not limited to financial information. As a result, these items lie on the boundary of ICFR – partly inside and partly outside. Similarly, authorizations and safeguarding of assets may relate to transactions or assets included in the financial statements or to operational matters not included in the financial statements. While authorizations and safeguarding of assets are not specifically mandated, they too lie on the boundary of ICFR. The challenge for audit committees in creating their charters is to assess the reasonableness of what is included in ICFR and what is not, particularly as formal reporting by management on internal control continues to evolve.

Figure 9 | **Internal Control Over Financial Reporting (ICFR)**

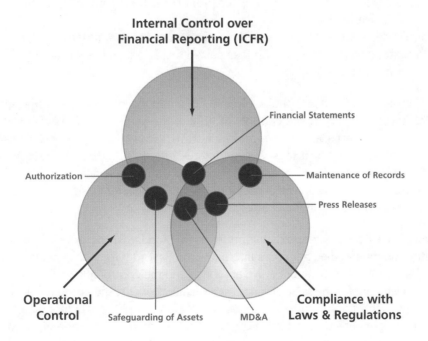

The CSA has stated that it is developing a proposed instrument to require a formal report by management on their assessment of the company's ICFR and is evaluating the extent to which auditor attestation of such report should be required. At the time of writing, it was not clear whether there would be an exemption for smaller companies. The reader should note that the SEC has recently issued rules to implement Section 404 of the *Sarbanes-Oxley Act*, which requires management to report on the effectiveness of their ICFR together with an auditor's attestation of that report.

In our opinion, the formal reporting by management on internal control is a positive development for audit committees. While most audit committees receive periodic reports from the internal and external auditors on specific audits, they seldom receive a comprehensive report from the CFO on the overall effectiveness of internal control. Such a formal reporting from the CFO will strengthen management's accountability for the effectiveness of internal controls.

In summary, the audit committee's responsibilities for ICFR are:

1) It is required to review the annual and quarterly financial statements, which define the scope of ICFR.

2) It is not required to perform or review a comprehensive assessment or evaluation of ICFR. (The CSA, however, is considering whether to require management to provide such a comprehensive assessment in a special report on ICFR with an attestation of this report by the external auditor.)

3) It typically deals with ICFR on an exception basis, i.e., the committee relies on the internal and external auditors to test ICFR as part of their work and report any control weaknesses or breakdowns to it.

MI 52-110 makes no reference to the involvement of either the internal or external auditor in evaluating and testing disclosure controls or ICFR. If the audit committee chooses to rely on the work of the internal and/or external auditors in discharging its responsibilities for the oversight of internal control, it must ensure that the internal and external auditors' evaluation and testing of internal control are commensurate with the reliance the audit committee intends to place on their work. The expectations of the audit committee in this regard must, therefore, be clearly stated in the charter.

In planning their audits, under existing professional standards, the external auditor must sufficiently understand the company's internal control in order to choose between two fundamental approaches – the substantive approach and the control reliance approach.

1) Auditors who opt for the *substantive approach* will directly verify the account balance or the transactions that comprise the account balance. For example, the auditor may choose to verify management's physical inventory counts performed at the year-end and verify the costing of this inventory to ascertain the proper value to be placed in the financial statements. Or, the auditor may choose to confirm the accounts receivable directly with third parties at the year-end to verify their accuracy. In these cases, the auditor places a minimal amount of reliance on internal control (e.g., reliance on control is limited to ensuring that all inventory is available for counting or all accounts receivable are available for confirmation).

2) Auditors who take a *control reliance approach* design their audit approach to obtain assurance from internal controls, including reliance on the work performed by internal audit, and support this reliance by a more detailed evaluation of the design of internal control systems and by testing their operation in practice. An auditor who utilizes a control reliance approach gains a much more detailed understanding of the operations of the company's accounting and control systems, and is better able to support the audit committee's oversight of internal control.

There is potential for confusion and misunderstanding between audit committees and external auditors with respect to the amount of control evaluation and testing that is performed during the external audit. This can create an "expectation gap" between what the audit committee thinks the auditor is doing and the assurance being provided, and what the auditor actually does and the assurance he or she intends to provide. For example, if the audit committee charter includes a broad oversight responsibility for ICFR, and the auditor is utilizing a substantive approach with few actual tests of internal controls, the audit committee may be relying on a false assumption about the amount of assurance they can derive from the auditor's work. This expectation gap is likely to decrease as auditors are required to formally attest to management's report on internal control and audit committees understand the scope and extent of audit work required to support this attestation.

Audit committees must understand the nature of financial control testing performed both by the internal auditor and the external auditor and how those tests are co-ordinated in order to achieve a comprehensive coverage. We note that the NYSE now requires that each listed company have an internal audit function to provide management and the audit committee with ongoing assessments of the company's risk management processes and system of internal control.

The audit committee should review the mandate of the internal audit function, its annual plan, proposed staffing and budget in order to understand and be in a position to approve the internal auditor's priorities and focus. The audit committee should receive regular reports on all aspect of the internal auditor's work whether they be on operational controls, ICFR or compliance with laws and regulations. This aspect of the audit committee's responsibility should be clearly articulated in its charter.

Today's rapidly changing reporting environment will have a significant impact on the company's internal control systems and, therefore, will also affect the audit committee's decisions regarding the degree of its involvement in the oversight of internal control. Issues for audit committees to consider are:
- the growing complexity of financial accounting standards and the information required to support their implementation;
- the growing importance of the MD&A and its integration with the financial statements;

- the new rules that shorten the deadlines for filing annual and quarterly financial statements in the United States and Canada;
- the potential for new legislation that expands civil liability remedies for continuous disclosure; and
- the growing importance of the board's and the audit committee's oversight of risk management policies and activities, and the NYSE proposals to extend the audit committee's role in this area.

All of these issues increase the importance of ensuring that the company has put in place properly designed systems of control that operate effectively. In our opinion, audit committees should now reassess:

- the role and responsibilities of the internal audit function, and if the company does not have an internal audit function, the audit committee should consider whether such a function should be instituted;
- the scope, nature and timing of the reporting by management and the auditors (internal and external) on internal control to the audit committee, and the need for external reporting to shareholders;
- the breadth and depth of the internal and external audit plans and resources, including the processes to evaluate and test internal control; and
- the role and responsibilities of the audit committee with respect to its oversight of internal control.

Risk Management

The existing TSX guidelines and the NP 58-201 both state that the board of directors should, as part of its responsibility for the stewardship of the company, state in its charter that the board is responsible for:[8]

> b) *adopting a strategic planning process and approving, on at least an annual basis, a strategic plan which takes into account, among other things, the opportunities and risks of the business;*
>
> c) *the identification of the principal risks of the issuer's business, and ensuring the implementation of appropriate systems to manage these risks.*

This raises the question of the audit committee's role in identifying principal risks of the company's business and ensuring the implementation of appropriate systems to manage these risks vis-à-vis the board's responsibilities. Should its role be different for financial risks as contrasted with non-financial risks?

---

[8] Canadian Securities Administrators' National Policy 58-201, "Corporate Governance Guidelines", Section 3.4.

We believe that, at a minimum, the audit committee's charter should state that the committee is responsible for oversight of risks related to amounts or disclosures in the financial statements and over the controls necessary to mitigate these financial risks. Given that the audit committee must approve the MD&A, and the MD&A contains information on both financial and non-financial risks and how they are mitigated or managed, this raises the question of the audit committee's oversight of non-financial risk. The existence of non-financial risk disclosure in the MD&A would appear to support a broader role for the audit committee in risk management.

MI 52-110 makes no reference to the role of the internal or external auditor with respect to risk management. The external auditor, however, is required by Generally Accepted Auditing Standards (GAAS) to include in the scope of the audit all major financial risks impacting the financial statements.

Neither MI 52-110 nor NP 58-201 distinguish between the board's responsibilities and those of the audit committee with respect to the oversight of internal control and risk management activities. Therefore, the board must decide what oversight responsibilities for risk management it will allocate to the audit and other board committees, and what responsibilities will be retained by the board. This allocation of responsibilities should be clearly stated in the charters of both the board and the audit committee.

There is considerable debate over what responsibilities for risk management are allocated to the audit committee. The listing requirements of the NYSE, for example, call for the audit committee to "discuss policies with respect to risk assessment and risk management". The following commentary is provided:[9]

> While it is the job of the CEO and senior management to assess and manage the company's exposure to risk, the audit committee must discuss guidelines and policies to govern the process by which this is handled. The audit committee should discuss the company's major financial risk exposures and the steps management has taken to monitor and control such exposures. The audit committee is not required to be the sole body responsible for risk assessment and management, but, as stated above, the committee must discuss guidelines and policies to govern the process by which risk assessment and management is undertaken. Many companies, particularly financial companies, manage and assess their risk through mechanisms other than the audit committee. The processes these companies have in place should be reviewed in a general manner by the audit committee, but they need not be replaced by the audit committee.

The NYSE listing requirements extend the audit committee's responsibilities for the governance of risk management beyond the financial risks that affect the financial statements. The NYSE also states that the audit committee's charter should include discussing with

---

[9] New York Stock Exchange Corporate Accounting and Listing Standards Committee, June 6, 2002, page 15.

management the policies that govern management's process for identifying and managing principal risks. Some companies have extended this principle further and established the audit committee as the audit and risk management committee.

In our view, there is merit to the approach put forward by the NYSE, and it should be seriously considered by audit committees in developing or revising their charter. Audit committees that choose to expand their responsibilities for the oversight of internal control and risk management beyond the minimum required for the preparation of accurate reliable financial statements must, however, ensure that they will have the information they require to discharge these expanded responsibilities effectively. They will require formal and regular reports by management on internal control, and regular reports by both the internal and external auditors on the adequacy of control and risk management policies and how effectively they are being implemented.

Dimension Four: Other Responsibilities

This dimension deals with the other roles and responsibilities that are often assigned to audit committees by the board of directors.

Often, audit committees are asked to take on additional responsibilities because the nature of their work allows them to develop a more in-depth understanding of the company's business and its operations than can be obtained by other board committees. Moreover, the audit committee has sources of information available to it through the internal and external auditors that are not as readily available to other board committees or to the board as a whole. As a result, the audit committee is often well positioned to add value in these areas.

However, audit committees can become victims of their own success and may be asked to take on responsibilities that are beyond their capability to deliver.

The following is an overview of some of the additional responsibilities more commonly delegated to audit committees.

Compliance with Laws and Regulations

Companies face a significant challenge in monitoring their compliance with all the laws and regulations that apply to them. This is particularly true for multinational companies with operations in several jurisdictions within Canada and around the world. The challenge is compounded when companies also operate different lines of businesses.

In our view, at a minimum, the audit committee's charter should include oversight of the company's compliance with tax and securities laws and regulations, an issue of particular complexity in multinational companies, which typically are subject to several tax and regulatory jurisdictions.

It is management's responsibility to develop a process for ensuring compliance with securities laws and regulations and with tax laws and regulations. It is the audit committee's responsibility to monitor this process. Management should provide the audit committee with a description of the process and regular reports explaining how senior management has satisfied itself that the company is meeting all of its financial reporting and tax filing requirements in all applicable jurisdictions. We believe this will be accomplished as part of the CEO and CFO certification process, when quarterly reports should be made to the audit committee on the CEO's and CFO's assessment and evaluation of disclosure controls.

Audit committees may wish to extend their responsibilities to include monitoring management's processes for ensuring that the company complies with other laws and regulations. If the audit committee decides to undertake this broader and more onerous set of responsibilities, it must work with, and receive regular reports from, legal counsel and internal audit to ensure that management has the appropriate procedures and policies in place throughout the company. The audit committee should also seek the advice of corporate counsel or outside counsel in developing programs to ensure compliance with these laws and regulations.

Whistle Blowing

MI 52-110 requires audit committees to establish procedures for:[10]

a) *the receipt, retention and treatment of complaints received by the issuer regarding accounting, internal accounting controls, or auditing matters; and*

b) *the confidential, anonymous submission by employees of the issuer of concerns regarding questionable accounting or auditing matters.*

It is important to note that the instrument does not require the audit committee to perform these whistle blowing procedures or investigate complaints; rather, the audit committee's role is to establish procedures for an effective whistle blowing process.

The audit committee should ensure that communication procedures appropriate to the company's size, business and circumstances have been established. In so doing, the audit committee should focus its attention on whether the company has the proper policies in place, and assess whether the culture of the company, and the "tone at the top" set by the CEO and CFO, encourages or inhibits the communication of concerns or complaints by employees and other persons.

---

[10] MI 52-110, Section 2.3 (7).

In circumstances where a recipient of these communications is identified, the audit committee should be satisfied that the recipient of such communications by employees and others is sufficiently independent of management (e.g., chief internal auditor, general counsel) to ensure that anonymity will be maintained, that all communications will be followed up and responded to in an appropriate manner, and that the rights of the employee will be protected. The recipient should have the authority, in consultation with the board or the audit committee, to investigate any matter and any person, including the CEO, CFO, board members and other senior executives. He or she should also have direct access to the audit committee and its chairman.

Moreover, the audit committee should require the executive responsible for receiving such communications to report regularly to the audit committee and then to the board on complaints received. Such reporting should include a summary of complaints received since the last meeting, the nature of the complaints, any observable trends and any complaints involving senior management, questionable business practices, intimidation of employees or the auditors, and possible fraud or illegal acts.

In some circumstances, the audit committee or its chairman may be the direct recipient of such communications. When the audit committee, or its chairman receives this type of communication, action must be taken promptly, but with discretion. The chairman of the audit committee should immediately inform the chairman of the board, the CEO, the general counsel and outside counsel. If the CEO and the CFO are the subjects of such communication, the chairman of the audit committee must act with considerable discretion but must inform the board immediately. The chairman of the audit committee should be wary in responding to any such communications because the communication might be the act of a disgruntled and frustrated employee who feels that he or she has been unfairly dealt with by management. However, it might also represent the concerns of a sincere employee who is disturbed about what he or she has found or observed. The chairman should refrain from making any response that has not been discussed with and approved by the board of directors.

In our view, any such communication should be taken seriously. The appropriate response depends upon the circumstances, but should involve the combined wisdom of both general counsel and outside counsel, supported by the external auditor if appropriate. In developing an appropriate response, the issues that need to be addressed include:
- the potential impact of the allegations, if validated, on the company's business operations and control systems;
- the potential number of persons involved, both inside and outside the company;
- the possible impact, if validated, on the financial statements or information that the company has already published or released to the market;
- the possibility, if validated, of fraudulent or illegal activities;
- the extent of investigation required and who should perform it;

- the need for forensic accounting/auditing expertise; and
- the potential restitution or recovery from insurance policies, and what actions are needed to maximize the potential success of such recoveries.

While the nature and extent of follow-up procedures will depend on the circumstances, the audit committee should carefully monitor the investigations of any such complaints and receive regular reports thereon. In some circumstances, it will be appropriate for the board to direct the audit committee to undertake the investigation or to supervise it.

Alternatively, the board may wish to create an *ad hoc* committee of the board to do so.

The most effective process will depend on the circumstances of the company and its business. Some of the questions that an audit committee should consider in reviewing and approving such a process include:

1) Who is responsible for the process? Does this individual and the process have a sufficient degree of independence and objectivity to be both effective and credible?
2) Has the CEO and senior management provided the right leadership and support for the process?
3) Is the process focused only on employees or is it open to third parties? How is this process integrated with other feedback, suggestion box and complaint systems?
4) Do the employees understand the process? What is their level of confidence that complaints will be dealt with quickly and effectively without reprisal?
5) Through what medium can complaints be submitted (e.g., mail, e-mail, voice mail, special secure phone line, etc.)? Will the process support the languages in which business is conducted and in which employees operate?
6) What is the decision-making process to determine whether a complaint is serious or frivolous?
7) How are decisions on whether to investigate, how to investigate, and who should investigate made (especially if the complaint involves senior management or the board of directors)?
8) How will investigations be managed to ensure they are effective, maintain confidentiality and minimize the risk of retaliation claims? Have appropriate considerations been given to protecting legal privilege?
9) What is the process for deciding what actions should be taken when investigations are completed? What is the involvement of the audit committee or board of directors? Is there an appeal process?
10) What reporting is provided to senior management, the audit committee and the board of directors on complaints received, investigated and actions taken?

In establishing a process, the audit committee should err on the side of simplicity and on the side of reporting more, not less, to the audit committee or its chairman. As experience is gained, these decisions can be revisited.

Corporate Ethics and Codes of Conduct

The proposed NI 58-101, "Disclosure Of Corporate Governance Practices" will require companies to:[11]

> *Disclose whether or not your board of directors has adopted a code of business conduct and ethics for its directors, officers and employees. In addition:*
>
> a) *disclose whether or not your board of directors monitors compliance with its code of business conduct and ethics; if not, explain why your board considers this to be appropriate; and*
>
> b) *if your board of directors has granted a waiver (including an implicit waiver) from a provision of the code of business conduct and ethics in favour of a director or officer, briefly describe the nature of the waiver, the name of the person to whom the waiver was granted, the basis for granting the waiver and the date of the waiver.*
>
> *If a code of business conduct and ethics has not been adopted, explain why your board considers this to be appropriate.*

In addition, NI 58-101 will also require:[12]

> 1) *Every issuer that has adopted a written code of business conduct and ethics must file a copy of such code on SEDAR no later than the date on which the issuer's audited annual financial statements must be filed, unless a copy of such code has been previously filed.*
>
> 2) *Any amendment to a code of business conduct and ethics that was previously filed under subsection (1) must be filed on SEDAR no later than 30 days after the final form of amendment has been approved by the board of directors.*
>
> 3) *If a board of directors grants, in favour of an officer or director of the issuer or a subsidiary entity of the issuer, a waiver of a code of business conduct and ethics that the issuer filed under this section 2.3, the issuer must promptly issue and file on SEDAR a news release that describes:*
>
>   a) *the nature of the waiver;*
>
>   b) *the name of the person to whom the waiver was granted;*
>
>   c) *the basis for granting the waiver; and*
>
>   d) *the date of the waiver.*
>
> 4) *For the purposes of subsection (3), where a waiver granted in favour of an officer or director is an implicit waiver, the news release referred to in subsection (3) must be issued and filed promptly upon the board becoming aware of such waiver.*

---

[11] Canadian Securities Administrators' National Instrument 58-101, "Disclosure of Corporate Governance Practices", Section 5.

[12] *Ibid*, Section 2.3.

Companies without a separate ethics or social responsibility committee may ask another committee to assume oversight responsibilities with respect to corporate ethics and codes of conduct. This role would include approving policies developed by management and monitoring their implementation. If the board delegates these responsibilities to a committee other than the audit committee, the audit committee should satisfy itself that these processes are appropriate and effective.

Audit committees may also have responsibilities for the code of conduct. In companies where another board committee has primary responsibility for the code of conduct, the audit committee's role is to monitor the code's implementation and the related employee accountability processes. If there is not another board committee responsible for the code of conduct, the audit committee may be asked to assume responsibility for both policy development and implementation.

Review of Senior Executive Expenses
Audit committees may also be asked to review the expenses of the CEO and the chairman of the board to ensure that they do not represent improper charges or reflect abuses. We believe very strongly that all audit committees should assume this responsibility.

Oversight of the Selection of Senior Financial Executives
We believe very strongly that the CEO should involve the audit committee in the selection of new senior financial officers, including the CFO and head of internal audit. At the very least, the chairman of the committee should be given the opportunity to interview potential candidates for CFO, head of internal audit and other senior financial executives. We believe that every member of the committee should be given the opportunity to interview a short list of candidates for CFO.

Review of Consulting Expenses
It is now common for audit committees to review the fees paid to the external auditor for audit and non-audit services. Many audit committees also review the consulting services provided by other professional services firms. This not only provides a basis for assessing the reasonableness of the fees paid to the external auditor for non-audit services, it also helps ensure that proper controls and accountability exist over the consulting services provided by other professional services firms, which are normally much greater than the fees for non-audit services paid to the external auditor.

Operating as Both an Audit and Finance Committee
In some companies, particularly not-for-profit organizations, the board of directors often asks the audit committee to provide more than an oversight role with respect to financial reporting. It may also ask the audit committee to take responsibility for the entity's financing, financing strategies and the implementation of those strategies. While this approach has the benefit of utilizing the financial expertise of the members on the audit committee and ensuring that issues related to financing strategies are addressed, there may be some

disadvantages. For example, the board and the audit committee may not always be clear as to when the committee is operating in the capacity of a financial advisor or as an audit committee. More importantly, the objectivity of the audit committee may be impaired if the same committee becomes the prime decision maker on financing issues including financing and tax structures.

Process for Creating an Audit Committee Charter

Audit committees should articulate carefully the responsibilities they are willing to assume to ensure that no expectation gap exists between the committee and the board with regard to the duties of the audit committee. The committee must also ensure that its responsibilities are disclosed publicly so investors also understand what they can expect from the audit committee.

The most effective way to accomplish this is to develop an audit committee charter, and disclose it as part of the corporate governance practices disclosures. (Some examples of audit committee charters are included in Appendix E.)

The following describes a process the authors have introduced to several audit committees and boards of directors. It is a process that should be led by the audit committee chairman.

Step One: Obtain the Support of the Board Chairman and the CEO

An audit committee should begin the process of creating the charter by obtaining the support of the chairman of the board and the CEO. The chairman of the audit committee should meet with the chairman of the board and the CEO to explain the reasons for and the benefits of developing a clear mandate and charter for the audit committee, and to obtain their agreement on the process for developing it.

Some of the concerns often expressed at these meetings are:
- the amount of time involved in allocating the appropriate responsibilities to the audit committee;
- articulating these responsibilities in the charter;
- the power the charter may confer on the audit committee; and
- whether the process will produce a charter that is both practical and achievable.

The chairman of the audit committee should address these concerns by concentrating on the advantages of creating and disclosing a well-articulated charter. The chairman should also articulate the risks of not having a clear allocation of responsibilities among the board, other board committees and the audit committee.

Step Two: Form a Steering Group

Once the required commitment has been received from the chairman of the board and the CEO, the next step is for the chairman of the audit committee to assemble a steering group to guide the activities in developing the charter. In our experience, the most effective steering groups are small ones consisting of the board chairman, CEO, CFO, the external audit partner and corporate counsel. Companies with internal audit departments should also consider including the head of that department in the steering group.

Step Three: Benchmark the Committee's Responsibilities

The steering group's first task is to benchmark the audit committee's existing responsibilities against minimum, best and leading edge practices. Because audit committee practices are evolving continuously, what was once a leading edge practice may now have become a best or even minimum practice. It is, therefore, prudent for audit committees to benchmark their activities on an ongoing basis.

A tool for audit committees to use in assessing their major areas of responsibility is provided in Appendix C. For each area of responsibility, the tool indicates traditional or minimal practice, common or best practices, and leading edge practices. Using this tool or a similar one, the steering group can initially identify the appropriate level of practice for its audit committee in each area of responsibility.

At this stage, it is important to focus on determining the specific responsibilities to be included in the audit committee's charter, but not on writing the specifics of the charter itself. Once completed, the benchmarking matrix, together with any recommendations of the steering group, should be submitted to both the audit committee and the board so that they can agree on the appropriate positioning for the audit committee.

Step Four: Review Benchmarking and Develop a Draft Charter

The audit committee should review the benchmarking matrix, and any recommendations of the steering group, to determine whether its responsibilities have been positioned appropriately in the company's circumstances with respect to minimum, best and leading edge practices. In our experience, this exercise will generate considerable discussion among committee members as they seek to understand the options available to them and to decide the most appropriate responsibilities for the committee.

After this meeting is concluded, the steering group will be in a position to begin drafting a charter — a task that may be undertaken by the chairman of the audit committee, a member of management or the external auditor.

Step Five: Review the Draft Charter

Once a draft charter has been produced, it should be reviewed first by the steering group and then by the audit committee. After the audit committee has approved it, the draft charter should be submitted to the board of directors for its approval.

After the board of directors has approved the charter, the company is required to disclose it in the AIF. We believe this is a positive step that will help investors understand the company's governance structure and how the audit committee's oversight contributes to accurate, timely and reliable financial reporting. This helps to build investor confidence and the company's overall reputation in the capital markets.

Step Six: The Final Step — Translate the Charter into a Work Plan

To help ensure that the responsibilities and duties contained in the charter are actually carried out, the charter should be translated into a work plan for the audit committee.

The process for doing this is quite simple. In consultation with the CFO, external auditor, and head of internal audit, the chairman of the audit committee should allocate every responsibility identified in the charter to a specific meeting agenda and date at which the item will be addressed. The work plan should also identify the kind of information and assurances that are to be provided to the audit committee at each meeting and identify who is accountable for providing this information and these assurances.

Once the work plan has been developed, it is the responsibility of the chairman of the audit committee to ensure that the commitments are met. In our view, liability for audit committees arises not from the responsibilities the committee undertakes, but from the failure to discharge these responsibilities in an effective manner.

Key Messages

- All *reporting issuers are now required to have a charter and to disclose the text of their charter.*
- *The text of the audit committee's charter should be clear and precise, so that the board of directors, management, the external auditor and investors clearly understand the roles and responsibilities of each in ensuring the integrity of internal control, risk management and financial reporting.*
- *The process for developing or reviewing a charter develops commitment by all parties to the committee's goals.*
- *After approving a charter, it is imperative that the audit committee carries out the duties under that charter. Carrying out those duties provides a good protection against liability.*

Audit Committees and the External Auditor

One of the key dimensions of audit committee responsibility is oversight of the external auditor. The *Sarbanes-Oxley Act* in the United States and MI 52-110 have now established, as a matter of securities regulation, that the external auditor works for and is accountable to the audit committee and board of directors as representatives of the shareholders. This is a change in the historical accountability relationship, under which the external auditor's essential relationship has been with management. This new accountability relationship between the external auditor and the audit committee and board of directors will likely be adopted by other organizations with public accountability, such as hospitals, crown corporations, etc. Understanding the way in which this new accountability relationship better enables audit committees and external auditors to work together more effectively is very important for all parties involved in the corporate reporting process.

The External Auditor's Responsibilities

Canadian statutes require that the external auditor be appointed at the annual meeting of the shareholders pursuant to a vote of the shareholders. The external auditor's duties are set forth in the statutes, MI 52-110 and the professional standards established by the Canadian Institute of Chartered Accountants. As prescribed in the CICA *Handbook*, in conducting an audit of a Canadian public company, the external auditor discharges his or her professional responsibilities by:

- Complying with the related rules of professional conduct (e.g., independence rules) issued by provincial institutes of chartered accountants and, if required, additional rules issued by regulators or professional bodies in other jurisdictions (e.g., the U.S. Securities and Exchange Commission).
- Complying with generally accepted auditing standards (GAAS) and supporting guidance as set forth in the CICA *Handbook*.

- Complying with the policies and requirements as set forth by the external auditor's own auditing firm.
- Communicating to the appropriate parties the nature and extent of the audit and the results of the auditor's work.

Generally Accepted Auditing Standards

An audit performed in accordance with generally accepted auditing standards (GAAS) is designed to provide reasonable assurance that the financial statements, taken as a whole, are free from material misstatement, whether caused by fraud or error. While a detailed discussion of GAAS is beyond the scope of this book, the following table provides a high level overview of the auditor's responsibilities and the audit committee's related role and responsibilities:

Generally Accepted Auditing Standards	Audit Committee Role and Responsibilities
1) The examination should be performed and the report prepared by a person or persons having adequate technical training and proficiency in auditing, with due care and with an objective state of mind.	Review the experiences of the lead audit partner and senior members of the audit team and assess their qualifications in relation to the company's business and financial reporting requirements. Monitor the auditor's independence and ensure that the auditor always operates with an "objective state of mind".
2) i) The work should be adequately planned and properly executed using sufficient knowledge of the entity's business as a basis. If assistants are employed they should be properly supervised.	Provide input to, discuss, review and approve the proposed audit plan, including its key areas of focus and staffing.
ii) A sufficient understanding of internal control should be obtained to plan the audit. When control risk is assessed below maximum, sufficient appropriate audit evidence should be obtained through tests of controls to support the assessment.	Review and understand the extent of the auditor's reliance on internal control and internal audit in their proposed audit plan.
iii) Sufficient appropriate audit evidence should be obtained, by such means as inspection, observation, inquiry, confirmation, computation and analysis, to afford a reasonable basis to support the content of the report.	Ask the auditor, at the conclusion of the audit, whether he or she has obtained sufficient and appropriate audit evidence to support his or her report and whether management has placed any restrictions on the audit.

Generally Accepted Auditing Standards	Audit Committee Role and Responsibilities
3) i) The report should identify the financial statements and distinguish between the responsibilities of management and the responsibilities of the auditor.	The responsibility for the preparation of the financial statements rests with management. In reviewing the statements, the audit committee should review the CEO and CFO certifications filed with the securities commissions, the supporting process leading to certification, and the formal written representations that management has provided to the external auditor with respect to the completeness, accuracy and presentation of the statements.
ii) The report should describe the scope of the auditor's examination.	Ensure that the scope of the auditor's examination, as set out in the audit plan and any subsequent changes to it, is properly reflected in their report.
iii) The report should contain either an expression of opinion on the financial statements or an assertion that an opinion cannot be expressed. In the latter case, the reasons therefor should be stated.	Review the auditor's opinion, and explore fully any reservation in the opinion or denial of opinion and the related implications.
iv) Where an opinion is expressed, it should indicate whether the financial statements present fairly, in all material respects, the financial position, results of operations and cash flows in accordance with an appropriate disclosed basis of accounting which, except in special circumstances, should be generally accepted accounting principles. The report should provide adequate explanation with respect to any reservation contained in such opinion.	Understand the critical accounting policies, significant accounting estimates and judgments made by management in the preparation of the financial statements, including consistency with prior periods. Review, understand and concur with the judgments made by management and the auditors with respect to materiality, including consistency with prior periods.

In addition to the standards and guidance set out in the CICA *Handbook*, each auditing firm also has its own policies and procedures, including those pertaining to quality and technical consultation, which they have developed to ensure that their audit engagements are performed in accordance with generally accepted auditing standards.

Reporting on Quality of Audit Work

Audit committees should ask the lead audit partner to describe how the auditor will ensure that the audit engagement is performed in accordance with GAAS and with his or her firm's specific auditing standards. They should also ask for information on how the lead audit partner will supervise the work to be performed, the nature and extent of other quality assurance reviews that may be undertaken, and whether or not any technical specialists will be consulted during the course of the audit.

In the United States, the NYSE requires that audit committees of listed companies obtain reports on the quality of audit work performed by the external auditor:[1]

> *...at least annually, [audit committees] obtain and review a report by the independent audi-tor describing: the firm's internal quality control procedures; any material issues raised by the most recent internal quality-control review, or peer review, of the firm, or by any inquiry or investigation by governmental or professional authorities, within the preceding five years, respecting one or more independent audits carried out by the firm, and any steps taken to deal with any such issues...*

Such detailed reporting requirements have not yet been adopted in Canada, although Canadian public companies listed on the NYSE are required to follow them.

The important message for all audit committees, however, is that they should obtain peri-odic reports from the external auditor on how the auditor ensures compliance with GAAS and should continually assess the capabilities and competencies brought by the auditor to the engagement, and the auditor's performance and independence.

Canadian Public Accountability Board
Background

The Canadian Public Accountability Board (CPAB) was created in 2002 by the CSA, the Superintendent of Financial Institutions and Canada's chartered accountants to promote high quality external audits of Canadian reporting issuers. CPAB's authority is set out in National Instrument 52-108, "Auditor Oversight", which requires all public accounting firms that provide external audit services for a reporting issuer to register with CPAB and be a "participant" in the CPAB "oversight program", which includes compliance with any restric-tions or sanctions imposed by CPAB.

---

[1] Final NYSE Corporate Governance Rules, paragraph 7.(c)(iii)(A).

This is the first time that public accounting firms have been required to comply with a national registration and inspection process. CPAB reports that, in its first year of operation, 230 public accounting firms registered with CPAB and approximately 200 firms chose to exit the market of providing external audit services to reporting issuers and, therefore, did not register with CPAB.

Structure
The overall responsibility for CPAB is given to a five-member Council of Governors. This council is made up of the chair of the CSA, the chair of the Ontario Securities Commission, the chair of the Québec Autorité des marches financiers, the Federal Superintendent of Financial Institutions and the president of the CICA. In addition to voting on by-law amendments, the council has the sole right to vote for the appointment of the independent directors and to appoint CPAB's chairman and vice chairman. It also has the power to remove the chairman and board members.

CPAB is governed by an 11-person board of directors that is appointed by the Council of Governors. Seven members, including the chairman, are from outside the accounting profession. Of the remaining four members, two are currently the CEOs of the provincial institutes of chartered accountants in Alberta and Ontario and one is the CEO of the Ordre des comptables agréés du Québec. Board members are appointed for a term of up to three years and are eligible for reappointment, provided that the total tenure does not exceed six years.

The operations of CPAB are conducted by full- and part-time staff, and directed by a chief executive officer who is appointed by and accountable to the board of directors. The costs of CPAB are billed, through the external auditors, to Canada's reporting issuers on the basis of audit fees.

Oversight Program
CPAB discharges its responsibilities through its oversight program that includes:
- establishing and maintaining participation requirements for public accounting firms that audit reporting issuers;
- maintaining a register of public accounting firms that audit reporting issuers;
- conducting inspections of registered public accounting firms to ensure compliance with professional standards and participation requirements;
- receiving and evaluating reports and recommendations resulting from the inspection process, including, if appropriate, reports from provincial accounting organizations on results of inspections of public accounting firms that audit reporting issuers that are not inspected directly by CPAB;
- imposing, where appropriate, sanctions and restrictions on public accounting firms that audit reporting issuers and, where necessary require remedial action;

- referring matters, as appropriate, to provincial accounting organizations for discipline purposes;
- referring matters, as appropriate, to securities regulators;
- providing comments and recommendations on accounting standards, assurance standards and governance practices to relevant standards-setting and oversight bodies; and
- providing recommendations to securities regulatory authorities.

Inspection Process

There are three categories of inspections. CPAB staff conduct annual inspections of the 12 participating public accounting firms that audit 50 or more reporting issuers; the Big Four firms are included in this category. CPAB conducts triennial inspections of other public accounting firms that register with the Public Accounting Oversight Board (PCAOB) in the United States. The rest of the participating firms will be inspected once every three years by provincial accountancy bodies, but subject to CPAB direction and review of results.

The CPAB inspections are designed to examine the public accounting firm's compliance with professional accounting and auditing standards, which include the extent to which each firm's system of quality control has been properly designed and effectively implemented. In this regard, it should be noted that the CICA's Auditing and Assurance Standards Board has issued new standards for quality control in public accounting firms that are effective January 1, 2005.

The inspections comprise a combination of procedures. CPAB staff conduct interviews of senior people (typically between 30 and 40 for a large firm) and review various documents, including policy and procedural manuals, quality-related communications, independence confirmations, client acceptance and continuance documentation, personnel files, training curricula and attendance records, staff satisfaction survey results, and quality assurance monitoring reports. CPAB staff also conduct focus groups to obtain input from partners and staff on quality related issues. Finally, they review audit working papers of completed audit engagements on a sampling basis.

Reporting

At the end of each inspection, CPAB provides the participating firm with a private report that contains the findings, recommendations and any other observations arising from the inspection. First, CPAB provides the firm with a draft report, which it discusses with the firm before it is finalized. The final report, by contractual arrangements with all participating firms and CPAB, cannot be made public or shared with any third party including companies audited by the inspected firm. CPAB does, however, publish an overall annual report on all inspections that is available on their website http://www.cpab-ccrc.ca.

Public accounting firms, other than those in Alberta, British Columbia and Manitoba, are required to provide notice, in certain situations, of any restrictions or sanctions imposed by the CPAB to their audit clients and to the securities regulator in each jurisdiction in which the audit clients are a reporting issuer.

Sanctions

Participating firms are expected to implement the recommendations contained in the final report within a prescribed period of time, normally 180 days. These recommendations may include a wide range of matters, such as changes to firm policy manuals, introduction of new compliance procedures, changes to professional education requirements or programs, etc.

If a firm fails to implement the recommendations, CPAB has indicated that it would make that fact public, and could impose other requirements, restrictions and sanctions on the firm.

CPAB has the authority to impose a number of restrictions and sanctions, such as a temporary or permanent limitation on the activities and operations of the firm or an individual in the firm. In extreme circumstances, CPAB could suspend or prohibit the firm from providing external audit services to reporting issuers.

Comment

CPAB will have an impact on the way in which external audits are conducted and documented. We expect that its presence and activities will have a positive effect. CPAB, however, is in its infancy and some of its practices will, no doubt, evolve.

One of the issues for audit committees to consider is that, at present, neither the external auditor nor CPAB are permitted to divulge the results of an inspection to a company or its audit committee. In our view, this can place an audit committee in a difficult position. Similarly, external auditors who wish to fulfill their obligation to communicate candidly to the audit committee may also be placed in a difficult position. We, therefore, encourage CPAB and external auditors to improve the communication process so that appropriate material information is provided to the audit committee.

The External Auditor's Accountability

Canadian statutes set out the formalities of the external auditor's appointment, and the financial statement reporting obligations of the board and the auditor to the shareholder. The statutes do not address issues such as the mechanisms by which the external auditor is selected and appointed, how the scope of the external auditor's work is determined, the fees to be paid to the auditor, how the audit is to be conducted, and what other services will be provided by the external auditor. Many of these matters, however, are addressed in MI 52-110. Given the current high level of scrutiny placed on external auditors and their work, audit committees and auditors need to redefine and strengthen their working relationships to ensure that they are able to address these issues appropriately. (This subject is discussed further in Chapter 8, Managing Relationships.)

MI 52-110 states that:[2]

2) *An audit committee must recommend to the board of directors:*
   a) *the external auditor to be nominated for the purpose of preparing or issuing an auditor's report or performing other audit, review or attest services for the issuer; and*
   b) *the compensation of the external auditor.*
3) *An audit committee must be directly responsible for overseeing the work of the external auditor engaged for the purpose of preparing or issuing an auditor's report or performing other audit, review or attest services for the issuer, including the resolution of disagreements between management and the external auditor regarding financial reporting.*
4) *An audit committee must pre-approve all non-audit services to be provided to the issuer or its subsidiary entities by the issuer's external auditor.*

In the companion policy that supports MI 52-110, the CSA provides the following explanations for these regulations and emphasizes the accountability of the external auditor to the audit committee:[3]

Although under corporate law an issuer's external auditors are responsible to the shareholders, in practice, shareholders have often been too dispersed to effectively exercise meaningful oversight of the external auditors. As a result, management has typically assumed this oversight role. However, the auditing process may be compromised if the external auditors view their main responsibility as serving management rather than the shareholders. By assigning these responsibilities to an independent audit committee, the Instrument ensures that the external audit will be conducted independently of the issuer's management.

An illustration of the relationship that should now exist among the external auditor, management, the audit committee and the board of directors is provided in Figure 10.

---

[2] Canadian Securities Administrators, *Multilateral Instrument 52-110*, "*Audit Committees*", Section 2.3.
[3] Canadian Securities Administrators, *Companion Policy 52-110CP to Multilateral Instrument 52-110*, "*Audit Committees*", Part 2.1.

Figure 10 | Key Relationships Among the External Auditor, Management, Audit Committee and Board of Directors

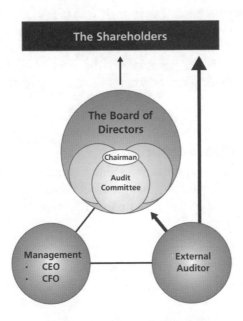

The essential message illustrated in Figure 10 is that the external auditor has two equal accountabilities. The first is to the shareholders, to whom the auditor must report on whether the financial statements are presented in accordance with generally accepted accounting principles. The second is to the audit committee and board of directors. While the external auditor must work closely with management, the auditor is not accountable to management. In simple terms — the external auditor reports to the shareholder, works for the audit committee and works with management in conducting his or her audit.

While MI 52-110 makes the external auditor accountable to the audit committee, this cannot compromise the external auditor's professional responsibilities to conduct his or her audit in accordance with generally accepted auditing standards and to report on the results of the audit to the shareholders. The companion policy to MI 52-110 emphasizes this point:[4]

> *Notwithstanding this responsibility, the external auditors are retained by, and are ultimately accountable to, the shareholders. As a result, subsection 2.3(3) does not detract from the external auditors' right and responsibility to also provide their views directly to the shareholders if they disagree with an approach being taken by the audit committee.*

[4] *Ibid*, part 2.2.

In order to discharge this dual set of accountabilities, the external auditor must understand the expectations that the audit committee and shareholders have for his or her performance. The shareholders' expectations can be satisfied by performing the audit examination in accordance with GAAS. A much different approach is required to satisfy the audit committee's expectations. The external auditor must meet with the committee to directly ascertain its expectations, ensure these expectations are properly articulated in the charter, and then take appropriate steps to ensure that those expectations are met. Audit committees clearly have an onus to express their expectations of the external auditor. This is the foundation of the accountability relationship between the audit committee and the external auditor.

The External Auditor's Independence

The independence of the external auditor is an essential component of the audit relationship. It is fundamental to the accountability that the external auditor has to the audit committee, to the performance of the audit and to preserving the confidence that investors place on the report of the auditor.

A *Summary of Auditor Independence Requirements*

New rules have recently been issued by the chartered accounting profession that clarify and strengthen the responsibilities of the external auditor to maintain the auditor's independence. These new rules require the external auditor to:[5]

1) First, identify any threats to their independence, which have been grouped in five categories:
   - A *Self-Interest Threat* – when a firm or a person on the engagement team could benefit from a financial interest in, or another self-interest conflict with, an assurance client.
   - A *Self-Review Threat* – when the external auditor is involved in auditing his or her own work.
   - An *Advocacy Threat* – when a firm, or a person on the engagement team, promotes an assurance client's position or opinion to the point that objectivity may be, or may be perceived to be, impaired.
   - A *Familiarity Threat* – when, by virtue of a close relationship with an assurance client, its directors, officers or employees, a firm or a person on the engagement team becomes too sympathetic to the client's interests.
   - An *Intimidation Threat* – when a person on the engagement team may be deterred from acting objectively and exercising professional skepticism by threats, actual or perceived, from the directors, officers or employees of an assurance client.

---

[5] The Canadian Institute of Chartered Accountants, *Guide to the New Independence Standard*, Section 2.0, "Overview of Independence Standard" and Section 3.0, "Threats to Independence", October 2003.

2) Having identified the potential threats to independence, the external auditor must then evaluate the significance of those threats. For each threat that is not clearly insignificant, the external auditor must determine if any of the following safeguards would eliminate the threat or reduce it to an acceptable level:
   - professional, legislative, or regulatory safeguards;
   - safeguards within the entity; and
   - safeguards within the firm.
3) Third, external auditors are to determine if any of the following prohibitions exist, which would preclude them from performing the engagement:
   - financial interests in the client;
   - loans and guarantees to or from the client;
   - close business relationships with the client;
   - family and personal relationships with the client;
   - future or recent employment with the client;
   - serving as an officer, director or company secretary of the client;
   - providing restricted non-assurance services to the client; or
   - making management decisions for the client.
4) Finally, for each threat identified by the external auditor as not clearly insignificant, the external auditor is required to document in the working papers a description of the nature of the engagement, the independence threat identified, a description of the safeguard applied to eliminate the threat or reduce it to an acceptable level, and an explanation of how the safeguard eliminates the threat or reduces it to an acceptable level.

Reporting to the Audit Committee

In April 2002, the CICA's Assurance Standards Board issued Section 5751 of the CICA *Handbook*, which provides standards and guidance for auditors with respect to communication with those having oversight responsibility for the financial reporting process. The auditor, at least annually, and prior to the issuance of the auditor's report, should in a letter to the audit committee:[6]

> a) *disclose to the audit committee, all relationships between the auditor and his or her related business or practice and the entity and its related entities that in the auditor's professional judgment may reasonably be thought to bear on the auditor's independence;*
>
> b) *confirm the auditor's independence with the audit committee; and*
>
> c) *disclose to the audit committee the total fees charged for audit and non-audit services provided by the auditor.*

---

[6] CICA *Handbook*, Section 5751, "Communications with Those Having Oversight Responsibility for the Financial Reporting Process", paragraph 32.

The CICA *Handbook* also requires the auditor to consider in reporting to the audit committee any relationships in which he or she:[7]
* holds a financial interest, either directly or indirectly, in a client;
* holds a position, either directly or indirectly, that gives the right or responsibility to exert significant influence over the financial or accounting policies of a client;
* has personal or business relationships of immediate family, close relatives, partners or retired partners, either directly or indirectly, with a client;
* has an economic dependence on a client; and
* provides services in addition to the audit engagement.

The disclosure of audit and non-audit fees should be in the form agreed with the audit committee (for example by type of services or within specific dollar ranges). The audit committee's expectations are normally determined and agreed before the auditor's letter is finalized.

Resolving Auditor Independence Issues

We believe it is very important to ensure that a candid dialogue on independence issues takes place between the audit committee and the external auditor.

The audit committee should make it clear that the external auditor must not refrain from disclosing to the committee any matter that could bear on the auditor's independence solely because the auditor has concluded that his or her independence is not impaired. The onus is on the external auditor to bring to the committee all matters that pose a potential threat to their independence. The audit committee is entitled to know, and should ask, about all matters that might have a bearing on the auditor's independence. If the auditor has judged a matter as not being one that might imperil his or her independence, the audit committee should ask the auditor to explain the reasons for such a judgment.

It is not, however, the audit committee's responsibility to form a conclusion regarding the external auditor's independence. That is the responsibility of the external auditor. The audit committee's role is to ensure that this conclusion has been formed in a professional and rigorous manner, taking into account all factors that affect the auditor's independence, and that the conclusion appears reasonable in the circumstances.

---

[7] *Ibid*, paragraph 5751.26.

It should be noted that while Canada has moved towards a more "rules-based approach" to independence, similar to that in the United States, some differences remain between Canadian and U.S. standards for independence. The United States continues to pursue an even more detailed, rules-based approach to auditor independence. These rules typically take the form of setting out a series of "independence impairing conditions", and if the auditor is not in violation of any of these conditions, he or she is entitled to conclude that they are independent.

In our view, the substance of auditor independence is the requirement for the auditors to perform their work with an "objective state of mind". While compliance with the new detailed rules is required, auditors must address the substance of independence. Therefore, the external auditor should be encouraged to focus on the substance of their independence rather than merely on its form.

Rotation of Audit Firms

There are some who believe that auditor independence can be assured by introducing a mandatory policy of regular rotation of audit firms. We do not support such a policy. A mandatory rotation of auditors would disrupt the audit process, make it more difficult for the auditor to develop and maintain a meaningful knowledge of the company's business and systems, and significantly increase the costs of auditing. In addition, the enforced brevity of the audit relationship could make the new auditor more dependent on management for information and, as a result, undermine the quality and effectiveness of the audit. While we are not in favour of the mandatory rotation of audit firms, we do support the policy of rotating the lead audit partner.

Partner Rotation

The new auditor independence rules state that a chartered accountant cannot continue as the lead engagement partner, or as the engagement quality control reviewer, on an audit engagement of a listed entity for more than five years in total, and cannot resume or assume either such role until a further five years have elapsed. Other partners who perform audit services, but not as the lead engagement partner, who provide more than 10 hours of assurance services in connection with the annual financial statement audit or the quarterly review of financial information cannot continue in such roles for more than seven years in total and may not thereafter perform the role of audit partner of the listed entity until a further two years have elapsed.

These new rules will have a substantial impact on the audit practices of public accounting firms. The audit committee should have an ongoing dialogue with the lead engagement partner and other senior partners in the firm as appropriate with respect to the plans the firm is making for the rotation of key partners on the audit engagement and the plans the firm has to develop partners to replace those partners who will have to "rotate off" the engagement.

Non-audit Services

Recently, most of the attention on auditor independence has been focused on the auditor's provision of consulting and non-audit services. In our view, however, this is not the crux of the independence issue. The most serious threat to an auditor's independence and objectivity stems from the fact that external auditors are paid by the companies they audit. It is this reality that requires audit committees to be increasingly vigilant in inquiring carefully into all matters affecting auditor independence.

The new independence requirements contain two categories of restrictions for non-audit services. The first category contains the following non-audit services, which cannot be provided to an audit client unless it is reasonable to conclude that the results of the services will not be subject to audit procedures performed by the external audit during the course of his or her examination:[8]

- bookkeeping and accounting services;
- financial information systems design and implementation;
- actuarial services;
- valuation services; and
- internal audit services.

The second category of restricted non-audit services are those that the external auditor may never provide to an audit client, even if they are not subject to audit procedures performed by the external auditor:[9]

- expert services including litigation support;
- legal services;
- management functions;
- human resources services; and
- corporate financial services.

If the non-audit service is not prohibited, then the external auditor may be engaged to deliver that service providing that it is pre-approved by the audit committee before work is commenced. In so doing, the audit committee can delegate to one or more independent members, usually the chairman, the authority to pre-approve such non-audit services. Any such pre-approved services, however, must be presented to the audit committee at its first scheduled meeting following such pre-approval.

---

[8]   The Canadian Institute of Chartered Accountants, *Guide to the New Canadian Independence Standard*, Section 5.0, "Prohibitions", October 2003.
[9]   *Ibid.*

If the audit committee has adopted specific policies and procedures for the engagement of non-audit services by the external auditor, then these policies and procedures are to be described in the AIF.

There is a *de minimis* exemption from the pre-approval requirement for small, routine type services. However, the aggregate amount of all the non-audit services that were not pre-approved is limited 5% of the total amount of audit and non-audit fees paid by the issuer to its external auditor.

We suggest the following process be put in place to help audit committees, management and the external auditor comply with these new requirements.

The external auditor should prepare an annual client service plan, which outlines to the greatest extent practically possible, the nature and planned fees of the various attest and non-audit services that management and the audit committee would expect the external auditor to provide in the next fiscal year. The annual client service plan would include quarterly reviews, provision for routine consultations on accounting, tax and other matters etc. The annual client service plan must be presented to the audit committee for its review and approval before such services are commenced.

Management may continue to engage the external auditor for other attest or non-audit services that were not included in the pre-approved annual client service plan, providing that:
- the external auditor is not prohibited from providing such services;
- management is satisfied that the external auditor is the preferred supplier for such services;
- the proposed terms of engagement for such services are approved before services are commenced, by either the full audit committee or a member of the audit committee, normally the chairman, to whom the audit committee has delegated the authority to pre-approve such services.

In our view, the auditor's provision of non-audit services does not, of itself, create independence issues, provided that:
- management has a proper process for defining its needs, seeking competitive bids and selecting the service provider;
- the audit firm's service provider takes the appropriate actions to educate management so they make informed decisions on all recommendations produced in a non-audit engagement (for example, in a complex tax planning assignment, the service provider should ensure that management understands the proposal, the alternatives being considered and the consequences associated with each alternative);

- the audit committee satisfies itself that the service provider's work and recommendations are appropriately scrutinized and audited by members of the audit team; and
- the audit committee has appropriate oversight and approvals, under which management discusses consulting and non-audit engagements with the audit committee or its chairman prior to awarding an engagement and provides a formal review, at least annually, of all non-audit services provided by the external auditor.

Non-audit Service Relationships: Benefits and Threats

Audit committees must clearly understand both the benefits and any potential threats involved when the external auditor has a broad-based professional service relationship with the company, and is not restricted to providing services that are narrowly defined to statutory auditing.

The most obvious benefit relates to management's ability to use the external audit firm's specialized expertise to solve problems and improve operating efficiencies, tax planning, financing, risk management and control effectiveness. Auditors that have a broad-based service relationship are able to develop a much deeper and more comprehensive understanding of their client's business, management structures, ethical culture, systems, principal business risks, controls and operating practices. Such knowledge increases the likelihood of the auditor detecting material errors in the accounting records or financial statements.

This potential for improved knowledge and reporting to the audit committee is illustrated in Figure 11. External auditors provide three major categories of services:
- basic audit services (e.g., audit of the consolidated financial statements, major subsidiaries, etc.);
- tax and audit related services (e.g., tax advice, comfort letters on financings, due diligence support, extended audit procedures or investigations, risk management services, extended control assessment and testing); and
- consulting and advisory services (e.g., operating efficiency reviews, organizational structure reviews, industry benchmarking studies, system benchmarking studies, etc.).

The arrows represent the reporting obligations. Horizontal arrows indicate the reporting responsibilities of the various engagements. The vertical arrows show how the findings, interpretations and reports are integrated into the overall audit and the reporting thereon to the audit committee.

Figure 11 | **Auditor's Services and Reporting Obligations**

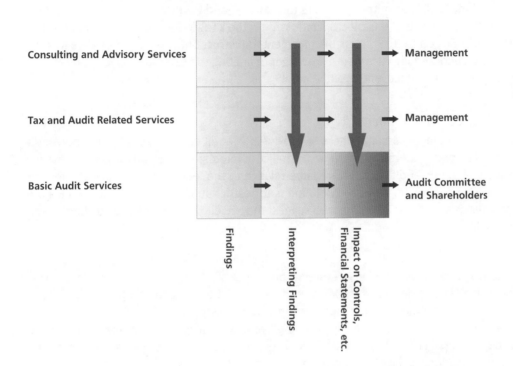

Auditors who undertake a number of engagements or assignments for a company, increase their knowledge of the company's business and systems, and thereby increase their likelihood of becoming aware of any control weaknesses, unauthorized operations/transactions, potential misstatements, disclosure matters or other issues that may impact the financial statements. The challenge for the auditors is to ensure that they effectively integrate the findings and knowledge obtained through these non-audit engagements into their audit process, so they can make more informed decisions and provide improved reporting to the audit committee. In our experience, while the integration of all non-audit engagement findings into the audit process may make some management teams uneasy, this anxiety should be mitigated when a well developed working relationship exists among the external auditor, management and the audit committee.

To ensure that the findings and knowledge gained through non-audit engagements are assessed for their effect on the financial statements and on controls, all service providers in the audit firm must understand their responsibility for reporting their findings to the lead audit partner. Similarly, the lead audit partner must monitor continually all non-audit services being provided. Finally, the lead audit partner must understand the audit committee's expectation that all significant findings will be explained and reported to the committee.

In our view there are advantages to having the external auditor engaged in various audit related and non-audit services provided the audit committee puts appropriate safeguards in place. If the audit committee prohibits the external auditor from providing these services, it must recognize that this places limitations on the knowledge the external auditor has, unless the audit committee directs management to instruct other service providers to keep the external auditor fully informed. The danger of limiting the external auditor's knowledge is its impact on the effectiveness of the audit.

Managing Conflicts of Interest

Critics of permitting external auditors to provide non-audit services suggest that non-audit relationships place external auditors in a conflict of interest, particularly when the fees for consulting and non-audit services are large relative to the fees for basic audit and related services. The commonly proposed solution is to restrict auditors from providing any non-audit services, and there are some who suggest they be allowed only to provide basic audit services.

We take a different view. We believe such a restriction could severely reduce the auditors' knowledge of the client's business, systems, operating issues/problems, risks and practices. It could also result in denying the company access to the best available resources, and thereby deprive shareholders of the benefits provided by these resources. Finally, it could increase the costs of audit and consulting services, since other professional service providers are not likely to have the detailed a knowledge of the company, its systems, strategies and operations as has the external auditor.

We recognize, however, that managing a broad-based service approach puts a burden on the lead audit partner to provide effective leadership to all members of the client service team. The partner who leads the client service team must directly ascertain the audit committee's expectations for the provision of non-audit services, and provide the committee with an unequivocal commitment to report promptly to it all findings that could have a material impact on the audit and the financial statements.

Audit firms must recognize that the lead audit partner's role is not that of a "salesman" or "account manager". Nor should the approach taken by the lead audit partner be confused with a selling strategy approach in which the audit is viewed as a "loss leader" that is used to sell more valuable non-audit services. In our view, these approaches violate the fundamental principles of the auditing profession, undermine the audit committee's integrity, and pose serious risks to the company. Using the audit to sell other services is not responsible auditing and should not be countenanced.

The Engagement Letter

The terms and conditions of all engagements, whether audit, audit-related or non-audit, performed by the external auditor should be clearly stated in an engagement letter and agreed to by the audit committee and the appropriate members of management. This letter should state the objectives and scope of the engagement, the anticipated nature and form of the reports to be provided, and the fees involved.

The engagement letter represents the contractual arrangements among the company, the audit committee and the external auditor. It should be signed by all three parties.

As a consequence of the auditor's legitimate concerns about legal liability, the chartered accounting profession has inserted exculpatory clauses designed to limit that liability. Audit committees should scrutinize these clauses carefully. Some audit committees are beginning to reject them, or modify them to the audit committee's comfort level. We encourage the audit committee to negotiate the terms of these clauses with the external auditor. In our experience, the audit committee and the external auditor can be successful in reaching an agreement that is satisfactory to both.

The Audit Plan

An important part of the external auditor's accountability to the audit committee is to engage the audit committee in developing the audit plan, including setting the priorities for the audit and reviewing the fundamental planning assumptions that determine the audit's scope and the extent of testing to be undertaken. The objective is to ensure that the proposed audit plan not only complies with professional standards but also meets the audit committee's expectations.

In our experience, meaningful input from the audit committee is achieved through direct communication with the chairman and members of the committee itself. This is not something that has been done well in the past. We suggest that the external auditor, particularly the lead audit partner, should make it a practice to meet separately with all members of the audit committee to obtain their views on audit plan priorities, including how significant business, financial and reporting risks are to be addressed. The external auditor should do this before formally presenting the audit plan to the audit committee.

Audit Plan

This section provides an overview of the key planning issues that audit committees must understand, review and discuss when approving the audit plan.

In reviewing the audit plan, the audit committee must understand the key planning parameters used in determining the audit's scope and extent of audit testing. Without this understanding, there is a danger that the audit committee will assume the audit addresses more than it does, particularly in the area of evaluating and testing controls.

Effectiveness vs. Efficiency

In its review of the proposed audit plan, the audit committee must differentiate between "effectiveness" and "efficiency" and understand how both dimensions are dealt with in the proposed plan put forward to the committee. The two concepts can best be explained by an example. Suppose an audit committee makes a request for proposals from two audit firms. Firm A submits a fee estimate that is 20% below that of Firm B. Without understanding and evaluating the effectiveness of the audit approaches of both, it may appear that Firm A is more efficient when, in fact, its scope may be more limited and hence provide a less rigorous audit. In assessing the appropriateness of audit fees, the audit committee needs to ensure that those fees reflect a common standard of effectiveness.

On the surface, efficiency is the easier dimension to understand and measure because most people assume the audit's efficiency is represented by its costs or fees. However, the cost of an audit must be related to its effectiveness, and this is the more challenging concept because it relates directly to the likelihood that the audit plan will be sufficiently comprehensive and rigorous to detect a material error in the financial statements, should such an error exist.

Audit effectiveness is only put to the test when a material error exists in the accounting records or disclosures. For example, a poorly designed, ineffective audit and a well-designed effective audit conducted in a company with high quality accounting records and controls will both yield the same results (i.e., an unqualified opinion). That is because neither audit will detect any errors or cause the auditor to qualify his or her report. In this situation, the ineffective audit will appear to be more efficient because its costs will likely be lower. The real question, however, is whether it provides reasonable assurance that management's processes and controls will prevent or detect material errors in the financial statements.

We do not believe the costs of the audit should be determinative. There have been many recent examples that demonstrate the tangible and intangible costs associated with ineffective audits. These can be extremely high and expose the audit committee, company, external auditor and shareholders to very significant risks. A constant pressure to reduce the audit scope and extent of audit testing, and limit audit fee increases or reduce them, can reduce the audit's effectiveness (i.e., the ability to detect material errors in the records or disclosures).

Considerations in Setting the Audit Priorities

When setting the audit priorities and approving the audit plan, audit committees should recognize that they face two types of risk. The risk is that the audit evidence will indicate that:

- a material misstatement does not exist, when it does, or
- a material misstatement exists when it does not.

These risks have different consequences. The first, which can be called the litigation risk, exposes the auditor, audit committee, board of directors and the company to litigation and regulatory investigation. The second, often called the false accusation risk, exposes the auditor, audit committee, board of directors and the company to embarrassment, unnecessary additional audit work and investigations or, in extreme instances, the restatement of financial statements when they are not warranted.

Both risks can be mitigated through the scope of the audit and the extent of audit testing being performed. The greater the scope and extent of the audit examination, the less the exposure to these risks. The only way to eliminate both risks is to conduct a 100% examination of all books and records — a very costly and largely impractical solution. Even then, there is a risk that incriminating evidence or transactions will be deliberately withheld from the auditor.

Dealing with Business Risk in the Audit Plan

In planning the audit, there are many sources of business risk that need to be addressed, such as those associated with financial structures, new acquisitions, environmental issues, new information technologies and systems, major new initiatives, potential asset impairments, etc. The audit committee should ask management and the internal and external auditors to identify the areas of significant business risk that might impact the financial statements, and therefore must be addressed in the audit plan.

The risk of fraud is one of the most important risks to address in planning the audit. This risk, which includes the risk of top management fraud, should be discussed with the audit committee and the external auditor. Both should reach a shared understanding as to how this risk is to be addressed in the audit plan.

In planning the audit, auditors are required by professional standards to make inquiries of management:[10]

a) to obtain an understanding of:
  i) management's assessment of the risk that the financial statements may be materially misstated as a result of fraud; and
  ii) the internal controls management has put in place to address such risk;

---

[10] CICA *Handbook*, Section 5135, The Auditor's Responsibility to Consider Fraud and Error in an Audit of Financial Statements, paragraph 5135.22.

b) to obtain knowledge of management's understanding regarding the internal controls in place to prevent and detect error;

c) to determine whether management is aware of any known fraud that has affected the entity, or suspected fraud; and

d) to determine whether management has discovered any material errors.

An audit plan that is based on an effective assessment of business risks, including the risk of fraud, will allocate the audit resources to the most critical areas. A well-designed audit plan based on risk will produce the most effective audit.

Materiality

Materiality is an important and related concept that impacts the effectiveness of the audit and the extent of audit work to be performed.

Under the concept of materiality, not all audit findings and misstatements, either individually or in the aggregate, are equally important in determining whether or not the financial statements are presented fairly in accordance with generally accepted accounting principles. Professional standards provide the following definition of materiality:[11]

> A misstatement or the aggregate of all misstatements in financial statements is considered to be material if, in the light of surrounding circumstances, it is probable that the decision of a person who is relying on the financial statements, and who has a reasonable knowledge of business and economic activities (the user), would be changed or influenced by such misstatement or the aggregate of all misstatements.

In approving the audit plan, audit committees should consider both the qualitative and quantitative aspects of materiality and pay close attention to both dimensions. The quantitative aspect has a significant impact on the extent of audit testing. For example, decreasing the materiality level from $20 million to $15 million will increase the amount of audit testing. The qualitative aspect is often more important in assessing the evidence obtained. For example, an audit finding that a control policy has been overridden by a senior officer is important not because of the amount involved, but because it may indicate culture that does not respect the integrity of controls.

The audit committee must consider materiality and audit risk together, especially at the planning and evaluation stages. To use a metaphor, risk determines where the spotlight should be focused and materiality determines how bright the spotlight should be.

---

[11] CICA *Handbook*, Section 5130, Materiality and Audit Risk in Conducting an Audit, paragraph 5130.05.

At the planning stage, materiality and various sources of audit risk determine the nature, extent and timing of the auditing procedures. At the evaluation stage, they are used to assess whether the results of those procedures support management's assertion that the financial statements are presented fairly in accordance with generally accepted accounting principles.

Fraud and Error Considerations[12]

The recent round of financial reporting scandals have thrust the issue of fraud into the public spotlight, resurrecting the question of "what is the external auditor's responsibility for the detection of fraud" while also raising questions about the audit committee's role around the detection of fraud.

When planning and conducting their audits in the past, external auditors have been entitled to assume management's good faith. Critics of the profession took the position that such an auditing standard allowed the external auditor to assume what investors expected them to prove. The practical reality, however, is that requiring external auditors to prove that material fraud does not exist would lead to very costly and time-consuming audits.

The CICA's Auditing Standards Board reached a compromise in the recently issued CICA *Handbook*, Section 5135, "The Auditors Responsibility to Consider Fraud and Error", which is effective for the audits of financial statements with periods ending after December 15, 2004.

Responsibilities

This new auditing standard defines the respective responsibilities of auditors, management, and audit committees with respect to fraud and error.

Management is responsible for establishing and maintaining a system of internal control that provides reasonable assurance as to the reliability of financial reporting, effectiveness and efficiency of operations, and compliance with applicable laws and regulations. A component of this responsibility is to establish an effective control environment that places a strong emphasis on fraud prevention. The most important duty management has is to set a tone of integrity that results in a culture of honest and ethical behaviour.

The external auditor's responsibility is to design and conduct sufficient audit procedures that, in the auditor's professional judgment, reduce to an appropriately low level the risk of not detecting a material misstatement in the financial statements.

---

[12] This section discusses the auditor's responsibilities to consider fraud when planning and conducting the audit. For a discussion of steps audit committees should take when an actual fraud is suspected or detected, refer to Chapter 14, The Tough Issues and How to Deal With Them.

Under the new auditing standard, the external auditor must now plan and perform every audit with an attitude of professional skepticism, recognizing the possibility that a material misstatement due to fraud could be present, regardless of past experience with the company or prior beliefs about management's honesty and integrity. It specifically requires the external auditor to make appropriate inquiries of management and the audit committee. The increased level of specificity of the inquiries that the external auditor must make of management, and the fact that the external auditor must now make inquiries of the audit committee, has led to some anxiety.

The audit committee's responsibility is to ensure, through oversight of management, that management establishes and maintains internal controls that provide reasonable assurance with respect to the reliability of financial reporting, effectiveness and efficiency of operations and compliance with applicable laws and regulations. The auditing standard stresses that active oversight by the audit committee can help reinforce management's commitment to creating a culture of honest and ethical behaviour.

The standard is based on the premise that management designs and implements internal controls, which employees are expected to follow. The risk for external auditors and audit committees occurs when management perceives that these internal controls prevent them from realizing their corporate and/or personal objectives. A review of past fraud cases indicates that, in certain circumstances, some management teams have overridden their own internal controls to report higher revenue and profits. For example, a study conducted in the United States found a high incidence of CEO (72%) and CFO (43%) involvement in fraud cases investigated by the SEC[13]. The new auditing standard recognizes this risk and requires the auditor to perform specific procedures related to the ability of management to override the controls.

It is important to emphasize that both the audit committee and the external auditor are fundamentally dependent on the integrity of management and management's commitment to adhere to the policies and internal controls they have put in place.

Inquiries of Management

The purpose of making inquires of management is to enable the external auditor to focus the audit plan on areas of greatest risk related to fraud and error. Under the standard, external auditors are required to make inquiries of management regarding:[14]

> a) *management's assessment of the risk that the financial statements may be materially misstated due to fraud;*

---

[13] Committee of Sponsoring Organizations of the Treadway Commission, *Fraudulent Financial Reporting: 1987-1997 — An Analysis of* U.S. *Public Companies*, March 1999, page 19.

[14] CICA *Handbook*, Section 5135, The Auditor's Responsibility to Consider Fraud and Error, paragraph 5135.33.

b) *management's process for identifying and responding to the risks of fraud in the entity, including any specific risks of fraud that management has identified or account balances or classes of transactions for which a risk of fraud is likely to exist;*

c) *management's process for identifying and responding to the risks of error in the entity;*

d) *management's communication, if any, to the audit committee or equivalent regarding its processes for identifying and responding to the risks of fraud and error in the entity; and*

e) *management's communication, if any, to employees regarding its views on business practices and ethical behaviour.*

Appendix Q provides examples of fraud risk factors typically faced by management, audit committees and auditors in a broad range of situations. The appendix is taken from the new auditing standard and provides some guidance to management and audit committees.

The new standard also requires the auditor to obtain written representations from management at the end of the audit that management:[15]

a) acknowledges its responsibility for the design and implementation of internal control to prevent and detect fraud and error;

b) has disclosed to the auditor the results of its assessment of the risk that the financial statements may be materially misstated as a result of fraud;

c) has disclosed to the auditor its knowledge of fraud or suspected fraud affecting the entity involving:
   i)   management,
   ii) employees who have significant roles in internal control, or
   iii) others, where the fraud could have a non-trivial effect on the financial statements;

d) has disclosed to the auditor its knowledge of any allegations of fraud or suspected fraud affecting the entity's financial statements communicated by employees, former employees, analysts, regulators or others; and

e) believes the effects of those uncorrected financial statement misstatements aggregated by the auditor during the audit are immaterial, both individually and in the aggregate, to the financial statements taken as a whole. A summary of such items should be included in or attached to the written representation and reviewed with the audit committee.

Inquiries of the Audit Committee

The new standard requires the external auditor to make specific inquires of the audit committee to determine whether it has knowledge of any actual, suspected or alleged fraud affecting the company. The way in which these inquiries may be made will vary. Some audit committees are opting for a formal questionnaire, while others prefer to have informal inquiries made of them *in camera*.

---

[15] *Ibid*, paragraph 5135.089.

The auditor also must obtain an understanding of the way in which the audit committee exercises its oversight of management's processes for identifying and responding to the risks of fraud in the company, and the internal control that management has established to mitigate these risks. The auditor can obtain this understanding by attending meetings where such discussions take place, reading the minutes from such meetings, or by making additional inquiries of the audit committee. Obtaining this knowledge will provide the auditor with insights into the company's susceptibility to management fraud, the adequacy of internal controls and the competence and integrity of management.

Audit Planning Considerations

In planning their audits, auditors must use the information obtained through their inquiries of management and their knowledge of the way in which the audit committee exercises its oversight responsibilities. Specifically, the auditor must:

a) put significantly more emphasis in their audit plan on management's ability to override internal controls and management fraud generally;

b) consider the fraud risk factors relating to incentives to commit fraud, opportunity to commit fraud and the ability to rationalize the fraudulent act;

c) include auditing procedures to address management's ability to override internal controls; in particular, requiring the testing of journal entries, reviewing accounting estimates for bias and understanding the business rationale for significant transactions outside the normal course of business; and

d) include auditing procedures to address the presumed risk of improper revenue recognition.

The Inquiry Process

We recommend that companies utilize the following process to implement this new standard. The first step is to hold a candid discussion among management, the audit committee and the external auditor about each party's responsibilities and expectations.

The process, as illustrated in Figure 12, begins with a consideration by the members of the audit team regarding the susceptibility of the company's financial statements to material misstatement due to fraud or error. This determines the nature and extent of the inquires they should make of management and the discussions and inquires they should hold with and about the audit committee. In our view, the inquiries of management should be held before the inquiries of the audit committee in order to enable the external auditor to discuss a summary of management's responses with the audit committee and to obtain the committee's reaction to that summary.

Figure 12 | **The Fraud Inquiry Process**

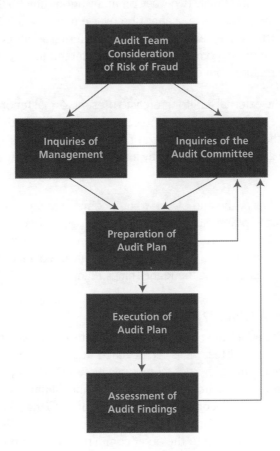

After making inquiries of both management and the audit committee, the auditor will develop the audit plan, which will be approved by the audit committee.

The audit plan will then be executed and the findings of the audit will be reported to the audit committee. The auditor should promptly assess and report to the audit committee any finding that:

a) raises questions regarding the honesty and integrity of management;

b) indicates possible fraud involving management;

c) indicates possible fraud involving employees who have significant roles in internal control;

d) indicates possible fraud (whether caused by management or other employees) that results, or may result, in a non-trivial misstatement of the financial statements; and

e) indicates matters that may cause future financial statements to be materially misstated or a material misstatement in prior financial statements.

Communications Between the External Auditor and the Audit Committee

The importance of candid and timely two-way communications among the external auditor, management and the audit committee cannot be over emphasized. It is critical that audit committees clearly articulate their expectations of the external auditors to them. It is equally critical that external auditors communicate how they intend to respond to those expectations and what they require from the audit committee.

It is not sufficient for the external auditor merely to present formal reports to the audit committee. Audit committees should make it a practice to communicate their concerns, priorities and the matters that "keep them awake at night" to their company's auditor. External auditors should make it a practice to promptly inform the audit committee of any concerns they have.

Holding *in camera* sessions at the end of every audit committee meeting provides an excellent opportunity for such communication. Regular meetings between the lead partner and the chairman of the audit committee also help establish more effective communication. A more detailed discussion of such communication is included in Chapter 8, Managing Relationships, and Chapter 9, Doing the Right Things Right.

What Should be Communicated?

Professional standards set out the nature of matters that external auditors are required to communicate to audit committees. It is left to each auditor's professional judgment to determine the form and timing of such communications. Obviously, matters that could affect the presentation or disclosure in the quarterly or annual financial statements should be brought promptly to the audit committee's attention prior to the meeting at which those matters are to be addressed. Matters that would not affect the financial statement's approval should be communicated to the audit committee at an appropriate time in relation to the matter's significance or urgency and the audit committee's meeting schedule.

We believe it is prudent practice for auditors to communicate directly with the CFO and the chairman of the audit committee on issues or findings that raise substantive concerns. In this way, they can work together to determine any additional investigations or work required, how the committee should address these matters, and in some circumstances, whether a special meeting of the committee is needed.

The CICA Handbook provides auditors with the following guidance regarding matters they should raise with the audit committee:[16]
1) the auditor's responsibility under generally accepted auditing standards and planning the audit;
2) weaknesses in internal control;

---

[16] CICA *Handbook*, Section 5751, "Communications with Those Having Oversight Responsibility for the Financial Reporting Process", paragraphs 5751.13 to 5751.23.

3) illegal acts;
4) significant transactions that appear to be inconsistent with the ordinary course of business, including fraud or possible fraud;
5) related party transactions;
6) significant accounting principles and policies;
7) management judgments and accounting estimates;
8) misstatements;
9) other information in annual reports;
10) disagreements with management;
11) consultations with other accountants;
12) major issues discussed that influence audit appointment;
13) difficulties encountered in performing the audit;
14) unusual actions which significantly increase the risk of loss to the entity; and
15) actions which, if they became public knowledge, might cause serious embarrassment to the entity, such as breaches of the corporate code of conduct.

Misstatements

An important yet controversial issue is the communication to the audit committee of known errors and possible misstatements detected during the course of the audit. We state unequivocally that audit committees must be informed promptly either by management or the external auditor of all misstatements that could have a material impact on the accuracy or reliability of the financial statements or other public disclosure documents.

Examples of the types of misstatements that should be communicated to the audit committee include:
*   material misstatements that have not been corrected or agreed to by management and, if not resolved, would result in a qualification of the auditors' report;
*   misstatements detected during the course of the audit, which are not considered material either individually or in the aggregate;
*   any misstatement or finding that represents a known or suspected fraud or illegal act;
*   misstatements or findings that indicate significant weaknesses in internal control, including the design or operation of the financial reporting or continuous disclosure process; and
*   misstatements that may cause future financial statements or public disclosures to be materially misstated.

Whether or not misstatements that are below the materiality threshold should be communicated to the audit committee should be based on the audit committee's expectations and the auditor's professional judgment. Today, professional standards and current practice place the emphasis on communicating more, rather than less.

U.S. standards require that any material and immaterial misstatements detected during the course of the audit be communicated to the audit committee. In Canada there is, as yet, more flexibility. But we repeat, the emphasis should be on communicating more rather than less. One practical approach is for the auditor to review all misstatements detected in the audit with management and the chairman of the audit committee in advance of the audit committee meeting. Together, they can determine which immaterial misstatements should be reviewed at the audit committee's meeting.

Auditors who identify a misstatement resulting from a fraud or suspected fraud should report this promptly to management and the audit committee. The audit committee is responsible for reporting such matters promptly to the board and, where appropriate (based on legal advice), the company will need to inform regulatory and enforcement authorities.

"Red Flag" Issues

The importance of candid and informed communication between auditors and audit committees has been emphasized in the Enron debacle. In its report, *The Role of the Board of Directors in Enron's Collapse*, The Permanent Subcommittee on Investigations of the Committee on Governmental Affairs of the United States Senate states:[17]

> *At the hearing, the Subcommittee identified more than a dozen red flags that should have caused the Enron Board to ask hard questions, examine Enron policies, and consider changing course. Those red flags were not heeded. In too many instances, by going along with questionable practices and relying on management and auditor representations, the Enron Board failed to provide the prudent oversight and checks and balances that its fiduciary obligations required and a company like Enron needed. By failing to provide sufficient oversight and restraint to stop management excess, the Enron Board contributed to the company's collapse and bears a share of the responsibility for it.*

Candid and informed communications between auditors and audit committees help ensure that any such "red flags" are identified, discussed, evaluated and responded to in an appropriate manner. Utilizing the collective knowledge, experience and capabilities of the external auditor and audit committee members to address "red flag" issues is one of the best ways for audit committees and auditors to discharge their responsibilities and serve the interests of shareholders.

[17] *The Role of the Board of Directors in Enron's Collapse*, Report Prepared by The Permanent Subcommittee on Investigations of the Committee on Governmental Affairs of the United States Senate, page 59, July 8, 2002.

While it is not possible to provide a definitive list of "red flags" issues, some of the more common ones are identified in the CICA Handbook:[18]

As described in paragraph 5135.43, the auditor may encounter circumstances that, individually or in combination, indicate the possibility that the financial statements may contain a material misstatement resulting from fraud or error. The circumstances listed below are only examples and in some cases other factors and circumstances may be present that mitigate or eliminate the possibility of fraud or error:

a) unrealistic time deadlines for audit completion imposed by management;

b) constant crisis conditions;

c) reluctance by management to engage in frank communication with appropriate third parties, such as regulators and bankers;

d) limitation in audit scope imposed by management;

e) identification of important matters not previously disclosed by management;

f) significant difficult-to-audit figures in the accounts;

g) aggressive application of accounting principles;

h) conflicting or unsatisfactory evidence provided by management or employees;

i) unusual documentary evidence such as handwritten alterations to documentation, or handwritten documentation that is ordinarily electronically printed;

j) information provided unwillingly or after unreasonable delay;

k) key employees have not taken vacations;

l) seriously incomplete or inadequate accounting records;

m) unsupported transactions;

n) unusual transactions by virtue of their nature, volume or complexity, particularly if such transactions occurred close to the year end;

o) transactions not recorded in accordance with management's general or specific authorization;

p) significant unreconciled differences between control accounts and subsidiary records or between physical count and the related account balance that were not appropriately investigated and corrected on a timely basis;

q) inadequate internal controls over computer processing (for example, too many processing errors; delays in processing results and reports);

r) evidence of the entity doing business with countries identified by international agencies as being prone to illegal or fraudulent activities;

s) significant differences from expectations disclosed by analytical procedures;

---

[18] CICA Handbook, Section 5135, The Auditor's Responsibility to Consider Fraud and Error in an Audit of Financial Statements, Appendix C.

t) *fewer confirmation responses than expected or significant differences revealed by confirmation responses;*

u) *evidence of an unduly lavish lifestyle by officers or employees;*

v) *unreconciled suspense accounts;*

w) *tips or complaints to the auditor by an entity's staff, customers, suppliers about fraud or irregularities occurring in the entity;*

x) *evidence of breaches in the entity's code of conduct or ethics, whether observed by the auditor or documented by the entity; and*

y) *long outstanding account receivable balances.*

Audit Fees

Auditors are responsible for providing the audit committee with an estimate, including supporting details, of the fees involved in the proposed audit plan. This normally occurs in conjunction with the audit committee's review of the audit plan, and should be reflected in the audit engagement letter(s).

Traditionally, audit fees have been negotiated between management and the auditor and then presented to the audit committee for approval. This is changing.

John Whitehead, the co-chair of the U.S. Blue Ribbon Committee on Improving Audit Committee Effectiveness, described the problems and challenges inherent in setting and approving audit fees. In his public submission to the New York Stock Exchange, he offered this idea for dealing with this issue:[19]

> "*An unfortunate practice has developed in the relationships between management, auditors, and board audit committees on the setting of auditor's fees. Fees are set annually by negotiation between management and the auditor and then approved by the audit committee. Management's objective, as it is with all expenses, is to keep the fees as low as possible. The auditor, at that stage, has no idea of how much time it will take, or how much extra work might be required to complete the audit and is often pressured to accept a lower fee and agree to a shorter time schedule than might be necessary in case questions arose. Audit committees often agree to the fee and the time schedule, unwilling to question what seems reasonable in relation to last year. If the auditor later does find questionable practices, he may have neither time nor money to pursue them under the terms of his agreement. A better practice would be to allow the auditor, at his option, to do work and charge fees up to a limit of, say, twice the original fee. This would tend to make management more aware of the authority of an independent auditor.*"

---

[19] Testimony of John C. Whitehead Before The Senate Committee On Banking, Housing and Urban Affairs as reported in the June 6th 2002 report of the NYSE Committee on Corporate Accountability and Listing Standards Committee.

In our view, the audit committee should now drive the process to set the audit fees. The committee should seek the input of management, but should not delegate this process to management. The audit committee and the auditor should together agree on the audit scope, the extent of audit testing, the relationship between the internal and external audit plans and the fees.

In order for audit committees to negotiate and approve appropriate fee schedules, they must gain a more complete understanding the factors affecting audit costs than most have acquired in the past. For example, audit committees must recognize that the time, effort and costs of conducting an effective audit increase as the company grows, enters new markets, develops more sophisticated financing arrangements, is listed on more exchanges, makes acquisitions, or becomes involved in joint ventures. Audit costs are also affected by new accounting and auditing standards or changes in securities regulations. Currently, standards are being changed more frequently than ever before, and it is imperative that management and audit committees be kept abreast of these changes.

In planning their audit approach and preparing their fee estimates, auditors have a responsibility to constantly assess how they can add greater value, improve the efficiency of their work and generate productivity improvements through the more effective use of technology, better utilization of company resources (e.g., internal audit), and development of more effective auditing procedures to minimize the cost of conducting the audit.

To assess the audit scope and fees, audit committees should address a number of factors, such as:
- Is the audit committee clear on its expectations for the scope of the external audit and the major risks that impact the financial reporting of the company?
- Is the audit plan geared to the most significant business, control and financial reporting risks?
- Has there been a disciplined and reliable assessment of such risks? Is this assessment of risks consistent with the areas of concern to the audit committee?
- Are there areas where costs could be curtailed without impairing audit effectiveness?
- Is there evidence that effectiveness has been reduced to meet cost expectations?
- Is there evidence that returns on other services are being used to subsidize poor returns on audit services? Is an assessment of the overall service relationship with the auditor used to rationalize holding audit fees flat, or reducing them?
- What are the components of the base audit fee? Can it be easily understood?
- Are the assumptions about risk, effectiveness of control and reporting timetables reasonable?
- Is the audit plan based on a "no errors expected" assumption in which follow-up error/system audits are negotiated when errors or control breakdowns are detected?
- Does the audit plan include an appropriate use of specialized resources (e.g., computer audit, financial instruments), or have such resources been limited to save costs?

- Have overall hours gone up or down, by how much and over what period of time? Is this consistent with the growth in the business, and business risks?
- Is there a change in the mix of hours (e.g., partner time being replaced by staff time) and is this reasonable? Is this change consistent with other periods?
- Has the auditor made the best use of technology (the auditor's and the company's) to reduce hours and improve effectiveness?
- What is the reliance on internal audit? Is it appropriate?
- What is the level of materiality used in planning the audit? How sensitive are overall audit costs to changes in materiality?
- What is the level of reliance on controls? Is it appropriate?
- What is the cost of auditing overseas subsidiaries, compared with domestic costs? How does the auditor manage and control such costs? What are the foreign exchange impacts and risks?
- Are audits of wholly owned subsidiaries required?

In the final analysis, the design of an effective audit entails a complex set of professional judgments made by experienced auditors, taking into account the needs and expectations of the audit committee and of management. While the costs can be measured precisely, the effectiveness cannot. The risks to the company, the audit committee, the auditor and the shareholders in focusing too much on efficiency and not enough on effectiveness can be severe. The objective for the audit committee is to understand the risk assessments and assumptions on which the audit plan and fees are based, ensure that the auditor works continually to improve the efficiency of the audit work and to arrive at a judgment as to whether the proposed fee is fair and reasonable.

Disclosure of Audit and Non-audit Fees

MI 52-110 requires the public disclosure to the shareholders of service fees paid to the external auditor in the AIF as follows:[20]

a) *Disclose, under the caption "Audit Fees", the aggregate fees billed by the issuer's external auditor in each of the last two fiscal years for audit services.*

b) *Disclose, under the caption "Audit-related Fees", the aggregate fees billed in each of the last two fiscal years for assurance and related services by the issuer's external auditor that are reasonably related to the performance of the audit or review of the issuer's financial statements and are not reported under clause (a) above. Include a description of the nature of the services comprising the fees disclosed under this category.*

---

[20] Form 52-110 F1, Part 9 "External Auditor Service Fees (By Category)".

c) Disclose, under the caption "Tax Fees", the aggregate fees billed in each of the last two fiscal years for professional services rendered by the issuer's external auditor for tax compliance, tax advice, and tax planning. Include a description of the nature of the services comprising the fees disclosed under this category.

d) Disclose, under the caption "All Other Fees", the aggregate fees billed in each of the last two fiscal years for products and services provided by the issuer's external auditor, other than the services reported under clauses (a), (b) and (c), above. Include a description of the nature of the services comprising the fees disclosed under this category.

These disclosures are virtually identical to those required in the United States.

Key Messages

- External auditors are accountable to the audit committee and board of directors as representatives of the shareholders.
- Audit committees must clearly communicate their expectations for the external auditor's performance and the auditors must communicate how they intend to respond.
- The auditors' provision of audit related and non-audit services can help both management and the effectiveness of the audit but the audit committee must approve all audit and non-audit services so that any potential threat to the auditor's independence is mitigated.
- Audit committees should ensure the prompt, candid and ongoing communication among management, the auditor and the audit committee regarding any material misstatements in the financial statements.
- While audit committees should seek management's input, they should not delegate the responsibility for negotiating audit fees with the external auditor.
- Disclosure to the shareholders must be provided in the AIF of the fees paid to the auditors for audit, audit related, tax and other services.

The Right People

Audit committees cannot function effectively if they do not have the "right people" as members and the "right chairman" as leader. Moreover, they must also be supported by the "right" attitudes on the part of management and the external auditor. This chapter discusses the meaning of "right" in all these contexts and also discusses the requirements of MI 52-110 with respect to the composition of audit committees.

In our experience, the audit committee's effectiveness depends first and foremost on the effectiveness of its chairman. Without a hard-working, qualified, persistent and committed chairman who is willing and able to devote a substantial amount of time to his or her duties, it is unlikely that the audit committee will fulfill its responsibilities as well as it should.

Composition of the Audit Committee

MI 52-110 requires that an audit committee be composed of at least three directors, each of whom must be independent and financially literate.

Independence

Section 3.1 states that, subject to certain exceptions, every audit committee member must be independent.

MI 52-110 sets out the meaning of independence as follows:[1]

1) A *member of an audit committee is independent if the member has no direct or indirect material relationship with the issuer.*
2) *For the purposes of subsection (1), a material relationship means a relationship which could, in the view of the issuer's board of directors, reasonably interfere with the exercise of a member's independent judgement.*

---

[1] Canadian Securities Administrators, *Multilateral Instrument 52-110, Audit Committees, Section 1.4.*

3) *Despite subsection (2), the following individuals are considered to have a material relationship with an issuer:*

   a) *an individual who is, or has been, an employee or executive officer of the issuer, unless the prescribed period has elapsed since the end of the service or employment;*

   b) *an individual whose immediate family member is, or has been, an executive officer of the issuer, unless the prescribed period has elapsed since the end of the service or employment;*

   c) *an individual who is, or has been, an affiliated entity of, a partner of, or employed by, a current or former internal or external auditor of the issuer, unless the prescribed period has elapsed since the person's relationship with the internal or external auditor, or the auditing relationship, has ended;*

   d) *an individual whose immediate family member is, or has been, an affiliated entity of, a partner of, or employed in a professional capacity by, a current or former internal or external auditor of the issuer, unless the prescribed period has elapsed since the person's relationship with the internal or external auditor, or the auditing relationship, has ended;*

   e) *an individual who is, or has been, or whose immediate family member is or has been, an executive officer of an entity if any of the issuer's current executive officers serve on the entity's compensation committee, unless the prescribed period has elapsed since the end of the service or employment;*

   f) *an individual who:*

      i) *has a relationship with the issuer pursuant to which the individual may accept, directly or indirectly, any consulting, advisory or other compensatory fee from the issuer or any subsidiary entity of the issuer, other than as remuneration for acting in his or her capacity as a member of the board of directors or any board committee, or as a part-time chair or vice-chair of the board or any board committee; or*

      ii) *receives, or whose immediate family member receives, more than $75,000 per year in direct compensation from the issuer, other than as remuneration for acting in his or her capacity as a member of the board of directors or any board committee, or as a part-time chair or vice-chair of the board or any board committee, unless the prescribed period has elapsed since he or she ceased to receive more than $75,000 per year in such compensation.*

   g) *an individual who is an affiliated entity of the issuer or any of its subsidiary entities.*

4) For the purposes of subsection (3), the prescribed period is the shorter of
   a) the period commencing on March 30, 2004 and ending immediately prior to the determination required by subsection (3); and
   b) the three year period ending immediately prior to the determination required by subsection (3).

5) For the purposes of clauses (3)(c) and (3)(d), a partner does not include a fixed income partner whose interest in the internal or external auditor is limited to the receipt of fixed amounts of compensation (including deferred compensation) for prior service with an internal or external auditor if the compensation is not contingent in any way on continued service.

6) For the purposes of clause (3)(f), compensatory fees and direct compensation do not include the receipt of fixed amounts of compensation under a retirement plan (including deferred compensation) for prior service with the issuer if the compensation is not contingent in any way on continued service.

7) For the purposes of subclause 3(f)(i), the indirect acceptance by a person of any consulting, advisory or other compensatory fee includes acceptance of a fee by
   a) a person's spouse, minor child or stepchild, or a child or stepchild who shares the person's home; or
   b) an entity in which such person is a partner, member, an officer such as a managing director occupying a comparable position or executive officer, or occupies a similar position (except limited partners, non-managing members and those occupying similar positions who, in each case, have no active role in providing services to the entity) and which provides accounting, consulting, legal, investment banking or financial advisory services to the issuer or any subsidiary entity of the issuer.

8) Despite subsection (3), a person will not be considered to have a material relationship with the issuer solely because he or she
   a) has previously acted as an interim chief executive officer of the issuer, or
   b) acts, or has previously acted, as a chair or vice-chair of the board of directors or any board committee, other than on a full-time basis.

In summary, independence means that to qualify for membership on the audit committee, a director must have no direct or indirect material relationship with the company — that is, no relationship that could, in the view of the board of directors, reasonably interfere with his or her exercise of independent judgment. It is important to note that it is the responsibility of the board of directors to make the judgment as to whether or not any relationship that exists between the director and the company could reasonably interfere with the exercise of independent judgment.

MI 52-110 sets out certain limited exceptions to the independence rule:[2]

3.2 Initial Public Offerings —

1) *Subject to section 3.9, if an issuer has filed a prospectus to qualify the distribution of securities that constitutes its initial public offering, subsection 3.1(3) does not apply for a period of up to 90 days commencing on the date of the receipt for the prospectus, provided that one member of the audit committee is independent.*

2) *Subject to section 3.9, if an issuer has filed a prospectus to qualify the distribution of securities that constitutes its initial public offering, subsection 3.1(3) does not apply for a period of up to one year commencing on the date of the receipt for the prospectus, provided that a majority of the audit committee members are independent.*

3.3 Controlled Companies —

1) *An audit committee member that sits on the board of directors of an affiliated entity is exempt from the requirement in subsection 3.1(3) if the member, except for being a director (or member of a board committee) of the issuer and the affiliated entity, is otherwise independent of the issuer and the affiliated entity.*

2) *Subject to section 3.7, an audit committee member is exempt from the requirement in subsection 3.1(3) if:*

    a) *the member would be independent of the issuer but for the relationship described in paragraph 1.4(3)(g);*

    b) *the member is not an executive officer, general partner or managing member of a person or company that*

        i) *is an affiliated entity of the issuer, and*

        ii) *has its securities trading on a marketplace;*

    c) *the member is not an immediate family member of an executive officer, general partner or managing member referred to in paragraph (b), above;*

    d) *the member does not act as the chair of the audit committee; and*

    e) *the board determines in its reasonable judgement that*

        i) *the member is able to exercise the impartial judgement necessary for the member to fulfill his or her responsibilities as an audit committee member, and*

        ii) *the appointment of the member is required by the best interests of the issuer and its shareholders.*

3.4 Events Outside Control of Member —

Subject to section 3.9, if an audit committee member ceases to be independent for reasons outside the member's reasonable control, the member is exempt from the requirement in subsection 3.1(3) for a period ending on the later of:

a) *the next annual meeting of the issuer; and*

b) *the date that is six months from the occurrence of the event which caused the member to not be independent.*

---

[2] Canadian Securities Administrators, *Multilateral Instrument 52-110*, "*Audit Committees*", Sections 3.2, 3.3., 3.4, 3.5 and 3.6.

3.5 Death, Disability or Resignation of Member —

Subject to section 3.9, if the death, disability or resignation of an audit committee member has resulted in a vacancy on the audit committee that the board of directors is required to fill, an audit committee member appointed to fill such vacancy is exempt from the requirements in subsections 3.1(3) and (4) for a period ending on the later of:

a) the next annual meeting of the issuer; and

b) the date that is six months from the day the vacancy was created.

3.6 Temporary Exemption for Limited and Exceptional Circumstances —

Subject to section 3.7, an audit committee member is exempt from the requirement in subsection 3.1(3) if:

a) the member is not an individual described in paragraphs 1.4(3)(f)(i) or 1.4(3)(g);

b) the member is not an employee or officer of the issuer, or an immediate family member of an employee or officer of the issuer;

c) the board, under exceptional and limited circumstances, determines in its reasonable judgement that

    i) the member is able to exercise the impartial judgement necessary for the member to fulfill his or her responsibilities as an audit committee member, and

    ii) the appointment of the member is required by the best interests of the issuer and its shareholders;

d) the member does not act as chair of the audit committee; and

e) the member does not rely upon this exemption for a period of more than two years.

Both the definition of independence and the exceptions are complex and the application of these criteria to any individual circumstance requires careful reading and consideration.

Some argue that the independence requirement imposes an unduly heavy burden on some smaller public companies. We believe, however, that the advantages that result from having a committee independent of management far outweigh any perceived inconvenience.

Financial Literacy

MI 52-110 sets out the meaning of financial literacy. Section 1.5 states that an individual is financially literate if he or she has the ability to read and understand a set of financial statements that present a breadth and level of complexity of accounting issues that are generally comparable to the breadth and complexity of the issues that can reasonably be expected to be raised by the company's financial statements.

The instrument does allow a director who is not financially literate at the outset to serve on the audit committee provided that the member becomes financially literate within a reasonable period of time following his or her appointment. While this may be a practical solution in some instances, for example in a small company, we are of the opinion that companies should exercise caution in appointing to the audit committee directors who are not financially literate. In circumstances where the audit committee has a majority of members who are financially literate and the director who is not financially literate has special skills or expertise that will add value to the audit committee, it may be appropriate to add that director. It should be noted that a company is permitted to take advantage of this more permissive approach only in circumstances where the board of directors determines that to do so will not materially affect the ability of the audit committee to satisfy all the other requirements of the instrument.

The qualities of independence and financial literacy, as defined, are the only two qualifications prescribed in MI 52-110. We believe that there are additional qualities to be looked for in selecting directors to serve on the audit committee.

Experience

There are some who suggest that audit committees should consist solely of people who have accounting or financial management experience, for example, former partners of accounting firms and former CFOs. We disagree. In our experience, accountants tend to become mired in technical details or wish to spend the committee's time auditing the auditor, while financial executives tend to identify too closely with management. This is not to suggest that both sets of backgrounds are not of value to an audit committee, rather that their contribution should be leavened with individuals with general business experience.

In some circumstances, one or two members with industry experience may be desirable and prudent (for example, a company heavily engaged in international financing may wish to have this kind of experience represented on the audit committee). As a rule, however, we do not advocate this as one of the criteria for membership on the audit committee. What is critical is that audit committee members have the capability to understand the accounting they are being asked to approve, whatever the business of the company. No audit committee member should sign off on anything that he or she does not understand and knowledge of the business in which the company is engaged can be very helpful in this regard. Indeed we strongly recommend that audit committee members should make every effort to get to know and understand the business or businesses in which the company is engaged. Such knowledge will make the audit committee more effective. A significant grasp of the company and its business will make the members of the committee much more sensitive to red flags that could be early warnings of potential problems.

Other Critical Qualifications

Much more than the appropriate knowledge, skills and experience are required to enable audit committee members to fulfill their responsibilities effectively. Those who serve on an audit committee have an obligation to devote the time required to carry out their duties at meetings, to prepare for meetings and, if required, to work between meetings. Indeed, the audit committee's duties have become so comprehensive and time-consuming that some boards of directors have made it a policy that audit committee members need not serve on any other board committee. While it is up to individual boards to decide whether or not to adopt such a policy, we believe that extending the offer to prospective audit committee members may help in recruiting busy people to serve on the committee.

Perhaps the most important characteristic of an effective audit committee member is to have the courage, discipline, and authority (force of personality and credentials) to ask demanding questions of both management and the external auditor, and to expect and obtain appropriate answers. The mind-set of members of an audit committee should be one of constructive skepticism.

The importance of being prepared to and willing to ask tough questions cannot be stressed too strongly. Management always possesses more information than audit committee members will ever have and therefore it is important to have a diligent process for questioning management on a variety of matters. We discuss this further in Chapter 9, Doing the Right Things Right. It should be obvious that the depth of the preparation that an audit committee member has made for a meeting of the committee will determine the ability of that member to ask the appropriate questions, as will his or her knowledge of the business or businesses of the company.

Continuing Education

Audit committee members have a duty to educate themselves about the business of the company and, more particularly, about issues that have the potential to affect the company's financial statements and disclosures. This education process should be facilitated by the audit committee chairman through the continuous education of members as part of meeting agendas, through appropriate orientation of new members, through encouraging and creating opportunities for members to get to know the senior executives so that appropriate relationships are established, and through regular dialogue between the chairman and the committee members.

The external auditor should be expected to play a role in educating the members of the committee by providing information about the external environment, including new accounting standards, and current best practices.

In addition, individual members also have a responsibility for their own education, and should spend sufficient time with management and others, including the external auditor, to understand the company's business and the issues facing it.

The best way to learn is to ask questions, and no audit committee member should be reluctant to ask a question that he or she feels may betray a lack of understanding of an issue. If a member does not understand something, the smart — indeed, prudent — thing to do is to ask. The failure to ask a question in such circumstances, which we call the "fear of looking stupid syndrome", can seriously cripple an audit committee member's effectiveness, and we strongly caution every member not to succumb to it.

Our message to members of audit committees is this: devote the time; educate yourselves; be demanding; be diligent; be prepared; and insist on timely, comprehensive briefings and responses both from management and the external auditor.

Recruitment

In the wake of the many recent corporate business scandals that have rocked the business community and caused investors, the media and the public to lose confidence in the integrity of corporate information and in the integrity of some management teams, there has arisen a much higher set of expectations of boards of directors. Whether or not some of these expectations are realistic, they are now a fact of corporate life. Much of the increased focus on the directors has centred on the audit committee. As a result, much more is now expected of members of the audit committee. The responsibilities of the committee have increased dramatically, and the attendant liabilities can be intimidating. Hence, a certain reluctance to serve on audit committees is beginning to appear. As a consequence, the pool of available candidates for membership on the committee appears to be shrinking. This is an unpleasant fact with which many boards of directors must now grapple. Recruitment of effective audit committee members has now become an issue.

We can offer little solace other than to state that, in our opinion, although the responsibilities are extremely onerous, individuals who are prepared to commit the time, diligence and toughness to their task need not be fearful. There are significant advantages to serving on the audit committee. Service on the audit committee can be very stimulating. While it may expose directors to a number of challenges, it provides them with a good understanding of the complex issues facing the company. They acquire a better appreciation of the ways in which the business is managed, how the major risks are controlled, how operating performance is measured, how the financial condition of the company is assessed and how it is disclosed to the public.

It may be that the time has come for boards, when they are searching for new members, to ensure that they recruit individuals who are willing (and, of course, able) to serve on the audit committee at some time during their tenure on the board.

The appropriate process for recruiting audit committee members from among the board members has also assumed significantly greater importance as the demand for increased vigilance on the part of audit committees has grown.

Many boards have established nominating or governance committees, or they have assigned responsibilities in this area to an existing committee. It is essential that such a committee be particularly sensitive to the special needs of the audit committee when recommending appointments to that committee, and that no recommendation for membership be made without first discussing it with the chairman of the audit committee and obtaining his or her concurrence. Indeed, we believe the chairman should be involved in the selection process and attend the meetings with potential candidates to determine their interest in joining the audit committee. Similarly, no candidate for audit committee membership should make a decision to serve on the committee without first meeting with the chairman to discuss the committee's expectations of its members and the demands that are likely to be made on his or her time.

Compensation

Several boards have increased the compensation provided to audit committee members in recognition of the demands made upon them with respect to the length of audit committee meetings, the time they must spend preparing for the meetings, the frequency of meetings and the increasingly onerous nature of audit committee responsibilities. Most frequently, this increased compensation is in the form of a meeting fee higher than the fee paid to members of other board committees. We support and encourage this trend.

The remuneration of the chairman of the audit committee has also been increased in many companies. Typically, this takes the form of a significantly increased chairman's retainer. Several companies have doubled the retainer for the audit committee chairman over that of other committee chairmen, and some have increased both the meeting fee and the retainer paid to the chairman.

Of those companies that have chosen to pay their directors a flat fee, which obviates the necessity to pay meeting fees, many have elected to pay the members of the audit committee a higher flat fee than that paid to other board members and to pay the chairman of the audit committee a fee higher than that paid to other committee chairmen.

Term

What is an optimum term for an audit committee member? The answer is obvious: there is no optimum term.

Our experience, however, leads us to offer the following advice. We believe it is most useful to focus on a minimum rather than a maximum term and we suggest that an audit committee member should be expected to serve for a minimum of five years. Such a term would be helpful to new members in meeting the demands of the learning curve involved in audit committee membership. It would also help provide the prudence of continuity among the members of the committee. If a committee member is performing well and contributing to the committee's effectiveness, we believe that there is no benefit in making a change for the sake of change, unless, of course, the member wishes to move to another committee.

More important than the term of membership is the evaluation of the member's performance while on the committee, which provides a much better tool for monitoring effectiveness than calculating the number of years he or she has served. A further discussion of performance evaluation is included in Chapter 10, Accountability and Striving for Continuous Improvement.

What is important, however, is to ensure an orderly turnover of members throughout the life of the audit committee. The chairman of the audit committee and the chairman of the board should discuss and develop succession plans.

The Chairman of the Audit Committee

The selection of the chairman of the audit committee is one of the more important decisions that the board will make. Chairmanship of the audit committee should never be regarded as a "reward" for long service or based on the popularity of the individual with his or her colleagues. Instead, assuming that an individual has the requisite experience, independence and qualifications, his or her selection should be based on the leadership, rigour, diligence courage, toughness and time available which the putative chairman will bring to fulfilling the chairman's duties.

The chairman must possess all of the traits and capabilities outlined above for members of the committee. But much more is required of the chairman because, in our experience, the audit committee's effectiveness depends upon the chairman's effectiveness. The leadership that the chairman provides is the defining element in audit committee effectiveness.

Throughout this book, we examine the chairman's role under a variety of topics, such as managing meetings; setting meeting agendas; forging and enhancing relationships with management, the internal and external auditors, and with the board of directors; creating an appropriate audit committee charter; ensuring the continuing education of the members of the committee; assessing the audit committee's performance and that of its members; and dealing with the tough issues. In this chapter, we confine our discussion to what we believe are the essential characteristics of a successful chairman.

Skills and Qualifications

The ability to provide leadership, the courage to break new ground, and the determination to hold both management and the external auditor accountable for their actions are the most important characteristics of an effective chairman. Also important are the ability and commitment to provide a vision for the audit committee and the ability to "sell" that vision to management, the board of directors and the external auditor. Although there are some risks inherent in these activities, they are ones that the chairman must be prepared to take.

In selecting the chairman, the board should be vigilant to select a qualified, independent-minded person who is able and willing to devote the time required to do the job properly. How much time is necessary will vary with the size and complexity of the company, but those considering the chairmanship of the audit committee should be aware that the time requirement will be very significant. Not only are audit committee meetings more frequent and of much longer duration than in the past, considerable time must be spent preparing for meetings, attending pre-audit committee meetings with both management and the external auditor, and meeting with the CFO, the internal auditor and the external auditor between meetings to deal with issues as they may arise.

The chairman must have the credibility, ability, authority and force of personality to ensure that he or she clearly controls the agenda, meetings and the discussions that take place at meetings of the committee. While the contributions of both the CFO and the external auditor are essential, neither should have the dominant voice in setting the agendas for the meetings, nor should they in any way control the discussions at the meeting. Their role is to provide information and to give the committee the benefit of their opinions.

Relationship-building Abilities

The chairman's experience and stature should enable him or her to establish very strong relationships with the external audit partner, senior members of the external audit team and other senior partners of the accounting firm who advise either the engagement team or the company.

The chairman should also establish a relationship with the external audit firm's managing partner or CEO. If this is not appropriate, given the company's geographic location or size, then this relationship should be established with the office or regional managing partner. There are many reasons for this, not the least of which is to ensure that the committee is not a captive of the engagement partner. Such relationships also help the chairman and the committee to remain current with evolving accounting standards and their effect on the company's financial reporting and disclosure, and to keep abreast of issues arising between management and the external auditor. In addition, this relationship will also help reinforce the fact that the external auditor works *for* and is accountable to the audit committee and the board, although the auditor works *with* management.

Obviously, the chairman must also establish effective relationships with the CEO, CFO and senior members of the company's finance team so that management and the chairman may share information, alert each other to concerns and issues as they arise, hold discussions in an atmosphere of trust and respect, and work productively together to meet the audit committee's needs. It is vital that management and the chairman of the audit committee always have easy access to each other. In our experience, it is also important for the chairman to establish relationships with the senior operating management of the company.

In the circumstances where the audit committee is the audit committee of a subsidiary, we believe that the chairman of that committee should establish relationships with the chairman of the parent company's audit committee and the appropriate executives of the parent.

The chairman's relationship with the audit committee members is also very important to the committee's success. No matter how strong the chairman's leadership abilities are, they will always be enhanced by the support of an informed committee. Therefore, the chairman must work diligently to keep the committee informed and to secure the committee's support for his or her objectives.

It is critically important that the members of the committee develop the right chemistry among themselves to enable them to work effectively as a group. We believe the chairman has a key role in developing the right chemistry.

The relationship that the chairman has with the chairman of the board and with the board of directors as a whole is another factor critical to the success of the audit committee.

Management

The integrity of a company's financial information, reporting and disclosure depends first and foremost on having a skilled management team that is committed to integrity, to transparency, to accountability and to fostering a culture or value system that reflects these values throughout the organization. In large part, this will depend on the attitudes of the CEO and the CFO. We cannot stress too strongly the importance of having the right corporate culture and values embedded in the company. A culture that values candid sharing of information among members of management, between employees and management, and between management and the board; a culture that encourages everyone to speak the truth without fear of reprisal; a culture that holds people accountable; a culture that does not punish the bearers of bad news, but encourages the giving of early warnings when these are warranted; such a culture will be significantly more successful in ensuring the integrity of information than volumes of laws and regulations.

Can the audit committee have any influence on this? We believe that it can.

Through the creation and annual review of its charter and operating principles, the audit committee can clearly communicate its expectations of management. If the chairman of the committee has developed an effective relationship with management these expectations can be reinforced regularly.

Of course, the expectations of the board of directors in this regard will be key.

To create an appropriate culture it seems self evident that statements of values alone are not enough. The real test is the actual practice, reinforced on a daily basis by the actions of the CEO and of senior management. For us, the issue is more than an issue of ethics. The CEO and his senior team lead by example and inappropriate, inconsistent actions by any leader in the organization, tolerance of such behaviour in them or in other employees, and, very importantly, reward systems that reinforce such behaviour will inevitably lead to the kinds of problems we have all recently witnessed.

Unless the board is prepared to hold the CEO and the CFO accountable for the values by which management operates, the task of the audit committee will be that much more difficult. This is another reason why the chairman of the audit committee must have the kind of relationship with the board that enables him or her to influence the board in this regard if the board seems reluctant to act.

The audit committee can be of assistance to the board in holding management accountable by virtue of the fact that the audit committee has access to an information stream from the internal and external auditors, which is not directly available to the board. This can provide the committee with early warnings of inappropriate behaviour or conduct contrary to the expectations set out in the audit committee's charter. Of course, the audit committee must clearly communicate to both the external and internal auditors its expectations that issues of this kind must be brought to its attention.

The committee can also adopt policies that specify its expected degree of conservatism in the company's accounting policies. Moreover, it can state, without ambiguity, that it will not tolerate any deviation from generally accepted accounting principles. In our opinion, audit committees should indicate in their charters that accounting policies should always be those that are the most appropriate.

The CEO

Whether or not the CEO is actively involved with the audit committee (and, we believe that he or she should be, and should attend all meetings of the committee), the CEO must support the expectations of the audit committee and the fulfillment of the requirements of its charter. It can be very difficult for the committee to be as effective as it should if the CEO does not actively support the committee and its objectives.

If the CEO consistently fails to support the audit committee, the audit committee has a responsibility to inform the board of directors and seek its support for holding the CEO accountable for that failure. The objective of the board should be to secure the CEO's support for the audit committee.

The CFO

We believe very strongly that the CEO should involve the audit committee in the selection of a new CFO. At the very least, the chairman of the committee should be given the opportunity to interview potential candidates for CFO, although we believe that every member of the committee should be given this opportunity. The CEO should also solicit the audit committee's views as part of the CFO's ongoing evaluation. In our experience, including the chairman of the audit committee on the board's management resources and compensation committee is helpful in this regard, and also in ensuring that the audit committee has input into the compensation of the CFO and other senior financial officers.

Our experience has been that an audit committee that also serves as a resource and "coach" for the CFO will add tremendous value to management. This is particularly true when a new CFO is appointed, especially one with limited experience in dealing with a board of directors or the external marketplace.

The relationship that the chairman of the committee has with the CFO will be a very significant element in the way in which the CFO interacts with the committee.

Quite apart from the insistence of the audit committee that the CFO be a person of skill and integrity, we believe the committee must insist that the CFO be prepared to share information with the chairman and with the committee in a candid and timely manner.

If the CFO consistently fails to support the audit committee, the audit committee has a responsibility first to inform the CEO and then, if the situation is not rectified, to inform the board of directors and seek its support for holding the CFO accountable for failing to support the committee. The objective of the board should be to secure the CEO's and CFO's support for the audit committee.

In summary, the CFO must be responsive to the expectations of the audit committee.

Internal Audit

The head of the internal audit function must have a clear and direct accountability to the audit committee and he or she must be comfortable having candid discussions with the chairman of the committee and with the committee itself.

We recommend that the chairman of the audit committee be consulted with respect to the appointment of the head of the internal audit function. As with the CFO, we believe that the chairman should have the opportunity to interview prospective candidates for the position. Moreover, we believe that the chairman of the audit committee should discuss with the CFO or CEO, as appropriate, the succession plan for the head of internal audit.

For a more detailed discussion of the relationship with internal audit see Chapter 8, Managing Relationships.

Communications with Management

Audit committees have a responsibility to communicate very clearly to management their expectations of the quality of the information that management presents to them. And management must respond to those expectations in terms of both quality and timeliness. The information must be presented clearly, fairly, comprehensively, and in a timely fashion. Management should be willing to communicate directly, candidly, and voluntarily. The audit committee should not have to "dig" for information, and should not have to resort to cross-examination in order to elicit information on any topic.

In Summary

While management should be supportive of the committee's objectives, the maintenance of an attitude of healthy tension between management and the committee is also important.

The External Auditor

The quality of the external audit team is an issue of the highest importance to the company and to the audit committee. We believe that the audit committee must ensure that the external auditor clearly understands its expectations. The committee must assure itself that the audit team has the requisite industry experience and skills. Indeed, the committee should question the audit partner closely in this regard. The committee should also be vigilant to ensure that, as far as possible, the team's skills are matched against the requirements of the audit committee charter and the needs of the company.

The external auditor must bring the "right" attitude to the engagement, beginning with a clear acknowledgement that the auditor works for and is accountable to the audit committee and the board. Many things flow from this. For example, while management's assessments of the external auditor's performance must be considered seriously, it is the audit committee's decision that must prevail. The audit committee must select the external auditor and decide on the external audit firm's continuing engagement. It should review and approve the senior audit team members to be assigned to the company by the external audit firm. Another consequence of the fact that the external auditor works for and is accountable to the committee is that, while management's views are important and should be taken into consideration, it is the committee that should negotiate and approve the fees paid to the external auditor.

The committee should clearly articulate its expectations of the external auditor. In part this can be done through its charter and operating principles, but only an ongoing dialogue between the committee and the external auditor will ensure that both parties clearly understand what is expected and can be delivered. The chairman of the committee has an important role to play in this.

The key message for the audit committee to send to the external auditor is that it will not tolerate anything less than complete candour and direct communication with the committee. The committee must be satisfied that it can rely on the external audit partner to have the courage of his or her convictions and to share with the committee any concerns he or she may have in a forthright manner. The audit committee must make it very clear that it expects the external auditor to stand their ground when dealing with management when circumstances warrant it.

The quality of the relationship between the chairman of the committee and the external auditor will have a significant effect on how successfully the committee is able to fulfill its duties. It is essential that management accept that a strong relationship must exist between the committee and the external auditor and not be threatened by it.

The role of the external auditor is discussed in Chapter 6, Audit Committees and the External Auditor.

Key Messages

- *All members of the committee must be independent and financially literate.*
- *Leadership by the chairman is critical to the audit committee's effectiveness.*
- *The membership of the audit committee should reflect a balance of business, industry and financial expertise.*
- *Audit committee members must be prepared to accept increasing work and time commitments.*
- *Members of the audit committee must be courageous, determined, demanding, prepared, diligent, willing and able to ask the appropriate and, when warranted, the tough questions, and must insist on timely and comprehensive briefings and responses from both management and the external auditor.*
- *Audit committee members must be committed to their continuing education regarding the business and developments in the external marketplace.*
- *Audit committee members must have the right "chemistry" among themselves, and be able to work effectively as a group.*
- *Management must be skilled and committed to integrity, transparency and accountability.*
- *Management must be responsive to the expectations of the audit committee.*
- *The external auditor is accountable to the audit committee and must be prepared to "tell it like it is".*

Managing Relationships

A central theme of the first edition of this book was that audit committees should make the transition from the old-style audit committee to the new-style audit committee. Recent events, new regulatory imperatives, and shareholder expectations have made it clear that boards of directors and audit committees now have little option but to make the necessary transition and to do so quickly. This chapter explores a fundamental element in this transition — the changing dynamics of the relationships among the audit committee, management and the external auditor, and the ways in which these relationships should be managed if the audit committee is to fulfill the expectations investors and regulators have of it.

Earlier in this book, we described briefly the attributes of the "old" and "new" audit committees and outlined some of the steps required to shift from the old to the new. Having established a clear understanding of what the audit committee will do, recruited the right people, chosen the right chairman, and established the external auditor's accountability, the next step is to forge the right relationships.

More than compliance with the new rules is required if audit committees are to fulfill their responsibilities effectively. Indeed, audit committees must guard against a "tick the box" approach to the new rules. To be effective, audit committees must manage a complex set of relationships, including those with the board of directors, management and the external auditor. Managing these relationships is not a simple task. It requires commitment on the part of both the committee and its chairman, as well as courage, determination, time and careful attention.

In making the transition from the "old" to the "new", a shift occurs in the relationship dynamic among the audit committee, management and the external auditor. In the "new" regime, the committee becomes the focal point of these relationships. It is important to manage this change carefully, to seize the opportunities it presents and to avoid the risks inherent in such a fundamental change. The risks revolve principally around the potential threats such a change may pose to management and the external auditor. The opportunities lie in more effective working relationships, which result in better information, more disciplined oversight and, ultimately, a more effective committee.

The Evolutionary Nature of the Relationships

For the most part, the audit committee's relationship with both management and the external auditor began as one of dependency. In many companies it has now evolved to one that can be characterized as a stage of independence. We believe the task for audit committees today is to strive to attain a stage of interdependence in their relationships with management and the external auditor.

The three stages in the evolution of relationships are depicted in Figure 13.

Figure 13 | **Stages of Relationship Evolution**

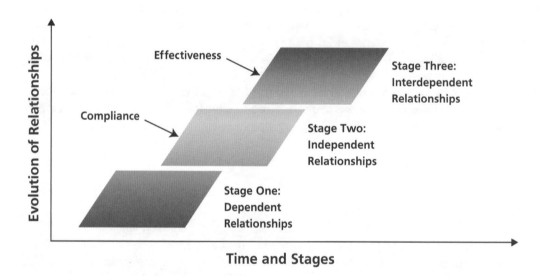

Stage One: Dependent Relationships

The traditional relationship that existed between boards of directors and management defined the original relationship between audit committees and management, and also affected the audit committee's relationship with the external auditor. In this stage, both the independent directors and the auditor were beholden to management.

Over the years, we observed that the increase in power of professional management was accompanied by a rising dependency by boards and audit committees on the CEO and on other senior executives. The CEO tended to select the independent directors and assign them to the board's various committees. Senior management also set board and committee priorities, created the meeting agendas and had virtually absolute control over the preparation and content of the materials to be discussed. The CEO, who often was the chairman of the board as well, evaluated the directors' performance, set their fees and decided whether or not to provide references on his own directors to other companies that might be seeking new directors.

While the external auditor had some safeguards (companies that fired their external auditors had to disclose their reasons), the auditor, too, was largely controlled by management. It was management who evaluated the auditor's performance; recommended whether the auditor should be retained or not and, if not, recommended a new auditor; negotiated and determined audit fees; and made all decisions on consulting and other non-audit assignments to be awarded to the auditor.

This state of affairs created a dependency on management — the very people the independent directors and the auditor were supposed to oversee and audit.

These dependent relationships were more common 20 years ago than they are today, but that does not mean they no longer exist! While the relationships in many companies evolved to a stage of independence during the 1990s, some companies have remained astonishingly resistant to change, despite the vastly different regulatory requirements and the increased expectations of shareholders and institutional investors.

Stage Two: Independent Relationships

By the early 1990s, there was considerable pressure to increase the board of directors' ability to function independently of management. In 1994, the Toronto Stock Exchange issued corporate governance guidelines that recommended that[1]:

> *Every board of directors should have in place appropriate structures and procedures to ensure that the board can function independently of management.*

Several changes were introduced to help the board function independently of management. In many companies, independent directors assumed an increased role and involvement in the selection of new directors. More boards were comprised of a majority of independent directors and either separated the roles of the CEO and chairman of the board, or appointed a lead director to guide the board, especially on issues such as the evaluation of the CEO's performance. Moreover, the audit committee's independence was strengthened.

---

[1] Toronto Stock Exchange Corporate Governance Policy — Proposed New Disclosure Requirements and Amended Guidelines, March 2002, Guideline 12.

At the same time, efforts were made to strengthen the external auditor's independence, make the auditor more accountable to the audit committee and increase the disclosure requirements when there was a change in the external auditor.

In 1999, in the United States, the Blue Ribbon Committee on Improving the Effectiveness of Audit Committees recommended that audit committees be composed entirely of outside directors, proposed additional criteria to strengthen their independence and recommended enhanced qualifications for committee members. These proposals were designed to increase the audit committee's ability to function more independently of management and thus, to oversee management's financial reporting more effectively.

Many companies embraced the concept of independence and real changes were made. In some companies, however, these changes consisted more of form than of substance. While an appearance of board and auditor independence was developed, it was often doubtful that such independence existed in reality. Other companies, which had the desire to improve, found the necessary changes difficult to implement.

In 2004, following the introduction of the *Sarbanes-Oxley Act* in the United States, the Canadian Securities Administrators introduced MI 52-110. Not surprisingly, it incorporated many of the requirements of *Sarbanes-Oxley* with respect to audit committees.

MI 52-110 made it mandatory for reporting issuers to have an audit committee, made it clear that the external auditor reports directly to the audit committee and that the audit committee must recommend to the board of directors both the external auditor and the external auditor's compensation. It also stated that the audit committee is responsible for overseeing the work of the external auditor and pre-approving all non-audit services performed by the external auditor. In addition, the instrument made it clear that the audit committee must be composed of independent directors who are financially literate, and that the committee must have the authority to engage independent counsel and other advisors when necessary[2].

These changes were introduced to increase the audit committee's and the external auditor's independence of management, and to strengthen the qualifications for membership on the committee. They are clearly changes for the better. The board's independence of management, the auditor's ability to conduct his or her work with total objectivity, and the audit committee's ability to function as an effective check on management are now widely considered to be essential to effective governance. We believe, however, that further refinements are required and that to be fully effective, audit committees must move beyond independence.

---

[2] MI 52-110 provides an exemption for venture issuers from the requirements prescribing the composition of the audit committee and the financial literacy qualification.

Stage Three: Interdependent Relationships

Achieving independence from management does not necessarily guarantee the effectiveness of either the audit committee or the external auditor. In our opinion, that occurs only when the audit committee, the external auditor and management recognize the interdependence of the relationship among them.

The effectiveness of all three parties will only be achieved fully when they:
- put in place channels of communication that permit all three to share information and matters of concern with each other and discuss them candidly;
- develop trust in and respect for each other's motives and goals; and
- generate constructive challenge and positive interaction among themselves.

We describe this stage as one of interdependency. It is this stage, we believe, that provides the most robust and sophisticated platform on which to construct the necessary checks and balances required to make a significant improvement in financial governance.

While we firmly believe that all boards and audit committees must strive to achieve this stage of interdependency, we also believe that the gains made in achieving the independent stage are essential. Indeed, it is our firmly held conviction that the interdependent stage can only be achieved by directors and auditors who have the ability to function independently of management.

The interdependent stage can best be described as one in which independent parties work together to serve better the interests of the shareholders. In the independent stage, the parties often put their individual interests first. In the interdependent stage, the parties work harder to fulfill more successfully their joint and mutual interest of better serving shareholders by enhancing the integrity of the company's financial reporting and the transparency of its disclosures.

In accepting that the optimum relationship among them is interdependency, audit committees, management and external auditors recognize that they share common objectives and that the means of increasing their effectiveness lies in working together. We emphasize, however, that the decision to move to interdependent behaviour can only be made by directors and auditors who are able to function independently of management. In other words, the independence of the directors and the auditors is the essential prerequisite for making the transition to interdependency.

The Need to Manage Relationships

Success in the interdependent stage depends to a very large extent on the strength of the relationships that are forged between the audit committee and management, between the audit committee and the external auditor, and between the external auditor and management. Managing these relationships is critically important.

In the dependent stage, there is no real need to manage relationships since management dominates all relationships. In the independent stage, there is also less need to manage relationships because the three parties tend to operate as three solitudes or in three silos. It is only in the interdependent stage that managing these complex relationships assumes critical importance. The remainder of this chapter discusses this matter and the roles that audit committees and their chairmen must play in the process.

Before proceeding with the substance of this chapter there is a further observation we would like to make, and it is of a public policy nature. In the system of checks and balances that control and govern a company's activities and its reporting to the public thereon, only two independent parties can serve as effective controls on the CEO and management: the independent directors and the independent external auditor. To us it seems self-evident that, to be effective, audit committees and external auditors must be truly independent of management, not only in terms of affiliations and other formalities but, more importantly, in terms of mindset and attitude. In our opinion, it is equally self-evident that they must work together. Rules, regulations, sanctions and penalties can only provide the framework within which the company and its management, directors and external auditors operate. It is the independent directors and the external auditor, working together, that provides the most effective checks on "egregious corporate behaviour".

Effective working relationships among audit committees, auditors and management cannot be legislated, no matter how sophisticated and detailed that legislation may be. Effective working relationships will only become a reality if the individual parties build, nurture and manage those relationships, and if they recognize and acknowledge the complexity of those relationships. Ultimately, it is the effectiveness of these working relationships that will ensure the integrity of financial reporting and, therefore, we believe that public policy makers should concentrate on encouraging and strengthening this dynamic, rather than relying solely on a rules-based regulatory regime.

Much of what has been written and promulgated about audit committee effectiveness has focused on structure (members' independence of management, qualifications for members, the number of meetings etc.). While structure is important, for us the critical issue is one of relationships. Audit committees that establish and nurture the right relationships and manage them effectively will have put in place a solid foundation for their effectiveness.

Indeed, we go further and state our belief that unless audit committees, management and the external auditor create productive relationships among themselves, they cannot be effective.

The changed expectations of audit committees will only reinforce the importance of these crucial relationships. For example, the requirement that audit committees have a formal charter has focused the spotlight on the importance of these relationships. There can be no real meaning behind the charter's words unless there has been a rigorous examination of and agreement on the respective roles that the audit committee, board and management will play in assuring the integrity of the company's financial information and its financial reporting; a clear enunciation of the expectations each has of the others; and a clear articulation of how these expectations will be realized.

The importance of candid and direct communication, and effective working relationships among the audit committee, management and the external auditor cannot be emphasized too strongly. Without them, audit committees will fail to be effective.

This chapter will discuss the chairman's role in establishing and managing these relationships; examine the kind of relationships an effective audit committee should have with management, the external auditor and the board of directors; and offer some suggestions as to how to achieve optimal, productive working relationships. It will also discuss briefly the relationship between the audit committee and the company's outside advisors.

The Chairman's Role in Managing Relationships

The responsibility for managing this complex set of relationships rests squarely with the chairman of the audit committee.

The chairman's objective can be stated simply: to initiate and manage effective working relationships among the audit committee, management, the external auditor and the board. The realization of this objective, however, is far from a simple task.

The chairman should strive to create an environment in which a system of interdependent relationships exists with the purpose of sharing information and concerns in an atmosphere of accountability, respect and confidence. While leading this process imposes a heavy burden on the chairman, similarly heavy burdens are also imposed on management, the external auditor and the board of directors to respond positively. Properly initiated and managed, however, the relationships that emerge will do more than anything else to ensure the integrity of a company's financial information.

Achieving productive relationships among the committee, the auditor and management will result in a system of checks and balances, based on candid two-way communication, constructive challenge, trust and accountability, that will reinforce the ability of both the board and management to carry out their respective duties to shareholders and the capital markets.

How can this critically important objective be achieved? There is no single set of strategies that will guarantee success. The most effective approaches will vary according to the stage of sophistication a company has reached in its governance policies generally, and in its audit committee practices. There are, however, some common principles and objectives and these are discussed below.

Relationship with the Board of Directors

The chairman of the audit committee cannot hope to be successful without the support of the board of directors. Therefore, the chairman must first articulate very clearly to the board his or her expectations of the roles of the audit committee, the external auditor and management, and then gain the board's support for these expectations.

An effective way for the chairman to initiate such a discussion is through a discussion of the audit committee's charter, which we believe to be the cornerstone of all these relationships. If the audit committee does not yet have a charter, then the process of drafting one and having it reviewed and approved by the board presents an excellent opportunity for discussions around expectations. For audit committees that do have a charter, the board's annual review of the charter, or the board's approval process for any amendments to the charter made by the audit committee in response to changing regulations, or changing views of the committee itself, provides the opportunity for the chairman to revisit both existing and changing expectations with the board.

Included in these discussions should be the expectations of the board and the chairman of the audit committee with respect to keeping the board informed about the audit committee's work. These expectations should focus on issues of timeliness and the degree of detail that is appropriate in the audit committee's reports to the board.

Once board-approved expectations have been determined, the chairman of the audit committee must communicate them to management and the external auditor. This presents the chairman with the opportunity to discuss ways in which management and the auditor can work together with the audit committee to fulfill these expectations. In communicating the board's and audit committee's expectations, it is often prudent for the chairman of the audit committee to enlist the participation of the chairman of the board to reinforce the fact that these expectations have the support of the entire board of directors.

The chairman of the audit committee must, of course, maintain a close relationship with the board of directors throughout the course of the audit committee's work. By reporting appropriately to the board at the first meeting of the board following an audit committee meeting, and, when necessary, by alerting the board to any concerns or issues that may arise between meetings of the committee, the chairman ensures that the board is kept informed. By so doing, the chairman also creates opportunities to educate the board and, when necessary, to secure the board's support for, or assistance in, the resolution of any difficult issues that may arise either with management or the external auditor. Moreover, a board that is fully informed by its audit committee is in a much better position to fulfill its statutory duties with respect to financial reporting.

Relationship with the External Auditor

Certain fundamental principles must be communicated to the external auditor, beginning with reinforcement of the fact that, while the auditor works with management, the auditor works for and is accountable to the audit committee and the board of directors. All aspects of the audit committee's relationship (and, indeed, the company's relationship) with the external auditor flow from this. Management can easily be threatened by this changed dynamic. Therefore, it is important that both management and the external auditor understand and accept the changed nature of the relationship, including the fact that the auditor will be encouraged to and should discuss any matter or matters with the chairman of the committee between meetings of the committee as required.

While under corporate law the external auditor is responsible to the shareholders, it is almost impossible for a diverse group of shareholders to exercise meaningful oversight of the external auditor. Traditionally, management has assumed this oversight role. To ensure that the external audit is not compromised and that it will be conducted independently of management, the audit committee must assume this oversight responsibility. Fortunately, MI 52-110 has put an end to the debate on this issue.

Expectations

A key message to communicate to the external auditor is that, because the auditor is accountable to the audit committee, the committee expects and insists upon clear, candid and direct communication between the auditor and the chairman and the committee. The chairman should also ensure that the auditor understands that both the chairman and the committee expect to be informed of any and all significant issues and all concerns the auditor may have at any given time, whether or not management agrees with those concerns.

In our opinion, audit committees should select the external auditor and abandon the traditional practice of reviewing and approving management's choice of an external auditor. We believe this new practice will logically flow from the requirements of MI 52-110. Moreover, it is the audit committee that should make the decision about the external auditor's continuing engagement. It follows that the audit fees should be negotiated with the chairman of the audit committee and not with management. We believe these practices will reinforce the external auditor's accountability to the committee and the board, and establish the foundation for the relationship between them.

While audit committees should retain sole responsibility for the above activities, it is important to seek management's views on these issues and give them careful consideration. However, as long as every attempt has been made to achieve agreement, the audit committee should never be reluctant to make a decision that management may not favour.

We strongly recommend that audit committees and auditors directly ascertain and document their expectations of each other in a letter, which should be reviewed annually. For example, when the auditor is first engaged, a letter should be prepared setting out these expectations. If and as expectations change, the letter should be amended appropriately. The process of creating this letter, even subsequent to the engagement of the external auditor, provides an excellent opportunity for both parties to participate in a rigorous analysis of their relationship.

Multilateral Instrument 52-110
This instrument deals with the relationship between the audit committee and the external auditors as follows.

Section 2.2 of the instrument states that a company must require its external auditor to report directly to the audit committee. Section 2.3, which prescribes the responsibilities of the audit committee, includes among them the duty to recommend the external auditor and the compensation to be paid to the external auditor to the board of directors; the responsibility for overseeing the work of the external auditor, including the resolution of disagreements between management and the external auditor; and the duty to pre-approve all non-audit services to be provided to the company or its subsidiary entities by the external auditor. Further, the instrument states that the audit committee must review and approve the company's hiring policies regarding partners, employees, former partners and former employees of the current and former external auditor.

Preparing for Audit Committee Meetings
While the chairman of the audit committee must be readily available to the external auditor and management at any time, it is important, when preparing for audit committee meetings, that the chairman of the audit committee be available to them on a regularly scheduled basis. In our experience, an effective way to ensure this is for the chairman to establish a regular series of face-to-face sessions prior to each audit committee meeting.
- *The first session* should be with the CFO to create the proposed agenda for the audit committee meeting and to agree on the information that will be provided to the committee. The agreed agenda should, of course, be submitted to the external auditor for his or her input.

- **The *second session*** should take place with the external auditor alone to obtain the auditor's input to the agenda, to discuss any concerns he or she may have and discuss the auditor's views on the progress of the audit and his or her findings.
- **The *third session*** should take place with both the external auditor and management present for the purpose of finalizing and prioritizing the agenda, and reviewing the materials management has prepared. This session has an additional purpose, that of providing the chairman with an opportunity to explore more fully any differences of opinion that may exist between management and the auditor, and to reach agreement on how best to present these matters to the audit committee.

To be effective, these sessions should take place sufficiently in advance of the audit committee meeting to allow enough time for any amendments to be made to the committee's briefing materials, for determining how best to present key issues to the committee, and for allowing the chairman to decide how to conduct the meeting. Materials should never be sent to audit committee members that have not been reviewed by the chairman, and discussed by him or her with management and the external auditor, ideally at the session when both are present.

We recommend that, in order to prepare for the third session referred to above, the chairman receive a binder containing all the material proposed to be included in the committee members' briefing books and that he or she review these materials, even though they may still be in draft form, prior to the joint session. This will enable the chairman to have a more intelligent discussion with management and the external auditor at the preparatory session, and will put him or her into a better position to suggest any amendments to the proposed materials before they are sent to the committee members.

While we believe all audit committee chairmen should follow these preparatory steps, we recognize that there may be circumstances that make in-person meetings less feasible, in which case conducting these sessions by telephone would be acceptable. Telephone sessions, of course, are less than optimal, and every effort should be made to have these sessions in person.

The Audit Committee Work Plan

Another responsibility of the chairman is to work with the external auditor and management to create an audit committee work plan for each fiscal year. This work plan should include regular matters that come before the committee in accordance with its charter, and any other matters of significant concern or interest that the chairman, management and/or the external auditor believe the committee should be aware of and should discuss during the period for which the plan is being created.

The audit committee work plan should always include an educational component. We recommend that it include subjects such as:
- a tour of the balance sheet;

- an analysis of the income statement;
- a review of major subsidiaries;
- a discussion of financing vehicles and arrangements;
- a review of tax structures and related risks;
- a review of principal enterprise risks;
- a series of presentations on the business or businesses of the company;
- a review of special corporate projects, such as a major information technology initiative or a new acquisition; and
- a review of new accounting and other external developments.

This educational component allows the committee to be better informed about issues that have the potential to affect the company's financial health and disclosure. In addition, it provides an opportunity for committee members to discuss issues with members of management who might not regularly attend audit committee meetings, such as executives responsible for a major subsidiary. In our view, it is important that audit committee members be exposed to a wider level of management than simply the CFO, the CEO, or members of the finance group. The importance of the educational component of such special agenda items cannot be over-emphasized. An audit committee that understands the business of the company and how it is carried out is a more effective audit committee.

Another educational expectation that audit committees should have of the external auditor is for the auditor to keep the committee apprised of new developments in accounting policies and standards, potential new accounting rules and the effect of these on the corporation. The chairman should communicate this to the auditor and make sure that there is time on each agenda of the committee for this purpose. This is especially important in today's environment in which changes in accounting policies and standards are occurring more frequently than ever before.

The audit committee work plan is not the same as the external auditor's audit plan. The external auditor should consult with the chairman and the committee members to obtain their views before finalizing the audit plan for the year. Although it seems self-evident, the audit committee should insist that the audit plan for the year be presented to the committee for their approval, ideally, prior to the beginning of the new audit year. If this becomes impossible, then no later than the last month of the first quarter.

Interaction with the Audit Firm
It is important to the success of the audit committee's relationship with the external auditor that the chairman be consulted with respect to the senior audit team members assigned to the company. The chairman should get to know the lead audit partner and his or her senior team members. This allows both parties to develop a sense of each other's working style and should help to promote both confidence in each other and respect for the responsibil-

ities of each party. It also establishes an environment in which clear, direct and candid communication can not only take place, but can flourish. Very importantly, it also permits the chairman to better assess the performance of the external auditor.

It is equally important that the chairman establish a relationship with the CEO or senior managing partner of the audit firm engaged by the board. If this is not appropriate due either to size or location of the company, then the relationship should be forged with another, but senior, partner of the firm.

Establishing these channels of communication permits ease of access when issues arise that require either consultation with, or intervention at, the highest levels of the audit firm.

Evaluation of the External Auditor

An important responsibility of the audit committee is to evaluate the external auditor's performance. Although the audit committee should bear the responsibility for ultimately assessing the auditor's performance, it should solicit the views of management. The assessment should cover the professional competencies in conducting the audit, value-added services provided by the auditor and client service issues. This process should be formalized by the audit committee and conducted annually.

In Camera Meetings

No meeting of the audit committee is complete without a series of *in camera* meetings with the external auditor, management, and the committee members only. It is the chairman's responsibility to include these meetings on every audit committee meeting agenda and ensure that sufficient time is set aside for them at each meeting. When *in camera* meetings with the external auditor occur regularly, they become less threatening to management, while providing an excellent opportunity for the external auditor to communicate privately and candidly with the committee. Similarly, they provide the committee with the opportunity for candid questioning of and private discussions with the external auditor. This process is an excellent relationship-building device.

Interaction with Major Subsidiaries

If a corporation has a major subsidiary or subsidiaries, whether domestic or foreign, we believe the audit committee of the parent and subsidiary companies must closely co-ordinate their activities and maintain close communication. Therefore, the chairman of the parent company's audit committee should establish a relationship with the chairman of the subsidiary's audit committee and with the lead partner of the subsidiary's external auditor. The audit committee should, however, seek legal advice on the kind of relationship it should have with the audit committee of a public subsidiary. We agree with the JCCG's recommendation[3]:

---

[3] Beyond Compliance: Building a Governance Culture, Final Report Joint Committee on Corporate Governance, November 2001, page 25.

With regard to audit committees, we believe that there needs to be close co-ordination and communication between audit committees of parents and subsidiaries. There should be a common appreciation of the control frameworks and cultures of the entities, and substantial sharing of information. Safeguards should ensure that the sharing of information is not used by the parent to disadvantage minority shareholders of subsidiaries.

Relationship with Management

It is often easier to manage the relationship between the audit committee and the external auditor than it is to manage the relationship with management. This is because, traditionally, management has sought to dominate the relationship with both the audit committee and the external auditor.

Clearly communicating the committee's expectations (and by definition, the board's expectations) to management can be very helpful in creating and managing an effective working relationship with management. It is critical that management not feel threatened by the audit committee's relationship with the external auditor and that the external auditor not be reluctant to stand up to management when that becomes necessary.

Importance of the Right Tone at the Top

The co-operation of the CEO and CFO with the audit committee and its chairman, and senior management's support for the committee's objectives, must be achieved if the committee is to be successful. Such co-operation and support are an integral part of the committee's success. The attitudes of both the CEO and CFO are critical, but the tone set by the CEO is likely to be determinative.

It is equally important that this co-operation and support not be given grudgingly or with reservations. Indeed, if such co-operation is not forthcoming, then the audit committee faces a significant challenge, which is discussed further in Chapter 14, The Tough Issues and How to Deal With Them. Suffice it to say here that, in these circumstances, the committee must report the situation to the chairman of the board, and enlist his or her help in discussing the matter with the CEO in an attempt to secure the CEO's co-operation. Should that initiative fail, then the committee has no choice but to report the matter to the board of directors and seek to have the board direct the CEO to reconsider.

Should this fail, the board may well have to consider whether or not the CEO is the right person for the job, or alternatively, whether the audit committee members feel they can continue to serve on the audit committee. This also has implications for the external auditor who faces a similar decision with respect to continuing as the external auditor.

The CEO has a key role to play in ensuring that the culture in the company is conducive to those constructive relationships between management and the audit committee that must be present if the audit committee is to be effective. It is the CEO's responsibility to create and communicate a culture that rewards integrity, demands it at all times, and holds people accountable for it. Moreover, it is the CEO's duty to state clearly his or her expectation that nothing less than a co-operative attitude in dealing with the audit committee and the auditors will be tolerated. This is not to say that disagreements will not be tolerated. Constructive disagreement is bound to happen and is, in fact, to be desired. What is not to be tolerated is withholding information or miserly doling out the bare minimum of information. The risk to the company is simply too great.

The expectations that the board and the audit committee have of management in this regard must be very clearly communicated, particularly to the CEO and the CFO. This task need not fall solely on the chairman of the audit committee, although the initiative must be his or hers. Ideally, this task should be undertaken by both the chairman of the board and the chairman of the audit committee. However, it is the responsibility of the chairman of the audit committee to encourage and monitor management's ongoing support and co-operation.

In his or her dealings with the CEO and the CFO, the chairman of the audit committee must create and foster an atmosphere in which both the CEO and the CFO have sufficient respect for, trust in, and comfort with the chairman that neither executive is reluctant to discuss any matter with him or her, either between committee meetings or in preparation for them. It is essential that the CEO, the CFO and the chairman be convinced they have the same objectives. A number of CEOs have told us that they sleep much better at night knowing they have a proactive, rigorous and challenging audit committee chairman.

Audit Committees and the CFO

Some CFOs, unfortunately, treat audit committees and their chairmen as necessary evils to whom they dole out information sparingly, grudgingly and only when absolutely necessary. This can be a recipe for disaster. One CFO told us that if asked the "right question" he would, of course, provide the answer, but that he felt no obligation to volunteer information unless the "right question" was asked. This kind of attitude puts audit committees and management at risk and no board of directors should tolerate it.

It is important, however, that the chairman and the committee demonstrate respect for, trust in, and confidence in the CFO and his or her financial team. The relationship between them should not be adversarial, but should be one that can best be described as containing a healthy element of constructive tension. Should the chairman and the committee cease to have confidence in the CFO, they have a duty to communicate their lack of confidence to the board of directors and the CEO, together with a recommendation for timely action.

While the practice is changing, it is a disappointing fact that many audit committees are not involved in the selection of a new CFO. Certification reinforces the fact that the CFO is publicly accountable for the company's financial reporting and, therefore, we strongly believe the audit committee should take an active part in his or her selection, while being appropriately sensitive to the fact that the CEO is accountable to the board for the selection of the senior management team. At the very least, the chairman should be consulted with respect to candidates, the criteria for the position, and should interview all short-listed candidates. Ideally, the committee members should also be involved in the selection process. The chairman, with the board's support, should make this request and make sure that it is honoured.

The members of the committee and the chairman can be very helpful to the CFO, mentoring him or her when required, acting as a sounding board when difficult decisions must be made, and supporting the CFO, if necessary, in circumstances where both the committee and the CFO agree on something and other members of senior management, including the CEO, do not.

Preparing for Audit Committee Meetings

As noted earlier, the chairman of the audit committee should make it a practice to hold sessions with management and the external auditor prior to every audit committee meeting to finalize the agenda and materials for the meeting. To reiterate: the first meeting should be with the CFO; the second with the external auditor and the third with the external auditor, the CFO and the appropriate members of management present.

Management should be aware that the third of these sessions — the one with both management and the external auditor present — is not to be regarded as either a perfunctory review or a substitute for the audit committee meeting. The purpose is to have an in-depth discussion of the agenda topics, a review of the presentations and reports that management has prepared for the audit committee, reach agreement on how the topics will be presented to the committee to allow sufficient time for discussion, and ensure that the chairman is properly briefed on all the issues and the actions to be taken.

These sessions should take place sufficiently in advance of the audit committee meeting to ensure that there is sufficient time to make any required amendments to the materials before they are sent to the members of the committee. Care, of course, should always be taken that there is enough time for members of the committee to review their briefing books prior to the meeting. We suggest that the briefing books be in the hands of the committee members not less than one week before the audit committee meeting. We recognize that with the shorter reporting times now in place, this will place an additional burden on management, but we feel strongly that management must re-engineer their closing procedures to accommodate this.

With regard to the briefing materials for the committee members, management should have a clear understanding of the quality and timeliness that the committee expects with respect to these materials, and that handouts at the meeting are unacceptable, other than in the most exceptional circumstances.

Audit Committee Work Plan

It is essential that management be involved in creating the audit committee work plan, which is also discussed above. When the chairman, management and the external auditor work together to create each year's work plan, it provides all parties with another opportunity to understand and appreciate more completely the expectations each has of the other. This can be very helpful in building and enhancing the relationship among them.

In Camera Meetings

In addition to holding regular *in camera* sessions with the external auditor at every audit committee meeting, as described above, *in camera* sessions should also be held with management. These sessions provide an opportunity for management to share with the audit committee their observations and any concerns they may have with respect to the external auditor's performance. *In camera* meetings also promote ease of communication, allow the articulation of concerns, and permit these activities to take place in a non-adversarial and routine environment. A practice of regular *in camera* meetings can be very effective in creating the kind of atmosphere in which healthy relationships between the audit committee and management can flourish.

Relationship with Internal Audit

We believe the relationship between the internal audit function and the audit committee should be clearly defined and addressed in the audit committee's charter.

A number of things flow from having the committee's relationship with internal audit clearly defined in its charter. For example, the audit committee should approve the annual internal audit plan, so far as it is related to those functions over which the audit committee has oversight. Also, the head of internal audit should report to the audit committee on all matters over which the audit committee has oversight. The chairman of the committee should make it clear that he or she expects the head of internal audit to raise any matters that could have an impact on the risks the company faces, its controls, the integrity of management, the quality of financial reporting, and the quality of the information systems that support financial reporting.

Administratively, internal audit should report to senior management, which in our opinion should be the CEO or CFO. However, this administrative reporting relationship should in no way impact internal audit's substantive accountability to the audit committee. In other words, internal audit should report, as a matter of substance, to the audit committee on all matters relating to controls and the integrity of financial reporting.

The chairman of the audit committee should make it a practice to meet privately with the head of internal audit prior to each audit committee meeting and the head of internal audit should attend all audit committee meetings. In our experience, it is helpful if the chairman of the audit committee schedules his or her meeting with the head of internal audit prior to the chairman's pre-audit committee session with both the external auditor and management. We also recommend that the audit committee meet *in camera* with the head of internal audit at least twice a year. The head of internal audit should have access to the chairman of the audit committee at any time.

Relationship with External Advisors

Many issues that come before the audit committee have a legal and/or corporate finance dimension, such as those related to tax, compliance, disclosure, financing and multinational structure, etc. Much of the time, legal issues will be discussed with the company's in-house corporate counsel, but there will be times when management will retain external legal counsel. Similarly, there will be times when the company retains other advisors, such as investment bankers, actuaries, geologists, valuation experts, etc.

One of the consequences of capital market reform is that management must retain additional advisors to substitute for the advice and services historically provided by the external auditor. This is because the external auditor has been prohibited from providing advice and services in a limited number of areas. As a result, the audit committee may also have to rely on advisors other than the external auditor in those areas that come within the committee's mandate and, therefore, it must have direct communication with these external advisors.

Clearly, the external advisors work for the company, except in those exceptional circumstances when they are retained by the committee itself. Usually, management retains the external advisors, such as the lawyers retained by the company's in-house counsel or the investment bankers retained by the CFO or the CEO. It is important that the external advisors and management understand the audit committee's expectations with respect to its relationship with these external advisors.

As a general rule, the audit committee should be comfortable using management's advisors. If, however, the committee finds itself in circumstances in which it believes it would be prudent to retain its own advisors, or it is not satisfied with the quality of the advice of management's advisors, then it should retain its own advisors. Audit committees should ensure that management clearly understands this general principle.

Audit committees should also ensure that management understands that there will be circumstances when the committee will wish to have the company's external advisors present at meetings. This will occur most often when the issue for which the external advisors have been retained is an agenda topic for discussion at a committee meeting. For example, the audit committee may wish to have the advisors present for any discussions around off balance sheet financing or accounting systems implementation. We encourage audit committees not to hesitate to take this step.

The audit committee should make it very clear to management that, whether or not the external advisors are retained by management or by the committee, it expects the advisors to report to it (or at least to its chairman) any and all significant concerns the advisors may develop with respect to matters that have the potential to have an impact on financial reporting. While we appreciate that rules of professional conduct may apply to these advisors, we do not believe they should be used as a shield behind which to hide, in order to justify not disclosing concerns about compliance with applicable securities regulations or concerns that may impact the integrity of the company's financial information and the manner in which its financial information is disclosed.

The relationship between the audit committee and other external advisors is becoming more important in light of the new and more onerous independence standards for the external auditor. Because of these new independence requirements, management is more often in a position of having to retain advisors other than the external auditor. The audit committee must make sure that it establishes a relationship with these advisors and that these advisors understand the audit committee's expectations of them with regard to advice given to the corporation in respect of matters within the mandate of the committee.

If these principles are clearly understood before the fact, there will be less chance that management will feel threatened or that an adversarial climate will ensue.

Key Messages

- The relationship among the audit committee, management and the external auditor should be an interdependent one.
- The changing accountabilities among audit committees, external auditors and management are changing the dynamics of their relationships and making the management of these relationships more complex.
- Strong relationships must be established and nurtured.
- The chairman is responsible for managing relationships and must have the support of the board of directors.
- The effective management of these relationships requires a climate in which each party trusts the motives of the others and recognizes that all parties have a common objective — the integrity of the company's financial information.
- Sustaining effective relationships requires constant monitoring, evaluation, assessment and the commitment to take corrective action if required.
- External advisors should have direct channel of communication to the audit committee or its chairman.

9

Doing the Right Things Right

The right mandate, the right members, and the ability to manage its relationships with the board, management and the external auditor are all critical to the audit committee's success. Financial governance will remain form without substance, however, unless the committee also has the information and processes it needs to be able to "do the right things the right way".

The processes that the audit committee adopts for carrying out its responsibilities and the information that comes to the committee are critical elements in its success. Without high quality, accurate, complete and timely information, the committee cannot function effectively. Fortunately, audit committees can and should influence how this goal is achieved. The important elements that will assist the committee in achieving this objective are illustrated in Figure 14.

It is our experience, however, that there is another essential component. If the audit committee is to be in a position to assess the information that comes before it in any meaningful way, or if the committee is to put in place processes that are effective, it must understand the business or businesses in which the company is engaged. While it is unlikely that the committee will ever have the depth of understanding possessed by management, it must develop a sufficient understanding of the business to enable it to ask the right questions, assess the quality and completeness of the information it receives, and initiate the appropriate processes for obtaining and testing that information.

As is the case with so many aspects of audit committee behaviour, the chairman's role is particularly important in making sure that the committee obtains the information and education it requires. These information needs are much more likely to be met when co-operative working relationships exist among the committee, management and the external auditor. Therefore, the audit committee chairman must set the stage for those relationships by ensuring that he or she clearly understands the committee's expectations and successfully manages the committee's relationships with management and the external auditor.

Figure 14 | **Doing the Right Things Right: Key Components**

It is important that the chairman never become complacent about his or her success in forging and nurturing these relationships. He or she should never rely solely on the existence of solid relationships to ensure that the elements illustrated in Figure 14 will produce the desired results. The chairman is responsible for continually monitoring best and leading edge practices to make sure that the most appropriate elements are in place to produce the high quality information required by the committee. Additionally, the chairman must be aware of developments in the internal and external environment that will affect the kind of information that should be provided to the committee and that might affect its practices.

Moreover, the chairman must also play a central role in encouraging the members of the committee to invest time and effort in developing an understanding of the business of the company, encouraging management to assist in the education of the members of the committee, and facilitating the members' education by including educational topics on each audit committee meeting agenda. In this endeavour, the chairman can be greatly assisted by a management with the right attitude and by the external auditor.

It is management's responsibility to produce the information required by the audit committee. The committee should always be aware, however, that it has an additional source of information that it should utilize in appropriate circumstances. That source, of course, is the external auditor. With the right relationships in place, the audit committee can and should explore areas where the external auditor can facilitate improvements in the completeness and reliability of the information that comes to the committee.

Setting Expectations of the Committee's Information Needs
Audit Committee Charter and Work Plan

The most effective way for an audit committee to begin communicating its expectations to management and the external auditor is through the audit committee charter and annual work plan. Properly drafted, the charter should set out the principles and procedures under which the committee intends to operate, and should articulate the committee's responsibilities and duties. The work plan should indicate the meetings at which the committee will address its various responsibilities and include any additional matters that the committee wishes to address in any particular year.

The charter and work plan, however, will not contain all facets of the committee's expectations. It is the chairman's responsibility to provide additional communication of these expectations, which may include such matters as the:
- timing of the delivery of the members' briefing books in order to afford members sufficient time to review the material before the audit committee meeting;
- quality and scope of the information contained in the briefing books;
- committee's expectations with respect to the presentations made at the meeting by management and the external auditor; and
- chairman's expectations with respect to the preparation for each meeting, including the creation of the agenda, his or her review of the material before it is sent to the committee members, his or her prioritization of the topics to be addressed, and his or her analysis of the principal issues to be considered in each information item.

The chairman's relationship with management and the external auditor should provide ample opportunity to communicate his or her wishes in this regard and, when the relationship is an effective one, it will form the basis upon which all the elements of high quality, complete and timely information are constructed.

Information to be Provided

Priorities and Level of Detail

The quality of discussion at audit committee meetings depends, in large part, on the quality of the information provided to the committee. Therefore, it is imperative that the committee insists on and receives high quality, complete, accurate and timely information. It is the responsibility of the chairman and the CFO to ensure that these information needs are met. The CFO's role is to produce the required information in a timely fashion and present it in a meaningful and effective manner. The chairman's role is to make the audit committee's expectations in this regard clear to management and to review the material prior to it being sent to the committee.

In today's environment, with more and more responsibilities thrust on the audit committee and with more frequent and much longer meetings, the effective use of the time spent at meetings is becoming more and more important. Thus, another task falls on the shoulders of the chairman. He or she must spend sufficient time with both management and the external auditor to enable him or her to prioritize the agenda and, even more importantly, to prioritize the issues contained in the material under each topic. Both the CFO and the external auditor should be made aware that the chairman expects their assistance in this task.

The audit committee charter should articulate the committee's priorities and define its information needs. The level of detail in the required information, however, must be determined through ongoing dialogue between management and the audit committee, and a shared understanding of why the committee requires the information that it does.

For matters that the audit committee addresses regularly — such as the financial statements, the litigation report, the treasury report, the review of provisions, and the certification report — the reporting format typically becomes a matter of routine, provided that the committee has clearly communicated its expectations to management. However, even regular reports should be reviewed periodically by the chairman, the CFO, and the committee to determine whether they can and should be improved.

For non-routine matters, the level of detail in the materials to be reviewed by the committee and in the presentations made to it should be agreed between the chairman and the CFO. It is important to strike a balance between burying the committee in voluminous data and providing it with insufficient information. When extensive or complex data must be presented (for example, in a transaction involving an acquisition), it is management's responsibility to highlight the critical components of the information and provide guidance to the committee in analyzing that information. Comprehensive executive summaries of voluminous material are a must.

Some audit committee members have told us of an infallible method they have developed to differentiate between the important and the less important information. This methodology is based on the timing and the presentation of information. Less important information arrives before the audit committee meeting and is provided in great detail. More important information is walked in to the meeting and presented on just a couple of slides. Need we say that such practices should not be tolerated!

Since the MD&A and the news release have become part of the financial reporting package, their review by the audit committee has assumed a much higher profile. It is imperative that the committee have sufficient time to review them prior to the audit committee meeting. Without a sufficient knowledge of the business, however, the audit committee will not be in a position to review effectively the content and structure of the MD&A.

It is also critical that the chairman have the opportunity to read the draft MD&A and news release carefully prior the session with management and the external auditor held to prepare for the audit committee meeting. These critical documents should not be sent to the audit committee members until the chairman and the external auditor have reviewed them. This puts an added stress on management to produce these documents some time in advance of the audit committee meeting. The shortened time frame for financial reporting and the expectations of the audit committee to have sufficient time to review these documents before their publication is proving to be a problem for many management teams. Certification also imposes additional stresses with respect to timing. The solution is not an easy one. We believe, however, that quarter-end and year-end closing procedures will require re-engineering to meet the needs of the audit committee.

Management and the external auditor should clearly understand that the audit committee will not tolerate last-minute handouts during the meeting unless the circumstances are truly exceptional and the chairman has agreed to the handouts.

Special Topics

In developing the annual work plan, the chairman should include a number of special topics for consideration by the committee. These should include educational topics, such as:

- new developments in accounting standards;
- new audit committee best practices;
- information about aspects of the company's business that will facilitate the committee's ability to assess the potential risk areas and assist it in determining appropriate areas for the audit focus;
- new business initiatives that have the potential to have an impact on either the financial statements or financial disclosure; and
- in-depth presentations on complex matters, such as variable interest entities, or foreign exchange policies.

An issue that has arisen recently is whether or not audit committees should review the presentations that the CEO and CFO intend to make to the analysts. Some companies ask the CEO to make the same presentation to the audit committee that will be made to the analysts. We believe this is a leading edge practice that all audit committees should consider, although we recognize that only some will want to include this in their charter, as timing imperatives may make this impractical.

Another matter of current debate is whether the letter of representation that management prepares for submission to the external auditor should be reviewed by the audit committee, should be addressed to both the external auditor and the audit committee, or should be copied to the audit committee. Some believe that such a practice would hold management accountable to the audit committee for the completeness and accuracy of the financial statements. Others have suggested that the introduction of certification has made this debate moot. We are of the opinion that since the audit committee itself is accountable to the shareholders, it must be part of the certification loop. In light of certification, we advocate that management's letter of representation be addressed to the external auditor and copied to the audit committee. This practice provides the audit committee with the opportunity to ask for additional representations, should the committee feel they are needed. (A further discussion of issues related to certification is provided in Chapter 12, CEO and CFO Certification.)

Preparation: Who and When

Management and the external auditor are responsible for preparing the information that is presented to the audit committee. The audit committee is responsible for communicating its expectations about the level of detail and the timing of the receipt of this information. Since the committee's effectiveness is so dependent on the information it receives, it is the chairman's responsibility to ensure that management and the external auditor understand and meet the committee's expectations.

Preparing for the Audit Committee Meeting

For audit committee meetings to be effective, the chairman must spend sufficient time preparing for them. Prior to each meeting, the chairman should consult with the CFO, head of internal audit, and the external auditor to create the agenda, agree on the information needed for the meeting, and discuss issues that have arisen since the audit committee's last meeting. Depending on the circumstances, these consultations may take place either in person or by telephone, though we believe that in-person meetings are much more effective.

The audit committee charter is the guide for the matters to come before the committee at its meetings, and the chairman should see to it that the committee fulfills all the responsibilities it has undertaken in its charter. One method to facilitate this is to publish a matrix setting out the committee's specific responsibilities and indicating the meeting date at which the committee will address each of them. This is called the "work plan". Both the charter and the work plan should be included in the committee members' briefing books for each audit committee meeting so the members can monitor the committee's progress throughout the year.

The chairman and the CFO should agree on the agenda for each audit committee meeting and agree on any additional matters not included in the charter that either management or the external auditor wishes to put before the committee. They should also agree on the kind of information to be presented and the level of detail required.

The work plan will set out the priorities for each meeting. Utilizing a risk-based approach in creating the work plan helps to focus the committee's time and attention on the most important issues. It is essential for the chairman to work closely with financial management and the external auditor so that the work plan will reflect their contributions. It is also advisable for the chairman to seek input from the company's internal audit and risk management groups.

In addition to meeting with the CFO to finalize the agenda, the chairman should also schedule a series of other meetings. He or she should hold separate sessions with the external auditor, and the head of internal audit, and should schedule a session with management and the external auditor together. It is important that these sessions take place well in advance of the audit committee meeting itself, so the preparation for that meeting, including the finalization of the material to be included in the briefing books for audit committee members, can be as complete as possible.

The session with the external auditor alone should occur in advance of the one at which both management and the auditor are both present. This provides the chairman and the external auditor with an opportunity to discuss candidly any matters of concern the auditor may have. It also enables the chairman to obtain the auditor's views on issues that have arisen since the committee's last meeting. We cannot emphasize too strongly the importance of creating this opportunity to provide both the chairman and the external auditor with a regular forum for the kind of candid discussion that must characterize the relationship between them. Such a dialogue also contributes to a more effective audit committee meeting since the chairman will have the benefit of the external auditor's assessment of what has arisen since the last meeting of the committee, thereby arming the chairman with the kind of knowledge he or she must have if the discussion and decisions taken at the meeting of the committee are to be as effective as possible.

Many chairmen meet regularly with the head of internal audit prior to each audit committee meeting. We believe that all audit committee chairmen should follow this practice. A session with the head of internal audit permits a candid discussion about any issues internal audit has identified that should be brought to the committee's attention and provides the chairman with an opportunity to review the reports that internal audit will present to the committee.

The last in the series of preparatory sessions should be held with both management and the external auditor present. Ideally, it should be scheduled at least eight or nine days in advance of the audit committee meeting itself. This means that the separate sessions with the CFO, the external auditor and internal audit should be scheduled sufficiently in advance of this plenary session so that input from those earlier meetings can assist the chairman in the conduct of the plenary meeting.

The purpose of this last session is to finalize the agenda, review the materials to be provided to the members of the committee, and agree on the presentations to be made by management and the external auditor. It is also to provide the chairman with an opportunity to identify and explore any differences of opinion that may exist between management and the external auditor and to reach agreement on how best to present these matters to the committee. The review at this session should not be a perfunctory one, but rather an in-depth consideration of the materials and the proposed presentations to be made to the committee. A key focus is to identify and prioritize the critical issues, concerns, risks and alternative solutions to be presented to the committee. There should be sufficient time between this meeting and the time when the briefing books for the audit committee meeting are to be distributed, for agreed amendments to be made to the briefing book materials. No materials should be sent to the committee members and no presentations should be made to the committee without having been previously reviewed by the chairman.

Given the complex nature of the matters that come before them, audit committee members have a right to expect that their briefing books will be available to them at least one week before the audit committee meeting. It is the chairman's duty to ensure that these expectations are met. It seems trite to state, but audit committee meetings are more effective if the committee members have had a reasonable time in which to digest the materials to be considered at the meeting. Of course, it is equally trite to observe that, for audit committee meetings to be effective, the members of the committee have an obligation to study their briefing books!

Audit Committee Meetings
Frequency
For most companies, the days of two or three audit committee meetings per year are long gone. The audit committee's review of the quarterly and year-end financial statements and the other elements of the financial reporting package, including a review of the certification report (which should include any issues that arose during the certification process) requires, at the very least, four meetings a year, and in today's environment many large public com-

panies schedule six meetings per year. We do not believe that audit committees of large public companies can discharge their obligations adequately in less than six meetings per year.

In setting the schedule for the audit committee meetings, consideration should always be given to adding an additional meeting to permit the committee to discuss matters of interest or concern identified in the committee's charter and work plan or that arise, due to changing circumstances, during the course of the year. Moreover, we strongly advocate the scheduling of one or two "off quarter" committee meetings to provide an opportunity for the audit committee to review and discuss special topics not directly related to the quarter-end. For example, the accounting and structural issues around variable interest entities, hedging, and accounting for executive compensation are among the complex matters that should not be dealt with perfunctorily at a meeting where the priority is the financial reporting package.

Ideally, the audit committee meeting should take place the day before the meeting of the board of directors. There are a number of reasons for adopting this practice, most importantly that it allows the audit committee to report to the board in a timely fashion. It is important to minimize the time during which some directors (the audit committee members) have knowledge of significant matters that are not known to other directors (the members of the board who are not on the audit committee). It is also important to ensure the timely disclosure of significant information. It should be unnecessary to state that no financial information should be disclosed by the company before the audit committee and the board have reviewed it and approved its disclosure.

Attendance

Regularly scheduled audit committee meetings should take place with all members present in person. In our experience, telephone meetings are less than satisfactory and, therefore, appropriate only in exceptional circumstances. We strongly advocate that even when meetings of the committee are held that are not on the regular schedule, committee members must make every effort to be present in person.

No meeting of the committee should be held without the external auditor being present.

The chairman is responsible for ensuring that the appropriate members of management for each agenda item are present at the meeting. Of course, he or she will want to consult with the CFO on this matter. It is our firm belief the CEO should attend all meetings of the audit committee. Certification makes this almost mandatory.

In short, committee members should show up and pay attention!

Managing the Meetings

In consultation with the chairman of the board, the chairman of the audit committee must schedule sufficient time for audit committee meetings. Ideally, audit committee meetings should take place the day before the meeting of the board. Experience indicates that a minimum of three to four hours should be set aside for audit committee meetings, and a growing number of large companies now allocate half a day for them. Much will depend on the number of meetings that are scheduled for the year. If more meetings of the committee are scheduled, the time spent at the meeting will not be as significant as it will be when only four or five meetings are scheduled. Today, a six-hour audit committee meeting is not as rare as it used to be. The work of the audit committee is increasing significantly, as is the complexity and the volume of the matters with which they must deal. Moreover, more time is needed to educate the committee on the intricacies of changing audit standards and practices and evolving regulatory imperatives, and to consider the impact these may have on the company's financial information and, indeed, on how the company manages its business.

It is the chairman's responsibility to ensure that sufficient time is allotted for audit committee meetings. In addition, he or she must also ensure that, at each meeting, sufficient time is set aside for presentations by management and the auditor and for as much discussion as members of the committee feel is required on any individual item. It is important that all questions be asked and answered to the full satisfaction of the committee. In our experience, the effectiveness of many audit committees is impaired by the amount of time devoted to presentations by management or the auditors, leaving insufficient time for discussion and questions. It is important that the audit committee assess the need for extensive oral presentations when, hopefully, the material in their briefing books is sufficiently comprehensive.

While it is to be expected that committee meetings will consume a significant amount of time, the chairman must use this time effectively. A risk-based approach helps make sure the committee's time and attention is focused on the most important issues.

Balancing presentation time and discussion time is not an exact science. While every effort must be made to do so, a certain flexibility will be required at the meeting. In this regard, the chairman should use his or her judgment at all times, but should also be prepared to utilize a judicious blend of diplomacy and control.

Some people believe that distinguishing between "information only" and "decision required items" on the agenda can be helpful in utilizing time appropriately. We are not convinced of this because many "information only" topics are of critical importance and are often a prelude to decision making. What is more helpful is for the chairman to articulate clearly the critical matters that require consideration and/or decision, not only on the meeting agenda but also during the course of discussions at the meeting. Having an in-depth discussion on priorities with management prior to the audit committee meeting will be enormously helpful.

The chairman should take careful notes at each audit committee meeting. These notes can be of great assistance in:

- reviewing the minutes;
- keeping a record of items on which follow-up is required, the form of the follow-up and the accountability for it;
- providing feedback to management and the external auditor;
- providing a record of the *in camera* meetings; and
- providing a basis for the chairman's report of the meeting to the board.

In Camera Meetings

No audit committee meeting is complete without separate *in camera* meetings with management and the external auditor. Time should also be set aside for an *in camera* meeting among the audit committee members themselves.

The purpose of meeting separately with management and the external auditor is to allow both to share candidly with the committee any concerns each may have about the other's performance or about the issues that arose during the meeting. Indeed, the committee should encourage both parties to feel free to raise and discuss any matter privately with the committee.

In a world in which auditors are required to be accountable to the audit committee, the *in camera* meeting with the external auditor is essential.

The *in camera* meeting among the members of the committee is perhaps the most valuable. In this environment, committee members often feel most comfortable in speaking freely, and sharing their observations and concerns. This provides important feedback to the chairman in managing the relationships and in addressing the priorities for future meetings.

These meetings provide the committee with an opportunity to get feedback, both positive and negative, about the meeting itself and to put any sensitive questions they may have separately to members of management and the audit team. The chairman has a responsibility to note carefully the matters discussed and to provide appropriate reports to each of management and the external auditor.

This is a healthy and valuable process and should be regarded by all as a routine invitation to speak freely. If *in camera* sessions are built into each meeting's agenda, they become part of the committee's routine and should not be threatening to either management or the auditor.

Meeting Dynamics

The chairman must have the qualifications, ability, authority and force of personality to ensure that he or she clearly controls the agenda, meetings and discussions that take place at the meetings. Neither the CFO nor the external auditor should have the dominant voice either in setting the meeting agenda or at the committee meetings, although the contribution of both is essential. At the meetings, it is the chairman's task to ensure that time is allowed for full and complete discussions of all matters before the committee and that all committee members are:

- satisfied they have the information they need to make decisions;
- understand the accounting policies, estimates and standards to be applied; and
- have received appropriate answers to their questions.

If the chairman is to manage the meetings effectively, another important task is to be vigilant about bringing timely, clear and definitive closure to all agenda items.

Reporting

Minutes

There is a need for a "due diligence" record of the committee's discussions. Traditionally, the view of the lawyers has prevailed and audit committee minutes have consisted principally of a record of decisions with only enough material included to indicate that the decisions were based on pertinent information. This minimalist approach to minutes has its obvious advantages, including maintaining the confidentiality of committee discussions. But does it provide a record of the committee's work? Today, it is more important than ever before that audit committees leave a clear record that they have fulfilled, to the best of their ability, their diligence obligations. Therefore, the content of the meeting minutes is being scrutinized more carefully.

The desire for confidentiality must be tempered with the need to leave a record of the diligence of the committee. This is the challenge facing audit committees as they consider the appropriateness of their minutes.

An exercise we have found useful is to check, periodically, the committee's minutes against the duties set out in the charter and work plan and evaluate whether or not the minutes appropriately reflect those duties.

The chairman should review the minutes carefully with the committee's secretary (usually the company's corporate counsel) and with the external auditor before asking the committee to discuss and approve them. Indeed, in addition to the chairman, the minutes should be pre-circulated for comments to the CFO, external auditor, internal auditor and other members of management who have presented an agenda topic at the meeting. Any amendments these individuals might suggest should be reflected in the minutes before they are circulated to the members of the committee.

Reporting to the Board

Reporting to the board of directors is a critical part of the audit committee's responsibilities. Since this should be done through the committee's chairman, reporting to the board on the committee's work becomes a key duty of the chairman — and one he or she must take very seriously.

The chairman should report to the board after every audit committee meeting and should do so at the next meeting of the board following the audit committee meeting. Ideally, the audit committee should meet the day before the board meeting. This is especially important when the audit committee has met to review the quarter-end or the year-end filings. It is less important when the audit committee has met to discuss other matters.

It is up to individual audit committees and boards of directors to determine whether the committee report to the board should be oral or written. What is important is that the report be comprehensive, while focusing principally on the matters of most significance to the board.

Audit committee chairmen are often pressured to keep their reports brief. While this is generally a laudable objective, the chairman should resist this pressure. This does not mean that the chairman should be disrespectful of the time and attention of the members of the board. It does mean, however, that the audit committee's report should be sufficiently comprehensive to inform the board of all matters about which the board requires either information or advice to permit it to carry out its own oversight responsibilities.

One final note on reporting to the board. The chairman of the audit committee should seek and obtain the assistance of the chairman of the board to ensure that the audit committee's report to the board is appropriately reflected in the minutes of the board meeting.

Reporting Externally

There are circumstances in which the audit committee has a responsibility to report to shareholders on its responsibilities and how it has discharged them. This obligation can be fulfilled by publishing the audit committee's charter and reporting on the committee's activities as part of the company's published governance practices in the annual report or in the information circular and AIF. An additional disclosure of its work will be contained in the publication of the external auditor's fees and the rationale behind the committee's recommendation thereof to the board of directors.

At the Annual General Meeting, shareholders have the opportunity to put direct questions to the audit committee chairman. The chairman should prepare carefully for this eventuality prior to the AGM by working with the chairman of the board, the CFO, the CEO and investor relations to create a list of possible issues and questions and the responses to them.

Additional Duties of the Chairman

Providing Feedback

The chairman has a responsibility to communicate to management and the external auditor any concerns expressed about their performance in the *in camera* meetings, or at any other time. Of course, he or she should also relay any plaudits. In addition, any concerns expressed about the issues discussed at the meeting should be communicated, as well as suggestions for improving materials or presentations, and for additional subjects to be added to the agenda for the next meeting.

This provides the chairman with an opportunity to establish an ongoing process of evaluating meetings and for follow up on matters arising from the meeting. It is also beneficial in reinforcing and managing the relationships among the committee, management and the external auditor. Whether or not the committee's expectations are met, the chairman must be prepared to provide the appropriate feedback.

In providing this feedback, the chairman should recognize that many people contribute to the preparation of the materials that come before the audit committee. Many of these people are never seen by the committee. We believe the chairman should acknowledge these efforts periodically and ask the audit committee to formally acknowledge their contribution.

Monitoring Best Practices

As stated earlier in this book, the chairman should constantly monitor audit committee best practices and educate the committee about them, including the process for adopting such practices. The external auditor should be asked to provide the chairman with his or her views about what constitutes best practices. The chairman should also discuss the subject of best practices with management (who quite often need education on the subject), and with the committee. When any changes to the committee practice are to be made, the chairman should discuss them with the chairman of the board.

Role of the Chairman of the Board

We strongly recommend that the chairman of the audit committee invite the non-executive chairman of the board or the lead director to attend all audit committee meetings. The advantages of having the chairman of the board attend the audit committee meetings are many, including facilitating the relationship-building process between the committee and the board.

Additional Thoughts

If we were to summarize in a very few words our advice to an audit committee chairman with respect to ensuring that the audit committee has the information it needs to make its decisions and that the committee continuously improve its practices, it would be this: Be proactive, not reactive.

Guidance on Information Content

It is not possible to provide much guidance on the content of the information that should be provided to the audit committee. So much of the content depends on the topic being addressed, the industry in which the company operates, the individual circumstances of the company and the issues facing the company. Chapter 13, Asking the Right Questions, may be of some help in that it provides a framework for preparing to ask some appropriate questions, although it does not address the issue of the content of the information. At best, this book can only address the issues around content.

Management is responsible for preparing and presenting all information related to the company. Only in special circumstances should the audit committee turn to parties other than management, such as the external auditor, for information on the company's operations.

Audit committees should insist that the content of the information provided to it by management be complete, accurate and comprehensive in approach. The information should provide:
- background and context;
- an assessment of inherent risks;
- a complete description of the recommendation being made and its impact on the company, investors and the market;
- a detailed discussion of alternatives; and
- the advice of any outside advisors, whether that advice is supportive or not of the recommendation being made.

The external auditor's role is to provide assurances. There will be circumstances, however, when the external auditor's knowledge of the company's operations and processes will be of significant assistance to the audit committee. Moreover, when appropriate, the auditor should provide the committee with assurances about the completeness of the information provided by management, the basis of its preparation, the assumptions used and reasonableness of the conclusions. In the appropriate circumstances, the external auditor can assist management in preparing the information and organizing and presenting it in ways best conducive to the committee's understanding of the issues. The external auditor can also help the committee in understanding how the information presented by management compares with industry trends and other peer group companies.

The following table illustrates some brief examples of the types of information and communications that management and the external auditor could provide to the audit committee for it to address three typical issues.

Issue	Management	Auditor
Financial Statements	Financial statements, supporting analyses, MD&A and related news releases and information on their preparation.	Assessment of compliance with GAAP, degree of conservatism, quality of presentation, and industry comparisons.
Internal Control	Report by senior management on effectiveness of internal control policies and systems. Reports by internal audit on their audit findings and management's response.	Review of control evaluation and testing performed in accordance with the audit plan, assessment of whether the work performed by the auditor supports the reports prepared by management.
Risk Management	Identification of principal financial risks and description of how they are being managed.	Assessment of the process used by management to identify risks, assessment of the completeness of the list of major financial risks, opinions on the processes used by management to mitigate or control these risks.

The Audit Committee's Role in Determining Information Content

The task of "influencing" the content to be provided by management is an ongoing one. It begins, however, with the audit committee's charter. In the course of creating or amending its charter, the committee has an excellent opportunity to communicate its expectations about information content to management and the external auditor. The preparatory sessions held by the chairman prior to audit committee meetings with the CFO, head of internal audit, and the external auditor, and the session held with management and the external auditor together, all provide further opportunities for the chairman to influence the content of information. Similarly, the *in camera* sessions held at the end of each audit committee meeting can be helpful in evaluating existing content and influencing future content.

Obviously, the time and attention the chairman devotes to preparing for the audit committee meetings will affect the degree to which the content will meet the committee's expectations and needs, as will his or her ability to provide management with the committee's evaluation of the content.

The audit committee should continually evaluate and, in consultation with management and the external auditor, strive to continually improve the content of the routine information that comes before it.

The "bottom line" on content: the information the audit committee receives will only be as good as it demands.

Key Messages
- Audit committees must clearly communicate their expectations with respect to the quality, accuracy and timeliness of the information it requires to management and the external auditor. The chairman has a leadership role in this regard.
- While management should produce the information, the external auditor is also a valuable source of information and should be utilized as a check on the completeness and accuracy of management's information.
- The chairman must undertake a significant amount of preparation for each committee meeting, including a series of preparatory sessions in advance of the audit committee meeting with management, the external auditor, internal audit and also a meeting with management and the external auditor together.
- Separate *in camera* meetings should be scheduled at the end of every audit committee meeting with the external auditor, management and the members of the committee alone.
- The committee's reports to the board of directors should be timely and comprehensive.

Accountability and Striving for Continuous Improvement

The final element in the audit committee effectiveness framework is the audit committee's assessment of its own effectiveness, and its report on its activities to the board and the shareholders. Both of these activities are an integral part of the audit committee's accountability to the board and the shareholders.

The audit committee's legal accountability is established by the legal framework under which the company operates and the requirements imposed by securities regulators. In addition, each audit committee has specific accountabilities (as the committee has defined them) in its charter, which often go beyond the bare imperatives. Indeed, audit committee effectiveness cannot be defined as mere compliance with regulatory requirements. Therefore, the charter is the principal yardstick against which the committee should evaluate its effectiveness.

All audit committees should monitor their performance and assess their effectiveness on a regular basis. Moreover, in today's environment where shareholders' and regulators' expectations have grown significantly, and continue to do so, audit committees must strive for continuous improvement. Monitoring performance and effectiveness is an exercise that requires strong leadership, discipline and diligence.

The responsibility for assessing audit committees effectiveness is a topic that is assuming more and more importance. In the United States, this has led the Public Company Accounting Oversight Board to issue "An Audit Of Internal Control Over Financial Reporting Performed In Conjunction With An Audit Of Financial Statements", which heightens the focus on evaluation of audit committee effectiveness:[1]

---

[1] Public Company Accounting Oversight Board, Release 2004-001, "An Audit Of Internal Control Over Financial Reporting Performed In Conjunction With An Audit Of Financial Statements", Paragraphs 56 to 59, March 9, 2004.

56. *The company's board of directors is responsible for evaluating the performance and effectiveness of the audit committee; this standard does not suggest that the auditor is responsible for performing a separate and distinct evaluation of the audit committee. However, because of the role of the audit committee within the control environment and monitoring components of internal control over financial reporting, the auditor should assess the effectiveness of the audit committee as part of understanding and evaluating those components.*

57. *The aspects of the audit committee's effectiveness that are important may vary considerably with the circumstances. The auditor focuses on factors related to the effectiveness of the audit committee's oversight of the company's external financial reporting and internal control over financial reporting, such as the independence of the audit committee members from management and the clarity with which the audit committee's responsibilities are articulated (for example, in the audit committee's charter) and how well the audit committee and management understand those responsibilities. The auditor might also consider the audit committee's involvement and interaction with the independent auditor and with internal auditors, as well as interaction with key members of financial management, including the chief financial officer and chief accounting officer.*

58. *The auditor might also evaluate whether the right questions are raised and pursued with management and the auditor, including questions that indicate an understanding of the critical accounting policies and judgmental accounting estimates, and the responsiveness to issues raised by the auditor.*

59. *Ineffective oversight by the audit committee of the company's external financial reporting and internal control over financial reporting should be regarded as at least a significant deficiency and is a strong indicator that a material weakness in internal control over financial reporting exists.*

The PCAOB standard makes it clear that the company's board of directors is ultimately responsible for evaluating the performance and effectiveness of the audit committee. The PCAOB does not suggest that the auditor is responsible for performing a separate and distinct evaluation of the audit committee. The standard, however, does require that should the auditor conclude during the course of the audit that oversight by the audit committee is ineffective, then the auditor must communicate any specific significant deficiency or material weakness to the board of directors in writing.

In our opinion, the responsibility for assessing the committee's overall performance and effectiveness, together with a continuous improvement program, should reside with the audit committee. Additionally, we believe that the audit committee has a responsibility to report to the board of directors on its assessment of its performance and effectiveness.

This chapter provides some guidance to audit committees in carrying out this responsibility.

Assessing Performance

We believe that the assessment of performance and effectiveness of the audit committee is best accomplished through a self-assessment process, and a subsequent report thereon to the board of directors. This should be done annually, or at least bi-annually.

The audit committee should review and assess:
- the appropriateness of its charter annually, and recommend to the board of directors any changes that the committee determines to be appropriate;
- the performance of the committee based on compliance of the audit committee with its charter;
- the performance of its members.

The board of directors also has responsibilities in this area. It must clearly enunciate in the board charter that it expects its committees to evaluate their effectiveness. The approach used by the board committees should, of course, be agreed among the board, the governance committee and the audit committee.

It is beyond the scope of this book to discuss the various processes that boards can use to assess their performance. We will, however, review the issues that audit committees should address as part of the overall assessment process.

Performance Assessment Tools

The starting point for assessing an audit committee's performance is its charter, and how it has discharged the duties and responsibilities set forth in the charter. For the charter to serve as an effective self-assessment tool, however, it must be well articulated, expressing duties and responsibilities in sufficient detail for progress against them to be measured and assessed. General questions on audit committee effectiveness should not be used as a substitute for a disciplined exercise in comparing the committee's performance against the responsibilities set out in the charter and in the work program that supports the charter.

In assessing their performance, audit committees should address two fundamental questions:

1) Is the committee satisfied that it has effectively discharged its responsibilities as set out in its charter?
2) How can the committee improve its operating efficiency and effectiveness?

Appendix F includes two examples of self-evaluation questionnaires as references for audit committee chairmen and members to use in evaluating their performance against their charter.

In its continuous quest for improvement, there are additional questions that audit committees may wish to consider. Some of these are:

- Are you satisfied with the assignment of priorities in the audit committee work plan and the allocation of work plan elements to the scheduled meetings of the committee?
- Would the efficiency and effectiveness of the committee be improved by adding more meetings to deal with specific issues not directly related to the quarterly and annual reporting process?
- Are you satisfied with the quality and timeliness of the material in your briefing books? Is the level of detail appropriate? Do you have any suggestions for improvement?
- Are you satisfied with the quality of presentations made by management? Made by the external auditor?
- Is the committee utilizing its time at the meetings effectively? For example, are the materials distributed in advance of a sufficient quality to obviate the need for oral presentations of the same material? Have the materials been distributed sufficiently in advance of the meeting to allow the members to digest the issues and recommendations in order to avoid an oral presentation of the same material?
- Has sufficient time at meetings been set aside for discussion and for answering your questions?
- Are you satisfied with the answers you receive?
- Are there any issues that you feel are not being addressed?
- Are the meetings too long or too short, given the matters that come before the committee at each meeting?
- Are there an appropriate number of audit committee meetings?
- Do you believe the committee takes full advantage of that *in camera* sessions?
- Are there sufficient educational opportunities covering both the external and internal environments?
- How would you evaluate the chairman's performance? Do you have any suggestions for improvement?
- Are all members of the committee contributing effectively?
- Are you aware of any audit committee best practices that the committee should adopt?

Reporting to the Board

Every board of directors will have processes in place for committee reports to the board. Many boards require written reports in advance of the board meeting. This may not be possible for audit committees, as we believe that audit committees should meet as close to the board meeting date as possible. Indeed, for approval of the quarterly and annual filings, we believe that the audit committee should meet the day before the board meeting to minimize the risk of inadvertent disclosures and to meet the filing deadlines. In these circumstances, the report of the audit committee is likely to be an oral one.

Factors to be considered in the audit committee's reporting are:

- *Timeliness of reports.* It is imperative that the audit committee report to the board in a timely fashion. Therefore, it is our opinion that the audit committee must report at the next board meeting following an audit committee meeting.
- *Time lapse between the audit committee meetings and the board meeting.* While the audit committee should report at the next board meeting, it is also important to consider the time lapse between the audit committee's meeting and that of the board. We believe the audit committee should meet the day before the meeting of the full board in order to minimize this time lapse. See Chapter 9, Doing the Right Things Right.
- *Format of reports.* Reports to the board may be made in writing or orally by the chairman of the audit committee, depending on the board's practices. It is important that the audit committee and the board agree on the level of detail of the committee's reports to the board.
- *Length of reports.* The chairman of the audit committee must be sensitive to the need to respect the board's agenda and time pressures, but given the nature of the committee's responsibilities for the integrity of financial information, unnecessary time constraints should not be placed on the audit committee's reports.
- *Provide activity-based reports.* It is very important that an expectation gap does not exist between what the board expects the audit committee to do and what it actually does. The consequences of such a communication breakdown could be very serious, especially if it involves the board's reliance on work done by the audit committee. The chairman's reports to the board should emphasize the committee's actual activities, the issues it has identified and the results of its deliberations.
- *Identify key issues.* In reporting to the board, the audit committee should clearly identify those matters for which board approval is required. For example, the board is responsible for approving the annual financial statements and reviewing financial reports. The minutes of the board should clearly reflect the basis for the board's reliance on the committee's work.

As stated earlier, the board should review the audit committee's charter at least annually, preferably early in the fiscal year. The charter then becomes the benchmark for the various reports that the chairman of the audit committee will make to the board as a whole during the year. We recommend that consideration be given to having the audit committee chairman provide the board with an annual report, which should include a report on the evaluation of the committee's performance against the charter.

Reporting to Shareholders

In our view, audit committees should report to the shareholders on how they have discharged their responsibilities. By publishing their charter, audit committees report on the responsibilities they have assumed. We believe, however, that audit committees must now go further and report on how they have discharged the responsibilities set out in the charter.

MI 52-110 requires Canadian companies to disclose the text of their audit committee's charter in the AIF. The instrument does not, however, contain a requirement for audit committees to report to shareholders on the committee's activities in satisfying its responsibilities as set out in its charter.

The TSX's current disclosure requirements for corporate governance practices and the CSA's proposed NP 58-201 require listed companies to disclose their system of corporate governance and also disclose the actual operation of their system of governance, i.e., their actual practices. This means that audit committees should not only disclose their responsibilities, but should also indicate how they discharge those responsibilities.

In the United States, audit committees are required to state, in a report to be included in the company's proxy or information circular, whether they have:
- reviewed and discussed the audited financial statements with management;
- discussed with the independent auditors the matters required by Statement on Auditing Standards No. 61; and
- received from the auditors disclosures regarding the auditors' independence required by Independent Standards Board Standard No. 1, and discussed with the auditors the auditors' independence.

The audit committee report must also include a statement that, based on the above, the audit committee recommends to the company's board of directors that the audited financial statements be included in the company's annual report. These disclosures must appear over the printed names of each audit committee member, which the SEC asserts "will emphasize for shareholders the importance of the audit committees' oversight role in the financial reporting process."

The U.S. rules also provide safe harbors for these reports by the audit committees to protect companies and their directors from certain liability under U.S. federal securities laws. Generally speaking, audit committee reports made pursuant to the SEC rules will not be considered "soliciting materials" "filed" with the SEC, and thus will not be subject to the antifraud provisions of the Securities Exchange Act of 1934.

We believe investor confidence is strengthened when investors clearly understand the audit committee's responsibilities and how they are discharged. In our opinion, audit committees should, therefore, publish both their charter and a summary report on how they discharged the responsibilities set out in their charter. We also encourage audit committees to consider new ways in which they may disclose their responsibilities, such as through the use of the corporate website and the Internet.

> **Key Messages**
> - *The audit committee should provide regular reports to the board on its activities.*
> - *Audit committees should evaluate their performance against the charter on an annual basis.*
> - *Audit committees have an accountability to shareholders, and therefore should publicly disclose both the charter and a summary of how they discharged the responsibilities contained in the charter.*

Corporate Reporting:
Issues and Trends

The corporate reporting environment continues to change and evolve. No one today should view corporate reporting as being restricted to the financial statements. Corporate reporting now encompasses a broad array of additional disclosure matters. No longer focused on historic accounting results, it now includes information on what drives performance and how value is created as well as prospective elements, such as guidance on future revenue and earnings targets. Moreover, disclosure of a growing number of non-financial performance metrics is being demanded by analysts, together with an ever-increasing number of financial metrics. These prospective elements raise several issues with which audit committees must now grapple.

Traditionally, the audit committee's primary role has been to monitor the integrity of the financial statements produced by management. As noted in Chapter 5, Doing The Right Things, MI 52-110 expands the audit committee's responsibilities beyond the annual financial statements to encompass the quarterly financial reports, MD&A and the earnings news release. As a result, the audit committee is becoming more involved in the oversight of corporate reporting matters as contrasted with financial reporting. A consequence of this is that the issues that must be addressed by the audit committee have been significantly expanded. Not only must it oversee the financial statements, its oversight responsibilities have been expanded to include a much broader range of financial disclosures. The audit committee must also address the controls over these disclosures, which range from internal controls over financial reporting to disclosure controls in general.

This chapter provides information on the changing corporate reporting universe, which should help audit committees determine the issues they should address in discharging this broader set of responsibilities.

The Corporate Reporting Universe

In this book, the term "corporate reporting" is used to encompass all the information and reports containing financial information that a company produces for its investors and other stakeholders. As such, it is much broader than the annual and quarterly financial statements.

The dimensions of corporate reporting and its fundamental components are illustrated in Figure 15.

Figure 15 | **Corporate Reporting Universe**

The effective functioning of our capital markets requires full disclosure of all material information on a timely basis. The outer circle represents all the continuous disclosure documents that a company either must file with securities regulators or that it provides voluntarily to analysts or other parties, such as banks or credit rating agencies. In the centre of the circle is the core reporting package comprising the financial statements, the MD&A and the earnings news release that companies must file quarterly and annually. While all of the elements in the diagram should come under the purview of the audit committee, the three elements in the centre of the circle must be reviewed by the audit committee. The extent of the audit committee's review of the elements in the outer circle will depend, to a large extent, on what the audit committee has agreed it should review, as expressed in its charter. We believe that audit committees should review all elements contained in the outer circle, although we recognize the challenges that this may present.

The elements shown in Figure 15 reflect Canada's existing securities legislation requirement that publicly-traded companies disclose all important changes in and about their business as these changes occur. This is sometimes referred to as the "continuous disclosure requirement". It should be noted that U.S. securities legislation is less rigorous, although the United States appears to be headed in this direction.

The Core Reporting Package

The two most important quarterly and annual filing requirements are the financial statements and the MD&A. The connection between them is becoming more and more important. Indeed, the requirements for review by the audit committee of these two documents, and certification of them by the CEO and CFO, have made the financial statements and the MD&A, together with the earnings news release, the core package for both quarterly and annual reporting.

Financial Reporting
Financial Statements
Audit committees have always been responsible for reviewing the annual financial statements. This responsibility has now been expanded to include the quarterly financial statements. The critical issue for the audit committee to address in performing these reviews is to ascertain whether the financial statements have been prepared in accordance with GAAP. While this is the primary responsibility with respect to the financial statements themselves, management and the audit committee must also ensure that the financial statements, together with the MD&A, provide a fair presentation of the results of operations and the financial condition of the company. This subject is discussed further in Chapter 12, CEO and CFO Certification. Other issues related to the overview of the financial statements, such as control issues, accounting policies, estimates and measurement uncertainties that impact the financial statements, are discussed later in this chapter.

In discharging its responsibility for reviewing the financial statements, the audit committee must understand what constitutes GAAP. In Canada, the authority for issuing the accounting standards that define GAAP has been given to the Accounting Standards Board of the CICA, and these standards are contained in the CICA *Handbook*.

The CICA *Handbook* contains recommendations that are presented in an italicized format. It also contains non-italicized paragraphs, and in the past there was some controversy over the authority of these non-italicized paragraphs. It is now clear that both types of paragraph have equal authority. The italicized recommendations indicate the main principles, while the material in the non-italicized paragraphs generally explains the recommendations or discusses their application to a particular situation. In addition, the non-italicized paragraphs may include guidance for practices that are encouraged or desirable, but not required.

The Accounting Standards Board issues *Accounting Guidelines* that provide additional material on how existing sections of the CICA *Handbook* should be applied in specific cases or present the board's conclusions on other issues of concern with respect to financial reporting.

The board also issues *Background Information* and *Basis for Conclusions* documents that set out the rationale for accounting guidelines and certain sections of the CICA *Handbook*. These documents are intended to explain how the board reached its conclusions.

The Emerging Issues Committee (EIC) reviews technical matters involving the interpretation of accounting standards and publishes *Abstracts of Issues Discussed*. These abstracts record the consensus views of the committee as to the appropriate accounting practice to be followed in the particular circumstances summarized therein. Some of the abstracts include material that illustrates the application of a consensus to assist in clarifying its meaning.

To be in accordance with GAAP, the financial statements must be in compliance will all the requirements of the CICA *Handbook*, *Accounting Guidelines* and EIC *Abstracts*. These are often referred to as the primary sources of GAAP. When there are different ways of interpreting or applying these requirements, management must select the treatment that is most consistent with the recommendations contained in the CICA *Handbook* and the audit committee and the external auditor must review management's rationale for its decisions.

It should also be noted that policies and Staff Accounting Bulletins issued by Canadian securities regulators may deal with accounting matters and should, therefore, be addressed when resolving an accounting or disclosure issue.

Canadian standards make is clear that it is not necessary to comply with guidance in U.S. or other international literature in order to comply with Canadian GAAP. Management and audit committees of Canadian companies, however, may wish to consider pronouncements issued by bodies authorized to issue accounting standards in foreign jurisdictions, such as the U.S. Financial Accounting Standards Board (FASB), or the International Accounting Standards Board (IASB). These are often important sources to consult when:
- issues arise on matters where primary sources of Canadian GAAP are silent; or
- the foreign source, typically U.S. GAAP, contains greater detail than the primary source of Canadian GAAP.

Management Discussion and Analysis (MD&A)

The requirement to provide an MD&A is set forth by the Canadian Securities Administrators, which describes the purpose of the MD&A as:[1]

> MD&A is a narrative explanation, through the eyes of management, of how your company performed during the period covered by the financial statements, and of your company's financial condition and future prospects. MD&A complements and supplements your financial statements, but does not form part of your financial statements.
>
> Your objective when preparing the MD&A should be to improve your company's overall financial disclosure by giving a balanced discussion of your company's results of operations and financial condition including, without limitation, such considerations as liquidity and capital resources — openly reporting bad news as well as good news. Your MD&A should:
> - help current and prospective investors understand what the financial statements show and do not show;
> - discuss material information that may not be fully reflected in the financial statements, such as contingent liabilities, defaults under debt, off-balance sheet financing arrangements, or other contractual obligations;
> - discuss important trends and risks that have affected the financial statements, and trends and risks that are reasonably likely to affect them in the future; and
> - provide information about the quality, and potential variability, of your company's earnings and cash flow, to assist investors in determining if past performance is indicative of future performance.

The CICA has published *Management's Discussion and Analysis — Guidance on Preparation and Disclosure*, which provides disclosure principles and recommended practices for the MD&A and guidance to help issuers prepare a meaningful and informative MD&A. Figure 16 illustrates the disclosure framework identified by the CICA.

---

[1] Canadian Securities Administrators, Form 51-102FI.

Figure 16 | **MD&A Disclosure Framework**

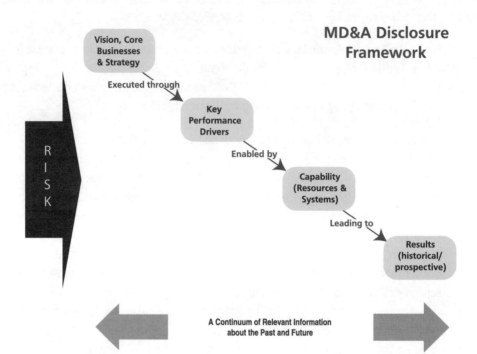

The MD&A must be fact-based. Its purpose is to provide readers with management's view as to what is critical to an understanding of the company's historical performance and its future prospects. The MD&A provides management with an opportunity to discuss the company's financial performance and critical non-financial performance indicators, future prospects and principal business risks. In so doing, the MD&A complements the financial statements and it, together with the statements and earnings news release, comprises the primary reporting package.

To illustrate: financial risks, exposures, contingencies and liabilities are an important component of the financial statements, and are presented in either the statements themselves or in the notes to them. The company, however, faces many more risks and exposures than just financial ones, including strategic risk, brand risk, reputational risk, competitive risk and environmental risk, to name but a few. The MD&A provides management with an opportunity to discuss its total approach to identifying and managing principal business risks and, in so doing, help investors to understand the company's global risk profile and how it is being managed.

The MD&A presents challenges for audit committees and their auditors. It is broader in scope than the financial statements; it is focused on the business, includes non-financial performance metrics, and contains prospective and historical information.

One of the most significant challenges for the audit committee is to understand and assess the process that the company follows in preparing the MD&A and obtaining both management and audit committee approvals. Since the MD&A involves prospective and non-financial information, non-financial management must be involved in its preparation. While this is necessary, there are some significant risks when a company adopts a silo approach, in which the CFO is responsible for the financial statements and other executives are responsible for the MD&A. These risks include a disconnect between the presentation of results and financial condition in the financial statements, the failure to address material issues, or the MD&A becoming either merely a marketing document or merely a restatement of financial results. We believe it is essential that the responsibility for co-ordinating the preparation of both the financial statements and the MD&A should reside in one executive, which in our view should be the CFO.

To be effective, the audit committee must review both the financial statements and the MD&A together, since these documents, in conjunction with the earnings news release, constitute the core reporting package. We have observed that, all too often, audit committees pay less attention to the MD&A than to the financial statements. In today's environment this can no longer be tolerated. Moreover, to adequately review the MD&A, the audit committee must have sufficient knowledge of the business in order to read the MD&A intelligently and must obtain the views of the external auditor. Most importantly, however, the audit committee should take sufficient time to review the MD&A appropriately.

Additionally, but very importantly, the audit committee must be satisfied that there is a consistent message in the financial statements, the MD&A, the earnings news release, and in the CEO's letter accompanying these disclosures.

Earnings News Releases
Ideally, the earnings news release should be issued simultaneously with the release and filing of the financial statements and MD&A.

When this is not the case, some challenging issues arise. The audit committee may be in a difficult position if a company issues a preliminary earnings release prior to the audit committee's review of the financial statements and MD&A. In these circumstances, the earnings news release should clearly state that all financial information contained in the release is preliminary, unaudited and, therefore, subject to change. When the audit committee actually reviews the final financial statements and MD&A, it must take care also to review the previously-issued earnings release. If the earnings release has not adequately or appropriately reflected the financial statements and MD&A, then another earnings release must be issued.

We do not agree with the practice of issuing a preliminary earnings release, except under exceptional circumstances. In our view, the earnings news release should only be issued when the financial statements and MD&A have been finalized, the work of the external auditor is complete, and the information is ready for filing with the appropriate regulatory authorities.

In reviewing the earnings news release, the audit committee must balance its "due diligence" responsibilities with the natural desire of its members to impose their personal preferences on the way information is expressed. If the audit committee has been diligent in reviewing the financial statements and the MD&A, then its review of the news release should focus on whether or not it is consistent with the financial statements and the MD&A and whether or not it contains the appropriate message to the investment community.

In reviewing the earnings news release, the audit committee should satisfy itself that the release:
- highlights the important messages, both good and bad;
- expresses the same facts that are presented in the financial statements and MD&A in a manner consistent with their presentation in the financial statements and MD&A; and
- expresses conclusions about the reported financial performance and financial condition that are consistent with those that could be derived from reading the financial statements and MD&A.

Other Dimensions of the Corporate Reporting Universe

The Pro Forma Earnings Issue

Audit committees should be particularly vigilant in reviewing news releases when the company uses other earnings metrics, often called "non-GAAP earnings measures" or "pro forma earnings", to help readers understand income and cash flows generated by the company's ongoing operations. Pro forma earnings normally exclude those expenses that management deems non-recurring or, in their view, are not critical to the understanding of the company's performance. Examples of expenses that management sometimes include in their presentation of pro forma earnings are:
- restructuring costs;
- depreciation;
- amortization; and
- losses on the sale of assets.

Pro forma earnings have been criticized for presenting only the "good stuff" and not the "bad stuff". To illustrate, the *Economist* magazine reported in its May 18, 2002 issue, that:[2]

- "In the first three quarters of 2001 the 100 biggest NASDAQ firms reported pro-forma earnings of $20 billion."
- "For the same period, they reported losses under America's Generally Accepted Accounting Principles (GAAP) of $82 billion."

An additional problem occurs when pro forma earnings are presented in a news release issued before the financial statements are released.

To minimize the problems attendant upon pro forma earnings, the OSC has published guidance for issuers that states:[3]

> *Staff expect issuers who choose to publish non-GAAP earnings measures to define the measures clearly, to demonstrate their relevance and to ensure that they do not have the potential to mislead investors. Specifically, issuers should:*
>
> - *state explicitly that the non-GAAP earnings measures do not have any standardized meaning prescribed by GAAP and are therefore unlikely to be comparable to similar measures presented by other issuers;*
> - *present prominently with the non-GAAP earnings measures the earnings measures for the period determined in accordance with GAAP;*
> - *describe the objectives of the non-GAAP earnings measures and discuss the reasons for excluding individual items required by GAAP to be included in determining net income or loss;*
> - *provide a clear quantitative reconciliation from the non-GAAP earnings measures to the GAAP financial statements, referencing the reconciliation when the non-GAAP earnings measures first appear in the disclosure document;*
> - *limit the number of non-GAAP earnings measures provided and avoid using multiple similar non-GAAP earnings measures that differ from each other only slightly;*
> - *present the non-GAAP earnings measures on a basis that is consistent from period to period and explain any changes in the composition of the measures when compared to previously published measures.*

While pro forma earnings can be helpful to a reader's understanding of the company's business, there can be a danger inherent in pro forma information. Most pro forma measures are not uniformly defined or commonly applied. As a result, they may not actually add to the reader's comprehension and may, in fact, cause confusion. These risks can be moderated if the pro forma measures are clearly explained and reconciled to GAAP.

---

[2] "Think of a Number", Matthew Bishop, *The Economist*, May 18, 2002.
[3] *Staff Notice* 52-303, "Non-GAAP Earnings Measures", Ontario Securities Commission, January 7, 2002.

Earnings Guidance

In recent years, more and more companies have begun to provide guidance to the market as to future revenue and earnings targets. This guidance is normally provided in news releases and is not a part of either the MD&A or of the financial statements. This practice is the subject of some controversy.

When the company provides earnings and revenue guidance, the audit committee needs to define its role and responsibilities with respect to such guidance. We believe audit committees should assume oversight responsibility for earnings guidance and suggest that the committee review how the guidance is developed, the monitoring and control mechanisms that exist to ensure its reasonableness, and the way in which information is to be presented.

Given the uncertainties involved in making such estimates, we believe any guidance should be presented in the form of a range rather than a single point estimate. For example, reporting that "management expects earnings per share to be between $1.10 and $1.15" is preferable to "management expects earnings per share will be $1.15."

The use of ranges provides the framework for management to determine what additional disclosure should be provided to investors when the actual results are not in accordance with expectations. Ranges also help address the issue of when such disclosure should be provided. Disclosure should take place at the time management determines that actual results will likely fall outside the range of estimates provided in the previously published guidance.

When actual results are not in accordance with the expectations management has provided in previous guidance, the company should issue revised guidance to ensure that it complies with the timely disclosure requirements of the securities regulations and does not expose itself to risk of selective disclosure. The MD&A produced for the reporting period in which such an updated disclosure is provided should include a description of the events and circumstances that led management to conclude that the previous guidance is no longer accurate and that revised guidance is required. This disclosure should be fact-based and prepared in a manner that helps readers understand the changes in business circumstances that led to the revised guidance.

The above discussion begs the question of whether such guidance should be provided at all. Since there are no requirements to provide guidance, boards of directors and audit committees should consider carefully the implications of providing this guidance. Unfortunately, companies are damned if they do and damned if they don't — this is the conundrum.

Accounting Policies, Estimates and Measurement Uncertainties

The accounting policies selected by the company should be proposed by management, agreed to by the external auditor, and approved by the audit committee.

To be in a position to do this effectively, audit committees must determine and approve the company's philosophy with respect to compliance with generally accepted accounting principles. Some suggest that minimal compliance with GAAP is all that is necessary. We do not advocate this approach. The preferred view, which we believe should be adopted by all audit committees, is that the accounting policies adopted by the corporation should be the most appropriate in the circumstances.

The CICA *Handbook* provides this discussion regarding changes in accounting policies:[4]

> *Accounting policies encompass the specific principles and the methods used in their application that are selected by an enterprise in preparing financial statements. There is a general presumption that the accounting policies followed by an enterprise are consistent within each accounting period and from one period to the next. A change in an accounting policy may be made, however, to conform to new Handbook Recommendations, Accounting Guidelines, Abstracts of Issues Discussed by the CICA Emerging Issues Committee or legislative requirements or if it is considered that the change would result in a more appropriate presentation of events or transactions in the financial statements of the enterprise.*

Audit committees should only countenance changes in accounting policy if those changes result in a more appropriate presentation or if the changes are necessary as a result of the implementation of new accounting standards.

Management is responsible for making the estimates required in the preparation of the financial statements. It is the audit committee's role to understand and evaluate the most significant accounting estimates. To do so, the audit committee must understand the methodology used in making the estimates, the major assumptions used, the sensitivity of the outcome (e.g., how would the accounting estimate change if changes were made in the assumptions), and the overall reasonableness of the result.

In assessing the overall reasonableness of accounting policies and estimates, audit committees should understand whether the policies or estimates are too conservative, too aggressive or appropriate. Each audit committee should set out its expectations in this regard in its charter.

[4] CICA *Handbook*, Paragraph 1506.02.

The evaluation of these policies and estimates involves a high degree of judgment. Management and the external auditor should provide the audit committee with information to enable it to assess whether the accounting policies and estimates used in the preparation of the financial statements were consistent with those used in prior periods, those used by other companies in the same industry or other similar businesses, and whether they were more conservative or more aggressive. The audit committee should ascertain the degree of conservatism in the accounting policies and estimates, both individually and in the aggregate, and should review the impact on the financial statements.

It is useful to portray the degree of conservatism in accounting policies and estimates using the form of a meter, as illustrated in Figure 17. Individual accounting policies or estimates can be portrayed using the meter and should generate discussion in the audit committee meeting as to why the policy or estimate was rated as it was, what should be done to change the rating if a change is appropriate, and why changes occur over time.

Figure 17 | **Conservatism Meter**

In assessing the evaluation of an accounting policy or estimate, the audit committee must be particularly sensitive to the fact that being overly conservative does not necessarily ensure a fair presentation. It must also be sensitive to the fact that the degree of conservatism in accounting estimates in one period may produce over-aggressive accounting in a subsequent period. For example, an over provision for doubtful accounts or inventory obsolescence will decrease earnings in Year One but could lead to inflated earnings in Year Two, when these amount are collected or the inventory is sold, especially if these amounts are greater than those estimated in Year One.

By their very nature, all accounting estimates involve some degree of measurement uncertainty. GAAP requires that the nature of a measurement uncertainty that is material should be disclosed when it is reasonably possible that the recognized amount could change by a material amount in the near term, except when disclosing the amount would have a significant adverse effect on the entity. When this amount is not disclosed, the financial statements should indicate the reasons for non-disclosure. It is important for audit committees to understand the above principle when assessing the presentation of accounting estimates and measurement uncertainties in the financial statements.

Audit committees should understand that securities regulators have been particularly concerned about companies that have "smoothed earnings" through the use of accounting estimates. The popular phrase "cookie-jar reserves" is used to describe situations where management has established reserves in good times and drawn down those reserves in bad times. This practice does not produce an accurate or reliable presentation of the company's actual earnings, but rather artificially smoothes earnings to present a picture of stable growth, when the reality is something different.

Audit committees should insist that management prepare a report for each quarterly audit committee meeting describing all significant estimates/reserves, indicating any changes made since the last report and the reasons for those changes. Audit committees should also require the external auditor to provide their opinion on the reasonableness of the estimates/reserves, including any changes to them.

Finally, audit committees should step back and assess the overall impact of the critical accounting policies, estimates and judgments, and determine whether they, individually and in the aggregate, fairly present the economic reality of the company and its performance in the accounting period.

Corporate Reporting: Its Future Evolution

Principles vs. Rules

The various accounting scandals and capital market reform initiatives have renewed interest in the long-standing debate on the respective merits of the different approaches taken by Canada and the United States in setting accounting standards and securities regulation.

While Canada takes a principles-based approach to accounting standards, the U.S. approach is a rules-based one. The difference in approaches is significant because accounting standards and securities regulations are the foundation of corporate reporting, and harmonization of specific standards requires agreement on the approach.

The principles-based approach has the merit of enabling management, the audit committee and the external auditor to exercise their judgment in determining what constitutes the most appropriate presentation of financial information. But this approach comes with a price. It compels audit committees and external auditors to be disciplined and very rigorous in examining and understanding all of the alternative accounting treatments available to them. It also compels them to make sure that the accounting policies that guide the presentation of the financial information are the most appropriate in the circumstances.

As will be discussed in the following chapter, the CEO and CFO certification requirements clearly indicate that mere compliance with GAAP may not be enough to achieve a "fair presentation" of the company's financial condition. As a result, failure to exercise appropriate judgment by audit committees and auditors, and their consequent approval of financial statements based on the minimum acceptable accounting alternative rather than on the most appropriate alternative, may result in pressure to remove the judgment factor and move to a rules-based system.

We support the concept of a principles-based approach. We find it difficult to accept that it is possible to create rules and regulations for corporate reporting that will fit all circumstances. We recognize, however, that a balanced approach incorporating the best of both principles and rules may be the most likely outcome of the current debate.

Co-ordinating the Evolution

The future evolution of corporate reporting, both in the United States and Canada, is being shaped by the accounting standard setters and the securities regulators as they set standards and requirements for the financial statements, the MD&A and, to a lesser degree, disclosures made in other documents such as the proxy information.

Accounting standard setters in the United States and Canada are focused on the annual and quarterly financial statements. Responsibilities for the other elements in the corporate reporting universe, such as the MD&A, lie with the securities regulators. The future of corporate reporting, and the core reporting package comprising the financial statements and the MD&A is, therefore, being shaped by the combined activities of these two groups — which often operate with different priorities.

Both groups, unfortunately, tend to be reactive and often focus their attention on issuing standards and regulations in response to criticisms or scandals involving corporate reporting failures. We believe that management, auditors and audit committees should take a more proactive approach, and strive to adopt best practices and develop new and innovative corporate reporting practices that enhance disclosure and provide meaningful information for investors. For their part, standard setters and securities regulators should strive to promote and, where appropriate, codify those innovative and leading-edge corporate reporting practices that gain general acceptance.

The activities of the standard setting groups that impact the MD&A and financial statements are, unfortunately, often not well co-ordinated. For example, one would expect that the disclosure of critical accounting policies would be located in the financial statements and not in the MD&A, as currently required by U.S. and Canadian securities regulators. This creates challenges for management, auditors and audit committees in understanding and keeping abreast of new developments and how disclosures in the financial statements and MD&A can best be co-ordinated and presented.

In this regard, we are very supportive of the CICA's efforts to develop and shape the disclosures in the MD&A and to co-ordinate these disclosures with those in the financial statements. In so doing, Canada may be able to lead the way in the evolution of the corporate reporting package into some more advanced and meaningful form of integrated business reporting.

Key Messages

- *Audit committees should be aware of the universe of corporate reporting and its various financial and non-financial components.*
- *Audit committees should review the financial statements, MD&A and related news releases as a single package of information.*
- *The effectiveness of the audit committee's review of earnings news releases, financial statements and MD&A depends not only on its understanding of accounting standards and regulations, but to a great extent on the committee's knowledge of the company's business and the industries in which it operates.*
- *In addition to approving the financial statements, MD&A and earnings news release, the audit committee must understand and agree with the process by which these documents were prepared.*
- *The audit committee should seek assurances from the CEO and CFO, as part of the CEO/CFO certification process, that they have put in place effective disclosure controls and procedures to ensure that all reports in the corporate reporting universe are prepared properly and filed with the appropriate authorities in accordance with applicable requirements (see Chapter 12, CEO and CFO Certification).*
- *Audit committees of inter-listed companies should understand the differences in the continuous disclosure systems in Canada and the United States and ensure their corporate reporting practices are in compliance with both Canadian and U.S. requirements.*
- *Audit committees should regularly review their oversight responsibilities to determine whether they should include additional financial and/or non-financial disclosures.*

CEO *and* CFO *Certification*

CEO and CFO certification has been enacted to provide a clear statement of the CEO's and CFO's accountability for the completeness and accuracy of the information included in annual and quarterly filings. The requirement for certification is a direct response to the notorious attempts on the part of some highly publicized CEOs and CFOs to avoid responsibility for the integrity of the information disclosed by their companies.

On January 16, 2004, the CSA issued Multilateral Instrument 52-109, "Certification of Disclosures in Issuers' Annual and Interim Filings", which requires CEOs and CFOs of public companies to certify certain documents and control procedures. These new regulations are based on those enacted in the United States, and when they are fully implemented, Canadian CEO and CFO certification requirements will be similar to those in the United States.

The wording of the CEO and CFO certificates is prescribed and cannot be altered.[1] When the CEO and CFO sign these certificates, they formally acknowledge in a public filing their personal responsibility and accountability for the accuracy, reliability and completeness of their company's financial disclosures.

Unlike the regulations in the United States, MI 52-109 does not specify the penalties that may be applied to CEOs and CFOs who are found to have provided a false certification.[2] However, the instrument states that an officer providing a false certification potentially could be subject to quasi-criminal, administrative or civil proceedings under securities law. Additionally, there are proposals under consideration for further sanctions and penalties for violations of securities laws, which may have an impact on the sanctions and penalties for false certification.

This chapter provides a brief overview of the CEO and CFO certification requirements and the issues related thereto. A more detailed discussion of certification can be found in the CICA publication CEO *and* CFO *Certification: Improving Transparency and Accountability.*[3]

---

[1] The certificates are presented in Appendix M.

[2] MI 51-109 is presented in Appendix N.

[3] The executive summary from the CICA publication, CEO *and* CFO *Certification: Improving Transparency and Accountability* is presented in Appendix L.

Application

MI 52-109 applies to all Canadian reporting issuers, except investment funds. It has been adopted by all Canadian jurisdictions except British Columbia, which is expected to enact its own, but similar, legislation.

Certifications designed to meet U.S. requirements, which are filed by Canadian companies that are SEC registrants, will satisfy the Canadian requirements provided that the company files the same financial statements and MD&A in both Canada and the United States. This means that Canadian public companies that comply with the U.S. certification requirements are exempt from the Canadian requirements. Such companies should be aware, however, that differences exist between the Canadian and U.S. continuous disclosure regimes, and while their U.S. certificates may be filed with Canadian securities regulatory authorities, the company must still comply with Canadian continuous disclosure rules.

It is important to note that the Canadian certification requirements do not provide any exemptions for smaller companies, unlike the exemptions from the financial literacy and independence requirements for audit committee members of TSX Venture Exchange-listed companies, which is provided under MI 52-110.

Implementation

The certification requirements are being implemented in three phases.

Phase One: Bare Certification

The first phase, which began in the first quarter of 2004 for companies with a December 31 year-end,[4] requires the CEO and CFO to certify that:[5]

1) I *have reviewed the interim filings (as this term is defined in Multilateral Instrument 52-109 Certification of Disclosure in Issuers' Annual and Interim Filings) of <identify the issuer>, (the issuer) for the interim period ending <state the relevant date>;*
2) *Based on my knowledge, the interim filings do not contain any untrue statement of a material fact or omit to state a material fact required to be stated or that is necessary to make a statement not misleading in light of the circumstances under which it was made, with respect to the period covered by the interim filings;*

[4] Companies with a year-end other than December 31 should refer to MI 52-109 to determine the implementation date applicable to them.
[5] Form 52-109F2 - Certification of Interim Filings during Transition Period.

3) *Based on my knowledge, the interim financial statements together with the other financial information included in the interim filings fairly present in all material respects the financial condition, results of operations and cash flows of the issuer, as of the date and for the periods presented in the interim filings;*

The certificate that must be signed in respect of the annual filing is identical except that it also extends to the information contained in the AIF.

The companion policy to MI 52-109 specifically states that the "fairly present" representation is not qualified by the phrase "in accordance with generally accepted accounting principles." This was designed to prevent management from relying solely upon compliance with GAAP as the basis for the certification, since GAAP cannot be expected to include all of the components of an overall fair presentation. Additionally, the term "financial condition" is much broader than the term "financial position", which GAAP defines as the net asset position presented on the balance sheet. For example, financial condition would include the impact of industry and competitive trends known to the company. This places greater emphasis on the focus, emphasis, integrity and completeness of the disclosures in the MD&A.

The statement in the certificate that the interim or annual filings do not contain an untrue statement of a material fact, or omit to state a material fact, is not limited to financial information. The statement applies to all of the information in the filings and, as a result, has a much broader reach than the "fairly present" certification.

By signing these certificates, the CEO and CFO undertake an accountability that is much broader than would at first appear. For example, the second and third paragraph of the certificate both begin with the phrase "Based on my knowledge...". At first glance, this phrase may seem to limit the CEO's and CFO's accountability, but it actually places a more stringent onus on the CEO and CFO.

CEOs and CFOs possess an extensive knowledge of the company's business, performance, financial condition and future prospects. The wording in the certificate emphasizes that they must take into account all of the information and knowledge they possess when determining whether the information presented in the filings "fairly present" the company's financial condition, results of operations and cash flows. This knowledge cannot be selective, nor is it confined to financial information.

When the certification of disclosure controls and procedures becomes effective (as discussed below), the onus on the CEO and CFO will be even greater. At that time, the CEO and CFO certificates will include an implicit assertion that the CEO's and CFO's knowledge is complete because they have put in place disclosure controls that ensure that all material information has been communicated to them for the purpose of making this certification.

When fully implemented, the way in which certification has been constructed puts an end to the "I didn't know" excuse for management. It does, however, impose a greater onus on the audit committee and the board to be satisfied as to the rigour of the design of the certification process, the discipline with which it is implemented, and the completeness of the communication of any issues that may arise from the implementation process in each filing.

Phase Two: Disclosure Controls and Procedures

In the second phase, the following requirements are added to the annual certificate:[6]

4) *The issuer's other certifying officers and I are responsible for establishing and maintaining disclosure controls and procedures and internal control over financial reporting for the issuer, and we have:*

   a) *designed such disclosure controls and procedures, or caused them to be designed under our supervision, to provide reasonable assurance that material information relating to the issuer, including its consolidated subsidiaries, is made known to us by others within those entities, particularly during the period in which the interim filings are being prepared; and*

   b) *designed such internal control over financial reporting, or caused it to be designed under our supervision, to provide reasonable assurance regarding the reliability of financial reporting and the preparation of financial statements for external purposes in accordance with the issuer's GAAP; and*

   c) *evaluated the effectiveness of the issuer's disclosure controls and procedures as of the end of the period covered by the annual filings and have caused the issuer to disclose in the annual MD&A our conclusions about the effectiveness of the disclosure controls and procedures as of the end of the period covered by the annual filings based on such evaluation; and*

5) *I have caused the issuer to disclose in the interim MD&A any change in the issuer's internal control over financial reporting that occurred during the issuer's most recent interim period that has materially affected, or is reasonably likely to materially affect, the issuer's internal control over financial reporting.*

The certification of disclosure controls and procedures will come into force for the annual certificate in 2005.

The interim certificate, which is not required until the first quarter of 2006, will contain all of the above requirements except the certification that the CEO and CFO have evaluated the effectiveness of disclosure controls. It should be noted that, in the United States, CEOs and CFOs are required to certify that they have evaluated the effectiveness of disclosure controls in both the quarterly and annual certificates.

[6] Form 52-109F1 — Certification of Annual Filings, paragraphs 4 and 5.

Phase Three: Internal Control Over Financial Reporting

The third phase will require the filing of a formal report by management on the effectiveness of internal control over financial reporting. At the time of writing, it was expected that this phase would include a requirement for some form of auditor attestation of this report, likely the auditor's opinion on management's process to assess the effectiveness of internal control and the auditor's opinion on the effectiveness of internal control. In October, 2004, the CSA announced that a proposed instrument outlining the requirements of this phase would be published for comment in late 2004 or early 2005.

Implications of Certification for the MD&A

As discussed in Chapter 11, Corporate Reporting: Issues and Trends, the MD&A is a key component of the core reporting package in both the quarterly and annual filings.

The "fairly present" certification applies to both the financial statements and the MD&A taken together. For example, if, as part of the certification process, the CEO and CFO concluded that the financial statements on their own would not yield a fair presentation, then the MD&A would be the only place to provide the additional disclosures and explanations necessary in order that the two documents together would constitute a fair presentation.

It should be noted that when the certification requirements of disclosure controls and procedures are implemented, the MD&A will be the document in which management must discuss deficiencies in their evaluation of disclosure controls and internal controls.

Since MI 52-110 requires audit committees to review the annual and quarterly MD&A, the CEO and CFO should brief the audit committee on any issues that arose in the certification process that impact the MD&A and describe how they plan to deal with these issues.

Implications for Management

Successfully implementing the certification requirements requires leadership and commitment from the CEO, CFO, corporate counsel, and senior executives in both the finance and business units. All of these parties must support the objective of ensuring that the company's financial reporting is transparent and of high quality. Without such a commitment — or without a detailed understanding of the certification requirements — it is unlikely that the company will achieve an effective certification process, a circumstance that would expose the CEO, CFO and the audit committee to a variety of risks.

The primary responsibility for the preparation of the financial statements and the effectiveness of internal control over financial reporting lies with the CFO. Therefore, it is not unreasonable to expect that the CFO will have the primary responsibility for ensuring that the proper processes and procedures are in place to support certification. However, the CEO cannot escape responsibility. Indeed, the requirement that the CEO sign a separate certificate was designed to prevent CEOs from abdicating their responsibilities. CEOs are required to take an active role in the process leading to certification. It is important that CEOs make their own assessments of fair presentation, based on their knowledge of the business and its strategies, risks and operating performance.

In these circumstances, audit committees should assess whether the CEO has fulfilled his or her certification responsibility or abdicated it to the CFO. One way in which the audit committee can make this assessment is by ensuring that it has a complete understanding of, and comfort with, the process and procedures supporting certification by the CEO. The assessment that the audit committee makes of the CEO's involvement in the certification process, and of the CEO's knowledge at the time he or she certifies, will help the audit committee monitor the "tone at the top".

Sub Certifications

CEOs and CFOs must have documentary evidence to support their assessment of fair presentation and, eventually, to support their design and evaluation of disclosure controls and internal control over financial reporting. MI 52-109 does not require sub-certifications from business unit leaders and finance executives in divisions or subsidiaries, however without some form of sub-certification process it is difficult to see how CEOs and CFOs can obtain the necessary knowledge and assurance to support their certifications. It is not surprising, therefore, that many large companies are establishing sub-certification processes, in which the direct reports to the CEO and CFO provide formal certifications to them on the:

- completeness and accuracy of the financial information pertaining to their area of responsibility; and
- effectiveness of disclosure controls and internal control over financial reporting.

While we believe some form of sub-certification must be established, we recognize that there are factors that may affect the decision as to whether a sub-certification process should be implemented. Among the most important are the size and complexity of the company's business. The further removed the CEO and CFO are from the business units, the more important sub certification processes become.

CEOs and CFOs should remember, however, that the signing of sub-certifications by junior officers and managers is not a substitute for diligence and knowledge on the part of the CEO and CFO. Nor are they a substitute for the CEO's and CFO's own evaluations of the effectives of disclosure controls and internal controls. If designed properly, a sub-certification process can add discipline to the disclosure process, positively reinforce the need for effective disclosure controls and help sustain a corporate culture that places a high value on accurate and timely public disclosures. An effective sub-certification process can also form the backbone of an accountability system for financial reporting. To achieve true accountability, however, the sub-certification process must focus on substance and not become just another documentation exercise.

The audit committee should receive reports on the sub-certification process, including the training elements that the CEO and CFO have put in place to fulfill their expectations of the process. It should satisfy itself that this process is well designed, effectively implemented and will contribute to improved controls and running the business better, as well providing documentation to support the certification process. The audit committee should also assess whether the certification process takes into account the principal business risks that could impair financial condition and the way in which those risks are being managed or mitigated.

Implications for Audit Committees

While MI 52-109 does not impose any review or governance requirements for audit committees, there are various implications of certification that they must address.

Audit committees must ensure that the CEO and CFO have developed an appropriate implementation plan to satisfy these new requirements as they become due. Developing such a plan will require management to review, assess and, if necessary, re-engineer financial reporting procedures to ensure that they have an effective certification process. The audit committee should also monitor the execution of this plan, keep the process under review, and be briefed each quarter on all issues that arose during that quarter's certification process and how those issues were resolved.

MI 52-110, "Audit Committees" requires audit committees to review the annual and interim financial statements, MD&A and earnings news releases, but not the AIF. Since the audit committee's review requirements and the CEO's and CFO's certification requirements are focused on the same documents, the audit committee's oversight of these documents, and the processes followed to prepare them, should include obtaining a comfort level on the effectiveness of the certification process put in place by management. It follows, therefore, that the audit committee should require quarterly reports from the CEO and CFO on the process followed and on any issues that arose during that process prior to the audit committee recommending the annual or interim financial statements or MD&A to the board.

The following questions are presented to stimulate thinking about the types of issues that audit committees should discuss with the CEO and CFO relating to the certification process:[7]

---

[7] The Canadian Institute of Chartered Accountants, CEO *and* CFO *Certification: Improving Transparency and Accountability*, pages 33-34.

1) *What supporting processes have the CEO and CFO put in place as part of the certification process? Do they cover all business units and corporate functions? Do they include business/operating executives as well as finance executives?*

2) *What criteria do the CEO and CFO use to assess fair presentation?*

3) *What guidance is provided to business unit managers, particularly on the assessment of fair presentation and communicating material information to the CEO and CFO?*

4) *Do the CEO and CFO meet with business executives and finance executives to review issues relating to certification? Do they have a standard list of questions? Have the questions changed from prior periods, and if so how?*

5) *If the company has a disclosure committee, what has it communicated to the CEO and CFO? What are the committee's processes and the results of its work?*

6) *What issues arose in the sub-certification process? How were they resolved?*

7) *Were there any "early stage" or other issues that were not disclosed because of a lack of sufficiently robust information to provide a useful disclosure?*

8) *How and by whom is the MD&A assembled and written?*

9) *Should the company file concurrently its financial statements, MD&A, AIF and the CEO and CFO certificates?*

10) *How have the CEO and CFO approached the design and documentation of disclosure controls and internal control over financial reporting?*

11) *Has a team been put in place to lead this process — with or without assistance of outside advisors?*

12) *Are the internal and external auditors involved in an appropriate manner?*

Implications for External Auditors

As with audit committees, MI 52-109 does not impose any specific responsibilities for external auditors with respect to the CEO/CFO certifications. Notwithstanding that, most audit committees, in our view, should obtain the external auditor's opinion on the rationale used by the CEO and CFO in making their "fairly present" assessment, the processes the CEO and CFO put in place to support the certifications, and any issues that arose with respect to the financial statements and the way in which those matters were resolved. The following questions are presented to stimulate thinking on the types of issues that external auditors should discuss with the CEO and CFO relating to the certification process:[8]

(8) *Ibid*, page 34.

1) Have the CEO and CFO *certificates been signed in respect of the period covered by the auditor's engagement (either interim reviews or annual audit)?*

2) Did the process identify any weaknesses in either disclosure controls and procedures or internal control over financial reporting? If so, what has management done to correct these deficiencies and what impact would these weaknesses have on the interim or annual financial statements?

3) Did the process detect any fraud or other illegal acts?

4) Did the process result in any revisions to the financial statements?

5) Did the process identify any errors in the financial statements that were not adjusted because they were not material?

6) Have the CEO and CFO communicated the results of their "material fact" and "fairly present" assessments and the process followed in reaching their assessments to the audit committee? What was the audit committee's reaction?

7) Are there any areas where the CEO and CFO concluded that, because the financial statements did not "fairly present" the company's financial condition, that additional material needed to be added to the MD&A? Is this the appropriate way of addressing this issue?

8) What process was followed in the review of the MD&A, particularly the disclosures in Sections 4(c) and 5 of the full certificate?

The audit committee and/or the CEO and CFO may request the auditor's involvement or assistance in some aspect of the certification process. If so, the auditor should carefully review the accounting profession's rules of professional conduct to determine whether or not he or she would be able to undertake such an assignment without impairing his or her independence, and then ensure that any such engagement is approved by the audit committee.

The CEO and CFO certification requirement should be viewed as more than a form-signing exercise. Perhaps the most practical benefit of a well-designed certification process is the opportunity for the CEO and CFO to engage, in a meaningful manner, the non-financial business unit leaders in the financial reporting process, which helps these operating executives better understand the importance of risk management and effective control and, in so doing, helps them run their business units more effectively. It also provides an opportunity to improve the information content of the MD&A and the internal reporting processes by which information is communicated from the business units to the people responsible for preparing the MD&A.

Key Messages

- The CEO and CFO certification process is not just a "form-signing" requirement. It should be viewed as a critical control step in the preparation of the annual and quarterly filings and as an opportunity to strengthen accountability and control throughout the organization.
- While the audit committee is not specifically referred to in the certification requirements, it should ask the CEO and CFO to provide it with a formal report on the certification process before it approves the annual or quarterly financial statements, MD&A and, where appropriate, the AIF.
- The CEO and CFO should report to the audit committee on their conclusions, the processes put in place to support their certification, and any issues that arose in the certification process and the way in which they were resolved.
- The audit committee should also ask the external auditor for his or her views on the certification process and whether they agree with the resolution of issues raised in the certification process and the overall conclusions reached by the CEO and CFO.

Asking the Right Questions

An element critical to the audit committee's effectiveness is its ability to obtain the information it requires in order to make informed decisions. In addition to the briefing materials provided by management and the auditor, one of the most effective ways for committee members to get the information they need is by asking the right qsuestions, in the right way, at the right time and to persist until the right answer is obtained. Obtaining satisfactory answers to their questions not only allows committee members to extract the information they require, it also assists them in developing valuable insights into the more intangible issues.

Some audit committee members have cultivated exceptional skills in asking the right questions. They seem instinctively to zero in on the "weakest link" in the argument, to distinguish between matters of importance and those that are trivial, and to focus on the critical issues. Effective audit committees also develop a form of "group expertise" in which members build on each other's questions, support one another in probing issues and assist the chairman in bringing closure to matters.

This chapter discusses ways in which audit committee members can enhance their skills in asking the right questions. It reviews some of the more important areas for questioning, and provides guidance as to the types of questions that should be asked. However, because every company's circumstances will differ, we have not attempted to provide comprehensive coverage of all topics for questioning or a standard checklist of questions to be asked.

Establishing the Right Environment

An effective audit committee will have a well-articulated charter, qualified members, leadership from the chairman and, very importantly, the courage to ask tough questions and insist on informative answers. It will also have established a meeting environment characterized by candid communication.

We believe the committee's success in this regard will be directly related to the evolution of the relationships among the committee, management and the external auditor. Figure 13, introduced in Chapter 8, Managing Relationships, illustrates the various stages in the evolution of these relationships.

Figure 13 | **Stages of Relationship Evolution**

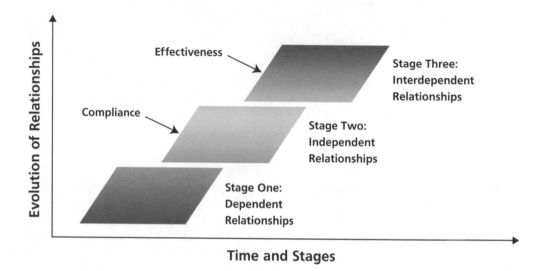

Audit committees in Stage One often feel compelled to pose questions to management in a way that is neither offensive nor embarrassing. If they do have tough questions, they will reserve them solely for queries about the audit fees. An environment of dependent relationships is not conducive to asking the tough questions, probing the sensitive issues, uncovering potential problems or suggesting alternatives. An exception may occur, however, when the company finds itself in a major crisis — a circumstance that can push the board and audit committee into a "take charge" role.

In Stage Two, audit committees and the external auditor become more independent and secure in their roles. The environment in which committee meetings are held becomes more conducive to asking substantive questions and management becomes more comfortable with sharing information, with the result that discussions become more constructive. Audit committee members become less cautious about asking "politically incorrect" questions of management or the auditor. The committee also becomes more demanding of the kind of information to be supplied by management and the external auditor, which in turn enables them to direct more substantive questions to both.

While the meeting environment is likely to improve when independent relationships exist, management and the external auditor may continue to be reluctant to speak candidly on important issues. Instead, they may adopt an approach of providing information only if the audit committee asks the "right question" to obtain it, and if the committee fails to ask that "right question" the information is not volunteered. This places the audit committee in the position of participating in a "guessing game" and trying to recognize and interpret the signals or hints provided by management or the external auditor. This situation is akin to a card game where some cards are placed on the table face up, and others are left face down. In these circumstances, the audit committee is forced to spend valuable meeting time trying to determine how many cards are face down, and which cards they are.

In Stage Three, when the relationships among the audit committee, management and the external auditor are interdependent, communication among these parties is significantly improved and more candid in nature. In this stage, all the cards are placed on the table face up. Discussions are focused on substantive review, understanding alternative approaches and solving problems. The audit committee is no longer regarded as having a mere oversight role, but is considered to be a valuable resource capable of playing an important part in solving difficult corporate reporting, risk management and control issues.

Interdependence increases the level of security and trust among the various parties and permits an environment in which audit committee members can ask difficult and sensitive questions without being concerned about how these questions will be perceived. In this environment, management is no longer reluctant to bring important and sensitive issues to the audit committee, and there is no longer a need to play the guessing game.

The Importance of Preparation

The ability to ask the "right questions" is highly dependent on both the information provided to the audit committee in advance of the meeting and the level of effort committee members make in preparing for the meeting. If complete and meaningful information on agenda topics is not provided to the committee in advance of the meeting, it is very difficult for committee members to ask meaningful questions and probe important issues. As discussed in Chapter 9, Doing the Right Things Right, audit committees should insist that complete and accurate information be provided in advance of the meeting on all matters that require decisions by the committee or have the potential to significantly affect the company's financial reporting.

When audit committee members have little, if any, time for advance study of complex material provided to them, they must spend most of their meeting time scrambling to absorb the information, understand it and consider its implications. In such circumstances, it is very difficult for the committee members to get beyond a high level understanding of the issues and an even higher level grasp of the implications. We cannot emphasize too strongly the importance of ensuring that committee members have sufficient time to do their homework carefully and diligently, and that the committee members do so.

Very few of the more significant non-routine issues that come before the audit committee will be of a "black-and-white" nature. Rather, they will be "shades of grey" and often will require the committee, the board and the company to make choices between various alternatives. Therefore, the audit committee must ask the questions that will provide it with the information it needs to understand all the available alternatives, including which ones were and were not considered by management and the reasons therefore. The committee must satisfy itself that the range of alternatives considered by management and the external auditor was complete and that no important alternatives were omitted from their consideration.

Questioning should be designed to achieve three objectives. These are to:

1) **Understand the material.** Before the committee can evaluate and challenge the conclusions reached by management or the external auditor, it must understand what is in the material, how the material was put together, whether people with specialist knowledge were involved or consulted, and the degree of the external auditor's involvement and assurance provided. It must also assess whether the information provided to the committee is complete, or whether additional information is required.

2) **Evaluate and challenge.** The committee must evaluate the logic and rationale supporting the proposals, paying particular attention to the assumptions made. The committee should be vigilant in trying to identify any unstated assumptions, such as "we have always operated this way" or "too much disclosure will confuse the reader" or "a focus on control will destroy our productivity". When assumptions such as these are identified, the committee has a responsibility to confront them. Moreover, it should ask the external auditor, or other advisors if appropriate, whether they would have reached a different conclusion or would have put forward a preferable alternative.

3) **Assess the overall conclusion.** The final step is for the committee to decide on the most appropriate course of action. In so doing, it must assess the reasonableness of the conclusion in the context of the external environment, the needs of shareholders, regulators and the market. It would be prudent for the committee to seek the external auditor's views and, where appropriate, the opinions of other external advisors, such as outside legal counsel.

Question Structure

Once the committee members have read and digested the material provided to them, they are in a position to determine the objectives for questioning, and frame the specific questions to be asked. If committee members are unclear about their objectives, they are unlikely to frame their questions properly.

Audit Enquiry: Seeking More Reliable Evidence from Audit Enquiry, a research report by the Canadian Institute of Chartered Accountants, provides information that will assist committee members in framing their questions. With the authors' permission, we have adapted the material to meet the needs of audit committees, rather than the needs of auditors for which it was intended.

Questions can be framed in various ways. How audit committee members should structure their questions depends on the circumstances, what kind of information is sought, what the information is to be used for, who is being asked, etc. But every question should have three characteristics:
1) It should make sense to the respondent;
2) It should use vocabulary that is common to the respondent and other members of committee; and
3) It should elicit the information required.

The following are ways in which questions can be structured.
- *Closed/open*: A closed question invites a concise, precise answer: yes, no, $1,600 per year and so on. They characteristically begin with "what", "when", "where", or "who". Usually, the responses comprise hard information, but lack descriptive detail and context. In contrast, open questions invite unstructured, discursive replies and do not limit the respondent to a narrow range of answers. Such questions may begin with "Please explain..." or "What's your opinion on...?"
- *Specific/general phrasing*: Specific questions focus on a particular, specifically defined topic. A closed question may lead to a specific one. For example, "Does the company have a revenue recognition policy for software sales?" could lead to "Please describe how this policy is applied in practice?" A general question is not focused on a particular topic and invites the respondent to choose what information will be given in reply. For example, "How do you apply the revenue recognition policy when new products are developed and sold?"
- *Clear/ambiguous*: Clear questions are unambiguous and easily understood. Questions beginning with "Why?", however, may put management or the auditors on the defensive and cause them to justify rather than describe. But ambiguous questions can sometimes be useful because they might reveal a cause/effect relationship as well as the respondent's assumptions about the situation.
- *Leading/non-leading*: The wording of leading questions betrays the answer that is expected, and usually should be avoided. A well-worded leading question, however, can serve as a devil's advocate, containing a deliberate assumption that provokes a complex or elaborate response. For example, one could ask: "Why would we not follow the U.S. guidance on revenue recognition?" Non-leading questions give no hint of the answer expected: "What do you think of the U.S. guidance on recognizing revenue?"

- *Direct/indirect*: A directly phrased question makes sense, and is explicit and understandable. For example, "Who reviewed the errors in revenue recognition detected in the audit and what actions did they take?" Indirect questions are used to avoid cueing the respondent, or when the same question is asked in a variety of ways to provide verification — circling by asking the same question in different ways. For example, "What happens if an employee questions whether revenue should be recognized on a particular sale?"
- *Simple/multiple*: Simple questions involve a single idea. They elicit information that is easy to manage and analyze. Multiple-phrased questions involve a string of ideas. They can serve exploratory purposes, leaving it to the respondent to choose which of several ideas to address. If not well thought through, however, they can confuse the respondent.

Guidance on Specific Areas

In this section, we provide suggestions for questions that audit committee members may wish to consider. We have resisted the temptation to provide a standard list of questions, and believe there can be a significant danger if audit committees rely on a "cookie cutter approach" to their questions.

Financial Reporting

An infinite variety of questions could be asked about financial reporting. The following questions have been selected as examples of ones audit committees might pose in their review of the quarterly and year-end financial statements. Our list is by no means comprehensive and audit committee members are encouraged to develop their own questions on issues of importance to them.

Questions for Management and the External Auditor

1) What is the quality, not just the acceptability, of the company's critical accounting policies? Have there been any changes in accounting policies or their application? Why were these changes made? If the changes were not made because of a new accounting standard, were they made to provide a more appropriate approach?

2) What are the critical accounting estimates? Have there been any changes in the methodologies or assumptions on which these estimates are based? Do the disclosures in the financial statements related to these estimates comply with the measurement uncertainty standards?

3) Has the audit committee been informed of all types of derivative, foreign currency or hedging transactions? Are the policies and controls over the use of such financial instruments appropriate? Are the levels of risk inherent in such transactions appropriate? Is the accounting and disclosure in the financial statements complete and understandable?

4) What is the inventory of "off-balance sheet" financing arrangements and transactions? What are the guarantees, warranties and contingent risks associated with each arrangement? Have there been any changes to these arrangements from prior years? Is the accounting treatment and disclosure appropriate?

5) Has the committee reviewed the potential litigation risk and satisfied itself that the accounting provisions and disclosure of contingent liabilities are appropriate?

6) Has the audit committee been provided with reports on any other financial risks faced by the company and on how these risks have been mitigated?

7) Has management conducted a formal review of all possible asset impairments, including non-operating assets, cost deferrals, intangibles and goodwill? Is the external auditor satisfied that all asset impairments have been identified and properly dealt with? Is the disclosure appropriate?

8) Are there any significant transactions that are not in the ordinary course of business? How have they been accounted for? Is the disclosure of such transactions appropriate?

9) Are there significant transactions or arrangements with related parties? Have they been properly disclosed? Are there any control or conflict of interest issues related to the involvement of senior management or directors with these parties? Do any of these transactions or arrangements violate the company's code of conduct?

10) Has management reviewed and updated the determinations of "operating segments" used in the disclosure of the segmented information? Are these classifications aligned with management's reporting structure? Are such classifications still appropriate?

11) Is the information presented in the financial statements consistent with that presented in the MD&A, related news releases, and other disclosures outside the financial statements? Does the financial statements, MD&A and news release taken together provide a fair presentation of the company's operating results and financial position? What is the audit committee's assessment of the clarity and understandability of financial statements, the MD&A and related news releases?

12) Has the company issued any pro forma earnings releases that were not reviewed by the audit committee? Does the committee understand how pro forma earnings reconcile to generally accepted accounting principles (GAAP) earnings and are they satisfied that such presentations are not misleading?

13) Have there been any disagreements between management and the external auditor? How have they been resolved? Were there any consultations with other accounting firms?

14) If the external auditor was responsible for preparing the financial statements, would he or she have used different principles or prepared them differently?

15) What were the major corrections made as a result of management's reviews in the closing process that were not anticipated?

16) What adjustments were proposed as a result of the auditor's work? What were the unadjusted differences that were considered by management to be immaterial? What follow-up procedures have been performed? What are the implications of these findings and adjustments with respect to quality of systems, the closing process and internal control?

17) Did the auditor encounter any major difficulties in performing the audit? Were there any restrictions placed on the scope or timing of the auditor's work? What are the implications arising from any such matters?

18) Were there any indications of fraud or illegal acts?

19) How does the company's financial statement presentation and disclosure compare to that of competitors and industry norms?

20) Are there any new or proposed accounting standards that impact the financial statements? Have the new accounting standards been implemented properly?

Other Questions for the External Auditor

Many audit committees ask questions of their external auditor with regard to the financial statements.

1) Is the financial statement disclosure followed in preparing the financial statements materially different from the disclosure practices generally employed by others in the industries or business in which the company is engaged?

2) Would you characterize as "inadequate" any of the significant accounting disclosure practices used by management in preparing the financial statements?

3) Could you characterize as "not the most appropriate" any of the significant disclosure practices used by management in preparing the financial statements?

4) Were immaterial items not discussed or disclosed in a manner that would have to be changed if such items became material in future?

5) Are you aware of any related party transactions involving the company, which have not been disclosed?

6) Are you aware of any existing failure by the company to comply with its covenants under loan agreements, trust deeds or similar instruments?

7) All things considered, is it your opinion that the financial statements contain a significant element of unfair reporting to shareholders and other third parties?

8) Are you aware of any accounting policies that are not in accordance with generally accepted accounting principles, irrespective of whether or not they are material?

9) Were there any disagreements with management about matters that individually or in aggregate could be significant to the company's financial statements?

10) Are you aware of any auditing and/or accounting matters where management decided to consult with other accountants?

11) Were there major issues discussed with management in connection to the application of accounting principles and auditing standards, and how were these matters resolved?

12) Were there any serious difficulties encountered in the performance of the audit?

CEO *and* CFO *Certification*

Chapter 12 provides a discussion of the CEO and CFO certification requirements, and that chapter includes several questions, which the audit committee may wish to ask of either management or the external auditor.

Relationship with the External Auditor

As discussed in Chapter 8, Managing Relationships, audit committees and external auditors are entering into new relationships in which the external auditor has a primary accountability to the audit committee as the representative of the shareholders. Audit committees may wish to ask the external auditor the following questions as a means of establishing and sustaining this new relationship.

1) Do you [the external auditor] understand our role as outlined in our audit committee charter? Do you understand our expectations for your performance? What are your expectations of us? What do you need from us to be successful?

2) Do you believe your working relationship with us [the audit committee] reflects the fact that your firm is accountable to the audit committee?

3) Do you have sufficient access to the audit committee and its chairman to permit candid communications, open sharing of concerns and confidential exchanges of information?

4) Have you been subject to what you consider to be unreasonable cost and fee pressures from management?

5) Has management put any pressure on you to accept accounting practices that you do not consider to be the most appropriate?

6) Are your audit team members empowered to communicate with the appropriate people in your firm on any professional issue or issues around independence, integrity or objectivity that may concern them?

7) What are your plans for rotation of partners on audit engagements? What succession planning do you have for the senior partners on our engagement?

8) What are your technical consultation and quality assurance policies, both for the firm and this engagement? What is your litigation record? What has your experience been with inspections conducted by the Canadian Public Accountability Board? What are you doing to continually improve the quality of your auditing?

Auditor Independence

In reviewing the auditors' letter on their independence, audit committees may wish to ask the following questions, which have been adapted from *Guidance for Audit Committees: Discussing Auditor Independence Matters with Your Auditor*, published by the CICA.

1) What policies and procedures does your firm have in place to identify interests and relationships that could have a bearing on your independence?

2) What procedures are in place on this engagement to identify any matters that could have a bearing on the firm's independence? Have all such matters been included in your annual independence report to the audit committee?

3) Have all non-audit services been reviewed and approved by the audit committee? How have you satisfied yourself that the firm's specialists and personnel providing the non-audit services do not assume a management role, develop structures or information that results in you auditing your own work, or create a mutuality of interest with management? What fees do non-audit services generate for your firm and how do they compare to the audit fees?

4) What percentage of your firm's revenue is derived from our company?
5) Have you been subject to any actual or threatened litigation by our company?
6) What financial relationships does your firm have with our company other than audit and consulting services?
7) What financial relationships does our company have with your firm? Consider:
   a) Our company is investing in the firm;
   b) Our company is acting as underwriter, broker-dealer or promoter for the firm.
8) What other business relationships exist between your firm and our company? Consider:
   a) The company is a significant supplier to the firm;
   b) The firm and the company are engaged in a joint venture;
   c) The firm and the company are engaged in an alliance or have a contractor/subcontractor relationship;
   d) The firm and the company have common investments.
9) What employment relationships exist between your firm and our company? Consider:
   a) Former partners or employees of your firm who are now employed by the company or serving on the board of directors;
   b) Close family members of your firm employed by the company;
   c) Former employees of the company employed by your firm.
10) What contingent fee arrangements exist between your firm and our company? Are they in accordance with the rules of professional conduct?

Audit Scope and Plan

When the audit committee reviews the proposed scope of the external audit plan and related fees, it must consider the comprehensiveness of the proposed approach. Audit committees may wish to ask the external auditor the following questions.

1) Have you reviewed the input received from audit committee members on the critical issues for the audit plan? How has this input been reflected in the proposed plan?
2) What options and alternatives did you consider in developing the external audit plan?
3) What is the level of materiality used in preparing the audit plan? What are the quantitative and qualitative dimensions? How were they determined? Has there been a change from prior years? Explain why?
4) What are the major risk areas and "key focus areas" of the audit plan? How were they identified? How have they changed from previous years? Does senior management agree with the risk assessments? What are the views of the internal auditor? Were they involved?
5) What is the depth of testing that you propose? What is the expectation of error assumed in the extent of testing? If no errors are expected, then how will you and management respond to the discovery of errors?
6) Are there any significant areas of the company's operations that have been excluded from the external audit plan or are being tested on a rotational basis?

7) What reliance is being placed on internal control and the internal audit function? How is this reliance established and supported? What is the overall approach to evaluation and testing of control? Does the control evaluation cover both headquarters and operating entities? What is the rotation plan for testing controls at divisions or operating business units?

8) What subsidiaries require statutory audits? What is the timing of such audits? Does the external auditor perform a review of the subsidiary's quarterly financial statements that is separate from the consolidated quarterly review? If yes, how are such reviews co-ordinated with the audit committees of both the subsidiary and the parent? What oversight should the audit committee of the parent company play in these audits?

9) What is the process for issuing management letters? What is the process for management to respond to the points raised in these management letters? Is there undue pressure exerted by management to minimize the points put forward in these management letters? What are the points or issues raised in prior letters that have not yet been addressed by management to your satisfaction?

10) How will you manage the engagement, monitor performance against the approved audit plan, supervise and review the work of the staff, consult on major issues, and report to the audit committee?

11) If there is more than one firm of external auditors involved in the audit of the consolidated financial statements, how is the reliance on the work of the other auditor established? Are there any issues the audit committee should be aware of?

12) How do the proposed audit fees compare with similar companies (recognizing that benchmarking audit fees is a very difficult exercise, because of the complex assumptions involved in planning audit scope and determining the appropriate extent of audit testing)? What are the trends in fees and hours spent on the engagement over the past few years? How do these trends compare with the growth in the company's business? Has the auditor generated ongoing productivity improvements in his or her approach to the audit and the tools he or she uses?

When management reporting on internal control with auditor attestation is implemented, the questions that audit committees should address to management and the internal and external auditors will become more extensive.

Internal Audit[1]

The internal audit function has a unique relationship with management. It serves as both an "independent critic" and a "constructive advisor" to management. Such a relationship requires that a healthy tension exist between internal audit and management, though obviously it should never degenerate into "open warfare" between the two groups. Nor should the relationship become too comfortable.

---

[1] The term "Internal Audit" refers to the internal audit function irrespective of what it may be called in each company.

Audit committees should question management and the head of internal audit to ensure that internal audit is effectively fulfilling both its "critic" and "advisor" roles. The committee should review and assess the proposed scope of the internal audit plan, its focus (e.g., operational review vs. control testing), the rotation cycles included, and the extent of testing. It should satisfy itself as to the quality of the leadership of the internal audit function and should ask questions relating to how the head of internal audit sets priorities, plans, supervises and reviews the various internal audit projects and activities.

In asking questions of the internal auditor, the audit committee should pay particular attention to following up on previous internal audit reviews and commitments made by management to correct deficiencies. It should receive regular reports on the status of outstanding issues raised by internal audit.

The audit committee should ensure that management has proper processes put in place to implement corrective actions in response to internal audit reviews, and that management is committed to ensuring that corrective actions are taken. In this regard, the committee should understand that operating management is often responsible for taking the corrective action and, when appropriate, the committee may consider asking the operating executives to appear before it to answer questions with respect to how control breakdowns occurred and what corrective action is being considered.

The following questions will help audit committees address the issues related to internal audit.

1) Does internal audit have a charter? Has the internal audit charter been presented to the audit committee for review/approval, and is it compatible with that of the audit committee? How often is this charter updated?

2) What are the priorities and overall strategy for the internal audit function?

3) Has the audit committee reviewed and approved the appointment or replacement of the leader of the internal audit function?

4) To whom does the head of internal audit report for administrative purposes (assuming that the internal audit function reports substantively to the audit committee)? Is this appropriate?

5) Does the head of internal audit have a strong reporting relationship with the audit committee and its chairman?

6) Are the internal audit function's budget and staffing adequate to support the necessary audit effort?

7) Is internal audit seen as an attractive place to work? Good from a career development perspective? Or, a dead-end function? What is the impact on the ability to recruit the right people?

8) How does the internal auditor maintain neutrality and objectivity?

9) What role does the internal audit function play in the CEO and CFO certification process, including the certification of disclosure controls and procedures, and internal control over financial reporting?

10) What role does the internal audit function play in enterprise risk management?

11) How does the internal audit staff stay abreast of technological advances and changes in the company's business?

12) Does the internal auditor work toward appropriate certification of his or her staff and does internal audit participate in professional development programs? Is the internal audit staff adequately trained? Does the staff have the right mix of skills?

13) Does internal audit outsource any or all of its activities? What are the outsourcing arrangements? How are these arrangements managed? What are the risks involved in such arrangements? How is the performance of the outsourcing service provider measured and evaluated?

14) Is the level of co-ordination between the internal and external auditor appropriate? If improvement is required, what is being done to improve it?

15) When there are significant findings from an internal audit, is management's response appropriate? What is the inventory of outstanding points raised by internal audit? How old are these points? How does management (headquarters, divisional, finance, IT, etc.) view internal audit and its audit reports?

16) Has internal audit assessed its compliance with the Institute of Internal Auditors Standards for the Professional Practice of Internal Auditing?

Risk Management and Internal Control

The CEO and CFO certification requirement has resulted on an increased focus on the importance of control. As discussed in Chapter 12, CEO and CFO Certification, audit committees should ensure that the certification process implemented by the CEO and CFO complies with the requirements, and is aligned with the principal business and financial reporting risks faced by the company. This requires management to make an assessment of principal business and financial reporting risks and requires the audit committee to understand those risks.

The issue of risk management and the alignment of controls with principal business risks is not addressed in the certification requirements. We believe that audit committees should satisfy themselves that an appropriate alignment does, in fact, exist.

When framing questions related to risk management and internal control, the audit committee's objective is to ascertain whether the company effectively manages its principal business risks and is "in control". Whether an organization is "in control" is not dependent solely on the risk management and control procedures built into computer networks and applications. It is also dependent on the culture of the organization and its ethical values, the adaptability and resourcefulness of its people, and the quality of its leaders.

To make this assessment, audit committees must address the issues of risk management and control at the business unit, subsidiary and corporate function levels. *Guidance for Directors: Dealing with Risk in the Boardroom*, published by the CICA,[2] identifies five factors directors can use in considering whether an organization is "in control". They are:

1) Members of the organization have a clear sense of corporate purpose, and are committed to achieving it.
2) They take risk knowingly, mitigate risk where appropriate and strive to be prepared for the unknown.
3) They trust each other and communicate openly to get the job done.
4) They have the human, physical and financial resources required.
5) They monitor progress and adapt to new circumstances.

The audit committee should consider these factors in framing their questions on risk management and control. Some questions that the committee might consider posing to management and the external auditor are:

1) What are management's overall objectives for internal control? Are these objectives consistent with the committee's view of the importance of control?
2) How are these control objectives aligned with the company's strategic plan?
3) How have the control responsibilities for corporate functions (e.g., finance, legal, IT) and operating management been assigned? Is the assignment appropriate? Are they understood?
4) Has the CEO set the right "tone at the top" with respect to managing risk and the importance of control? Is the CEO actively engaged in the certification process?
5) Does the behaviour of the CEO, CFO and other senior executives set an appropriate example? Do they "walk the talk"? Do they encourage a "push the envelope" type of culture?
6) Has management made a comprehensive assessment of principal business risks? Who performed this assessment (e.g., operating management or internal audit, corporate functions or operating management)? How often is it updated? Does this assessment of risk cover:
   a) Strategic risks, including business transformation and acquisitions;
   b) Operational risks, including IT risks and compliance with laws and regulations;
   c) Financing and liquidity risks, including off balance sheet financing arrangements;
   d) Corporate reporting risks, including financial and non-financial reporting and continuous disclosure;
   e) Crisis and emergency response risks, including lawsuits, regulatory investigations, environmental, technology and reputational risks.
7) Has the company established a threshold or appetite for risk in each of these categories? Have these thresholds been approved by the board?

[2] (Toronto 2000, CICA).

8) Are the control systems established by management aligned with this assessment of risk? Does management change and adapt the control systems to changes in business operations and risk? Have "mission critical" systems that require high reliability been identified?

9) How has the board organized its oversight of the management of these risks between itself and the various board committees? Is there an enterprise approach to risk management?

10) Do managers with risk management and control responsibilities have the necessary capability (e.g., knowledge, skills, technology, budget)? Are the compensation and reward systems aligned with the organization's risk management and control objectives?

11) Are control systems evaluated and tested by internal audit or by the external auditor? What is the scope of their evaluation and testing? Are controls evaluated and tested on a rotational basis? Are the control evaluation and testing activities of internal and external audit effectively co-ordinated?

12) How are control deficiencies detected in audits dealt with by management? What is the inventory of outstanding points raised by the internal and external auditors? How old are these points?

13) Are there any indications of senior management overriding corporate policies or the system of control?

14) Are there different standards or expectations of control for the company's subsidiaries, business units or operations in other countries?

Information Technology Issues

The board of directors should assume responsibility for the integrity of the company's internal control and management information systems.

Information technologies are central to both internal control and management information systems. As these technologies change and evolve, they create new risks and new opportunities for improved control and effectiveness. They also make it more challenging for boards of directors and audit committees to discharge their oversight responsibilities. The following questions, from the CICA publication *20 Questions Directors Should Ask About* IT, will help boards and audit committees focus on the important issues, irrespective of how they allocate the oversight responsibilities between them.

1) Does management have a strategic information systems plan in place that is monitored and updated as required? Does this plan form the basis for the annual plans, annual and long-term budgets and the prioritization of information technology projects?

2) Have appropriate procedures been established to ensure that the company is aware of technology trends, periodically assessing them and taking them into consideration when determining how it can better position itself?

3) Have key performance indicators and drivers of the IT department been determined? Are they monitored from time to time and are they benchmarked against industry standards?

4) How is the company managing its relationships with third-party service providers?

5) Does management have appropriate procedures to address information technology employee turnover, training and project assignment?

6) How has management ensured that it has identified the required technology expertise and how is top talent attracted and retained?

7) Has the board considered the creation of an IT subcommittee or assigned a board member specific responsibility for the organization's investment in, and use of, information technology?

8) Who on the management team has responsibility for IT corporate governance? Is this person in a sufficiently senior management position?

9) What is management doing to ensure that employees are aware of, and are in compliance with, the company's information and security policies?

10) Does management have a plan to periodically conduct risk assessments covering the company's use of information technology, including internal systems and processes, outsourced services and the use of third-party communications and other services? If it does, are the results of the assessments acted on where appropriate or required?

11) How does management ensure data integrity, including relevance, completeness, accuracy and timeliness, and its appropriate use within the organization?

12) What arrangements does the company have for the regular review and audit of its systems to ensure risks are sufficiently mitigated and controls are in place to support the major processes of the business?

13) Has the company assigned someone the responsibility for privacy policy, privacy legislation and compliance therewith?

14) Has the company identified the various legislative and regulatory requirements for protecting personal information and developed a policy and procedures for monitoring compliance with them?

15) If the company uses e-business to buy or sell products or services, has there been a specific review of the risks and controls over the e-business activities?

16) Are the company's e-business activities appropriately protected from external attack by hackers or others that, if successful, would result in loss of customer satisfaction or public embarrassment?

17) Has the company adopted formal availability policies? Has it implemented effective controls to provide reasonable assurance that systems and data are available in conformity with availability policies?

18) Does the company understand the impact of an interruption in service and are there plans in place to deal with potential interruptions? Has a business continuity plan been adopted? If it has been adopted, is it tested regularly and are the results used to improve the plan?

19) Has management considered and addressed legal implications that pertain to the use of software, hardware, service agreements and copyright laws?
20) Have policies covering licences, agreements and copyright been formulated and disseminated to all personnel?

Compliance with Laws and Regulations

Ensuring compliance with laws and regulations is becoming a greater challenge for all companies. It is particularly challenging for those that expand their operations into different markets and list their shares on foreign exchanges. The following are some questions for the audit committee to consider:

1) Has management (the legal department or outside counsel) identified all the laws and regulations with which the company must comply in conducting its business? How does management ensure that it keeps current with changes in laws and regulations and with the compliance implications arising from such changes? What are the compliance implications arising from changes in the company's businesses?
2) How does management monitor compliance with these laws and regulations? Does the company have the requisite capabilities to monitor compliance and manage the legal affairs of the company?
3) Which laws and regulations present the most serious risk to the company from a non-compliance perspective?
4) Which laws and regulations present the most serious risk to the board of directors from a non-compliance perspective?
5) Has the company had a "legal audit" of its processes to ensure compliance with laws and regulations and to manage litigation by outside counsel? Should the audit committee hear directly from outside counsel on their findings and conclusions?
6) How are estimates of litigation exposure developed? Are they reasonable? How are they reflected in the financial statements?

Mergers and Acquisitions

In a merger or acquisition transaction, the audit committee faces a number of very significant challenges. While the audit committee's focus is primarily on the accounting and disclosure implications of the transaction, the board of directors may ask it to also consider issues relating to the strategy, structure and control aspects of the proposed transaction. As a result, the first issue for audit committees to address is its role and responsibilities, which should be discussed and agreed with the chairman of the board and the board itself.

Some questions that audit committees might consider when a transaction comes before them are presented below.

Audit, Financial Reporting and Disclosure Questions

1) What are the continuous disclosure requirements (e.g., material change report, news release, quarterly financial statements)? Do all parties understand what these obligations are and when disclosure should be made?

2) What will be the impact of the transaction on the company's financial reporting (balance sheet, earnings, cash flow)? What impact will the financing proposals for the transaction have on the company's ability to raise capital? What is the impact on existing covenants?

3) What goodwill will be generated on the transaction? What are the nature and magnitude of "intangibles" involved in the transaction? What valuations will be obtained to support the recording of this amount? Will the valuations be from an independent and reputable source?

4) What is the scope, timing and extent of due diligence activities? Who performed the due diligence review? What are their qualifications? What is their objectivity and independence?

5) Who are the legal advisors? Should the audit committee or board meet privately with them? Should the audit committee or board retain its own advisors?

6) Who are the tax advisors? What is their reputation and experience in the industry? What are the terms and conditions of their engagement? What was the process for selecting them? Who approved the recommended firm?

7) Who are the investment advisors? What is their reputation and experience in the industry? What are the terms and conditions of their engagement? What was the process for selecting them? Who approved the recommended firm?

8) Is there a single lender or syndicate? If a syndicate is involved, have the advantages and disadvantages been considered? What are the terms and conditions of the banking syndicate?

9) Is a fairness opinion required? If so, who will provide it? What are their qualifications? Are they independent?

10) Are there any related party aspects of the transaction?

11) Are there any conflict of interests (in fact or appearance) involving any of the directors, management, advisors, strategic partners, joint ventures and outsourcing partners or the auditor or any other parties involved in the transaction?

12) What services does the external auditor provide? Is there adequate protection that the auditor's independence will not be impaired, or perceived to be impaired?

Pension Plans

Companies today have a range of pension, retirement savings, profit sharing and other plans that are administered for the benefit of employees. Often these plans are established with independent trustees that have fiduciary responsibilities to the plan. The division of risks between the company and the pension plan may be quite different (e.g., investment risk in a defined benefit plan is borne by the company whereas the employee bears the investment risk in a defined contribution plan). The following questions may be considered by audit committees in addressing governance and reporting issues in these plans (referred to in the questions as "pension plans").

1) What is the governance structure for the pension plan? Are the trustees independent? What accountability (if any) do they have to the company's board of directors and audit committee vis-à-vis the employee and retiree stakeholder groups?

2) If there is a pension committee of the board, what are its responsibilities vis-à-vis the audit committee? What are the board's responsibilities vis-à-vis the audit committee?

3) Are there any potential conflict of interest issues related to the structure of the pension plan, its management, its trustees, its investments or its governance? How are these potential conflict of interest situations managed or mitigated?

4) What financial statements are prepared by the pension plan? To whom are they distributed? What regulators are they filed with? What accounting standards are used in their preparation? Should the audit committee review the financial statements and regulatory filings?

5) What are the major risks in the pension plan? What risks are borne by the company or guaranteed by it?

6) What is the funding status of the pension plan? Is it over funded or under funded? When was the last actuarial valuation performed?

7) Is an independent auditor appointed for the pension plan? Should the audit committee review the terms of that appointment and provide its expectations for that auditor's performance?

8) What audit reports and management letters have been issued by the external auditor of the pension plan? What is that auditor's assessment of the control systems in the pension plan and the ability of the pension plan management to effectively manage risk?

9) How does the pension plan management satisfy itself that the pension plan complies with all applicable laws and regulatory requirements?

In Summary

This chapter has focused on asking some of the right questions. But there is another fundamental part of the right question equation. Audit committees must be persistent in obtaining appropriate answers to their questions. If, for some reason, appropriate answers are not immediately available at the meeting, the committee must be vigilant in following up with management and in making sure that the answers it has requested are forthcoming in a timely fashion. Audit committees should never be satisfied with less than complete answers to their questions.

Key Messages

- One of the most effective ways for committee members to get the information they need is by asking the right questions, in the right way, at the right time and to persist until the right answer is obtained.

- The stage to which the relationship among the audit committee, management and the external auditor has evolved will affect the committee's effectiveness in asking questions.

- The ability to ask the "right questions" is highly dependent on both the information provided to the audit committee in advance of the meeting and the level of effort committee members make in preparing for the meeting.

- Questions should be designed to enable the audit committee to understand the material, evaluate and challenge the proposals being made, and assess the appropriateness of the overall conclusion.

- Questions may be phrased in different ways, and audit committees should structure their questions to reflect the circumstances of the kind of information being sought, what the information is to be used for, who is being asked, etc. It is important, therefore, to know your objectives in asking a question.

- All questions should make sense to the respondent, use vocabulary common to the respondent and other committee members, and elicit the information required.

- Audit committees must be persistent enough to get appropriate answers to their questions.

The Tough Issues and How to Deal With Them

Inevitably, there will be times when audit committees will face some difficult issues in discharging their responsibilities, and this chapter discusses some of them. We have tried to provide general suggestions for approaching these matters and to identify some of the items that audit committees should address in resolving the problem. Every situation will be different and the best way for an audit committee to approach an issue will depend on the circumstances.

In some circumstances, the tough issues discussed in this chapter may develop into a crisis in which the audit committee must launch a formal or informal investigation. Such a situation is discussed in greater detail in Chapter 15, Audit Committees in Crisis Situations.

A critical decision that audit committees must make in resolving some of these tough issues, or when dealing with a crisis, is determining whether the committee should get independent advice, particularly independent legal advice. Naturally, audit committees will utilize the auditors, lawyers, actuaries, geologists, valuation experts and other professionals who have already been engaged by the company to help deal with the issue. There may be times, however, when the committee will wish to obtain its own independent expert advice.

The following are some of the tough issues that an audit committee may encounter.

Second Accounting Opinions

Circumstances may arise where management and the external auditor cannot reach an agreement on a particular accounting issue. In these situations, the audit committee may have to arbitrate the matter, or approve a recommendation from management or the external auditor that another independent accounting firm be engaged to provide a second opinion to help resolve the dispute.

We believe it is prudent for audit committees to establish a policy that second opinions on accounting matters are to be obtained only after the audit committee has reviewed the matter and concurred with the decision to seek a second opinion. The purpose of such a policy is not to curtail or limit obtaining second opinions. Instead, it is to ensure that the committee fully understands:

- the available options and alternatives;
- the reasons why management and the external auditor cannot reach an agreement;
- the nature of the question to be asked (for example: What accounting is acceptable in accordance with GAAP? What is the most appropriate accounting? What is the most conservative? What is the most aggressive?); and
- the information, assumptions and facts to be provided to the second accounting firm.

By reviewing this information before the "second opinion" is sought, the audit committee is better able to determine the reasonableness of the positions taken by management and the external auditor, ensure that the right questions are being asked, and better assess and interpret the second accountant's report.

Audit committees should select the accounting firm to provide the second opinion, known as the "reporting accountant", in consultation with management and the external auditor. The reporting accountant should be accountable to the audit committee, in the same way as the external auditor is accountable, and their report should be addressed to the audit committee.

Under the rules of professional standards, a reporting accountant is required to:[1]

- obtain written permission from the company to contact its external auditor. A reporting accountant should not accept an engagement if permission to contact the external auditor is not obtained;
- obtain, from the entity, a written statement of all relevant facts and assumptions, and a description of the circumstances and nature of any relevant disagreements between the entity and its external auditor or another third party such as an investment banker; and
- contact the external auditor in writing to confirm that the information provided by the company is complete and consistent with the external auditor's knowledge of the circumstances or transaction.

---

[1] CICA *Handbook*, Section 7600, "Reports on the Application of Accounting Principles, Auditing Standards or Review Standards", paragraph 7600.12.

When reporting accountants complete their work and form an opinion based on the information provided to them, they should issue a written report that:[2]
- describes the nature of the engagement;
- states that the engagement was performed in accordance with generally accepted standards for such engagements;
- includes or refers to the statement of relevant facts and assumptions, and the source of this information; and
- expresses an opinion on the appropriate accounting principles, auditing standards or review standards to be applied to the matters described in the statement of relevant facts and assumptions, and refers to available authoritative support and supporting rationale.

The report of the reporting accountant will contain certain technical caveats, including any restrictions placed on distributing the report to third parties. The audit committee should consider these restrictions carefully. A prudent audit committee will agree on these restrictions at the time the reporting accountant is engaged.

The audit committee should review the "second opinion" report in the presence of the reporting accountant, management and the external auditor so it can evaluate the views and recommendations of each party.

There may be circumstances in which the audit committee and/or management may wish to retain another accounting firm to provide accounting advice on a difficult or particularly complex issue where a "second opinion" is not necessary and there is no disagreement between management and the external auditor. The audit committee should be aware that the professional standards that govern these engagements are similar to those that govern the "second opinion" engagements, but these are less onerous. In our view, the audit committee should approve all such engagements.

Top Management Fraud or Improper Actions

Perhaps the most difficult issue that an audit committee must address is top management fraud or improper action on the part of senior management. While the vast majority of senior management officers are honest, capable people who have integrity, audit committees must be alert to the possibility that some executives may engage in improper behaviour. A study in the United States of 204 companies that had been the subject of SEC fraud findings between 1987 and 1997 found that the CEO was involved in 72% of the frauds examined.[3]

[2] CICA *Handbook*, Section 7600, "Reports on the Application of Accounting Principles, Auditing Standards or Review Standards", paragraph 7600.24.
[3] Fraudulent Financial Reporting: 1987-1997 — An Analysis of U.S. Public Companies, Committee of Sponsoring Organizations (COSO) of the Treadway Commission, March 1999.

In an address to Congress in 2002, Alan Greenspan, the Federal Reserve Chairman, said:[4]

> *Why did corporate governance checks and balances that served us reasonably well in the past break down? At root was the rapid enlargement of stock market capitalizations in the latter part of the 1990s that arguably engendered an outsized increase in opportunities for avarice. An infectious greed seemed to grip much of our business community. Our historical guardians of financial information were overwhelmed. Too many corporate executives sought ways to "harvest" some of those stock market gains. As a result, the highly desirable spread of shareholding and options among business managers perversely created incentives to artificially inflate reported earnings in order to keep stock prices high and rising. This outcome suggests that the options were poorly structured, and, consequently, they failed to properly align the long-term interests of shareholders and managers, the paradigm so essential for effective corporate governance. The incentives they created overcame the good judgment of too many corporate managers. It is not that humans have become any more greedy than in generations past. It is that the avenues to express greed have grown so enormously.*

Recent events illustrate that fraudulent and improper activities continue!

To address these and other issues of improper behaviour, audit committees and external auditors must be alert to certain "red flags" that signal possible fraud, or illegal, improper or unethical actions and activities by senior management. The CICA *Handbook* provides these examples of such red flags:[5]

> i)   *a significant portion of management's compensation is represented by business, stock options or other incentives, the value of which is contingent upon the entity achieving unduly aggressive targets for operating results, financial position or cash flow;*
> ii) *there is excessive interest by management in maintaining or increasing the entity's stock price or earnings trend through the use of unusually aggressive accounting practices;*
> iii) *management commits to analysts, creditors and other third parties in achieving what appear to be unduly aggressive or clearly unrealistic forecasts;*
> iv) *management has an interest in pursuing inappropriate means to minimize reported earnings for tax-motivated reasons;*
> v)   *management displays a significant disregard for regulatory or legislative authorities; and*
> vi) *control has changed, especially if the price paid by new management was high.*

---

[4] Testimony of Mr. Alan Greenspan, Chairman of the Board of Governors of the U.S. Federal Reserve System, on the occasion of the Federal Reserve Board's semi-annual monetary policy report to the Congress, before the Committee on Financial Services, U.S. House of Representatives, July 17, 2002.

[5] CICA *Handbook*, Section 5135, "The Auditor's Responsibility to Consider Fraud and Error in an Audit of Financial Statements", Appendix A.

There will be occasions when it will be very difficult to interpret the indicators and related evidence. The audit committee and the external auditor are exposed to two types of risk:

1) false accusation risk (for example, the audit committee launches an investigation or accuses the CEO and senior management of fraud, illegal, or improper activities when such actions are not warranted); and

2) false acceptance risk (for example, the audit committee or the external auditor accept the actions and activities of the CEO and senior management as being appropriate when they are not).

There are justifiable concerns about making a false accusation risk and its related consequences. However, those concerns should not cause audit committees to resist the conclusion that senior management is committing improper or fraudulent activities or insist on seeking more evidence of improper activity before reaching a conclusion.

While both actions may cause undue delay or, indeed, a rationalization that the evidence does not suggest fraudulent or improper activities, these concerns about a false accusation risk should not prevent the audit committee from conducting an appropriate inquiry. Such an inquiry can range from merely asking questions to asking the internal and external auditors to expand the scope of their audit activities to conducting a formal investigation.

Whenever there are concerns about possible improper actions, it is imperative that the audit committee and the external auditor candidly discuss their concerns and observations and together plan the way to respond to them. An advantage of holding regular *in camera* sessions is that it provides an opportunity for the audit committee and the external auditor to discuss any warning signs. When the audit committee and external auditor pool their knowledge and experience, they can be an effective check on improper behaviour.

A note of caution: There are significant consequences to either overreacting and risking a false accusation, or underreacting and assuming that management's behaviour is appropriate. Therefore, prudent audit committees will proceed with caution, but will do so expeditiously.

In deciding how best to proceed, the audit committee is well advised to seek expert advice. In most circumstances, the external auditor will be a valuable advisor, given his or her wide experience with issues of this nature. Outside legal counsel is another important source of advice.

When any suspicion arises of improper behaviour by management, the chairman of the audit committee should immediately inform the independent chairman of the board and, in most circumstances, the CEO.

The external auditor can be helpful in confirming the existence of improper behaviour and, indeed, may often be the one who uncovers the information that management is engaged in what may be inappropriate actions. In the latter situation, the audit committee will find itself squarely in the midst of a potentially fraught situation. In these circumstances, the only course of action for the audit committee is to summon both management and the auditor to meetings at which the views of both can be discussed, and then to launch an immediate investigation. The nature and organization of such an investigation will be dictated by the circumstances and by legal advice.

Obviously, the involvement of the CEO or top management in fraudulent or improper activities has the potential to explode into a major crisis for the company. Chapter 15, Audit Committees in Crisis Situations, will address this and other matters that may lead to a crisis, and provide advice on how the audit committee should respond.

Discovery of Errors in Published Financial Statements

When management or the directors become aware of errors in published financial statements, they must respond promptly and appropriately. Canadian law requires directors or officers who become aware of an error in a published audited financial statement to notify the audit committee and the auditor.

When the audit committee is notified of an error, it should immediately seek the advice of legal counsel. The audit committee, the external auditor and the legal advisors need to consider various options including:

- whether a further investigation of the discovered errors should be undertaken to ensure there are not additional errors of a similar nature;
- whether a follow-up investigation is needed, and who should conduct it;
- what public disclosure is required in the event the error is material;
- whether previously issued financial statements and auditor's reports need to be withdrawn or restated; and
- whether a special board committee needs to be established for the purposes of the investigation.

In these situations, litigation is always a distinct possibility and, therefore, careful consideration must be given to legal issues such as privilege.

The discovery of errors in previously issued financial statements requires audit committees to make some very important decisions with very significant implications for it, the external auditor, the company and its shareholders. The decisions must be made promptly and decisively, utilizing the best legal, accounting and auditing advice the audit committee can obtain.

If the error is of a nature or magnitude that a restatement of previously issued financial statements may be required, then the reader's attention is directed to Chapter 15, Audit Committees in Crisis Situations.

Reviews and Investigations by Securities Regulators

Today, securities regulators in the United States and Canada have implemented comprehensive review programs to monitor the quality of financial statements and continuous disclosure reporting. In addition, there are specific review and approval processes for the filing of registration statements and prospectuses.

Management should brief the audit committee on all communications received from securities regulators that require an explanatory response and explain how these communications are being responded to and whether the company is required to take any corrective action. The audit committee should seek the external auditor's views on these matters, and determine what action, if any, the committee should take. In these situations, the audit committee's role is to understand the questions and concerns raised by the regulators and approve management's response strategy. In our opinion, the audit committee or its chairman should review and approve all responses made by management, including any and all materials provided to the regulators.

If a securities regulator or taxation authority launches a formal investigation, this should be regarded as a challenge to the integrity of the company's reporting and behaviour, and the audit committee should act accordingly. It should review and approve the response strategy, and should be consulted on any major decision taken during the course of the response.

Whether the request for information is informal or formal, a prudent audit committee will engage expert outside counsel to advise it on both its response strategy and developing the substance of its response.

Conflicts of Interest

Circumstances may arise where a member of the audit committee satisfies all of the independence requirements of MI 52-110, but finds himself or herself in a situation where he or she believes that they may have a conflict of interest with respect to a matter being discussed by the audit committee.

In such circumstances, the member should discuss the situation with the chairman of the audit committee and the chairman of the board, and absent himself or herself from the discussions or decisions with respect to that matter. The chairman may wish to raise the matter with the committee and solicit their views.

If the conflict of interest is such that either the audit committee member or the chairmen believe that it may impair that member's objectivity and independence, then the director should resign from the audit committee.

Public Subsidiaries

Members of an audit committee of a public company that is a subsidiary may experience difficult situations when the interests of the subsidiary or the minority shareholders are in conflict with those of the parent company.

The options available to the independent members of the subsidiary's audit committee are limited. Either the subsidiary's independent directors are successful in achieving an appropriate resolution or, if the matter is sufficiently material and they are not successful, they may have no option but to resign.

Independent members of a public subsidiary's audit committee may also experience difficulty in obtaining access to the information they require from the parent company. In these circumstances, the subsidiary's audit committee has an obligation to make every effort to obtain all information that is critical to its financial reporting. The audit committee may need to obtain legal advice as to how far it can go in gaining access to this information without putting the parent in jeopardy of contravening securities laws. Similarly, the audit committee may need to obtain legal advice when the parent company requests financial information from the subsidiary that is not disclosed.

When the external auditor of the subsidiary is also the external auditor of the parent, the external auditor may be helpful to the audit committee in navigating through the shoals of the issues that surround the distribution of information in corporate groups. The external auditor, however, cannot share the parent's information with the subsidiary without the approval of the parent.

Compliance with Laws and Regulations

Large corporations face a significant challenge in ensuring that they are in compliance with all the laws and regulations that govern them in all the jurisdictions in which they operate.

When the audit committee's charter includes oversight responsibility for compliance with laws and regulations, the committee should ask management, and more specifically the general counsel, to report formally to it on the systems and processes that have been put in place to ensure such compliance. The committee should also satisfy itself that the compliance with these procedures is evaluated and tested periodically by internal audit, the external auditor and in-house counsel.

Appropriate action must be taken whenever a failure to comply with laws and regulations is reported to the audit committee by management or the internal or external auditors. While it is management's responsibility to investigate such failures, assess their implications and implement corrective action, the audit committee is responsible for satisfying itself that management has taken the appropriate steps to comply and to ensure that such failures will not occur in the future.

Audit committees may wish to consider retaining experienced outside counsel from time to time to review the systems and processes that have been put in place to ensure compliance. The benefit of so doing lies not only in an objective review but, very importantly, in providing the committee with a tool for benchmarking the corporation's systems and processes against best practices.

Systems Weaknesses and Control Breakdowns

When the internal or external auditors report a systems weakness, control deficiency or failure to comply with laws and regulations, it places the audit committee in a difficult position.

Management is responsible for fixing such deficiencies, investigating their impact and, if necessary, making changes in management personnel or responsibilities. The audit committee is responsible for ensuring that management provides the committee with an assessment of the impact of such weaknesses and control breakdowns.

Management should present to the committee a plan of corrective action for all significant system weaknesses and control breakdowns included in its assessment. The internal and external auditors, as appropriate, should monitor the implementation of these actions and report to the audit committee on the progress of implementation.

In many cases, the responsibility for a control breakdown and its correction rests with the operating executives (for example, a divisional manager or president of a foreign subsidiary). The audit committee would be well advised to consider asking these executives to appear before the committee to explain why the control breakdown occurred and what their plans are for correcting them. This will help reinforce the importance of a strong control environment, and the fact that operating management is accountable for maintaining effective control systems.

As discussed earlier in this book, the CSA is likely to introduce some form of management reporting on internal control over financial reporting, together with auditor attestation. This requirement will formalize management's reports to investors and the audit committee on control breakdowns and should provide more comprehensive information on system weaknesses. This, of course, will increase the audit committee's oversight responsibilities.

Replacing the Audit Partner and/or External Audit Firm

There may be situations where the working relationship among management, the external auditor and the audit committee is not functioning to the audit committee's satisfaction. The causes of such strained working relationships can be varied, and may include concerns over costs, personality conflicts, competency problems or the inability of the lead audit partner to work effectively with management and the audit committee. It can also, however, indicate serious disagreements over accounting principles, control weaknesses or risk exposures. The audit committee needs to understand the causes clearly before it can take action to remedy the situation.

The audit committee must determine whether the breakdown results from a failure of management, the external audit firm, or the lead audit partner. It is unlikely that the audit committee will recommend a change of CFO except in extraordinary circumstances, though such an action should be considered in appropriate situations. However, the audit committee should carefully monitor the CFO's ability to work effectively with the external auditor, accept constructive criticism and respond appropriately to audit findings, and ensure that this assessment is reflected in the evaluation of the CFO's performance.

If the audit committee concludes that the source of the problem lies with the external auditor, it faces two choices: to replace the lead audit partner, or replace the external audit firm.

When considering the replacement of the lead audit partner or the external audit firm, it is important to remember that the auditor's independence must be protected. If the audit committee wants the auditor to utilize professional skepticism, and constructively challenge the positions put forward by management, then it must expect that "healthy tensions" will develop between management and the external auditor. At times, these healthy tensions can become quite strained, and the audit committee must ascertain whether management's desire to change the audit partner or firm simply reflect the fact that the auditor is doing his or her job, or whether the desire for change represents a more serious deficiency that should be addressed by a change in the lead audit partner. Sometimes, the positions may become so entrenched that it becomes very difficult for management and the lead audit partner to work effectively together, which may then require a change in the lead audit partner, management or both.

Another cause of strained working relationships is when the lead audit partner's knowledge, skills and capabilities are no longer aligned with or relevant to the business and professional needs of the company. The lead audit partner might have established highly effective personal relationships with senior management and the audit committee, but the committee may now have doubts about the lead partner's experience and qualifications for conducting an effective audit. This should prompt the audit committee to give serious consideration to replacing the lead audit partner. In today's environment, it is too risky to ignore such concerns.

If the audit committee and its chairman have established effective working relationships with the lead audit partner, they will have firsthand information and knowledge of the individual, and be better able to assess the validity of any concerns put forward by management.

Without such an effective working relationship, the audit committee and its chairman are in a much more difficult position to assess the validity of any proposal to replace the lead audit partner. Similarly, if the chairman of the audit committee has established a relationship with other senior management partners in the external audit firm, he or she has the ability to discuss problems in the service relationship with them to obtain another perspective on and to develop options for resolving the matter. In some cases, no matter how hard all parties try, the chemistry between the audit committee and/or management and the lead audit partner or other senior members of the audit team simply does not work. In these situations, the external auditor should replace those individuals.

The option of replacing the external audit firm should be considered only in exceptional circumstances. The constant threat of being replaced or having the audit engagement put out for proposal could make the external auditor reluctant to confront issues with management or raise concerns with the audit committee, which in turn could weaken the effectiveness of the audit. While the audit committee provides a source of security for the external auditor, it should not be reluctant to replace the audit partner or external audit firm when the circumstances warrant that action.

Replacing or Reprimanding Management

When significant errors, control breakdowns and systems weaknesses are detected in the course of the audit or in previously issued financial statements, a presumption of concern is raised about the competencies, capabilities and, possibly, the integrity of the responsible executives. This presumption of concern is further strengthened when there is not a timely resolution of control weaknesses or deficiencies in managing business or financial risks.

It is appropriate for the audit committee to seek the external auditor's views on the competencies and integrity of the CEO, CFO and other members of senior financial management. The committee should understand, however, that, while the external auditor brings an independent perspective and broad professional experience, the auditor is not an operating executive, and therefore his or her views, while worthy of respect, must be placed in proper perspective.

The audit committee has a responsibility to communicate to the CEO and the board's compensation committee any concerns it may have with the performance, competency or integrity of the CFO, head of internal audit , treasurer, CIO or other senior executive. In situations where the CEO is directly involved, the audit committee should communicate its concerns to the chairman of the board.

Guidance to Analysts and Investors

Today, many companies provide guidance to analysts and investors regarding the company's future revenue and earnings targets. Although such guidance is not technically considered to be a forecast, management must ensure that the methodology and assumptions used in providing it reflect the planned course of action, and that the final guidance is a reasonable estimate of what will likely be achieved if the assumptions are attained.

In our opinion, audit committees should review any guidance before it is released, including the supporting methodologies and assumptions. (For a further discussion of this, see Chapter 11, Corporate Reporting: Trends and Issues.)

Resistance to the Audit Committee

The audit committee and its chairman may encounter resistance from management or the external auditor in either providing information to the committee or in executing its directives. Such resistance may be open and direct, or passive, in that while no one overtly opposes the committee's decisions or requests, nothing ever happens or the information is never produced.

Open and direct resistance is often the easiest to deal with because the concerns and arguments are clearly on the table to be addressed. Passive resistance is more challenging because the audit committee may have difficulty in determining the source of the resistance and reasons for it.

Audit committees must deal with both kinds of resistance or the behaviour will inevitably undermine the committee's effectiveness. If the resistance cannot be overcome, the chairman should raise the matter with the chairman of the board and determine an appropriate course of action.

When the Audit Committee Gets Sued

Audit committees may encounter situations where they are named as a defendant in civil litigation or regulatory proceedings. In such cases, the audit committee must ensure that it obtains the best legal advice and counsel. The best defence against being sued successfully is for audit committees to ensure that they discharge their duties in a responsible manner, with due care and appropriate reliance on experts when entitled to do so. The audit committee should also ensure that the corporation has an appropriate indemnification policy and Directors and Officers Insurance.

Dealing with an Incompetent Audit Committee

Sometimes the audit committee itself may be incompetent or less than effective. If so, what should be done, and who should do it?

An ineffective or incompetent audit committee poses a significant risk to the company, the board of directors and, ultimately, the shareholders. The committee plays a key role in establishing the company's expectations with respect to the control and compliance cultures, and to the integrity of financial information and disclosure. Therefore, the company cannot afford to tolerate ineffective performance from the committee. Moreover, because the committee also plays a key role in mitigating the potential for management to override the company's control procedures, there is an added incentive for the board and the company to take corrective action. If an ineffective audit committee exists in a situation in which management is either incompetent or lacks integrity, the potential for disastrous consequences increases substantially.

There are, of course, varying degrees of audit committee incompetence or ineffectiveness. Four of the more obvious circumstances are addressed below.

An Incompetent Audit Committee and an Incompetent Chairman

The highest risk occurs when the audit committee as a whole is incompetent or ineffective, including its chairman. In these circumstances, it is likely that the board also faces competency issues. Who, then, can act?

We believe the external auditor has an obligation to take action since he or she is ultimately accountable to the shareholders, even though this may pose a danger to the auditor. The auditor's professional responsibilities do not change simply because the audit committee is ineffective. Assuming that the external auditor has apprised the board of his or her concerns and no action is forthcoming, the auditor may have a duty to resign from the engagement and make public the reasons for doing so.

An Incompetent Audit Committee with a Competent Chairman

In these situations, the chairman of the audit committee has a clear duty to act. His or her concerns must be communicated to the chairman of the board, the board as a whole and, if the board has a governance or nominating committee, to that committee's chairman.

The chairman of the audit committee must do everything in his or her power to influence a change in the personnel of the audit committee, including soliciting the help of the external auditor. Until corrective action can be taken, the external auditor should also work with the chairman to compensate for the weaknesses of the committee members.

Some Committee Members are Incompetent

Sometimes, situations arise where one or more members of the audit committee are not contributing or "pulling their weight" on the committee. The demands placed on audit committees today, together with the expectations for their performance and the liability exposure, make it very risky to tolerate incompetent or unproductive members.

If the chairman has established an effective working relationship with the lead audit partner, CEO and CFO, they can be valuable sources of input on the performance of audit committee members, and also potential sources of corroboration for the chairman's concerns.

The chairman must provide non-performing members with feedback and, if their performance is not improved, must raise the matter with the chairman of the board and chairman of the governance or nominating committee and ask that the ineffective member or members be replaced. In the final analysis, the chairman of the audit committee is responsible for initiating corrective action.

An Incompetent Chairman with a Competent Committee

When the audit committee is of the opinion that its chairman is either incompetent or not performing in accordance with the committee's expectations, the committee members have a duty to take corrective action. The external auditor can be helpful in assisting the committee members in making their views known to the chairman of the board and chairman of the governance or nominating committee.

The audit committee members should, however, be careful that their opinion of the chairman is not based on personality issues. A discussion of the matter with the external auditor can be helpful in achieving a degree of objectivity that committee members may not always have.

When the Auditor and Management Disagree

The audit committee should expect that there will be situations when the auditor and management disagree. This is a normal part of the audit process, and is not necessarily indicative of a crisis. What is the role of the audit committee?

Traditionally, audit committees have been reluctant to participate in resolving such conflicts. Indeed, some audit committees have explicitly stated that they did not want to discuss an issue unless management and the auditor are in agreement. The message was that management and the auditor should solve their own disagreements.

Today, given the changed nature of the relationship between the audit committee and the external auditor, audit committees are expected to be informed of significant disagreements, and how they were resolved. If they are unresolved, the committee should require them to be brought to it for resolution.

By participating in the resolution of disagreements, the audit committee has the opportunity to avoid the escalation of the disagreement to crisis proportions. Should, however, the committee fail to have the issue resolved, it will find itself in a crisis situation. The committee may find itself in a position of having to accept a qualified opinion, having to find another auditor because the auditor resigns or having to take action with respect to management.

Key Messages

- *When faced with tough issues to resolve, audit committees will need to determine whether they should get independent advice, particularly independent legal advice.*
- *Audit committees should establish a policy that second opinions on accounting matters are to be obtained only after the audit committee has reviewed the matter and concurred with the decision to seek a second opinion.*
- *When tough issues arise, such as errors discovered in previously issued financial statements, management is responsible for fixing the problem and the audit committee is responsible for ensuring that management has done so.*
- *As part of its monitoring of internal control, the audit committee should ask management to report on the systems and processes in place to ensure compliance with the laws and regulations of each jurisdiction in which the company operates.*
- *The audit committee, management and the external auditor all play important roles in the financial governance system. If one party is incompetent, the other two parties must work together to effect the changes necessary to resolve the problem.*

Audit Committees in Crisis Situations

There will come a time in the life of every audit committee when it will have to deal with events that are out of the ordinary. Most of the time, hopefully, these events will be relatively minor ones that can be addressed discretely, though forcefully, by the audit committee and its advisors. Recent history, however, has provided several examples of major events occurring in a number of companies with which a number of audit committees and their advisors have had to grapple — or appear to have failed to grapple — either at all or inadequately. It is these latter events that have found their way onto the front pages of newspapers and forced some audit committees to carry out the task of addressing a crisis in the full glare of public attention.

It is a sobering fact of business life today that audit committees should expect to find themselves in the position of having to deal with extraordinary events. This is a major new development in business life — vastly different from what audit committees might have envisaged even 10 years ago. Clearly, it is a significant result of the spotlight that has been turned on audit committees, which itself is the inevitable consequence of the skepticism that has arisen about the information published by companies. Audit committees must now conduct themselves with this possibility, perhaps probability, in mind.

This chapter will attempt to offer some advice for audit committees that find themselves faced with the task of addressing either a minor or major extraordinary event.

The Dimensions of a Financial Reporting Crisis

The crises that audit committees may need to address will be related to financial reporting, since problems in other areas will be matters to be resolved either by the full board or another of its committees. We define a crisis in financial reporting as regulatory, investor or public criticism of a company's financial disclosures or reporting, including the controls over the information contained in these disclosures. A crisis in financial reporting, however, can quickly move beyond mere "criticism" into litigation, regulatory investigations, loss of investor confidence, or falling stock prices and, in some cases, even criminal investigations.

As an audit committee plans its response to a financial reporting crisis, it should consider the impact the crisis might have on the company's liquidity, financial condition and future viability. Moreover, it should always consider the extent to which the financial reporting crisis may raise questions about the integrity of top management, particularly the CEO and CFO. Figure 18 illustrates the relationship between these issues.

Figure 18 | **Assessing the Impact of a Financial Reporting Crisis**

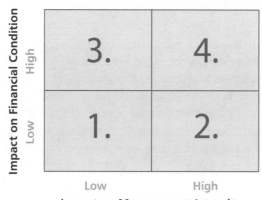

In the first quadrant are financial reporting crises that likely have little impact on either the company's financial viability or the perceptions about the integrity of management. A restatement of the financial statements of prior periods that results from an imperfect systems installation that was promptly reported and corrected by management, when detected by the external auditor, would fall into this category. The damage to the company's reputation is real and the competence of management might be questioned by disgruntled shareholders. Such a financial reporting crisis, however, is not likely to raise questions about top management's integrity.

In the second quadrant are actual or potential financial reporting crises that are unlikely to impact the company's financial condition but will have a serious effect on perceptions about the integrity of management. Disclosing the use of corporate resources for personal purposes or improperly computed compensation payments made to senior executives are examples of crises that would fall into this category. While these crises would likely have relatively small economic impact on the company, they could raise serious questions about the integrity of senior management. Such disclosures could lead to regulatory investigations, and terminations or sanctions of top management.

In the third quadrant are financial reporting crises that have a serious impact on the company's financial condition, but will not affect perceptions about the integrity of management. A restatement of prior years' financial statements caused by the discovery of unrecorded contracts and commitments in the records of a recently acquired subsidiary is an example of a crisis that would fall into this category. While the integrity of the previous management of the acquired subsidiary would no doubt be challenged, the integrity of the acquiring company's top management would not likely be questioned. The unrecorded contracts and commitments, however, could have a material impact on the company's financial condition.

In the fourth quadrant are those extremely serious financial reporting crises that can have a direct impact on both the company's financial condition and perceptions of the integrity of top management. Off balance sheet partnerships are, unfortunately, becoming a classic example of a crises that would fall into this category. These partnerships often contain some significant contractual arrangements which, when triggered, threaten the company's ability to continue as a going concern. Should senior management officers have a material financial interest in these partnerships and receive significant amounts of money from them, questions would certainly be raised not only about the integrity of top management, but also about the oversight of a board of directors that allowed such arrangements under the company's code of conduct. A financial reporting crisis that falls into this quadrant would likely have the most serious consequences for the audit committee and the external auditor.

The Audit Committee's Role in a Crisis

Generally, extraordinary events will fall into three categories: errors leading to a restatement or a major write-down; events arising from top management fraud; or events arising from or surrounding a liquidity crisis. Each of these events may give rise to a number of differing situations. In some circumstances, management may be offside with the auditor and the audit committee may side with management. In others, management may be offside with the auditor and the audit committee may side with the auditor. The potential for complexity is enormous, especially if one factors in the possibility that within the audit committee itself, there may exist differing views and/or there may be differing views between the company's auditor and the "second opinion" auditor.

The role of the audit committee in these extraordinary situations can be problematic. In what circumstances should it shift from its oversight role to that of crisis investigator? Should it ever make that shift? Does it ever have a positive duty to make that shift? What are the criteria that would compel such a shift? Does the duty that audit committee members owe to the company *qua* director differ from their duty as audit committee members? For example, if the result of the audit committee's investigative work is to sink the company's stock value and thereby imperil the future of the company, wherein lies the duty of directors to the company and its shareholders? Is the duty of the audit committee different if the investigation is internal or external?

When audit committees find themselves having to deal with events that are out of the ordinary, they face a number of other potential challenges that could impact the audit committee's ability to function effectively. How will the committee obtain the information it needs? In responding to the audit committee's requests for information, what is the role of management? Of the external auditor? Of subsidiaries, private and public, and their management? Of divisional management? How does the audit committee evaluate the information it receives? Is the situation exacerbated when either management or the external auditor is under attack? Suppose both management and the external auditor are under attack. How does the committee educate its advisors, both legal and accounting. How should the committee deal with the regulators? How should it deal with the media? How should it deal with the investment community?

The remainder of this chapter will address some of these issues and provide some generic advice with respect to dealing with them. Of course, each audit committee must respond to these questions in the unique circumstances in which the company finds itself. But there is one imperative that is common to all audit committees that are forced to deal with events that are extraordinary: that imperative is to act quickly to formulate a plan.

Responding to a Crisis

The audit committee's plan may — in all probability, will — have to be refined as the work evolves. No audit committee, however, can be effective in addressing extraordinary events without a plan for doing so.

Formulating The Plan

The audit committee should meet as soon as possible after the chairman of the audit committee is apprised of a serious issue or problem. If the chairman of the board has not been made aware of the issue, the chairman of the audit committee should immediately inform him or her, and invite the board chairman to attend the audit committee's emergency meeting. The chairman of the committee should also contact the external auditor to discuss the issue from his or her perspective and to invite the external auditor to attend the meeting. If it is the external auditor who apprises the chairman of the audit committee of the problem, the chairman should contact the CEO and CFO to discuss the matter prior to the audit committee's meeting.

At the meeting, the chairman should report the issue or problem to the committee, and the appropriate members of management should be asked to comment on the situation. The external auditor should also provide the committee with his or her perspective on the issue.

The purpose of this meeting is to discuss and decide on the way in which the committee wishes to proceed. There are a number of issues to consider, which are discussed below.

Retaining Advisors

The first decision is whether the committee should retain its own advisors. If it chooses to do so, the chairman should be empowered to retain the appropriate advisors. In our experience, the committee should begin by retaining an experienced legal advisor to advise the committee on the optimum way in which it should address the issue or problem. In addition to providing the committee with legal advice, such an advisor can also assist the committee in retaining other advisors, foreign or domestic, that may be required. The outside legal advisor should attend all meetings of the audit committee at which the problem is discussed. In most circumstances, it is not prudent for the committee to rely solely on the advice of the company's own internal and external counsel because of the potential for a conflict of interest.

Whether or not the committee should retain another accounting firm to assist it in its work will depend on the issue to be addressed, but the committee should not shy away from taking this step if the circumstances warrant it. The external auditor, however, should be involved in this decision and the views of the external auditor should be taken into consideration.

Role as Investigator

A critical issue for the committee and its advisors is whether or not the committee itself should conduct the investigation, or whether the committee should delegate the investigation to internal audit or other appropriate members of management.

Reporting to the Board

It is very important that the board of directors be kept informed of the plans and the work of the audit committee. Inviting the chairman of the board to attend all meetings is a step in that direction, but the committee, through its chairman, should make it a practice to make a status report to the board as often as may be appropriate.

The committee's crisis response plan should be presented to the board of directors and, if necessary, the board's authorization should be obtained. The plan should also be discussed with senior management and the external auditor.

Detailed Planning and Information Needs

Once the committee has retained its advisors, formal planning for how it will proceed can take place. The committee's plan, developed with the assistance of its advisors, should identify the information it will need to address the issue, the sources of that information, and the timetable for its receipt. It should also address the methods by which the committee will evaluate the information it receives. As soon as it is possible, the committee should also develop a timetable for its meetings to address the crisis.

Setting a Reporting Date

The audit committee should also set a preliminary, but realistic date for its report on the crisis. While this date may have to be moved because it is impossible to predict the way in which a crisis may evolve or the time required to conduct the inquiries, it is a good discipline for the committee to have a reporting date in mind. Of course, the reporting date may not be in the purview of the committee if regulatory deadlines are involved.

Dealing With the Media

In a crisis situation, control of communication with the media is essential. It is helpful if the committee has access to experienced media relations advisors to assist it in this regard. The committee's crisis response plan should address the way in which it will deal — or not deal — with the media.

There may be circumstances in which news releases will be necessary. All news releases should be approved by the audit committee and the board. A media relations advisor should assist the committee in drafting the releases and the committee's legal advisors should review them and any other form of communication with the media or the investment community prior to their release.

Should the media ever have direct access to the committee? Our experience indicates that this would be unwise. There will be circumstances, however, when the committee may wish to correct misinformation in the media. The prudent course of action in such circumstances is to issue a news release.

A Hypothetical Case

Having dealt generically with the steps the audit committee should take when formulating a plan for responding to the crisis it is facing, we believe it will be instructive to pose a hypothetical case to illustrate how an audit committee might respond to a crisis, and formulate and implement its plan of action. In the course of doing so, we will attempt to give some advice on many of the issues that are sure to arise for any audit committee that finds itself responding to a crisis.

We emphasize that it is in times of crisis that the mettle of the audit committee will be subjected to its most severe testing, and that the committee has the highest obligation to act quickly, decisively and courageously, observing and displaying the most rigorous standards of integrity and judgment.

The following case is entirely fictional and is organized in four parts. The first part sets out the facts, the second describes the emerging crisis, the third addresses the full-blown crisis, and the fourth summarizes the audit committee's response to the crisis. At each stage, we describe the issues that the audit committee should consider in determining its course of action, the steps the audit committee should take, and how the committee should implement its decisions.

Part One: The Facts

ABC Company Limited is a construction company that went public 10 years ago. It has consistently posted excellent growth in revenue and earnings. The return to shareholders has been impressive. The CEO is known as a visionary, and is a flamboyant, aggressive and skilled engineer who involves himself actively in major projects and with major customers. He has a reputation for being the "king of the deal". His CFO is a financial genius, known to be ambitious, with a reputation on the street for pioneering new and innovative ways of financing large projects. Government contracts are a significant part of ABC's revenue.

The company has put in place an independent board of directors and the audit committee is composed of an experienced group of dedicated directors who take their roles and responsibilities very seriously.

As part of its duties in implementing the requirements of MI 52-110, the audit committee oversaw the creation and implementation of a "whistle blower" policy. The policy requires any communication of that nature to be directed to the company's corporate counsel who, in turn, must report all such communications to the chairman of the audit committee on a quarterly basis. The chairman has made it a practice to report all complaints, and the recommendations of management for responding to them, to the audit committee.

In the most recently ended quarter, the chairman of the audit committee is advised that three communications were received in response to the company's whistle-blowing policy. The first related to the dismissal of an employee. The second involved pay equity practices for employees working on contracts outside Canada. The third questioned the way in which certain government contracts were obtained. The company's corporate counsel is of the opinion that all three matters are minor in nature and proposes that he should follow up on the first two and ask the CFO to investigate the third.

The chairman of the audit committee recalls some concerns about ABC's controls over revenue recognition that were expressed by the lead audit partner at the last *in camera* session of the audit committee. As a result, he has kept this matter on the agenda of the audit committee, and has asked the external auditors to keep the committee informed.

Commentary

Audit committees must be constantly vigilant for and alert to any signals, information or "red flag" indicators that might indicate serious problems lying beneath the surface. (See Chapter 13, Asking The Right Questions and Chapter 14, The Tough Issues and How to Deal With Them.) Unfortunately, the sources of information for audit committees are relatively few — management, the external auditor and public information about the company and its industry in the business media. Diligent and "educated" audit committees that have a good working knowledge of the business and how it is carried on, and have established relationships with the people who manage the business, may have other sources of information. The "whistle-blower" policy provides yet another source of information.

In determining what action it should take, the audit committee must choose between two risks:
- The risk of reaching a conclusion that a potential problem exists when, in reality, a problem does not exist; and
- The risk of concluding that no potential problem exists when, in reality, one does exist.

In the circumstances of this hypothetical case, the corporate counsel's recommendations require careful attention. The first two reported incidents present some significant issues relating to the company's human resource practices and have possible consequences for the company's reputation. They are, however, unlikely to have significant potential to affect the company's financial statements or to reflect badly on the company's internal controls. As a result, the recommendation of the corporate counsel that he investigate these two matters appears reasonable.

The third matter, however, could be more serious because it does have the potential to affect financial reporting and could reflect on the effectiveness of internal controls. Government contracts are often highly politically sensitive and can have a significant impact on the company's reputation. The process for obtaining them requires compliance with detailed and specific bidding policies and procedures. From an accounting standpoint, the terms and conditions negotiated in the contract could affect the ways in which revenue is recognized and income is reported over the life of the contract. In these circumstances, the chairman and the committee, once having been apprised of the matter, should question whether the CFO is the appropriate investigator.

Part Two: A Crisis Begins to Emerge

From its review of the financial statements, the audit committee knows that government contracts have been an important source of business and growth in the past two to three years. From presentations that have been made to both the committee and the board, the audit committee knows that the CEO and CFO, together with senior sales executives, often actively participate in the final negotiations, including the way in which the contract will be financed. Moreover, the audit committee is aware of the external auditor's concern about the controls over revenue recognition.

In attempting to determine whether the audit committee should accept the corporate counsel's recommendation that the CFO should investigate the matter, the chairman concludes that he and the committee will require more information before making that decision.

ABC Company does not have an internal audit department, so this avenue of investigation and information is not available to the committee.

An audit committee meeting is scheduled to take place within the week. The chairman decides to raise the matter in the *in camera* sessions.

The order in which the *in camera* sessions are held is adjusted so the committee will hear first from management. In that session, the audit committee explores the types of contracts in issue and is informed that they are large contracts with substantial enhancements and "extras" that are awarded after the initial contract. The audit committee asks management to describe the process by which the company secured the contracts, and management informs the committee that there was nothing unusual about the process.

The second *in camera* session is with the external auditor. In that session, the audit committee learns more about the discomfort that the auditor expressed in the previous *in camera* session. The auditor's concerns centre on the involvement of the CEO and CFO, the large sales commission paid by the company on these government contracts, the way in which the contracts are financed, and the way in which the "percentage completion" approach to revenue recognition is being applied at ABC. After considerable discussion, the auditor states that, in his view, an independent investigation of the matter would be appropriate.

In the third *in camera* session for audit committee members only, the committee discusses the direct involvement of the CEO and CFO in these contracts. It concludes that it is inappropriate for the CFO to conduct the investigation because of the CFO's potential to be, or be perceived to be, in a conflict of interest position.

The audit committee decides that the company's corporate counsel, together with the external auditor, should conduct a preliminary investigation. Some members, however, express reservations about the corporate counsel because of his potential to also be in a conflict of interest position. All agree that the external auditor should be involved in order to provide accounting and internal control expertise to the investigation.

The audit committee provides the preliminary investigators with a mandate to review the contracts and facts alleged in, or related to, the complaint and to assess whether any of these facts, if proven to be true, would suggest a violation of any applicable laws or regulations, the company's policies or code of conduct or generally accepted accounting principles. The corporate counsel and the external auditor are instructed to conduct their work quickly, thoroughly and discretely, and to report back to the audit committee at a special meeting, which will be called for the purpose of receiving their report.

In approving this engagement of the external auditor, the committee instructs the corporate counsel to retain the external auditor for this specific purpose in order to establish and protect "privilege" as far as possible. The committee also suggests that the external auditor should be free to ask one of their forensic accountants to assist in the investigation if the external auditor believes this would be helpful.

Commentary

The audit committee is responding in a deliberate and careful manner. It is gathering information from both management and the external auditor, is focusing on the complaint that has the highest potential for affecting the company's financial reporting, and is taking action to ensure that an objective assessment will be made and that the information obtained is protected to the greatest extent possible from being available to other parties at a later date.

It should be noted that the committee's decision is to conduct a preliminary investigation, as distinct from a more formal investigation. By so doing, the committee has moved quickly, and has kept open the option of conducting a more formal investigation should one be required as a result of the preliminary findings.

Part Two Continued: The Plot Thickens

The work of the corporate counsel and the external auditor is well organized and conducted in a highly competent manner. They examine the contracts that were the subject of the whistle-blower's concerns and discover that the contracts involved one of ABC's most senior sales vice-presidents, who was hired specifically to secure government business. The vice-president is very experienced in the way the government works in this area, knows many of the decision makers, has considerable chutzpah, and is known to be skilled at charming government officials. He has a large expense account that is approved by the CEO only, and was paid a seven figure commission on the contracts he was instrumental in securing.

The corporate counsel and the external auditor also discover some troubling documents in this individual's files. The files appear to include several confidential government memoranda and other classified documents, none of which appear to be publicly available. It also appears that these documents had a significant influence on the way in which ABC structured and priced its bid. Moreover, the investigation of the individual's expense reports indicates that considerable sums of money appear to have been spent entertaining government officials, with little or no documentary support. The individual's explanation is that this is what it takes to get the job done.

The external auditor's concerns about certain revenue recognition accounting issues deepens as a result of the investigation.

Just as the corporate counsel and the external auditor are about to report to the audit committee, a leading newspaper runs a feature article alleging misconduct by government employees and the waste of taxpayer dollars on what they describe as highly inflated contracts awarded to ABC.

Commentary

While the newspaper article might or might not have been anticipated, the fact that the audit committee initiated this preliminary investigation promptly was the right thing to do, and should stand it in good stead if a storm of public criticism gathers. The committee should always be prepared for the unexpected.

Part Three: A Full-blown Crisis Develops

Before calling a meeting of the audit committee, the chairman meets with the corporate counsel and the external auditor to discuss their preliminary findings. He also discusses these findings with the chairman of the board. An audit committee meeting is then called to receive and discuss the findings of the preliminary investigation.

Meanwhile, the media controversy escalates rapidly. Questions are raised in the legislature, further exacerbating the situation. There are calls for a public inquiry.

Management is now in full damage-control mode. The CEO releases some public statements that were not discussed with the board, or approved by it or the audit committee. In these public statements, the CEO states that ABC's conduct was proper at all times, in accord with government and company policies, and that his executives acted in accordance with the highest standards of business conduct. He tells the media that he, his executives and ABC Company will be exonerated from all allegations of wrongdoing.

Some of the directors of ABC are concerned that these public statements could actually encourage further investigations, more newspaper articles, greater regulatory scrutiny and civil litigation. All of the directors are worried by the public outcry, and by the fact that the CEO has issued statements without consulting the chairmen of either the board or the audit committee, to say nothing about consulting the board itself. A number of directors ask the chairman of the board to call a board meeting to discuss the situation.

To complicate matters, the CFO informs the chairman of the audit committee that he has received a continuous review letter from the securities commission inquiring, *inter alia* about the company's revenue recognition policies. The CFO tells the chairman that this is a routine matter and is not in any way related to the controversy over the government contracts.

As the corporate counsel and external auditor prepare to meet with the audit committee, they discover some correspondence that seems to indicate that the CEO and CFO may have a financial interest in a vehicle that was used to finance the contracts in question. They immediately communicate this new information to the chairman of the audit committee. The chairman, in turn, informs the chairman of the board and the two chairmen agree to meet.

The audit committee and the board now find themselves in the eye of the storm. Each day brings new revelations and new allegations. There are calls for the government to take legal action to recover the alleged excessive and improper payments made to ABC. "Where were the directors?" howls the media.

At their meeting, the chairman of the audit committee and the chairman of the board discuss a number of matters:
- Should the board obtain independent legal advice on how it should proceed?
- Should the audit committee now launch a more formal investigation?
- Should the board and the audit committee insist that all statements to the media be reviewed and approved by the board or the audit committee prior to their release?
- How should the board now deal with the CEO and CFO?

The audit committee meets and the chairman of the board attends. Based on the information obtained from the preliminary investigation, the audit committee decides to seek advice from the company's outside counsel, and from a senior partner of another prestigious law firm who has had considerable experience advising boards and audit committees in similar circumstances. The committee authorizes its chairman, in company with the chairman of the board, to meet with the two outside lawyers and to formulate a plan of action.

The two lawyers and the two chairmen meet and agree that the audit committee should now conduct a more formal investigation. The audit committee can either conduct the investigation itself or retain an external investigator, such as an experienced law firm. They decide that, in the circumstances, it would be more appropriate for the audit committee to retain an external investigator who will report to it. This decision is based on the fact that the matter involves government contracts, may potentially involve the CEO and CFO, and the audit committee wants to demonstrate to investors and the public that it has put in place an independent and qualified investigator. At the meeting, it is further agreed that the investigator's task will be to determine whether or not a problem exists, and if a problem does exist what the size and scope of the problem is, who is responsible for it, and what remedial action is needed.

It is also agreed that it is essential that a detailed plan be developed to respond to the crisis, complete with a realistic timetable. While a key element of the response plan will be the conduct of the external investigation, the plan must also address communications with government, securities regulators, investors (especially institutional investors), employees, analysts, and key customers. The two lawyers and the two chairmen decide that all news releases are to be reviewed and approved by the audit committee, and that the company should co-operate fully with any government or regulatory queries. Such co-operation, however, is not to involve any admissions of guilt, wrongdoing or improper accounting unless the audit committee's own external investigators determine that such wrongdoing has occurred and legal advice has been obtained.

Since the investigation is, by its very nature, unpredictable, the lawyers and the chairmen also conclude that the response plan must be flexible and continually monitored and refined.

The chairman of the audit committee calls a meeting of the committee to discuss the proposal that he, with the concurrence of the chairman of the board, intends to make with respect to a response plan. He invites all members of the board to attend the audit committee's meeting, and most directors do so.

The audit committee agrees with the chairman's proposal. But the issue as to whether to retain an outside law firm to conduct the investigation under the supervision of the audit committee or whether the committee itself should conduct the investigation, not surprisingly, provokes considerable discussion.

Some committee members argue that an experienced outside law firm, completely independent from any prior engagements for the company, is invaluable because such a firm brings a wealth of experience to the investigation and its retention helps enormously with the optics by demonstrating that the board is conducting a thorough and impartial investigation. These directors suggest that the law firm engaged to conduct the investigation should be encouraged to retain an independent forensic auditor, with no prior involvement with the company, to assist it in its work.

Other members of the committee, however, argue that retaining an outside investigator could result in the committee losing control over the way in which the investigation is organized and conducted. These directors have observed that such investigations often acquire a life of their own, and the audit committee will not wish to be seen to be interfering with it. They also express concerns about the costs of such an investigation, which they believe will be very, very high. They question whether the benefit is worth the cost.

The chairman argues that whenever the committee learns about a potential material wrong-doing involving senior management and affecting financial reporting, it has a duty to investigate and report to the board. He states that there is sufficient evidence from the preliminary investigation to suggest that independent, specialized expertise and objectivity in the investigation are essential. He also expresses his conviction that conducting a thorough and completely independent investigation will be viewed positively by the street, the regulators, government and key customers and is in the best interests of the company, its shareholders and directors.

After much discussion, the committee agrees with the chairman and unanimously adopts the proposal to launch a formal investigation conducted by a third party. The committee states its expectation that the law firm selected to conduct the investigation should be retained by the committee, should report to the committee and that the ability to establish privilege should be maximized. The committee also states that the law firm should not have had any prior involvement with ABC, must have the requisite investigatory experience and must have a high degree of credibility with the securities commission and the government. Furthermore, the committee states that the law firm should have the ability to retain forensic accountants other than the external auditor to assist it in the investigation.

The chairman of the board, having consulted with all the members of the board, authorizes the audit committee to proceed as proposed.

The chairman of the audit committee reminds the committee that, while the purpose of the investigation is to determine whether any unlawful activity or any improper financial reporting has occurred, the committee and the board have an obligation to take remedial measures should such be indicated, and should be prepared for that possibility. These measures might include: disciplining or terminating culpable employees; modifying and enhancing existing company policies, or developing new policies; enhancing internal controls; and identifying any loss to investors and others, and considering what actions might be required in this regard.

The committee instructs the chairman to identify and retain the appropriate law firm to conduct the investigation. It adopts the response plan, recognizing that the plan will likely have to be refined and modified as the investigation moves forward and events occur. The committee also decides to retain its own legal advisors.

Commentary

The audit committee has now moved from the board's normal governance role of overseeing and monitoring management to investigating management, first through a preliminary investigation and then through a more formal investigation. Some might argue that the audit committee should not move across the governance/management divide. Under the circumstances in which this audit committee has found itself, we believe that it had no other choice.

In the past, an audit committee would have retained an external investigator only in exceptional circumstances. Today, especially in the United States, an external investigation is becoming the norm. As a few commentators have observed, it appears that we are now living in an era of special investigations.

Audit committees should be aware that such investigations can shift quickly from focusing on "what is the problem?" to "we must now look for all other potential problems". This can result in a very broad inquiry. They should also be aware that investigations of this type have become much more adversarial in nature. As a result, the investigation can have a significant effect on employee morale and may result in the company having to respond to employee requests for independent legal advice.

Where are the CEO and CFO? The reader will have noticed that the CEO and CFO do not appear to be part of this process. Why?

The preliminary investigation indicated that these officers might be directly involved in the problem and might have obtained personal financial benefits through the financing of these contracts. The committee does not yet know what the actual involvement of these officers might be, or whether they have acted improperly or not. In these circumstances, we believe that both the CEO and CFO should be isolated from the investigation process itself, although they will be required to co-operate fully with it and will be expected to provide any information the investigator may request. It is likely that the CEO and CFO will retain their own legal advisors, which, while it is prudent for them to do so, may cause additional complexity with respect to the investigation.

Part Four: Preparing for the Investigation

Following the audit committee's retention of a law firm to act as its independent investigator, the committee selects a senior executive to support the law firm's investigatory work. This individual, after consultation with the independent law firm's investigator, prepares a number of communications that:

- Advise all employees that the investigation is taking place and that employees are to co-operate with the investigation. After much discussion with the investigator and the chairman of the audit committee, a decision is taken not to include in this communication that employees who refuse to co-operate will be disciplined or, possibly, terminated. The discussion included the following questions: should employees who don't co-operate be disciplined and terminated? If they will be subject to sanction, why should this fact be omitted from the communication?
- Instruct all relevant employees to preserve all paper documents and electronic files within their control.
- Instruct the chief information officer to preserve all e-mails and instant messages and to arrange for electronic mail to be copied onto a searchable hard drive.
- Announce the appointment of a document custodian to collect paper documents from the appropriate employees and maintain a record of the document collection process.
- Prepare a certificate of compliance with the documentation instructions to be signed by employees.
- Instruct all employees not to talk to the media, as the company has appointed a spokesman who will speak on its behalf.

The individual assigned to support the investigation also arranges a special education session for members of the law firm and its accounting advisors to brief them on the company, its business, industry, etc. The purpose is to provide the investigators with background and information as they begin their investigation.

Commentary

The effectiveness of the investigation will depend to a large extent on the quality of the planning preparations, the choice of the investigating body, the internal and external communication of the process to be followed and the choice of the person who will support the process.

It is essential that the audit committee and the investigating law firm clearly agree on and articulate the role that each will play. The audit committee must make its expectations of the investigation clear and must clearly understand the manner in which the investigator will approach the investigation. For example, some firms conduct these investigations in a highly adversarial fashion. Although this approach can be very threatening to those who must respond to requests for interviews and for information, and can sometimes be counter productive, the investigator must have the freedom to conduct a thorough investigation.

Companies and their executives should always be aware that an examination of e-mails will feature prominently in the investigation. A note of caution to all e-mail senders and respondents.

The Investigation

We leave the reader to speculate on the outcome of this hypothetical investigation. We can state, however, that such an investigation will follow its own course. Interviews will be conducted both internally and externally. Paper and electronic documents will be reviewed and e-mails will be examined. Status reports will be made to the audit committee at various intervals.

We cannot emphasize too strongly the need for the audit committee to maintain open and effective lines of communication with the investigator. The committee should always be aware that the investigator is appointed by the committee and is accountable to it and should conduct itself accordingly. For its part, the investigator must conduct a thorough and objective examination of the matter, but be sensitive to the relationship it has with the committee.

The chairman of the audit committee must take a leadership role in creating and implementing the response plan and in overseeing the conduct of the investigation. The chairman will be the chief point of communication between the committee and the investigator and should request frequent status reports from the investigator. After each report is received, the chairman must decide whether a meeting of the committee is required and, if so, call one. Audit committee members should expect to be called to frequent meetings, and sometimes on short notice. The time demands on the chairman and the committee members are likely to be significant.

There are implications for the external auditor throughout this process. First, the external auditor will be a significant contributor to the investigation. Second, the investigation may have an impact on the ability of the external auditor to complete its usual work and to issue its reports on the quarterly or annual financial statements. In the facts of our hypothetical case, the accounting for these contracts may become an issue, in which case the auditor may not be in a position to form an opinion on the financial statements until the investigation is complete. Nor can the CEO and CFO certify the financial statements and the MD&A. Hence, the audit committee will not be in a position to approve the financial statements, or recommend their approval to the board.

There may be nothing that the audit committee and the external auditor can do about this. They must await the results of the investigation.

Reporting

Once the investigation is complete, the investigator will issue its final report to the audit committee. In its turn, the audit committee will report to the board. It may be efficient to invite the board to attend the meeting of the audit committee at which the final report is received. The committee must then decide whether or not the report should be made public. Sometimes, there is little choice, especially if the issue has become the subject of significant media attention and regulators are of the view that the report should be disclosed. Much will depend on the nature and the facts of the crisis that the committee is dealing with. In our hypothetical situation, the committee may well decide to make the report public.

Developing a Generic Response Plan

The discussion in this chapter, including the hypothetical case, illustrates the many complex considerations facing an audit committee at a time when it must respond quickly to an emerging crisis.

Although the specific nature of the response will depend upon the unique circumstances in which the committee and the company find themselves, the existence of a generic response plan will better position an audit committee to react more quickly and with greater certainty in a crisis. Developing a generic response plan in advance provides the audit committee with time to make important decisions in an atmosphere free of the complications created by a breaking crisis.

The chairman of the audit committee and the chairman of the board should collaborate on the generic plan proposal to be put before the audit committee. The generic plan should focus on:

- The way in which the specific crisis response plan is to be developed;
- How experienced outside legal advisors will be identified and retained;
- The processes used for communications during the crisis, including the way the company will deal with the media, regulators, investors and employees;
- Steps to be taken to ensure the retention of documents important to the investigation;
- Instructions to be provided to management regarding the required consultation with the audit committee and the board in their damage control efforts;
- Steps the audit committee will take if it does not agree with the position of the external auditor;
- Steps the committee will take in situations when management and the external auditor are in disagreement;
- The roles of the chairman of the audit committee and the chairman of the board during the crisis;
- The nature of the audit committee's reporting to the board during the crisis and any investigation.

In Summary

Conducting an investigation is challenging, time-consuming, and expensive. Moreover, it calls for resolve on the part of the audit committee. Swift and decisive action is essential. This is true not only for the conduct of the investigation but also, and very importantly, for the remedial steps that must be taken as a result of the investigation. The board and the audit committee must understand that their actions will be highly influential in shaping the future tone at the top.

Key Messages

- *In today's environment, audit committees should seriously consider creating a generic plan of procedure (as opposed to a response plan), in the event a crisis does arise.*

- *The audit committee should be alert to any "red flags" or other indicators that trouble may be in the offing. In this regard, the external auditor can be helpful, especially if the right relationships have been created among the audit committee, the external auditor and management, and the audit committee has educated itself about the business and the people that manage it.*

- *The actions taken by the audit committee in the initial stages of any crisis will have a significant effect on how the investigation and resolution of the matters in issue will play out in the public arena and internally.*

- *There is no perfect response plan. Each response plan will have to be tailored to the fact situation and the nature of the crisis with which the audit committee must deal.*

- *Not all crises can be avoided, even by the most diligent audit committees. Audit committees that are diligent, have knowledge of the business and how it is carried on, know the senior management, have put in place the right relationships among the committee, the external auditor and management, and have the appropriate relationships with the other committees of the board, will have a better chance of anticipating a potential crisis and taking steps to manage it effectively.*

- *There will always be a difficult balance to maintain between undertaking preliminary investigations of too many minor issues and not investigating enough to prevent a major crisis.*

Opportunities for Audit Committees in Smaller Public Companies

When a company issues securities to the public, it has to comply with the various regulations of the securities commissions and the listing requirements of the stock exchanges. It also assumes a greater degree of public accountability for its actions than it had while it was a privately-owned company and, therefore, must address corporate governance issues.

Ensuring that smaller companies have access to capital and increasing the confidence of investors in the performance and reporting of smaller public companies is an extremely important public policy issue for Canada. It is also a challenge — at both the macro and micro levels.

Smaller public companies have struggled with the issues of effective corporate governance. In 2001, Deloitte conducted a survey for the Canadian Venture Exchange, which provided a snapshot of board practices at smaller companies listed on the CDNX. Some of the survey findings were:

- More than 86 per cent of respondents had no succession plan for senior management;
- Almost three-quarters had a chairman who was also a member of management;
- 65 per cent of boards did not have a definition of an independent director;
- A large majority had no written job descriptions for board members, no code of conduct for directors and no education program for new directors;
- 84 per cent of boards never had the independent directors meet separately as a group.

However, on a somewhat more positive note, two-thirds of the companies said it would be helpful to have corporate governance guidelines that apply to the CDNX, but more than half said they did not want to disclose their practices on an annual basis.[1]

---

[1] A commentary on this survey can be found in "Small firms lack governance: survey Most don't have code of conduct for board" by Richard Blackwell in the Globe and Mail, June 27, 2001. The survey findings can be obtained on the CDNX website — www.cdnx.com.

Unfortunately, smaller companies are sometimes perceived as wanting the benefits of other people's money without the obligations that go with it. We believe sound corporate governance practices and effective audit committees can be implemented in smaller public companies and these practices should not be viewed as a "technical compliance exercise" but one that will help build investor confidence.

In general, we believe that public companies, whether large or small, should be held to the same standards. This is especially true of their audit committees.

Exemptions for Venture Exchange Issuers

MI 52-110 exempts audit committees of venture issuers from the requirements pertaining to the composition of the committee and its reporting obligations.[2] As a result, the members of a venture issuer's audit committee are not required to meet the independence or financial literacy requirements (these requirements are discussed in Chapter 7, The Right People).Venture issuers must, however, comply with the other requirements of MI 52-110, and provide, on an annual basis in their AIF, some alternative disclosure as set forth in Form 52-110F2.[3]

Although venture issuers are not required to meet the independence or financial literacy requirements imposed by MI 52-110, we believe there are many advantages for them in doing so. It is our opinion that independent and financially literate directors add great value to smaller and larger companies, and we encourage venture issuers to seek directors with these qualifications to sit on their audit committees.

The Challenge for Smaller Public Companies

To be successful as a public company and to achieve the benefits that this brings, smaller companies must attract analyst attention, generate ongoing investor interest in their performance and build market confidence in their reporting. This is a critical issue for smaller companies and for many it represents a significant challenge.

The consolidation of the brokerage industry, the increasing size and significance of institutional investors and the geographical diversity of Canada compound that challenge. Smaller companies complain that there are fewer people undertaking investment research and that investment decisions are concentrated in a relatively few large organizations, which negatively impact smaller companies' ability to gain access to the capital markets and to generate investor interest in the shares of their company. Smaller companies believe that analysts and institutions are focused primarily on larger companies and give little time and attention to following and researching the smaller companies.

---

[2] MI 52-110, Audit Committees, Part 6.1.
[3] A copy of Form 52-110F2 is included in Appendix B.

We believe that an effective audit committee can play a valuable role in helping the company solve these challenges. In fact, we suggest that such a committee can be an extremely valuable asset to smaller public companies. The purpose of this chapter is to provide some thoughts and ideas on how smaller public companies can develop effective audit committees.

The Role of the Venture Capitalist

Venture capitalists are a very important source of capital for new companies. They also provide financial and management expertise for companies that they believe have the potential to become successful public companies. This expertise often complements the owners' business experience, which is often focused in areas such as innovation, research and development, production or marketing.

Venture capital funding is remarkably localized in Canada. Most venture funding is invested in firms located within 400 kilometres of the venture capitalist and, on a per-capita basis, there is less venture capital funding in Canada than in the United States. For example, emerging companies in Massachusetts are reported to receive four to six times the venture capital funding that Ontario companies do.[4]

It has been argued that this restriction in venture capital funding in Canada, together with its localized nature, makes it necessary for Canadian companies to "go public" faster than their American counterparts. This creates more pressure for Canadian smaller public companies to attract and sustain an analyst following when they go public, which in turn creates an imperative to ensure investor confidence in the company's financial reporting.

During the melt down of the technology sector, the venture capitalist community was criticized for hyping the stock of the companies they invested in and not putting enough focus on things such as business plans, cash flow generation, earnings and the integrity of corporate reporting. Today, many venture capitalists are much more focused on these "back to basics" business issues, and play a more active role on the boards of directors of the companies in which they invest and take a greater interest in their corporate governance practices.

The involvement of venture capitalists on the boards of the companies in which they invest has many positive features, but their participation gives rise to some concerns. Many venture capitalists are stretched very thin, in terms of the numbers of private and public company boards on which they sit, which often limits their effectiveness as directors. Their participation can also create more conflict of interest situations especially when these companies undertake transactions with other companies in which the venture capitalist has a financial interest.

[4] "21st Century, Companies Must Be In An Environment That Fosters Invention", Brian Silverman, National Post, May 27, 2002, page 9.

There are also challenges when the venture capitalist sits on the board of a company after it goes public. As long as the company is privately held, the interests of both the venture capitalists and the owners coincide. When the company goes public, however, there are public shareholders to consider, and there is a need for broader accountability and enhanced corporate governance practices. Once a company goes public, the importance of having independent and financially literate directors and an independent and highly qualified audit committee is critical to their credibility.

In summary, venture capitalists can play an important role in helping to finance emerging companies and in providing managerial expertise. Their contribution to corporate governance issues and their participation on the board, however, should not be considered as a substitute for qualified independent directors or a rigorous audit committee.

Building Confidence in Financial Reporting

Many people have expressed the view that compliance with the recommend changes in governance practices and the more stringent requirements for audit committee practices may be more costly and difficult for smaller public companies to achieve. In smaller public companies, resources are more limited, making compliance with these new standards more difficult.

We share this concern, but suggest the objective of continually enhancing investor confidence in the company's financial reporting is extremely important for both large and small public companies. Today, any suspicion about the integrity of a company's financial reporting can have serious repercussions. For a smaller public companies trying to establish themselves in the capital markets, any such concerns can be disastrous.

Mark's Work Wearhouse is a good example of a company that used quality financial reporting to differentiate itself and gain recognition in the capital markets. Mark's was a small retail company headquartered in Calgary. Soon after becoming a public company, its management and board decided that Mark's would establish a reputation in the marketplace for the comprehensiveness and quality of its corporate reporting. Mark's focused not just on the financial statements, but on the annual report and on its corporate governance practices. The company won numerous awards for the quality of its annual reports and corporate governance practices, and in so doing, became recognized across Canada's investing community, adding to the value of the Mark's Work Wearhouse brand. Today, Mark's is a thriving part of Canadian Tire Corporation.

Some Cautionary Notes

The financial reporting of smaller public companies has traditionally been perceived by analysts and the capital markets as being more "error prone" than that of "large cap" companies. Correcting this perception should be a priority for the CFO, CEO and audit committee of every smaller company. The following are four areas that deserve focus and attention:

1) *Senior management override* — Unfortunately, many entrepreneurs tend to run their companies after the IPO in the same manner as they did when the company was private. When companies are privately held, the entrepreneur often has considerable flexibility with respect to issues such as internal control, risk management and tax planning. In a private company the owner-manager is all-powerful, and accountable only to himself or herself, since the owner-manager ultimately bears the risk. In a public company, the entrepreneur must ensure that his or her actions are always taken in the best interests of all shareholders. Investors are very suspicious of entrepreneurs who appear to run their public companies as if they were still private companies.

2) *Revenue recognition problems* — A smaller public company is often under great pressure to gain recognition as a "high growth company", which can result in pressure to report consistent increases in significant revenue growth. Issues around revenue recognition (recording revenue that is not yet earned) are common and lead to many of the accounting problems and restatements that have occurred. Many analysts believe that smaller public companies don't have the internal policies or resources to prevent these problems from occuring.

3) *Inadequate systems and controls* — Rapidly growing companies often outpace their accounting and administrative systems leaving them exposed to errors in financial reporting. Today, however, information technologies and integrated software packages provide smaller companies with cost effective solutions to these challenges that, in the past, were only available to larger companies, providing the smaller companies have appropriate systems installation and migration planning processes to benefit fully from these packages.

4) *Inadequate focus on earnings and cash flow* — In the hey-day of the "tech bubble", many small and not so small technology companies downplayed the importance of generating cash and profitability. Those days have passed. Today, investors are more focused on the company's financial reporting, and smaller companies must be responsive to those expectations. The MD&A and financial statements should clearly explain the company's results and how they are aligned, or not aligned, with the company's published strategy, capabilities and published guidance (if any).

Independent and financially literate directors and an effective audit committee can be a valuable resource to companies in addressing these and other concerns. Smaller companies should be encouraged to recruit experienced directors who can act as mentors and assist them in enhancing the integrity of their financial reporting. An independent and effective audit committee, supported by an independent external auditor, will generate confidence in the investors that they can rely on the information provided by the company.

Preparing for the Initial Public Offering (IPO)

We do not believe that a company should wait until the IPO to establish effective corporate governance practices, including an independent audit committee. The entrepreneur, together with the venture capitalist and investment advisors, should put in place an independent board and audit committee before the IPO is taken to the market. The independent board and audit committee can help guide the IPO process and ensure that the required financial reporting practices, for example formal quarterly reporting, are established and implemented before the IPO. This will generate greater confidence in potential investors and make the IPO more attractive. It will also help ensure that the company's financial reporting and governance practices do not "crash and burn" in public view immediately after the IPO.

A qualified audit committee can play an important governance role in the IPO process and in the review and approval of the prospectus and the regulatory filings. The audit committee should approve the appointment of the external auditor, and have a voice in the appointment of outside legal advisors, investment advisors and other specialists — including the terms and conditions of their respective appointments. The audit committee should also approve their reporting relationships and state what information or reports it expects to be provided directly to the committee by these external advisors.

Applying the Effectiveness Framework in Smaller Public Companies

The following sections of this chapter provide some thoughts and guidance on how the framework for an effective audit committee can be applied in a smaller public company. For a more detailed discussion of these matters, see chapters 5 through 10.

Doing the Right Things

It is just as important for the audit committee of a small public company to have a clearly articulated charter describing its role and responsibilities as it is for a large company. Its charter will often be shorter and simpler than that of a larger company, because the business, control and reporting issues that its audit committee has to consider in defining its role are less complex. The same process followed by the larger companies in creating their charters should be followed by smaller companies (as discussed in Chapter 5, Doing The Right Things). Smaller companies should resist the temptation to merely copy the charters of other companies, as this will prevent them from creating a cost effective and appropriate charter tailored to their circumstances.

We also believe that smaller companies can derive a huge advantage in terms of enhancing investor confidence from the disclosure of their audit committee charters.

Getting the Right People

We believe that an independent and effective audit committee can be a valuable resource and strategic asset for smaller public companies. As discussed earlier, we strongly recommend that smaller companies should adopt the same requirements for independence and financial literacy as required for larger companies. Moreover, smaller companies should focus their efforts on recruiting experienced directors.

It has been suggested that the recommended corporate governance reforms and new audit committee requirements may make it more difficult for smaller companies to attract qualified and experienced directors, especially those willing to serve on the audit committee. In our experience, smaller companies can be successful in recruiting the directors they want, especially if they are made aware of the actual extent of the qualified director pool. Establishing a genuine and sincere commitment to integrity in the operations of the company and in its financial reporting will likely be very important to potential directors who are concerned about legal liability.

Many smaller public companies have used stock options as a method of compensation for both management and directors — an attractive method of remuneration since many smaller public companies have limited cash resources. While they are often controversial, in the circumstances of smaller companies the use of stock options is often appropriate, providing there is full disclosure of the options granted to each director and the compensation plan is presented to the shareholders for their approval.

The quality of the directors who serve on the boards and audit committees of smaller companies will be scrutinized more carefully than in the past. Investors will likely be more cautious about small companies with boards that are comprised of a significant number of management directors and where outside directors have close ties to the company, its founder or venture capitalist. The challenge for smaller companies is not the investment they will have to make in attracting qualified directors and establishing an effective audit committee, but earning a return on this investment.

Managing Relationships

In addition to managing its relationships with the board, management and the external auditor, audit committees of smaller companies (more particularly, the chairman) must also be prepared to work with the venture capitalists. The audit committee's role may also include serving as a mentor to the CEO and CFO, particularly when these executives do not have extensive experience in managing public companies. The external auditor can be a significant source of assistance in this process.

Doing the Right Things Right

Setting the priorities, developing agendas and preparing information for audit committee meetings may be a less complex task in smaller companies than it is in larger ones, but it is no less important. The chairman of the audit committee, in consultation with the CFO and external auditor, should be able to agree on the agenda and the information to be present-ed to the committee quite easily. While it may be possible to streamline the number of preparatory sessions and *in camera* meetings outlined in Chapter 8, Managing Relationships and Chapter 9, Doing the Right Things Right, the same processes should be followed.

Accountability and Striving for Continuous Improvement

As is the case in larger companies, the chairman of the audit committee has a responsibil-ity to report to the board of directors at the board meeting following each audit committee meeting and should assess, at least annually, the ways in which the committee can improve its effectiveness.

While the audit committee's charter must now be disclosed, a description of how the com-mittee has discharged its responsibilities thereunder should be included in the company's corporate governance disclosures in either the annual report or information circular. This is not merely a compliance exercise. The company should view this reporting as an opportu-nity to demonstrate to its investors why they should have confidence in the integrity of the company's financial reporting.

There is no doubt that smaller public companies face many challenges in building investor confidence, attracting qualified directors and establishing effective governance practices, including effective audit committees. It is also clear to us that an effective audit committee can be a valuable asset to smaller public companies in building investor confidence in their financial reporting and enhancing their image in the capital markets.

Key Messages

- Adopting a "beyond mere compliance" approach to the role of the audit committee in smaller companies should increase investor confidence and make it easier for the company to attract qualified directors.

- Smaller companies must guard against the "red flag" issues that will undermine investor confidence: senior management override, revenue recognition problems, inadequate systems and controls, and inadequate focus on earnings and cash flow.

- Implementing effective corporate governance process, including an audit committee, before the IPO, will help generate investor confidence and make the IPO more attractive.

- While the business, control and reporting issues of smaller companies may be less complex than larger ones, their audit committees should follow the same processes for establishing a charter and discharging their responsibilities.

- Smaller companies should focus on recruiting experienced outside directors whose presence will help boost investor confidence.

Capital Market Reform:
Late Breaking News

On October 29, 2004, the CSA released proposed governance guidelines (National Policy 58-201, "Corporate Governance Guidelines") and disclosure requirements (National Instrument 58-101, "Disclosure of Corporate Governance Practices").[1] Also on that date, regulators in the participating jurisdictions proposed amendments to MI 52-110, "Audit Committees".[2] On November 22, 2004, the Government of Ontario introduced legislation to provide civil liability for secondary market reform disclosure.

This book was just about to go to print on October 29. In order to discuss these new initiatives, while also respecting our publishing deadline, we deemed it more efficient to do so in a new chapter, rather than to revise those sections of the book that had already been written. This chapter, therefore, is designed to provide readers with an overview of the new proposals and a sense of their effect, should they be implemented. As of the date of writing, the CSA had not indicated when the new requirements would take effect.

Proposed Governance Guidelines and Disclosure Requirements

The CSA issued its governance proposals in the form of a national policy (NP 58-201) and a national instrument (NP 58-101). There is a difference between instruments and policies. In order for an instrument to come into force, a securities commission must submit it to the provincial Minister of Finance for review and approval. Once approved, the rules contained in instruments are mandatory for reporting issuers in that jurisdiction. (National instruments are enacted by securities regulators in all Canadian jurisdictions, while multilateral instruments are enacted only in those jurisdictions that choose to participate.) Policies, on the other hand, do not contain mandatory rules; instead, they contain recommended guidance. Policies do not require ministerial approval to become effective.

[1] NP58-201 and NI 58-101 are presented in Appendix O.
[2] The participating jurisdictions are all Canadian jurisdictions except British Columbia. The proposed amendments to MI 58-110 are presented in Appendix P.

NP 58-201, "Corporate Governance Guidelines" is a policy, and therefore contains proposed recommended practices. NI 58-101, "Disclosure of Corporate Governance Practices" is an instrument and, when finalized and approved by the Minister of Finance, will become mandatory.

With the releases of NP 58-201 and NI 58-101, the CSA has issued proposals that go beyond financial reporting to address the broader issues of corporate governance. The CSA describes these governance proposals as representing the best practices in corporate governance, and companies (with some exceptions) will be required to disclose their compliance with them on a "comply or explain" basis. Should a company not adopt the recommended approach, it will be required to explain how it achieves the same governance objective. Placing the emphasis on disclosure, rather than on the "rule" or recommended approach, is intended to provide companies with the flexibility to tailor their governance practices to their own circumstances while also giving investors sufficient information to assess those practices. The objective of the TSX Guidelines, therefore, has been preserved — namely, to allow pressure from investors to be an effective catalyst for change.

When NP 58-201 and NI 58-101 are implemented, however, they will supersede the existing TSX governance guidelines and governance-related listing requirements. Thus, the TSX will relinquish its historical role as Canada's corporate governance standard setter. To this end, the TSX announced, also on October 29, that it will revoke its own corporate governance policy. In its stead, it will monitor compliance with the proposed governance disclosure rule.

The significance of the move by the securities regulators into the field of pure governance should not be overlooked. Through this initiative, they are becoming more involved in the oversight of boards of directors and of committees of the board. In other words, the securities regulators are now promulgating governance standards. This incursion into the boardroom, coupled with the securities regulators' new and broader investigative and enforcement powers, has important implications for boards and their committees.

Securities regulators will likely be able to enforce corporate governance disclosure more effectively than could the TSX. Failure to provide adequate disclosure in the management proxy circular will be a breach of the securities law, and could expose the company to enforcement proceedings and sanctions. It seems likely that the regulators will use their continuous disclosure reviews to ensure that a company's governance practices actually conform with what that company discloses them to be.

Many Canadian companies recently improved their governance practices to bring them into line with the TSX Guidelines, and have rethought their disclosure of these practices. For those that have not — or those that have not done enough — the proposed disclosure rule will require them to renew their focus on better governance and better disclosure.

NP 58-201 sets out 18 best practices drawn from existing Canadian and U.S. standards, including those of the *Sarbanes-Oxley Act* and the listing standards of the New York Stock Exchange and the NASDAQ Stock Market.

The areas of recommended best practices are described below.

Board Composition and Independence

It is proposed that a majority of the board should be independent. A director is independent if he or she has no direct or indirect material relationship with the company or any subsidiary or parent of the company. This definition of "independence" is based on, though not the same as, the one provided in MI 52-110, "Audit Committees". The definition is, however, consistent with the definition provided in the proposed amendments to MI 52-110 (which are discussed later in this chapter).

If a director is not independent, the company must describe what the board does to facilitate the exercise of its independent judgment in carrying out its duties. It should be noted that this disclosure is only required if a majority of the directors is not independent.

It is also proposed that the chairman of the board should be independent. If he or she is not independent, an independent lead director should be appointed.

NP 58-201 recommends that the independent directors meet regularly *in camera*. Under NI 58-101, the number of such *in camera* meetings held in the past 12-month period must be disclosed. If such meetings are not held, the company must disclose what the board does to facilitate open and candid discussion among its independent directors.

Board Mandate

The proposed policy is that the board should have a written mandate that includes certain specified responsibilities. These responsibilities relate to organizational integrity, strategic planning, risk identification and risk management, succession planning, communications, internal controls, management information systems and corporate governance. It is proposed that the board's mandate should also include the expectations and responsibilities of the directors, including those regarding the review of meeting materials before board and committee meetings, and attendance at meetings. Under the proposed disclosure rules, the board's mandate must be disclosed in the company's information circular. If there is no mandate, the company must disclose how the board delineates its roles and responsibilities.

It is also recommended that the board's mandate should contain procedures by which security holders can provide feedback to the board.

Role of the Board in Integrity

The proposed policy recommends that the board should have an oversight role with respect to the ethical framework of the company. It should satisfy itself about the integrity of the CEO and other senior officers, and should also be satisfied that the CEO and his or her officers have created a culture of integrity throughout the company.

It is also recommended that the board should approve the company's code of business conduct and ethics. At a minimum, this code should address: conflicts of interest; protection and proper use of company assets; confidentiality of corporate information; fair dealing with security holders, customers, suppliers, competitors and employees; compliance with laws, rules and regulations; and the reporting of any illegal or unethical behaviour. The board should also be responsible for monitoring the ongoing compliance with such a code.

Once a company has a written code of conduct, it must file a copy of it and any amendments to it on SEDAR. If the company does not adopt such a code, it is proposed that it will be required to disclose the steps it takes to encourage and promote a culture of ethical business conduct. Should it be determined that a material departure from the code has occurred, the company must treat that occurrence as a material change, as defined under National Instrument 51-102, "Continuous Disclosure".

Board Effectiveness

The proposed policy recommends that there should be a comprehensive orientation program for new directors and continuing education for all directors with respect to the business of the company and the duties of directors. If a company does not provide continuing education for its directors, it is proposed that it must disclose the way in which the board ensures that its directors maintain the skill and knowledge necessary for them to fulfill their responsibilities as directors.

To promote effectiveness, the policy recommends that the board should develop position descriptions for the chairman of the board and the chairmen of each board committee. If no such position descriptions exist, the proposed disclosure rule would require the company to disclose the way in which the board assesses the performance of individuals in these roles.

The proposed policy recommends that the board, working with the CEO, should develop a position description for the CEO that delineates management's responsibilities.

Board Assessments

NP 58-201 recommends that the board, its committees and individual directors be regularly assessed regarding their effectiveness and contribution. If such assessments are not performed on a regular basis, the company must disclose the way in which the board satisfies itself that it and its committees and individual directors are performing effectively.

Nomination of Directors

The proposed policy recognizes that the board should be responsible for nominating directors. In doing so, the policy recommends that the board should consider the competencies and skills it requires, after assessing the skill set that the board currently possesses.

NP 58-201 recommends that the board should appoint a nominating committee that is composed entirely of independent directors to assist it in making its nominations. The nominating committee should have a written mandate that is disclosed in the proxy circular. It also recommends disclosing the operating procedures of the nominating committee. If no nominating committee exists, the company must disclose the way in which the board encourages an objective nominating process.

Executive Compensation

The proposed policy recommends that the board should establish a compensation committee composed entirely of outside directors, and set out its responsibilities in a written charter. This committee should be responsible for reviewing the executive compensation disclosure before it is publicly disclosed, in addition to making recommendations to the board with respect to the CEO's compensation and compensation matters in general. If there is no compensation committee, the company must disclose the way in which the board encourages an objective process for determining compensation.

Venture Issuers

NP 58-201 provides exemptions for venture issuers. They are exempt from the disclosure requirements with respect to the board mandate and position descriptions, and the disclosure of the board's structures and procedures that are put in place to ensure independence.

Disclosure Generally

All of the disclosures described above must be made in the company's management information circular. In addition, the following specific matters must be disclosed in the circular:

• Each independent director must be identified. In the case of directors who are not independent, the basis of the determination that they are not independent must be disclosed;

• Companies must disclose any other public company directorships held by its directors; and

• Companies must identify and describe the function of all of their board committees.

Proposed Amendments to Audit Committee Rules

For the most part, the proposed amendments to MI 52-110 relate to the definition of independence. The proposed definition is based on the one contained in the *Sarbanes-Oxley Act*, and it clarifies certain of the existing provisions while updating others in response to changes that occurred in the U.S. definition in recent months.

The most significant change affects directors who have or have had, directly or through a family member, a relationship with the company's internal auditor or external auditor. Currently under MI 52-110, a director would not be independent if any member of his or her immediate family was an employee or partner of the company's internal auditor or external auditor over the past three years. Given the very broad definition of "immediate family", boards were faced with the prospect of directors not being considered independent because their siblings or in-laws worked for the internal or external auditor. This provision has now been amended so that it applies only to a spouse, minor child or stepchild, or adult child or stepchild who shares a home with the director.

The proposed amendments also include an addition to the companion policy dealing with the independence of shareholders, which are intended to highlight the range of relationships that a company may have with significant shareholders.

Finally, the proposed amendments would extend to venture issuers the disclosure required for TSX-listed issuers regarding the education and experience of audit committee members.

These proposed changes are intended to make the definition of independence in MI 52-110 consistent with that contained in proposed NI 58-101. The definition has also been expanded to more closely match the definition used by both the SEC and the NYSE.

The first step in determining whether or not an individual is independent remains consisted with that of the current MI 52-110. In other words, an individual will be considered independent if he or she has "no direct or indirect material relationship with the issuer". Similarly, the definition of "material relationship" has not changed. The specific situations in which an individual is considered to have a material relationship with the issuer, however, have been expanded. The specific situations that have been changed in the proposed amendments are as follows:

- *Employment with the company's internal or external auditor*: Previously, the restriction included the individual's "immediate family" (spouse, parent, child, sibling, mother- or father-in-law, son- or daughter-in-law, and anyone other than an employee who shares the individual's house). In the proposed amendment, these relationships have been restricted and "immediate family" has been replaced with an individual's spouse, minor child or stepchild, or adult child or stepchild who shares a home with the individual. Furthermore, the circumstances in which the employment by the audit firm of an individual's spouse or child would constitute a material relationship are slightly more limited in the proposed amendments. As in the original instrument, any compensation received from an audit firm by a fixed income partner for prior service with that firm, and which is not contingent on continued service, will not indicate a material relationship.

- *Compensation by the company*: In the original instrument, if an individual or their immediate family member received more than $75,000 in direct compensation from the issuer, they were considered to have a material relationship. The proposed amendments would limit the restriction on immediate family members to those who were employed as executive officers of the issuer.

- *Definition of material relationships*: The proposed amendments would include restrictions on consulting arrangements — i.e., situations in which an individual, their spouse, minor child or stepchild or adult child or stepchild who shares the individual's home accepts directly or indirectly any consulting, advisory or other compensatory fee from the company or any of its subsidiaries.

- *Definition of an issuer*: The proposed amendments would include subsidiary entities and the parent of the issuer in the definition of an issuer for the purposes of determining independence.

It should be noted that British Columbia has adopted its own definition of independence, which will be applicable to those companies that are reporting issuers only in British Columbia. If a company is a reporting issuer in another Canadian jurisdiction as well as in British Columbia, it will be governed by the independence definition contained in MI 52-110.

Civil Liability for Secondary Market Disclosure

In late November, the Ontario Government introduced revised legislation originally contained in Bill 198, which, if passed, would provide a statutory right to sue public companies and their officers, directors and experts when there is false or misleading information (or when required information is not disclosed) in materials that a public company discloses to investors on an ongoing basis. These materials include the company's annual and quarterly financial statements and news releases issued by the company.

Civil liability for secondary market disclosure means that more investors will be able to hold companies legally responsible for the accuracy and completeness of information they provide. Although the securities legislation currently makes it an offence for companies to provide inaccurate disclosure in required documents, the provisions of the new Ontario legislation will give investors the right to bring civil action based on damages suffered from relying on inaccurate information. At present, securities legislation limits the right to sue for inaccurate information to inaccuracies in a prospectus.

Civil liability for secondary market disclosure is not without controversy. Some fear that it will encourage frivolous actions. In response to these concerns, the proposed legislation requires that court approval be obtained before a case can proceed. It also caps the liability of a company or its officers or directors. In the case of companies, the limit sat at either 5% of market cap or $1 million, whichever is greater. For directors and officers, it is the greater of either $25,000 or 50% of annual compensation.

It remains to be seen whether or not there will be a flood of these actions. Irrespective of the efforts to limit the amount of monetary damage, the costs to the company, its officers, directors and experts in defending these actions, even in the court approval stage, are likely to be significant — especially in terms of damage to reputations.

In our opinion, the best defence is a proactive one. The best protection for the company, its officers and directors is effective disclosure controls and effective oversight of these controls by the CEO and CFO (as part of the certification process), the external auditor and the audit committee. The company, its directors and officers should also gain increased comfort with respect to the integrity of financial reporting when management's report on internal control and auditor attestation of this report comes into force.

Continuing Capital Market Reforms

Capital market reforms in Canada can be divided into three phases, and these reforms are the result of pressures applied by the groups illustrated in Figure 19.

Figure 19 | **Three Phases of Capital Market Reform**

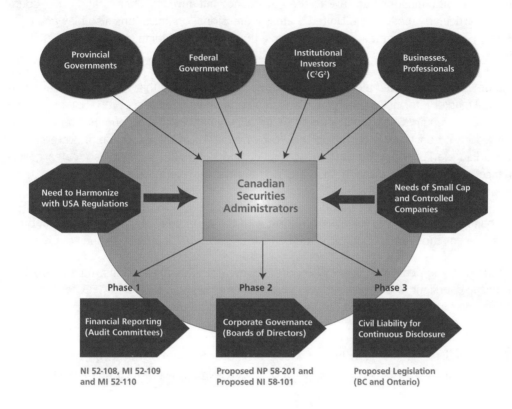

As discussed earlier in this book, the financial and accounting scandals that have occurred recently in the United States and Canada have provided the impetus for reform. These scandals put pressure on politicians to enact enabling legislation, which is the foundation for capital market reform. The regulators, in turn, have issued the rules that comprise these reforms and continue to issue new rules, while also playing an important role in monitoring and enforcing the rules.

Another group pressuring for capital market reform have been the institutional investors, who are exerting more and more influence on corporate governance. The institutional investors' objectives are two-fold: to promote good governance practices and to align the interests of management and the board with those of the shareholders. Increasingly, these investors are making investment decisions in favour of companies that comply with their objectives.

Yet another pressure for reform comes from the business community. Companies that seek to raise capital must be sensitive to the governance initiatives in Canada and other countries, particularly those in the United States. Professional organizations also play an active role in supporting capital market reforms that make Canadian markets attractive to investors.

Figure 19 also illustrates the two conflicting economic realities that are shaping Canadian capital market reform. On one hand, Canadian companies need access to U.S. capital markets, which requires a harmonization of securities regulations and accounting standards so they do not constitute a barrier to the flow of capital. On the other hand, however, the Canadian market's high proportion of smaller and controlled companies creates governance challenges for Canada that are not always the same as the challenges being addressed in the United States.

To balance the pressures for market reform with the economic realities of Canadian business, recent capital market reforms are being introduced in Canada in a series of phases.

The first phase dealt with financial reporting when the CSA released instruments dealing with the oversight of external auditors, audit committees and CEO and CFO certification. These instruments were based on the U.S. *Sarbanes-Oxley Act* requirements, but were adapted to the Canadian market.

The second phase was launched in a series of proposals that moved beyond financial reporting to address the broader issue of corporate governance, which we discussed earlier in this chapter.

The third phase will impose civil liability for secondary market disclosures, which is also discussed earlier in this chapter. Boards and audit committees, together with management, therefore, should now start to address seriously the various secondary market liability issues raised in these proposals.

Capital market reform is an evolving and dynamic activity and the business community has a key role to play in the process. If, however, businesses choose not to become actively involved, they will undoubtedly get the regulatory environment they deserve.

Key Messages

- The securities regulators are becoming more involved in the oversight of boards of directors and committees of the board. The CSA's proposed national policy contains recommended governance best practices, while its proposed national instrument will require mandatory disclosures by companies indicating whether or not they comply with those best practices.

- The CSA has proposed amendments to its audit committee rules to clarify the definition of "independence", align it with the definition proposed in its policy on corporate governance guidelines and more closely match the definition used in the United States.

- Ontario has introduced legislation that will impose civil liability for secondary market disclosure.

- Capital market reforms are ongoing, and the business community has a key role to play in the process. If they choose not to become involved, however, they will be able to blame only themselves if they disagree with the resultant regulatory environment.

Change in a High Risk World

Many investors have lost confidence in the integrity of corporate information, in the integrity of senior management, and in the discipline and rigour applied by boards and audit committees. They have also suffered a loss of confidence in the outside advisors to corporations.

Given the examples of notorious lapses in good corporate conduct that we have seen during the recent past, some loss of confidence is justified. But a few — even several — examples of egregious corporate misconduct should not be taken to indicate a universal problem, despite what the media would have us believe. The vast majority of managements, boards of directors, and external auditors do their jobs well and are diligent about observing high standards of integrity. Unfortunately, the many examples of good governance, good audits, comprehensive and timely disclosure, and effective audit committees are not reported because they are not newsworthy. Even more fundamental is the fact that actions taken by boards, audit committees and auditors to correct inaccuracies in financial reporting prior to disclosure, are intrinsically not discoverable by persons outside the company — and must remain so.

That is not to say, however, that more rigorous corporate governance should not be encouraged. We believe that many of the improvements that have been mandated by new securities law rules both in Canada and in the United States are in the best interests of companies, boards of directors, and the investing public. As we stated in the first edition of this book, we believe that the business community has a positive duty to enhance, continually, the manner in which it governs itself, to clearly demonstrate the integrity of the information it discloses to the investing public, and to increase investor confidence in its processes and standards. An important component of improved and more rigorous governance is, of course, a more effective audit committee.

But we question the intensity of the spotlight that has been turned on corporate governance. Corporate governance is now seen as the key to eradicating management malfeasance and to maximizing value. Blame for almost every corporate scandal is imputed to deficiencies in corporate governance. While in some instances such deficiencies may well be a contributing factor, they are generally not the cause. This focus on the board, by the media and regulators alike, has obscured the fact that boards are only part, albeit an important part, of corporate governance. Boards do not manage and their ability to effectively supervise management, while assumed by many, is not, and cannot be, absolute.

At a time when it is becoming more and more important to have the best possible talent in the boardroom, the intensity of the spotlight that has been turned on the directors, has caused many of the very people who should serve or remain on boards of directors to question whether they are willing to take on the risks of the role in today's climate. While this attitude may be understandable, it will do little to further the cause of better governance. In fact, it has the potential to hinder it. If the pool of available talent shrinks so that companies have difficulty finding skilled directors, governance will suffer.

Similarly, concerns are beginning to emerge in the accounting profession about the attractiveness of auditing in this new environment, and the profession's ability to attract and retain "top talent". Moreover, if the impact of some of the profession's new rules is to restrict the external auditor's role to that of simply policing accounting standards, then a disservice is being done to both investors and the business community. External auditors have a lot more to offer in terms of added value, without compromising their independence, and it is counterproductive to deprive companies of the total value they can provide.

We also question the reliance on rules as the means to improve the oversight of the board. Rules are not enough. They are just the beginning. In our opinion, it would be more effective if the focus was also directed towards encouraging companies to take more care in selecting appropriate persons to serve as directors and to chair the board and its committees, and encouraging them to manage the relationship between the board and management more effectively. We believe that establishing, managing and continually improving the relationship between the "right board" and management will produce more lasting and more rewarding results. Hence, the emphasis in this book on the value of managing relationships between the audit committee and management, between the audit committee and the external auditor, between the audit committee and the board, and between the board and management.

It is not difficult to understand why the focus has centred on rules. Clearly, it is easier to promulgate rules than it is to address the more complex and sophisticated issues involved in relationships between the board and management. Perhaps the more important reason, however, is that it is the regulators, rather than the business community itself, that have seized the lead in attempting to restore investor confidence. Not surprisingly, the regulators both in Canada and in the United States have taken a rules-based approach.

While we believe that well thought out rules are necessary as they form a foundation on which to build the appropriate relationships, rules alone will not get the job done. We are fearful that the emphasis on rules will lead to the triumph of form over substance. For example, in our opinion, independence is an attitude of mind, rather than merely a list of regulator proscribed business connections. And how do you legislate the most important element of a director's duty, judgment? Only a rigorous and demanding approach to selecting directors will result in more directors who display judgment and are independent-minded. Moreover, rules cannot guarantee integrity. We are beginning to observe the emergence of a "tick the box" mentality, and such an attitude will do little to encourage companies to invest properly in the rules themselves in order to create value, to say nothing about providing the incentive to invest heavily in establishing the right relationships.

There is a huge need for more directors who do a better job, sit on fewer boards and who understand and accept that hard work, homework and the investment of substantial amounts of their time is essential. The courage to be a minority of one should be a *sine qua non* when it comes to selecting a director. Being prepared to take unpopular and difficult decisions and positions is an integral part of a director's job, as is being prepared to demand better information from management and its advisors. Needed: directors who are prepared to rock the boat. Therein lies true independence.

The "we are here to support management" philosophy that was so rampant when we began to serve on and advise boards of directors, must give way to a philosophy that can best be stated as: "we are here to hold management and advisors accountable, and while we will not manage, we will form the relationships with management and advisors that will permit us to more effectively fulfill our responsibilities to the shareholders, and that will provide us with an effective platform on which to build the necessary checks and balances that will encourage the highest standards of corporate behavior and corporate reporting".

We would like to sound another note of caution. It has become very fashionable to speak in terms of diversity when selecting directors. But if "diversity" means that persons with little business experience are selected to sit on boards because they bring the "community view" or the "philanthropic view", or simply represent the so-called "minority view", then we have to disagree with the trend. Appropriate business experience is a must when it comes to selecting directors. It is not too difficult to find diversity of business experience, while respecting the imperative of securing the appropriate skill sets that may be required on any individual company's board of directors. Companies can no longer afford to waste a single board seat. Each one must be filled with a director who has the requisite knowledge and experience to contribute to the success of the business.

It is imperative for companies and their boards to derive value from their investment in compliance with the new initiatives. The costs for public companies of compliance with the *Sarbanes-Oxley Act* and the new Canadian securities law directives are soaring and will continue to climb. Companies should use their investment in the new initiatives to improve the management of their businesses.

And there is yet another cost beginning to be felt. While it is an unintended consequence — and, hopefully, one that will be short lived — differences are being observed in the way in which companies go about their business. There appears to be a large measure of risk aversion among CEOs and their boards. Moreover, if they are spending increasing amounts of time meeting the new requirements, they have less time and fewer resources to devote to thinking ahead. Staying on side with the SEC or the OSC is becoming a significant focus. Some board members have reported that they are spending a disproportionate amount of time coping with the new governance rules, rather than spending their available time overseeing the business and planning for its future.

Securities regulators have opted for the "quick fix" of promulgating rules and exercising more and more control over the boardroom. Regulators should recognize that corporate governance in and of itself does not drive market value. An over emphasis on compliance with rules creates a risk of undermining economic growth by reducing risk taking and entrepreneurship.

Two other key issues have been overlooked in the past, but are now beginning to be addressed. The first issue is the importance of having a culture of integrity and the right values embedded in a public company, and, in particular, in its CEO. Statements of values endorsed by the board and the CEO are common today, but the real test is the actual practice of those values, reinforced every day by the actions of the CEO and the management team. CEOs and senior managers lead by example and inappropriate, inconsistent actions by leaders, tolerance of such behaviour in other employees, and reward systems that reinforce such behaviour, will inevitably lead to the kinds of excesses and problems we have all recently witnessed.

The second issue is that the board and its committees must rely on the information they receive through the CEO. This dependency can be mitigated if the appropriate relationships have been created between the board and management and if the directors have spent time educating themselves about the business or businesses being conducted by the company, and becoming acquainted with the senior managers. One advantage of creating these relationships is that doing so expands the sources of information available to the directors. It is critical, however, that the CEO be committed to an open and candid sharing of information, whether good or bad, with the board and that he or she be prepared to demand the same candidness from the CFO and the senior management team in their dealings with the board. It is equally critical that the board make its expectations in this regard very clear, and that it be prepared to hold management to account should its expectations not be met.

Problems can arise when the CEO and the senior managers withhold or filter information to the board. Serious situations can arise if this is excessive and the true picture is hidden from the board until it is too late. Boards should have a zero tolerance for such behaviour.

Fear of reprisal within a company, combined with the wrong culture can make it difficult for middle management, and, indeed, members of the senior management team to speak out if they see major problems or risks that have not been disclosed to the board. Establishing a culture of integrity and the right value systems will be more effective than rules alone in encouraging people to tell the truth and to give early warnings when these are warranted.

The perspectives of the external and internal auditors can be valuable to the board and the audit committee as they assess the company's culture and the information provided by management.

The good news is that these issues can be addressed productively and effectively if the board, management and the external auditors have got their relationship right. The bad news is that managing relationships is hard work and very time consuming. All the new governance rules in the world will be inadequate to protect the company and its directors and its shareholders if the company's real culture is inappropriate or dysfunctional.

Assuming a Leadership Role

In the first edition of this book we urged the private sector to assume a leadership role in improving governance and disclosure practices and communicating their initiatives to the investing public. We said then, and continue to believe today, that market regulation is preferable to government regulation. Events may have overtaken us, but that does not mean that the private sector does not continue to have a significant role to play in shaping its future destiny.

The risk for the business community of not taking a prominent leadership role in improving its governance and disclosure systems, both in terms of their credibility and integrity, is that government will be pressured to introduce even more rules, accompanied by greater enforcement measures. It is business itself that must be seen to be taking the steps necessary to restore confidence in the credibility and integrity of corporate information. It is not, however, sufficient for a company to simply disclose its commitment to this. It must also disclose the commensurate action that it is taking to continually improve its governance practices, and to foster a culture of accountability. This, together with stringent enforcement of the rules, will be very effective in restoring investor confidence.

There is yet another obligation for business. It should not hesitate to speak out when it believes that the rules that are proposed are not well thought out, or when it believes that the existing rules should be reconsidered. If business is apathetic, it will deserve the regulation it gets.

At the same time, we urge boards of directors and management not to lose their focus and perspective as they strive to enhance their governance practices and to improve the integrity of their financial reporting. The struggle to keep up with the plethora of unprecedented and fast-moving change can take its toll with respect to the time and attention that both boards of directors and management must give to responding to it. The primary responsibility of the board is to manage the company. Boards do this by delegating the day-to-day management to professional managers. The goal of both the board and management is to create value for the shareholders. That means managing the business of the company for success. With the increased emphasis on improving governance (and we support better governance unreservedly), boards of directors, and indeed, management, must be careful not to become distracted from their primary responsibility of ensuring that the business is successfully managed, thereby enhancing shareholder value.

We believe enhancing corporate governance and the integrity of corporate reporting will produce more successful companies. While good governance cannot and should not prevent companies from taking business risks that may prove to be unsuccessful, good governance can ensure that the business risks they do take are properly assessed and managed. A company's success is determined primarily by the quality of its management. Good governance focuses on the quality of that management, on management's accountability to the board of directors and through them to the shareholders, and on the quality of management's reports to investors. When there is good governance, accountability, and transparent reporting there is no place for an under-performing management to hide. There is no place for a management group that acts primarily in its own self-interest. There is also no place for a management that displays a lack of integrity.

We urge regulators and politicians to proceed with some caution in initiating new measures. Understandably, they will be under pressure to introduce more and more initiatives. In so doing, however, they must be careful not to over-burden companies with excessive, overly complex or unnecessary regulation. It is important that regulators constantly monitor the cost and effectiveness of their initiatives, both new and old.

Canadian companies must be particularly vigilant to retain their focus on creating shareholder value. They operate in an increasingly competitive North American market. They struggle with productivity issues as they compete for capital and the best people. They face large research and development challenges and operate in a high tax, high entitlement environment. Therefore, Canadian companies cannot afford to be distracted from their primary purpose for too long. If they do, shareholder value may well be adversely affected. And in today's environment, it is imperative that they strike a balance between appropriate responses to the plethora of changing standards that govern their activities and keeping the principal focus on the successful management of the business.

Future corporate failures cannot be eliminated. The best that governance can achieve is to raise the standards of vigilance and scrutiny expected of boards of directors and to hold management to higher standards of integrity, accountability and risk management.

Challenges

Today's environment poses a number of challenges for boards of directors, audit committees and external auditors as they struggle to meet new standards and to improve the ways in which they oversee the work of management.

Perhaps the most obvious challenge is coping with the overwhelming nature of the compliance agenda. The sheer volume and pace of capital market reform has been an enormous challenge for boards of directors, management and the external auditors. This has put a strain on the resources of all three. We believe that this challenge is far from over and will continue to test the mettle of directors, management and the auditors.

Another challenge is the critical need for strong leadership from the board and its committees, especially from the chairmen of the board and the board's committees. Without effective leadership from the various chairmen, the board simply will fail to improve its oversight. Great care, therefore, must be taken in the selection of the chairmen of the board and its committees. Providing the necessary leadership in these roles will require a substantial time commitment, substantial leadership ability and the inclination, the will, and the determination to hold the board and management accountable.

A third challenge is the need to upgrade the quality, skills and commitment of directors. This challenge is far broader than that of ensuring independence from management. The starting point for good governance is to select the right people to serve as directors. More care must be taken with this task. Selection criteria are not about friendship, or about political correctness, but about how the knowledge and experience of a candidate can contribute to the proper functioning of the board. It is about commitment, about the courage to be a minority of one, about devoting the time needed to fulfill one's duties, about integrity, about the courage to ask the difficult questions, and about the persistence to obtain the appropriate answers to those questions. It is also about a commitment to continually upgrade personal knowledge and skills.

A fourth challenge is the need to overcome reluctance to serve on the audit committee in today's climate. The time demands, the number of meetings, the sheer volume and complexity of the briefing materials, the increasingly onerous duties and the ever-present spectre of significant liability, are causing directors to say "no" to service on the audit committee. Overcoming this reluctance poses a challenge for boards, governance committees and audit committees.

Yet another challenge is the issue of compensation, for both management and the directors. Designing effective management compensation programs that reward management appropriately while not encouraging self interested behaviour, or misleading financial reporting, is becoming increasingly important to boards. While these matters are beyond the purview of this book, audit committees must be sensitive to the compensation plans in place for management as they consider a number of issues during the course of their work.

With respect to board compensation, it is now becoming the practice for directors to serve on fewer boards, partly because the time required to fulfill one's duties as a director has increased substantially, and partly because companies are becoming more reluctant to appoint directors who sit on a large number of boards. Moreover, directors' accountability has assumed more onerous proportions, and their exposure to liability continues to increase. All of these factors lead to the inescapable conclusion that directors will have to be paid substantially more. Some significant increases in directors' fees are beginning to be seen. We support this trend and believe it will continue.

A sixth challenge is the fact that business is becoming more complex, accounting standards are becoming increasingly complicated and disclosure requirements are becoming less straightforward. We are concerned that the objective of producing more comprehensive and meaningful financial reporting is being lost in the complexity. The solution may lie in returning to a principles-based approach to corporate reporting rather than relying on detailed and mechanistic rules.

Another challenge is unrealistic expectations. We believe there is an expectation gap between what boards and audit committees can deliver and what the public believes they can. There is no easy way to overcome this challenge. We believe, however, that well articulated and appropriately disclosed mandates for the board and its committees are an important step in bridging this gap. This is particularly true for the audit committee.

A final challenge is one of a public policy nature. The lack of a single securities regulator in Canada and the lack of national securities regulation is both problematic and an embarrassment. Creating a single national securities regulator should be a high priority for the federal and provincial governments. It's time.

The Key Message

All the initiatives being taken by boards of directors today should be focused on enhancing shareholder value by improving corporate governance, corporate reporting and the effectiveness and accountability of management. Only higher standards of governance, greater transparency and a management held to higher standards of accountability can reduce the potential for further egregious examples of corporate misconduct.

This book has been about providing directors with some guidance on the subject of improving audit committee performance. It is a compilation of ideas and techniques that have been tried and found to be effective. It does not pretend to be definitive. Indeed, if we have learned anything in the more than 20 years that we have served on and advised audit committees, it is that the best of them are committed to continuing always to find new and better ways of fulfilling their responsibilities.

But the ideas in this book can and will make a difference. We think of them as the basis upon which effective audit committees are built.

The fundamental thesis behind the ideas and techniques in the book is that more effective audit committees are all about doing the right things, having the right people, doing the right things right, and striving for continuous improvement. Central to these elements of audit committee effectiveness is managing critical relationships.

If relationships among the board, the audit committee, management and the external auditor are managed effectively, the committee will work effectively. As the task of managing these relationships falls squarely on the shoulders of the chairman of the committee, the importance of selecting the right chairman is critical, as is the chairman's commitment to the task. There is no doubt that managing these relationships will take time, effort, courage, persistence and diplomacy. But most of all, it takes leadership.

If this book has a key message, it is this: audit committees, boards of directors and management should accelerate their transition to an environment in which the relationships among them are interdependent.

Much of the focus so far has been on the transition from dependent to independent relationships, hence the attention paid to the independence of directors, the independence of the external auditor, financial literacy, and other structural issues. The real challenge is to move to interdependent relationships, and thus the emphasis in this book, as it was in the first edition, on the importance of developing and nurturing relationships.

As we have said before, the interdependent stage is best described as one in which independent parties work together to better serve the interests of the shareholders. The shareholders' interest is best served when the audit committee, the board and management recognize that the relationship among them is interdependent, since it is only when this recognition occurs that the effectiveness of their activities will be substantially improved. In the interdependent stage, channels of direct and prompt communication are put in place that permit the three parties to inform each other of and discuss matters of concern candidly; trust in and respect for each other's motives and goals is established; positive interaction occurs; accountabilities are clear; and the information flow is facilitated, all of which contributes to the effectiveness of the audit committee's oversight.

An audit committee must start the journey to more effective oversight by clearly articulating its duties and responsibilities, recruiting the right people and the right chairman, doing the right things in terms of the information it requires and the processes it follows, making its expectations of both management and the external auditor very clear, committing itself to self-evaluation and dedicating itself to continuous improvement. Leadership and commitment from the chairman of the committee is critical.

But the single most important achievement an audit committee can make is to lead the way to a recognition and acceptance of the interdependent nature of the relationships that exists among the committee, management and the external auditor. All else flows from this.

Audit Committees:
The Legal Overview

By Carol Hansell[1]

Overview

The legal requirement for public companies to have an audit committee was first introduced in Canada in 1970. For more than 30 years, statutory provisions relating to audit committees remained largely unchanged. However, in the two years since *Integrity in the Spotlight* was first released, the regulatory environment for audit committees in Canada has changed radically. To some extent, change was already underway in Canada prior to the introduction of the *Sarbanes-Oxley Act* of 2002 ("SOX"), but most of the current requirements were adopted in order to align Canadian governance regulation with the rigorous standards imposed under SOX and by the NYSE and NASDAQ.

All reporting issuers in Canada[2] must now have an audit committee, although there are differences in the requirements imposed on audit committees of TSX-listed issuers and other issuers. These requirements relate generally to the composition of the audit committee on the one hand and the responsibilities of the audit committee on the other. There are also disclosure requirements with respect to the audit committee. For the purposes of this overview, a "Listed Issuer" is an issuer listed on a "major exchange", which includes the TSE, the NYSE and NASDAQ.

---

[1] Carol Hansell is a senior partner of Davies Ward Phillips & Vineberg LLP. She is a transaction lawyer, specializing in mergers and acquisitions and is recognized internationally as an expert in corporate governance.

[2] British Columbia is the exception to this statement. British Columbia has not adopted audit committee requirements comparable to those adopted in other parts of the country. For the readers' convenience, this exception is referred to only in this footnote.

Composition of the Audit Committee

The audit committee of every listed issuer must be comprised of at least three directors, each of whom is "independent" (subject to certain limited exceptions).

Individuals who are or have been employed by the issuer or by the issuer's internal or external auditor (and certain family members who are or have been partners of or employed in certain capacities with those entities) are precluded from serving on the audit committee for a period of three years after that relationship ends. The same applies to executive officers of an entity if any of the issuer's executives serves on the entity's compensation committee and to individuals who receive (or whose immediate family members receive) more than $75,000 per year from the issuer (other than for board service). Individuals who are consultants or advisors to the issuer may not serve on the audit committee. The same applies to individuals affiliated with the issuer or its subsidiaries. It is then up to the board to determine whether there are any other relationships between a director and the listed issuer, which should preclude a director from being considered "independent".

Every member of the audit committee of a listed issuer must be "financially literate" or must become so within a reasonable period of time following his or her appointment. "Financially literate" means:

> *The ability to read and understand a set of financial statements that present a breadth and level of complexity of accounting issues that are generally comparable to the breadth and complexity of the issues that can reasonably be expected to be raised by the issuer's financial statements.*

This standard is more rigorous than the U.S. standard, which is found in the stock exchange listing requirements. For example, the NYSE listing standards provide that each member of the audit committee must be financially literate, as such qualification is interpreted by the company's board in its business judgment.

There is no requirement in Canada for there to be financial experts on the audit committee. There is, however, a requirement to disclose the qualifications of each of the members of the audit committee. Listed issuers are required to disclose each audit committee member's relevant education and experience, including any education and experience that would provide the member with:

- an understanding of the accounting principles used by the issuer to prepare its financial statements;
- the ability to assess the general application of such accounting principles in connection with the accounting for estimates, accruals and reserves;

- experience preparing, auditing, analyzing or evaluating financial statements that present a breadth and level of complexity of accounting issues that are generally comparable to the breadth and complexity of issues that can reasonably be expected to be raised by the issuer's financial statements, or experience actively supervising one or more persons engaged in such activities; and
- an understanding of internal controls and procedures for financial reporting.

What Canadian Audit Committees Are Required by Law to Do

The audit committee of every reporting issuer must have a written charter setting out its mandate and responsibilities. The written charter must include the following responsibilities:

- *Supporting the Independence of the External Auditor* — The audit committee must be responsible for:
  - nominating the external auditor;
  - setting the compensation of the external auditor;
  - overseeing the work of the external auditor (with the issuer requiring the external auditor to report directly to the audit committee, although this does not detract from the external auditor's accountability to shareholders of the issuer);
  - pre-approving all non-audit services (subject to certain exceptions, including for *de minimis* services) to be provided to the issuer or its subsidiary entities by the external auditor, although certain delegation of this function is permitted, with reporting back to the audit committee required; and
  - reviewing and approving the issuer's hiring policies regarding partners, employees and former partners and employees of the issuer's external auditor (present and former);
- *Financial Statements and Financial Information* — The audit committee must:
  - review the following before its public disclosure:
    - financial statements;
    - MD&A; and
    - annual and interim earnings news releases;
  - satisfy itself that there are adequate procedures in place for the review of the issuer's disclosure of financial information derived from the issuer's financial statements (and periodically assess the adequacy of those procedures);
- *Whistle Blowing Procedures* — Every audit committee must establish procedures to deal with:
  - complaints the issuer receives about its accounting, internal accounting controls or auditing matters;
  - employee concerns about accounting or auditing matters.

Standards of Performance

In discharging their responsibilities as members of the audit committee, directors are required to act in a manner consistent with two basic duties — the fiduciary duty and the duty of care. These are, of course, the same duties that govern the behaviour of directors in the discharge of their duties — whether in connection with the audit committee or otherwise.

Fiduciary Duty

The fiduciary duty requires the director to act honestly and in good faith, with a view to the best interests of the corporation. As obvious as this standard of conduct seems, honest, well-intentioned directors may fall short as a result of their relationship with persons other than the corporation. For example, a director's fiduciary duty prohibits the director from preferring the interest of any other person to the interests of the corporation. Accordingly, if a director approves a particular accounting treatment to accommodate the wishes of a majority shareholder, the director may have breached his or her fiduciary duty if he or she did not approve that treatment with a view to the best interests of the corporation. Fiduciary duty also brings with it a duty of confidentiality. If the director discloses information acquired in his or her capacity as a member of the audit committee to a third party (including a controlling shareholder), this could under some circumstances constitute a breach of the director's fiduciary duty. It could, of course, also constitute a breach of Canadian securities laws, which prohibit the selective disclosure of undisclosed material information.

Duty of Care

The duty of care requires each director to exercise the care, diligence and skill that a reasonably prudent person would exercise in comparable circumstances. This requires that the director spend the time and apply the resources necessary to make an informed judgment. Directors who are being careful and diligent will ask themselves whether they have the information they need in order to make a decision, consider that information critically and question management and outside advisors closely until they are satisfied with the responses they receive.

How careful and diligent must a director be? The test is what a "reasonably prudent person" would do in "comparable circumstances". The words "reasonably prudent" suggest that directors are not held to a standard of infallibility nor that they must be extraordinarily conservative in their judgments. There is risk involved in running a business. The standard of the "reasonably prudent person" takes this into account. It does, however, require the director to examine the facts and analysis before him in order to achieve a reasonable level of understanding and comfort.

"In comparable circumstances" allows a court to consider all aspects of an impugned decision in determining whether a director has acted in accordance with his or her duty of care. This may include the kind of business carried on by the corporation, the nature of the transaction in question, the relationship of the director to the corporation (for example, whether the director is also a member of management) and the expertise and experience of that director.

Directors are often concern about the degree of "skill" required of them. Will they be criticized for not recognizing a problem that they do not have the expertise to detect? Courts will deal harshly with directors who turn a blind eye to a problem or issue. However, directors are not required to have any particular skill set. They are only expected to apply the skills they do possess for the benefit of the corporation. When a particular skill or expertise is required that they do not possess, they must seek the experience and expertise of others.

Are All Directors Subject to the Same Duty?

Directors are often concerned about whether they will be subject to a different standard if they sit on the audit committee. Although all directors are subject to the same duty of care, two factors may expose audit committee members to greater criticism (and therefore potentially greater liability) than may be the case for directors who do not sit on the audit committee.

The first factor is the skill set that members of audit committees may possess. Changes in governance regulations and best practices have emphasized the importance of audit committee members being "financially literate" and of at least some of the members of the committee having financial expertise. As discussed above, each director must apply to the business of the corporation whatever skill he or she may possess. This includes his or her ability to interpret financial statements and any accounting or related financial expertise he or she may have. Although an expectation may be developing that a member of an audit committee will have these skills, the courts have not given any indication that they will hold directors responsible under the "duty of care" for skills which they do not possess. The increased exposure for audit committee members who are financially literate or who have accounting or related financial management expertise may come from a need to demonstrate that they applied their expertise diligently and that, under the circumstances, a reasonably prudent person would not have acted differently.

The second factor which may affect audit committee members' exposure to liability is the circumstances in which audit committee members find themselves. As discussed above, a director must exercise the care, diligence and skill that a reasonably prudent person would exercise *in comparable circumstances*. In its 1992 Standard Trustco decision, the Ontario Securities Commission stated that if a director has received information or insight about a particular matter as a result of sitting on a committee, that information or insight becomes part of the "comparable circumstances" against which a court may judge the director's conduct. Members of the audit committee will have more detailed information and more contact with the executives responsible for financial reporting, with the internal auditors and with the external auditor. They may be exposed to greater criticism if they do not respond to the information they receive in the way that a reasonably prudent person would respond.

There is no doubt that recent developments will focus attention on members of audit committees. There should be little question that if accusations are made about the integrity of the financial reporting system or the reliability of the financial statements, the conduct of the audit committee members will be scrutinized. This highlights the importance of the audit committee having a clear and actionable mandate and having a thorough understanding of how to discharge its responsibilities under that mandate from a legal perspective.

What the Courts Have Said About Audit Committees

There has been little case law in Canada dealing with audit committees. The courts have considered whether an audit committee chair becomes an expert witness by virtue of that office (the answer was no) and whether instructions given by an audit committee chair to a valuator were binding on the corporation (the answer was yes). In one case, deficiencies in the governance practices of a board of directors (in areas which would fall within the mandate of most audit committees, although this board did not have an audit committee) led to a finding of contributory negligence in a lawsuit by the corporation against its external auditor. In other words, the court found that the auditor had been at fault, but that the resulting damage would not have been as extensive if the board had done a better job.

Canadian courts have also dealt with the responsibilities of auditors. In one case, an Ontario court confirmed that the ultimate duty of the auditor is owed to the shareholders, noting that an audit conducted solely for management would be of questionable utility. The Supreme Court of Canada has held that auditors are not accountable to investors who may use the audited financial statements to make investment decisions. It adopted the following role of the auditor from a leading decision of the House of Lords:

> It is the auditors' function to ensure, so far as possible, that the financial information as to the company's affairs prepared by the directors accurately reflects the company's position in order first, to protect the company itself from the consequences of undetected errors, or, possibly wrongdoing ...and second, to provide shareholders with reliable intelligence for the purpose of enabling them to scrutinize the conduct of the company's affairs and to exercise their collective powers to reward or control or remove those to whom that conduct has been confided.

How Directors Protect Themselves

Liability is top of mind for all directors in the current environment. There are two things that directors need in order to protect themselves if they are sued.

First, they need a successful defence. Typically, this involves evidence that the directors discharged their fiduciary duty and duty of care and that they took the steps necessary to ensure that the corporation complied with its statutory obligations.

Second, directors need to make sure that defence costs are not financially crippling. They therefore need reliable indemnities and directors' and officers' insurance (D&O insurance). An indemnity creates an obligation on the part of the corporation to pay a director's legal expenses, and in some cases, any fine or judgment imposed on the director. D&O insurance covers many of the same types of costs, but will be particularly important to the director if the issuer is unable or unwilling to pay the director's costs as promised under the indemnity.

Directors are wise to keep copies of their D&O insurance and all indemnities in their personal files. There is no way to tell what a director's relationship with the corporation will be at the time when he or she needs to rely on the indemnity or insurance. In some cases, the corporation itself may not have kept complete files and will therefore not be able to provide the directors with the necessary documents when it becomes critical.

Multilateral Instrument 52-110

Audit Committees

PART 1 — DEFINITIONS AND APPLICATION

1.1 Definitions —

In this Instrument, "accounting principles" has the meaning ascribed to it in National Instrument 52-107 *Acceptable Accounting Principles, Auditing Standards and Reporting Currency*;

"AIF" has the meaning ascribed to it in National Instrument 51-102;

"asset-backed security" has the meaning ascribed to it in National Instrument 51-102;

"audit committee" means a committee (or an equivalent body) established by and among the board of directors of an issuer for the purpose of overseeing the accounting and financial reporting processes of the issuer and audits of the financial statements of the issuer, and, if no such committee exists, the entire board of directors of the issuer;

"audit services" means the professional services rendered by the issuer's external auditor for the audit and review of the issuer's financial statements or services that are normally provided by the external auditor in connection with statutory and regulatory filings or engagements;

"credit support issuer" has the meaning ascribed to it in section 13.4 of National Instrument 51-102;

"designated foreign issuer" has the meaning ascribed to it in National Instrument 71-102 *Continuous Disclosure and Other Exemptions Relating to Foreign Issuers*;

"exchangeable security issuer" has the meaning ascribed to it in section 13.3 of National Instrument 51-102;

"executive officer" of an entity means an individual who is:
a) a chair of the entity;
b) a vice-chair of the entity;
c) the president of the entity;
d) a vice-president of the entity in charge of a principal business unit, division or function including sales, finance or production;
e) an officer of the entity or any of its subsidiary entities who performs a policy-making function in respect of the entity; or
f) any other individual who performs a policy-making function in respect of the entity;

"foreign private issuer" means an issuer that is a foreign private issuer within the meaning of Rule 405 under the 1934 Act;

"immediate family member" means an individual's spouse, parent, child, sibling, mother or father-in-law, son or daughter-in-law, brother or sister-in-law, and anyone (other than an employee of either the individual or the individual's immediate family member) who shares the individual's home;

"investment fund" has the meaning ascribed to it in National Instrument 51-102;

"marketplace" has the meaning ascribed to it in National Instrument 21-101 *Marketplace Operation*;

"MD&A" has the meaning ascribed to it in National Instrument 51-102;

"National Instrument 51-102" means National Instrument 51-102 *Continuous Disclosure Obligations*;

"non-audit services" means services other than audit services;

"SEC foreign issuer" has the meaning ascribed to it in National Instrument 71-102 *Continuous Disclosure and Other Exemptions Relating to Foreign Issuers*;

"U.S. marketplace" means an exchange registered as a 'national securities exchange' under section 6 of the 1934 Act, or the Nasdaq Stock Market;

"venture issuer" means an issuer that does not have any of its securities listed or quoted on any of the Toronto Stock Exchange, a U.S. marketplace, or a marketplace outside of Canada and the United States of America.

1.2 Application —

This Instrument applies to all reporting issuers other than:

a) investment funds;

b) issuers of asset-backed securities;

c) designated foreign issuers;

d) SEC foreign issuers;

e) issuers that are subsidiary entities, if

    i) the subsidiary entity does not have equity securities (other than non-convertible, non-participating preferred securities) trading on a marketplace, and

    ii) the parent of the subsidiary entity is

        A) subject to the requirements of this Instrument, or

        B) an issuer that (1) has securities listed or quoted on a U.S. marketplace, and (2) is in compliance with the requirements of that U.S. marketplace applicable to issuers, other than foreign private issuers, regarding the role and composition of audit committees;

f) exchangeable security issuers, if the exchangeable security issuer qualifies for the relief contemplated by, and is in compliance with the requirements and conditions set out in, section 13.3 of National Instrument 51-102; and

g) credit support issuers, if the credit support issuer qualifies for the relief contemplated by, and is in compliance with the requirements and conditions set out in, section 13.4 of National Instrument 51-102.

1.3 Meaning of Affiliated Entity, Subsidiary Entity and Control —

1) For the purposes of this Instrument, a person or company is considered to be an affiliated entity of another person or company if

    a) one of them controls or is controlled by the other or if both persons or companies are controlled by the same person or company, or

    b) the person or company is

        i) both a director and an employee of an affiliated entity, or

        ii) an executive officer, general partner or managing member of an affiliated entity.

2) For the purposes of this Instrument, a person or company is considered to be a subsidiary entity of another person or company if

    a) it is controlled by,

        i) that other, or

        ii) that other and one or more persons or companies each of which is controlled by that other, or

        iii) two or more persons or companies, each of which is controlled by that other; or

    b) it is a subsidiary entity of a person or company that is the other's subsidiary entity.

3) For the purpose of this Instrument, "control" means the direct or indirect power to direct or cause the direction of the management and policies of a person or company, whether through ownership of voting securities or otherwise.

4) Despite subsection (1), a person will not be considered to be an affiliated entity of an issuer for the purposes of this Instrument if the person:
   a) owns, directly or indirectly, ten per cent or less of any class of voting securities of the issuer; and
   b) is not an executive officer of the issuer.

1.4 Meaning of Independence —

1) A member of an audit committee is independent if the member has no direct or indirect material relationship with the issuer.

2) For the purposes of subsection (1), a material relationship means a relationship which could, in the view of the issuer's board of directors, reasonably interfere with the exercise of a member's independent judgement.

3) Despite subsection (2), the following individuals are considered to have a material relationship with an issuer:
   a) an individual who is, or has been, an employee or executive officer of the issuer, unless the prescribed period has elapsed since the end of the service or employment;
   b) an individual whose immediate family member is, or has been, an executive officer of the issuer, unless the prescribed period has elapsed since the end of the service or employment;
   c) an individual who is, or has been, an affiliated entity of, a partner of, or employed by, a current or former internal or external auditor of the issuer, unless the prescribed period has elapsed since the person's relationship with the internal or external auditor, or the auditing relationship, has ended;
   d) an individual whose immediate family member is, or has been, an affiliated entity of, a partner of, or employed in a professional capacity by, a current or former internal or external auditor of the issuer, unless the prescribed period has elapsed since the person's relationship with the internal or external auditor, or the auditing relationship, has ended;
   e) an individual who is, or has been, or whose immediate family member is or has been, an executive officer of an entity if any of the issuer's current executive officers serve on the entity's compensation committee, unless the prescribed period has elapsed since the end of the service or employment;
   f) an individual who
      i) has a relationship with the issuer pursuant to which the individual may accept, directly or indirectly, any consulting, advisory or other compensatory fee from the issuer or any subsidiary entity of the issuer, other than as remuneration for acting in his or her capacity as a member of the board of directors or any board committee, or as a part-time chair or vice-chair of the board or any board committee; or

ii) receives, or whose immediate family member receives, more than $75,000 per year in direct compensation from the issuer, other than as remuneration for acting in his or her capacity as a member of the board of directors or any board committee, or as a part-time chair or vice-chair of the board or any board committee, unless the prescribed period has elapsed since he or she ceased to receive more than $75,000 per year in such compensation;

g) an individual who is an affiliated entity of the issuer or any of its subsidiary entities.

4) For the purposes of subsection (3), the prescribed period is the shorter of

a) the period commencing on March 30, 2004 and ending immediately prior to the determination required by subsection (3); and

b) the three year period ending immediately prior to the determination required by subsection (3).

5) For the purposes of clauses (3)(c) and (3)(d), a partner does not include a fixed income partner whose interest in the internal or external auditor is limited to the receipt of fixed amounts of compensation (including deferred compensation) for prior service with an internal or external auditor if the compensation is not contingent in any way on continued service.

6) For the purposes of clause (3)(f), compensatory fees and direct compensation do not include the receipt of fixed amounts of compensation under a retirement plan (including deferred compensation) for prior service with the issuer if the compensation is not contingent in any way on continued service.

7) For the purposes of subclause 3(f)(i), the indirect acceptance by a person of any consulting, advisory or other compensatory fee includes acceptance of a fee by

a) a person's spouse, minor child or stepchild, or a child or stepchild who shares the person's home; or

b) an entity in which such person is a partner, member, an officer such as a managing director occupying a comparable position or executive officer, or occupies a similar position (except limited partners, non-managing members and those occupying similar positions who, in each case, have no active role in providing services to the entity) and which provides accounting, consulting, legal, investment banking or financial advisory services to the issuer or any subsidiary entity of the issuer.

8) Despite subsection (3), a person will not be considered to have a material relationship with the issuer solely because he or she

a) has previously acted as an interim chief executive officer of the issuer, or

b) acts, or has previously acted, as a chair or vice-chair of the board of directors or any board committee, other than on a full-time basis.

1.5 Meaning of Financial Literacy —

For the purposes of this Instrument, an individual is financially literate if he or she has the ability to read and understand a set of financial statements that present a breadth and level of complexity of accounting issues that are generally comparable to the breadth and complexity of the issues that can reasonably be expected to be raised by the issuer's financial statements.

PART 2 — AUDIT COMMITTEE RESPONSIBILITIES

2.1 Audit Committee —

Every issuer must have an audit committee that complies with the requirements of the Instrument.

2.2 Relationship with External Auditors —

Every issuer must require its external auditor to report directly to the audit committee.

2.3 Audit Committee Responsibilities —

1) An audit committee must have a written charter that sets out its mandate and responsibilities.
2) An audit committee must recommend to the board of directors:
    a) the external auditor to be nominated for the purpose of preparing or issuing an auditor's report or performing other audit, review or attest services for the issuer; and
    b) the compensation of the external auditor.
3) An audit committee must be directly responsible for overseeing the work of the external auditor engaged for the purpose of preparing or issuing an auditor's report or performing other audit, review or attest services for the issuer, including the resolution of disagreements between management and the external auditor regarding financial reporting.
4) An audit committee must pre-approve all non-audit services to be provided to the issuer or its subsidiary entities by the issuer's external auditor.
5) An audit committee must review the issuer's financial statements, MD&A and annual and interim earnings press releases before the issuer publicly discloses this information.
6) An audit committee must be satisfied that adequate procedures are in place for the review of the issuer's public disclosure of financial information extracted or derived from the issuer's financial statements, other than the public disclosure referred to in subsection (5), and must periodically assess the adequacy of those procedures.
7) An audit committee must establish procedures for:
    a) the receipt, retention and treatment of complaints received by the issuer regarding accounting, internal accounting controls, or auditing matters; and
    b) the confidential, anonymous submission by employees of the issuer of concerns regarding questionable accounting or auditing matters.

8) An audit committee must review and approve the issuer's hiring policies regarding partners, employees and former partners and employees of the present and former external auditor of the issuer.

2.4 *De Minimis* Non-Audit Services —
An audit committee satisfies the pre-approval requirement in subsection 2.3(4) if:

a) the aggregate amount of all the non-audit services that were not pre-approved is reasonably expected to constitute no more than five per cent of the total amount of fees paid by the issuer and its subsidiary entities to the issuer's external auditor during the fiscal year in which the services are provided;

b) the issuer or the subsidiary entity of the issuer, as the case may be, did not recognize the services as non-audit services at the time of the engagement; and

c) the services are promptly brought to the attention of the audit committee of the issuer and approved, prior to the completion of the audit, by the audit committee or by one or more of its members to whom authority to grant such approvals has been delegated by the audit committee.

2.5 Delegation of Pre-Approval Function —
1) An audit committee may delegate to one or more independent members the authority to pre-approve non-audit services in satisfaction of the requirement in subsection 2.3(4).

2) The pre-approval of non-audit services by any member to whom authority has been delegated pursuant to subsection (1) must be presented to the audit committee at its first scheduled meeting following such pre-approval.

2.6 Pre-Approval Policies and Procedures —
An audit committee satisfies the pre-approval requirement in subsection 2.3(4) if it adopts specific policies and procedures for the engagement of the non-audit services, if:

a) the pre-approval policies and procedures are detailed as to the particular service;

b) the audit committee is informed of each non-audit service; and

c) the procedures do not include delegation of the audit committee's responsibilities to management.

PART 3 — COMPOSITION OF THE AUDIT COMMITTEE

3.1 Composition —
1) An audit committee must be composed of a minimum of three members.

2) Every audit committee member must be a director of the issuer.

3) Subject to sections 3.2, 3.3, 3.4, 3.5 and 3.6, every audit committee member must be independent.

4) Subject to sections 3.5 and 3.8, every audit committee member must be financially literate.

3.2 Initial Public Offerings —

1) Subject to section 3.9, if an issuer has filed a prospectus to qualify the distribution of securities that constitutes its initial public offering, subsection 3.1(3) does not apply for a period of up to 90 days commencing on the date of the receipt for the prospectus, provided that one member of the audit committee is independent.

2) Subject to section 3.9, if an issuer has filed a prospectus to qualify the distribution of securities that constitutes its initial public offering, subsection 3.1(3) does not apply for a period of up to one year commencing on the date of the receipt for the prospectus, provided that a majority of the audit committee members are independent.

3.3 Controlled Companies —

1) An audit committee member that sits on the board of directors of an affiliated entity is exempt from the requirement in subsection 3.1(3) if the member, except for being a director (or member of a board committee) of the issuer and the affiliated entity, is otherwise independent of the issuer and the affiliated entity.

2) Subject to section 3.7, an audit committee member is exempt from the requirement in subsection 3.1(3) if:
   a) the member would be independent of the issuer but for the relationship described in paragraph 1.4(3)(g);
   b) the member is not an executive officer, general partner or managing member of a person or company that
      i) is an affiliated entity of the issuer, and
      ii) has its securities trading on a marketplace;
   c) the member is not an immediate family member of an executive officer, general partner or managing member referred to in paragraph (b), above;
   d) the member does not act as the chair of the audit committee; and
   e) the board determines in its reasonable judgement that
      i) the member is able to exercise the impartial judgement necessary for the member to fulfill his or her responsibilities as an audit committee member, and
      ii) the appointment of the member is required by the best interests of the issuer and its shareholders.

3.4 Events Outside Control of Member —

Subject to section 3.9, if an audit committee member ceases to be independent for reasons outside the member's reasonable control, the member is exempt from the requirement in subsection 3.1(3) for a period ending on the later of:
a) the next annual meeting of the issuer, and
b) the date that is six months from the occurrence of the event which caused the member to not be independent.

3.5 Death, Disability or Resignation of Member —

Subject to section 3.9, if the death, disability or resignation of an audit committee member has resulted in a vacancy on the audit committee that the board of directors is required to fill, an audit committee member appointed to fill such vacancy is exempt from the requirements in subsections 3.1(3) and (4) for a period ending on the later of:

(a) the next annual meeting of the issuer, and

(b) the date that is six months from the day the vacancy was created.

3.6 Temporary Exemption for Limited and Exceptional Circumstances —

Subject to section 3.7, an audit committee member is exempt from the requirement in subsection 3.1(3) if:

a) the member is not an individual described in paragraphs 1.4(3)(f)(i) or 1.4(3)(g);

b) the member is not an employee or officer of the issuer, or an immediate family member of an employee or officer of the issuer;

c) the board, under exceptional and limited circumstances, determines in its reasonable judgement that

    i) the member is able to exercise the impartial judgement necessary for the member to fulfill his or her responsibilities as an audit committee member, and

    ii) the appointment of the member is required by the best interests of the issuer and its shareholders;

d) the member does not act as chair of the audit committee; and

e) the member does not rely upon this exemption for a period of more than two years.

3.7 Majority Independent —

The exemptions in subsection 3.3(2) and section 3.6 are not available to a member unless a majority of the audit committee members would be independent.

3.8 Acquisition of Financial Literacy —

Subject to section 3.9, an audit committee member who is not financially literate may be appointed to the audit committee provided that the member becomes financially literate within a reasonable period of time following his or her appointment.

3.9 Restriction on Use of Certain Exemptions —

The exemptions in sections 3.2, 3.4, 3.5 and 3.8 are not available to a member unless the issuer's board of directors has determined that the reliance on the exemption will not materially adversely affect the ability of the audit committee to act independently and to satisfy the other requirements of this Instrument.

PART 4 — AUTHORITY OF THE AUDIT COMMITTEE

4.1 Authority —

An audit committee must have the authority

a) to engage independent counsel and other advisors as it determines necessary to carry out its duties,

b) to set and pay the compensation for any advisors employed by the audit committee, and

c) to communicate directly with the internal and external auditors.

PART 5 — REPORTING OBLIGATIONS

5.1 Required Disclosure —

Every issuer must include in its AIF the disclosure required by Form 52-110F1.

5.2 Management Information Circular —

If management of an issuer solicits proxies from the security holders of the issuer for the purpose of electing directors to the issuer's board of directors, the issuer must include in its management information circular a cross-reference to the sections in the issuer's AIF that contain the information required by section 5.1.

PART 6 — VENTURE ISSUERS

6.1 Venture Issuers —

Venture issuers are exempt from the requirements of Parts 3 (*Composition of the Audit Committee*) and 5 (*Reporting Obligations*).

6.2 Required Disclosure —

1) Subject to subsection (2), if management of a venture issuer solicits proxies from the security holders of the venture issuer for the purpose of electing directors to its board of directors, the venture issuer must include in its management information circular the disclosure required by Form 52-110F2.

2) A venture issuer that is not required to send a management information circular to its security holders must provide the disclosure required by Form 52-110F2 in its AIF or annual MD&A.

PART 7 — U.S. LISTED ISSUERS

7.1 U.S. Listed Issuers —

An issuer that has securities listed or quoted on a U.S. marketplace is exempt from the requirements of Parts 2 (*Audit Committee Responsibilities*), 3 (*Composition of the Audit Committee*), 4 (*Authority of the Audit Committee*), and 5 (*Reporting Obligations*), if:

a) the issuer is in compliance with the requirements of that U.S. marketplace applicable to issuers, other than foreign private issuers, regarding the role and composition of audit committees; and

b) if the issuer is incorporated, continued or otherwise organized in a jurisdiction in Canada, the issuer includes in its AIF the disclosure (if any) required by paragraph 5 of Form 52-110F1.

PART 8 — EXEMPTIONS

8.1 Exemptions —

1) The securities regulatory authority or regulator may grant an exemption from this rule, in whole or in part, subject to such conditions or restrictions as may be imposed in the exemption.

2) Despite subsection (1), in Ontario, only the regulator may grant such an exemption.

PART 9 — EFFECTIVE DATE

9.1 Effective Date —

1) This Instrument comes into force on March 30, 2004.

2) Despite subsection (1), this Instrument applies to an issuer commencing on the earlier of:

a) the first annual meeting of the issuer after July 1, 2004, and

b) July 1, 2005.

FORM 52-110F1
AUDIT COMMITTEE INFORMATION REQUIRED IN AN AIF

1. The Audit Committee's Charter

Disclose the text of the audit committee's charter.

2. Composition of the Audit Committee

Disclose the name of each audit committee member and state whether or not the member is (i) independent and (ii) financially literate.

3. Relevant Education and Experience

Describe the education and experience of each audit committee member that is relevant to the performance of his or her responsibilities as an audit committee member and, in particular, disclose any education or experience that would provide the member with:

a) an understanding of the accounting principles used by the issuer to prepare its financial statements;

b) the ability to assess the general application of such accounting principles in connection with the accounting for estimates, accruals and reserves;

c) experience preparing, auditing, analyzing or evaluating financial statements that present a breadth and level of complexity of accounting issues that are generally comparable to the breadth and complexity of issues that can reasonably be expected to be raised by the issuer's financial statements, or experience actively supervising one or more persons engaged in such activities; and

d) an understanding of internal controls and procedures for financial reporting.

4. Reliance on Certain Exemptions

If, at any time since the commencement of the issuer's most recently completed financial year, the issuer has relied on

a) the exemption in section 2.4 (*De Minimis Non-audit Services*),

b) the exemption in section 3.2 (*Initial Public Offerings*),

c) the exemption in section 3.4 (*Events Outside Control of Member*),

d) the exemption in section 3.5 (*Death, Disability or Resignation of Audit Committee Member*) or

e) an exemption from this Instrument, in whole or in part, granted under Part 8 (*Exemptions*), state that fact.

5. Reliance on the Exemption in Subsection 3.3(2) or Section 3.6

If, at any time since the commencement of the issuer's most recently completed financial year, the issuer has relied upon the exemption in subsection 3.3(2) (*Controlled Companies*) or section 3.6 (*Temporary Exemption for Limited and Exceptional Circumstances*), state that fact and disclose

a) the name of the member, and

b) the rationale for appointing the member to the audit committee.

6. Reliance on Section 3.8

If, at any time since the commencement of the issuer's most recently completed financial year, the issuer has relied upon section 3.8 (*Acquisition of Financial Literacy*), state that fact and disclose

a) the name of the member,

b) that the member is not financially literate, and

c) the date by which the member expects to become financially literate.

7. Audit Committee Oversight

If, at any time since the commencement of the issuer's most recently completed financial year, a recommendation of the audit committee to nominate or compensate an external auditor was not adopted by the board of directors, state that fact and explain why.

8. Pre-Approval Policies and Procedures

If the audit committee has adopted specific policies and procedures for the engagement of non-audit services, describe those policies and procedures.

9. External Auditor Service Fees (By Category)

a) Disclose, under the caption "Audit Fees", the aggregate fees billed by the issuer's external auditor in each of the last two fiscal years for audit services.

b) Disclose, under the caption "Audit-Related Fees", the aggregate fees billed in each of the last two fiscal years for assurance and related services by the issuer's external auditor that are reasonably related to the performance of the audit or review of the issuer's financial statements and are not reported under clause (a) above. Include a description of the nature of the services comprising the fees disclosed under this category.

c) Disclose, under the caption "Tax Fees", the aggregate fees billed in each of the last two fiscal years for professional services rendered by the issuer's external auditor for tax compliance, tax advice, and tax planning. Include a description of the nature of the services comprising the fees disclosed under this category.

d) Disclose, under the caption "All Other Fees", the aggregate fees billed in each of the last two fiscal years for products and services provided by the issuer's external auditor, other than the services reported under clauses (a), (b) and (c), above. Include a description of the nature of the services comprising the fees disclosed under this category.

INSTRUCTION

The fees required to be disclosed by this paragraph 9 relate only to services provided to the issuer or its subsidiary entities by the issuer's external auditor.

FORM 52-110F2
DISCLOSURE BY VENTURE ISSUERS

1. The Audit Committee's Charter

Disclose the text of the audit committee's charter.

2. Composition of the Audit Committee

Disclose the name of each audit committee member and state whether or not the member is (i) independent and (ii) financially literate.

3. Audit Committee Oversight

If, at any time since the commencement of the issuer's most recently completed financial year, a recommendation of the audit committee to nominate or compensate an external auditor was not adopted by the board of directors, state that fact and explain why.

4. Reliance on Certain Exemptions

If, at any time since the commencement of the issuer's most recently completed financial year, the issuer has relied on

a) the exemption in section 2.4 (*De Minimis Non-audit Services*), or

b) an exemption from this Instrument, in whole or in part, granted under Part 8 (*Exemptions*), state that fact.

5. Pre-Approval Policies and Procedures

If the audit committee has adopted specific policies and procedures for the engagement of non-audit services, describe those policies and procedures.

6. External Auditor Service Fees (By Category)

a) Disclose, under the caption "Audit Fees", the aggregate fees billed by the issuer's external auditor in each of the last two fiscal years for audit fees.

b) Disclose, under the caption "Audit-Related Fees", the aggregate fees billed in each of the last two fiscal years for assurance and related services by the issuer's external auditor that are reasonably related to the performance of the audit or review of the issuer's financial statements and are not reported under clause (a) above. Include a description of the nature of the services comprising the fees disclosed under this category.

c) Disclose, under the caption "Tax Fees", the aggregate fees billed in each of the last two fiscal years for professional services rendered by the issuer's external auditor for tax compliance, tax advice, and tax planning. Include a description of the nature of the services comprising the fees disclosed under this category.

d) Disclose, under the caption "All Other Fees", the aggregate fees billed in each of the last two fiscal years for products and services provided by the issuer's external auditor, other than the services reported under clauses (a), (b) and (c), above. Include a description of the nature of the services comprising the fees disclosed under this category.

INSTRUCTION

The fees required to be disclosed by this paragraph 5 relate only to services provided to the issuer or its subsidiary entities by the issuer's external auditor.

7. Exemption

Disclose that the issuer is relying upon the exemption in section 6.1 of the Instrument.

Companion Policy 52-110CP
to Multilateral Instrument 52-110
Audit Committees

Part 1 — General

1.1 Purpose.

Multilateral Instrument 52-110 *Audit Committees* (the Instrument) is a rule in each of Québec, Alberta, Manitoba, Ontario, Nova Scotia and Newfoundland and Labrador, a Commission regulation in Saskatchewan and Nunavut, a policy in New Brunswick, Prince Edward Island and the Yukon Territory, and a code in the Northwest Territories. We, the securities regulatory authorities in each of the foregoing jurisdictions (the Jurisdictions), have implemented the Instrument to encourage reporting issuers to establish and maintain strong, effective and independent audit committees. We believe that such audit committees enhance the quality of financial disclosure made by reporting issuers, and ultimately foster increased investor confidence in Canada's capital markets.

This companion policy (the Policy) provides information regarding the interpretation and application of the Instrument.

1.2 Application to Non-Corporate Entities.

The Instrument applies to both corporate and non-corporate entities. Where the Instrument or this Policy refers to a particular corporate characteristic, such as a board of directors, the reference should be read to also include any equivalent characteristic of a non-corporate entity.

E.g., for an income trust to comply with the Instrument, the trustees should appoint a minimum of three trustees who are independent of the trust and the underlying business to act as an audit committee and fulfil the responsibilities of the audit committee imposed by the Instrument. Similarly, in the case of a limited partnership, the directors of the general partner who are independent of the limited partnership (including the general partner) should form an audit committee which fulfils these responsibilities.

If the structure of an issuer will not permit it to comply with the Instrument, the issuer should seek exemptive relief.

1.3 Management Companies.

The definition of "executive officer" includes any individual who performs a policy-making function in respect of the entity in question. We consider this aspect of the definition to include an individual who, although not employed by the entity in question, nevertheless performs a policy-making function in respect of that entity, whether through another person or company or otherwise.

1.4 Audit Committee Procedures.

The Instrument establishes requirements for the responsibilities, composition and authority of audit committees. Nothing in the Instrument is intended to restrict the ability of the board of directors or the audit committee to establish the committee's quorum or procedures, or to restrict the committee's ability to invite additional parties to attend audit committee meetings.

Part 2 — The Role of the Audit Committee

2.1 The Role of the Audit Committee.

An audit committee is a committee of a board of directors to which the board delegates its responsibility for oversight of the financial reporting process. Traditionally, the audit committee has performed a number of roles, including

- helping directors meet their responsibilities,
- providing better communication between directors and the external auditors,
- enhancing the independence of the external auditor,
- increasing the credibility and objectivity of financial reports, and
- strengthening the role of the directors by facilitating in-depth discussions among directors, management and the external auditor.

The Instrument requires that the audit committee also be responsible for managing, on behalf of the shareholders, the relationship between the issuer and the external auditors. In particular, it provides that an audit committee must have responsibility for:

a) overseeing the work of the external auditors engaged for the purpose of preparing or issuing an auditor's report or related work; and

b) recommending to the board of directors the nomination and compensation of the external auditors.

Although under corporate law an issuer's external auditors are responsible to the shareholders, in practice, shareholders have often been too dispersed to effectively exercise meaningful oversight of the external auditors. As a result, management has typically assumed this oversight role. However, the auditing process may be compromised if the external auditors view their main responsibility as serving management rather than the shareholders. By assigning these responsibilities to an independent audit committee, the Instrument ensures that the external audit will be conducted independently of the issuer's management.

2.2 Relationship between External Auditors and Shareholders.

Subsection 2.3(3) of the Instrument provides that an audit committee must be directly responsible for overseeing the work of the external auditors engaged for the purpose of preparing or issuing an auditor's report or performing other audit, review or attest services for the issuer, including the resolution of disagreements between management and the external auditors regarding financial reporting. Notwithstanding this responsibility, the external auditors are retained by, and are ultimately accountable to, the shareholders. As a result, subsection 2.3(3) does not detract from the external auditors' right and responsibility to also provide their views directly to the shareholders if they disagree with an approach being taken by the audit committee.

2.3 Public Disclosure of Financial Information.

Issuers are reminded that, in our view, the extraction of information from financial statements that have not previously been reviewed by the audit committee and the release of that information into the marketplace is inconsistent with the issuer's obligation to have its audit committee review the financial statements. See also National Policy 51-201 *Disclosure Standards*.

Part 3 — Independence

3.1 Meaning of Independence.

The Instrument generally requires every member of an audit committee to be independent. Subsection 1.4(1) of the Instrument defines independence to mean the absence of any direct or indirect material relationship between the director and the issuer. In our view, this relationship may include commercial, charitable, industrial, banking, consulting, legal, accounting or familial relationships. However, only those relationships which could, in the view of the issuer's board of directors, reasonably interfere with the exercise of a member's independent judgement should be considered material relationships within the meaning of section 1.4.

Subsection 1.4(3) of the Instrument sets out a list of persons that we believe have a relationship with an issuer that would reasonably interfere with the exercise of the person's independent judgement. Consequently, these persons are not considered independent for the purposes of the Instrument and are therefore precluded from serving on the issuer's audit committee. Directors and their counsel should therefore consider the nature of the relationships outlined in subsection 1.4(3) as guidance in applying the general independence test set out in subsection 1.4(1).

3.2 Derivation of Definition.

The definition of independence and associated provisions included in the Instrument have been derived from both the rules promulgated by the SEC in response to the *Sarbanes-Oxley Act* and the corporate governance rules issued by the NYSE. The SEC rules set out requirements for a member of the audit committee to be considered independent. The NYSE corporate governance rules define independence and outline conditions for a director to be considered independent and also require that audit committee members be independent directors as defined by both the SEC provisions and the NYSE rules. We have mirrored this composite approach to the definition of independence for audit committee members in the Instrument.

3.3 Safe Harbour.

Subsection 1.3(1) of the Instrument provides, in part, that a person or company is an affiliated entity of another entity if the person or company controls the other entity. Subsection 1.3(4), however, provides that a person will not be considered to be an affiliated entity of an issuer if the person:

a) owns, directly or indirectly, ten per cent or less of any class of voting equity securities of the issuer; and

b) is not an executive officer of the issuer.

Subsection 1.3(4) is intended only to identify those persons who are not considered affiliated entities of an issuer. The provision is not intended to suggest that a person who owns more than ten percent of an issuer's voting equity securities is automatically an affiliated entity of the issuer. Instead, a person who owns more than ten percent of an issuer's voting equity securities should examine all relevant facts and circumstances to determine if he or she is an affiliated entity within the meaning of subsection 1.3(1).

Part 4 — Financial Literacy, Financial Education and Experience

4.1 Financial Literacy.

For the purposes of the Instrument, an individual is financially literate if he or she has the ability to read and understand a set of financial statements that present a breadth and level of complexity of accounting issues that are generally comparable to the breadth and complexity of the issues that can reasonably be expected to be raised by the issuer's financial statements. In our view, it is not necessary for a member to have a comprehensive knowledge of GAAP and GAAS to be considered financially literate.

4.2 Financial Education and Experience.

1) Item 3 of Form 52-110F1 requires an issuer to disclose any education or experience of an audit committee member that would provide the member with, among other things, an understanding of the accounting principles used by the issuer to prepare its financial statements. In our view, for a member to have such an understanding, the member needs a detailed understanding of only those accounting principles that might reasonably be applicable to the issuer in question. For example, an individual would not be required to have a detailed understanding of the accounting principles relating to the treatment of complex derivatives transactions if the issuer in question would not reasonably be involved in such transactions.

2) Item 3 of Form 52-110F1 also requires an issuer to disclose any experience that the member has, among other things, actively supervising persons engaged in preparing, auditing, analyzing or evaluating certain types of financial statements. The phrase active supervision means more than the mere existence of a traditional hierarchical reporting relationship between supervisor and those being supervised. A person engaged in active supervision participates in, and contributes to, the process of addressing (albeit at a supervisory level) the same general types of issues regarding preparation, auditing, analysis or evaluation of financial statements as those addressed by the person or persons being supervised. The supervisor should also have experience that has contributed to the general expertise necessary to prepare, audit, analyze or evaluate financial statements that is at least comparable to the general expertise of those being supervised. An executive officer should not be presumed to qualify. An executive officer with considerable operations involvement, but little financial or accounting involvement, likely would not be exercising the necessary active supervision. Active participation in, and contribution to, the process, albeit at a supervisory level, of addressing financial and accounting issues that demonstrate a general expertise in the area would be necessary.

Part 5 — Non-Audit Services

5.1 Pre-Approval of Non-Audit Services.

Section 2.6 of the Instrument allows an audit committee to satisfy, in certain circumstances, the pre-approval requirements in subsection 2.3(4) by adopting specific policies and procedures for the engagement of non-audit services. The following guidance should be noted in the development and application of such policies and procedures:

• Monetary limits should not be the only basis for the pre-approval policies and procedures. The establishment of monetary limits will not, alone, constitute policies that are detailed as to the particular services to be provided and will not, alone, ensure that the audit committee will be informed about each service.

• The use of broad, categorical approvals (*e.g.* tax compliance services) will not meet the requirement that the policies must be detailed as to the particular services to be provided.

- The appropriate level of detail for the pre-approval policies will differ depending upon the facts and circumstances of the issuer. The pre-approval policies must be designed to ensure that the audit committee knows precisely what services it is being asked to pre-approve so that it can make a well-reasoned assessment of the impact of the service on the auditor's independence. Furthermore, because the Instrument requires that the policies cannot result in a delegation of the audit committee's responsibility to management, the pre-approval policies must be sufficiently detailed as to particular services so that a member of management will not be called upon to determine whether a proposed service fits within the policy.

Part 6 — Disclosure Obligations

6.1 Incorporation by Reference.

National Instrument 51-102 permits disclosure required to be included in an issuer's AIF or information circular to be incorporated by reference, provided that the referenced document has already been filed with the applicable securities regulatory authorities.[1] Any disclosure required by the Instrument to be included in an issuer's AIF or management information circular may also [be] incorporated by reference, provided that the procedures set out in National Instrument 51-102 are followed.

---

[1] See Part 1, paragraph (f) of Form 51-102F2 (*Annual Information Form*) and Part 1, paragraph (c) of Form 51-102F5 (*Information Circular*).

Creating the Charter:
A Benchmarking Tool

This benchmarking tool examines nine key elements of audit committee responsibility, and identifies practices for each that relate to minimum statutory requirements, current best practices, and current leading-edge practices. The use of this benchmarking tool is described in Chapter 5, Doing The Right Things Right.

Audit committees should match their current responsibilities and practices to those identified in the table. They should then examine the practices in the table to identify those they wish to change or improve.

NOTE: Audit committees operating at a "Best Practices" level would perform all of the activities identified as best practices as well as those identified as minimum requirements. Audit committees operating at a "Leading Edge" level would perform all of the activities at all levels.

Composition of the Committee		
Minimum Requirement	**Best Practices**	**Leading Edge Practices**
• Consists of a minimum of three members, all of whom are outside directors of the company. • All members are independent (i.e., as defined by MI 52-110: an audit committee member is considered independent if they have no material relationship with the issuer, such a relationship being one that could, in the view of the issuer's board, reasonably interfere with the exercise of a member's independent judgment). • The majority of members are financially literate (i.e., as defined by MI 52-110, as having the ability to read and understand a set of financial statements that present a breadth and level of complexity of accounting issues that are generally comparable to those that can be reasonably expected to be raised by the issuer's financial statements). • Although it is preferred that the audit committee members attend meetings in person, a quorum may be achieved through a majority of members being present in person, by teleconferencing or by videoconferencing.	• Composition of the committee complies with all applicable requirements of the stock exchanges on which securities of the company are listed and of security regulatory authorities. • All members of the audit committee are financially literate.	• If any audit committee member serves on the audit committee of more than three public companies, in each case the board determines that such simultaneous services would not impair the ability of that member to effectively serve on the company's audit committee and this determination is disclosed in the company's annual proxy statement. • All audit committee members are financially literate, and at least one member can be considered a financial expert. • A regular part of audit committee meetings involves the appropriate orientation of new members as well as the continuous education of all members. Items to be discussed include specific business issues as well as new accounting and securities legislation that may impact the organization.
Current Positioning		
Desired Positioning		

Financial Reporting		
Minimum Requirement	**Best Practices**	**Leading Edge Practices**
• The review and discussion of financial reporting is restricted to the annual and interim financial statements and is focused on minimal compliance with accounting principles, presentation/disclosure standards (i.e., GAAP). • Reviews and recommends approval to the board financial statements, MD&A and related annual and interim news releases before they are publicly disclosed. • Satisfies itself that adequate procedures are in place for the review of the company's public disclosure of financial information extracted or derived from the financial statements, and periodically assesses the adequacy of those procedures.	• Discusses with management and the external auditor the quality of GAAP, not just acceptability of GAAP. • Discusses with management any significant variances between comparative reporting periods and across comparable reporting units. • In discussion with management and the external auditor, identifies problems or areas of concern, and ensures such matters are satisfactorily resolved. • Engages the external auditor to perform a review of the interim financial statements, reviews their findings, but no formal report is issued. • Reviews financial statements of subsidiaries as well as the consolidated financial statements, pension plans, joint ventures, etc. • Reviews major accounting issues regarding accounting principles and financial statement presentation, including any significant changes in the selection or application of accounting principles to be used. • Reviews disclosure contained in the proxy circular and statement or any other public disclosure document of the organization of the services performed and the fees paid to the external auditor.	• Requires a representation letter from management similar to that provided by the external auditor (e.g., recommendation of NACD in the United States). • Reviews financial information and earnings guidance provided to analysts and ratings agencies. • Reviews other public disclosures containing material audited or unaudited financial information (including, but not limited to: prospectuses; annual and interim reports; Form 10-K: and Form 10-Q). • Receives from the external auditor a formal report on the auditor's review of the interim financial statements.
Current Positioning		
Desired Positioning		

Accounting Policies		
Minimum Requirement	**Best Practices**	**Leading Edge Practices**
• Reviews accounting policy note to ensure completeness and acceptability with GAAP as part of the approval of the financial statements.	• Proactively discusses and reviews the impact or proposed changes in accounting standards or securities policies or regulations. • Reviews with management and the external auditor any proposed changes in major accounting policies, and key estimates and judgments that might be material to financial reporting. • Discusses with management and the external auditor the *acceptability, degree of conservatism and quality* of: — underlying accounting policies; — key estimates and judgments. • Discusses with management and the external auditor the clarity and completeness of the company's financial disclosures. • Benchmarks the company's accounting policies to those followed in its industry. • Reviews analyses prepared by either management or the external auditor of significant financial reporting issues and judgments made in connection with the preparation of the financial statements including the following: — effects of alternative GAAP; — effects of regulatory or accounting initiatives; and — off balance-sheet structures.	• Discusses with management and the external auditor to ensure that the underlying accounting policies, disclosures and key estimates are considered to be the most appropriate in the circumstances (within the range of acceptable options and alternatives). • Discusses with management and the external auditor the clarity and completeness of the company's financial and non-financial disclosures made with respect to continuous disclosure requirements. • Reviews with management and the external auditor all related party transactions and the development of policies and procedures related to those transactions.
Current Positioning		
Desired Positioning		

Risk and Uncertainty		
Minimum Requirement	**Best Practices**	**Leading Edge Practices**
• Reviews, as part of its approval of the financial statements: — uncertainty note disclosures; — MD&A disclosures.	• The board of directors, in consultation with management, identifies the principal business risks, decides on its "appetite for risk", approves related risk management policies, and assigns oversight responsibilities to board committees and the board as a whole. • The audit committee's focus is on financial risks and ensuring that they are being effectively managed or controlled by: — reviewing the appetite for financial risks as set forth by management and the board; — reviewing the company's policies for the management of significant financial risks; — reviewing management's assessment of the significant financial risks facing the company; — reviewing management's plans, processes and programs to manage and control such risks. • Requests the external auditor's opinion of management's assessment of significant financial risks facing the company and how effectively they are being managed or controlled. • At least annually reviews insurance programs in place for the company and evaluates their appropriateness.	• Same as "best practice", except the audit committee's role is expanded to cover policies and programs related to principal business risks as well as financial risks (NYSE). • The audit committee serves as a "risk management committee" as well as an audit committee. • Discusses with management, at least annually, the guidelines and policies utilized by management with respect to financial risk assessment and management, and the major financial risk exposures and the procedures to monitor and control such exposures in order to assist the committee to assess the completeness, adequacy and appropriateness of financial risk disclosure in management MD&A and in the financial statements. • Ascertains that policies and procedures are in place to minimize environmental, occupational health and safety and other risks to asset value and mitigate damage to or deterioration of asset value and review such policies and procedures periodically. • Reviews foreign currency, interest rate and commodity price risk mitigation strategies, including the use of derivative financial instruments.
Current Positioning		
Desired Positioning		

Controls and Control Deviations

Minimum Requirement	Best Practices	Leading Edge Practices

• Reviews the:
  — plan and scope of the annual audit with respect to planned reliance and testing of control;
  — major points contained in the auditor's Management Letter resulting from control evaluation and testing.
• Receives reports from management when significant control deviations occur.
• Reviews the CEO/CFO certifications. Inquires as to practices and procedures adopted to permit management's assurance on the underlying controls.
	• Sets a clear expectation for a "tone at the top" that conveys basic values of ethical integrity as well as legal compliance and strong financial reporting and control.
	• Reviews the plans of the internal and external auditors to ensure the combined evaluation and testing of control is comprehensive, well co-ordinated, cost effective and appropriate to risks, business activities, changing circumstances, etc.
	• Receives from management, the auditors, legal department, etc., regular reports on all major control deviations, or indications/detection of fraud, and how such control breakdowns have been corrected.
	• Reviews appointments of key people involved in financial reporting (CFO, head of internal audit, etc.)
	• Periodically reviews and monitors practices and procedures adopted to assure compliance with applicable laws and requirements of the applicable stock exchanges including officer certification. *(Sarbanes-Oxley Act).*
		• Management prepares a formal report, at least annually, on the effectiveness of the company's control systems with auditor attestation. *(Sarbanes-Oxley Act)*
		• Reviews fraud prevention policies and programs, and monitors their implementation.
		• Extends its oversight of control systems into non-financial areas (e.g., operations).
		• Reviews business practices followed by senior management to assess compliance with appropriate corporate policies and the Code of Business Conduct and to address deficiencies in such compliance.

Current Positioning		
Desired Positioning		

Compliance with Laws and Regulations

Minimum Requirement	Best Practices	Leading Edge Practices
• Discusses the company's compliance with tax and financial reporting laws and regulations, normally if and when issues arise.	• Reviews regular reports from management and others (e.g., internal and external auditors) concerning the company's compliance with financial related laws and regulations, such as: — tax and financial reporting laws and regulations; — legal withholdings requirements; — environmental protection laws; — other matters for which directors face liability exposure. • Provides input to and reviews the company's code of ethics or conduct. • Periodically discusses with the chief legal officer any significant legal, compliance or regulatory matters that may have a material effect on the financial statements or the business of the company (including material notices to, or inquiries received from, governmental agencies).	• Expands its review to include a broader set of laws and regulations that must be complied with (e.g., compliance with privacy laws in electronic commerce systems). • Annually reviews or receives reports from other board committees (e.g., social responsibility committee) on management's processes to ensure compliance with company's code of ethics.

Current Positioning

Desired Positioning

Relationship with the External Auditor		
Minimum Requirement	**Best Practices**	**Leading Edge Practices**
• Has sole authority to recommend the hiring and firing of the external auditor. • External auditor reports directly to the audit committee. • Reviews: — proposed audit plan.	• Establishes effective communication processes with management and the external auditor so it can objectively monitor the quality and effectiveness of the external auditor's relationship with management and the audit committee. • Reviews the terms of engagement of the external auditor, including their qualifications, professional competence, experience and performance. • Reviews and approves: — proposed audit scope, focus areas, timing, staffing and key decisions (e.g., materiality, reliance on internal audit) underlying the audit plan; — appropriateness and reasonableness of proposed audit fees.	• Reviews management's plans for an orderly transition to a new external auditor if required. • Receives at least annually a report by the external auditor on the audit firm's internal quality control. The review includes any material issues raised by the most recent quality control review, or peer review, of the firm, or any governmental or professional authorities of the firm within the preceding five years, and any steps taken to deal with such issues. • The review of communications from the external auditor includes: — immaterial unadjusted items; — communications between the audit firm and their national office regarding accounting issues identified; — management letter issued or proposed to be issued.
Current Positioning		
Desired Positioning		

Relationship with the External Auditor (cont'd)		
Minimum Requirement	**Best Practices**	**Leading Edge Practices**
• Has sole authority to recommend compensation of the external auditor to the board. • Directly responsible for the resolution of any disagreements between management and the external auditor regarding financial reporting.	• Receives regular reports from the external auditor on: — progress against the approved audit plan; — important findings; — recommendations for improvements; — the auditor's final report. • Obtains assurances from the external auditor that the audit was conducted in a manner consistent with the applicable standards for the conduct of an audit in accordance with Canadian (and U.S. if applicable) generally accepted auditing standards.	• Reviews a report from the external auditor concerning the audited financial statements describing the following: — all critical accounting policies and practices used; — all alternative treatments of financial information within generally accepted accounting principles that have been discussed with management; — ramifications of the use of alternative disclosures and treatments; — treatment preferred by the external auditor; — any material written communications between the external auditor and management (i.e., management representation letter; internal control letter; schedule of unadjusted differences).
Current Positioning		
Desired Positioning		

Relationship with the External Auditor (cont'd)		
Minimum Requirement	**Best Practices**	**Leading Edge Practices**

• Is directly responsible for overseeing the work of the external auditor.
• Reviews and pre-approves, in accordance with an established pre-approval policy, all services (audit and non-audit) to be provided to the company or its subsidiary entities by the external auditor. In performing such a review, assures itself that none of the services to be provided would breach the external auditor's independence.
• If the authority to pre-approve non-audit services has been delegated to one or more independent members of the audit committee, any such pre-approvals granted are presented to the audit committee at its first meeting following such pre-approval.
• The pre-approval policy encompasses the following:
   − policies and procedures are detailed as to the particular service;
   − audit committee is informed of each non-audit service;
   − the procedures do not include delegation of the audit committee's responsibilities to management.
	• Meets regularly in private with the external auditor.
	• Reviews communications from external auditor regarding:
	   − any identified weaknesses or deficiencies;
	   − any audit problems or difficulties encountered in performing the audit;
	   − management's response and actions taken to remedy the issues identified.
	• Ensures there is a direct channel of communication with the external auditor to discuss and review specific issues as appropriate.
	• Discusses with the external auditors the audit partner rotation plan including the timing and process for implementing the plan (i.e., succession plan set).
	• Reviews, at least annually, a report from the external auditor on all relationships and engagements for non-audit services that may reasonably be thought to bear on the independence of the auditor.	

Current Positioning		
Desired Positioning		

Relationship with the External Auditor (cont'd)		
Minimum Requirement	**Best Practices**	**Leading Edge Practices**
• Reviews and approves the company's hiring policies regarding partners, employees and former partners and employees of the current and former external auditor. • The external auditor is provided notice of and is entitled to attend and participate in every meeting of the committee. (CBA). • Discusses with the external auditor the rotation plan for all audit partners active on the engagement. (CICA). • At least annually, reviews and discusses with the external auditor, the policies and procedures followed to ensure the maintenance of the external auditor's independence. (CICA).		
Current Positioning		
Desired Positioning		

Relationship with the Internal Auditor		
Minimum Requirement	**Best Practices**	**Leading Edge Practices**

• Accepts:
  — appointment of internal auditor;
  — overall scope and approach of internal audit;
  — selected reports issued by the internal auditor.
	• At least annually, reviews:
	  — internal auditor's terms of reference;
	  — plan and budget of internal audit (financial and operational activities);
	  — majority of reports issued by internal auditor (including any identified weaknesses or deficiencies);
	  — management's response to internal auditor's reports (including any actions taken to remedy the issues identified).
	• Approves the reporting relationship of the internal auditor to ensure appropriate segregation of duties is maintained and internal auditor has direct access to the audit committee.
	• Ensures the internal auditor's involvement with financial reporting is co-ordinated with the activities of the external auditor.
	• If no internal audit function exists, the audit committee regularly reviews the need for such a function (NYSE).
	• Ensures there is a direct channel of communication with the internal auditor to discuss and review specific issues as appropriate.
	• Meets regularly, in private, with the internal auditor.
		• Assumes primary reporting relationship for the internal audit function.
		• Periodically reviews the adequacy of internal controls, including reports from management of any deficiencies in the design or operation and/or major issues in the adequacy of these controls, including evidence of fraud. Makes reports or recommendations to the board.
		• Reviews communications from internal auditor concerning any audit problems or difficulties encountered in performing the audit and management's response to same.

Current Positioning		
Desired Positioning		

Other Responsibilities and Issues

Minimum Requirement	Best Practices	Leading Edge Practices
• Establishes procedures for the receipt, retention and treatment of complaints received by the company regarding accounting, internal accounting controls or auditing matters, as well as the confidential, anonymous submission by employees of the company of concerns regarding questionable accounting or auditing matters.	• The chairman and the audit committee take responsibility for setting forth their expectations for their information needs (e.g., nature level of detail, timing, preparer, etc.) and ensure that the information they receive is responsive to important performance measures and to the key risks the committee oversees.	• Overall, the committee assists the board in its oversight of: — the reliability and integrity of the accounting principles and practices used; — financial statements and other financial reporting; — disclosure principles and practices followed by management of the company and its subsidiaries; — oversight of the qualifications, independence and performance of the external auditor of the company; — establishment by management of an adequate system of internal controls and procedures; — performance of the internal controls and procedures; — performance of the internal audit function; and — compliance by the company with legal and regulatory requirements. (NYSE).

Current Positioning

Desired Positioning

Other Responsibilities and Issues (cont'd)		
Minimum Requirement	**Best Practices**	**Leading Edge Practices**
• Has the explicit authority to engage and to set and pay the compensation for independent counsel and other advisors as the committee determines necessary to carry out its duties. • Has a written charter that sets out its mandate and responsibilities. • The audit committee reports directly to the board of directors.	• Receives reports from the internal and/or external auditors on their review of officer and senior executive expense accounts. • Approves policies and receives reports from the internal and/or external auditors on their review of political donations and commissions paid to suppliers or customers to ensure compliance with these policies. • An evaluation of the performance of the audit committee in relation to the mandate is performed annually. • In consultation with management and the external auditor, develops an annual audit committee work plan to ensure all responsibilities as set out in the charter are adequately met.	• Reviews and provides its views on funding matters, financing strategies, capital structure, etc., as well as the appropriate accounting and presentation issues related thereto. • Reviews information and disclosures (e.g., posting of annual report and financial statements) made through the corporate website, including web casts of analyst calls, etc. • Audit committee mandate is reviewed and assessed annually.
Current Positioning		
Desired Positioning		

Other Responsibilities and Issues (cont'd)		
Minimum Requirement	**Best Practices**	**Leading Edge Practices**
• Meetings of the committee may be called by the board of directors, chairman of the board, committee chairman or any other member of the committee or by the external auditor. (CBA). • The audit committee meets at least quarterly.	• The audit committee meets at least six times per year. • Minutes of each committee meeting are prepared and circulated to the board of directors. • Committee meets regularly with only members present. • Committee meets regularly in private with management.	• A report on each meeting is prepared for the board of directors, and includes: — any issues with respect to quality or integrity of the financial statements; — compliance of the company and its subsidiaries with respect to legal or regulatory requirements; — performance and independence of the external auditor; and — performance of the internal audit function of the company and its subsidiaries. • The audit committee meetings are scheduled the day before the meetings of the board of directors to allow the audit committee to report to the board in a timely fashion. • In setting the committee's meeting schedule, an additional meeting is added to permit the committee to discuss matters of interest or concern identified in the committee's work plan or that arise over the course of the year.
Current Positioning		
Desired Positioning		

Example of a
Whistleblower Policy

This appendix contains an example of a whistleblower policy, which was created by Finning International Inc.

General

The Finning International Inc. Code of Ethics and Conduct ("Code") requires directors, officers and employees to observe high standards of business and personal ethics in the conduct of their duties and responsibilities. As employees and representatives of the Corporation, we must practice honesty and integrity in fulfilling our responsibilities and comply with all applicable laws and regulations.

Reporting Responsibility

It is the responsibility of all directors, officers and employees to comply with the Code and to report violations or suspected violations in accordance with this Whistleblower Policy.

No Retaliation

No director, officer or employee who in good faith reports a violation of the Code shall suffer harassment, retaliation or adverse employment consequence. An employee who retaliates against someone who has reported a violation in good faith is subject to discipline up to and including termination of employment. This Whistleblower Policy is intended to encourage and enable employees and others to raise serious concerns within the Corporation rather than seeking resolution outside the Corporation.

Reporting Violations

The Code addresses the Corporation's open door policy and suggests that employees share their questions, concerns, suggestions or complaints with someone who can address them properly. In most cases, an employee's supervisor is in the best position to address an area of concern. However, if you are not comfortable speaking with your supervisor or you are not satisfied with your supervisor's response, you are encouraged to speak with someone in the Human Resources Department or anyone in management whom you are comfortable in approaching. Supervisors and managers are required to report suspected violations of the Code of Conduct to the Company's Compliance Officer, who has specific and exclusive responsibility to investigate all reported violations. For suspected fraud or securities law violations, or when you are not satisfied or uncomfortable with following the Corporation's open door policy, individuals should contact the Corporation's Compliance Officer directly.

Compliance Officer

The Corporation's Compliance Officer is responsible for investigating and resolving all reported complaints and allegations concerning violations of the Code and, at his discretion, shall advise the President and CEO, the CFO and/or the audit committee. He has direct access to the audit committee of the board of directors and is required to report to the Committee at least annually on his compliance activity. The Company's Compliance Officer is John Struthers, Corporate Secretary. John's direct telephone line is (XXX-XXX-XXXX). If you are not comfortable speaking with John or John is unavailable and the matter is urgent, you may contact the Chairman of the audit committee, Mr. Andrew Simon via email at XXXX@XXX.com

Accounting and Auditing Matters

The audit committee of the board of directors shall address all reported concerns or complaints regarding corporate accounting practices, internal controls or auditing. The Compliance Officer shall immediately notify the audit committee of any such complaint and work with the committee until the matter is resolved.

Acting in Good Faith

Anyone filing a complaint concerning a violation or suspected violation of the Code must be acting in good faith and have reasonable grounds for believing the information disclosed indicates a violation of the Code. Any allegations that prove not to be substantiated and which prove to have been made maliciously or knowingly to be false will be viewed as a serious disciplinary offense.

Confidentiality

Violations or suspected violations may be submitted on a confidential basis by the complainant or may be submitted anonymously. Reports of violations or suspected violations will be kept confidential to the extent possible, consistent with the need to conduct an adequate investigation.

Handling of Reported Violations

The Compliance Officer will notify the sender and acknowledge receipt of the reported violation or suspected violation within five business days. All reports will be promptly investigated and appropriate corrective action will be taken if warranted by the investigation.

Examples of
Audit Committee Charters

This appendix contains examples of the audit committee charters from:
- *Canadian Tire Corporation, Limited*
- *O&Y Properties Corporation*
- *Royal Bank of Canada*
- *Nortel Networks Corporation*
- *General Electric Company (U.S. Issuer)*

CANADIAN TIRE CORPORATION, LIMITED
AUDIT COMMITTEE MANDATE AND CHARTER

I. THE BOARD OF DIRECTORS' MANDATE FOR THE AUDIT COMMITTEE

1. **The Board of Directors ("Board")** bears responsibility for the stewardship of Canadian Tire Corporation, Limited (the "Corporation"). To discharge that responsibility, the Board is obligated by the Ontario Business Corporations Act to supervise the management of the business and affairs of the Corporation. The Board's supervisory function involves Board oversight or monitoring of all significant aspects of the management of the Corporation's business and affairs.

Financial reporting and disclosure by the Corporation constitute a significant aspect of the management of the Corporation's business and affairs. The objective of the Board's monitoring of the Corporation's financial reporting and disclosure (the "Financial Reporting Objective") is to gain reasonable assurance of the following:

a) that the Corporation complies with all applicable laws, regulations, rules, policies and other requirements of governments, regulatory agencies and stock exchanges relating to financial reporting and disclosure;

b) that the accounting principles, significant judgements and disclosures which underlie or are incorporated in the Corporation's financial statements are the most appropriate in the prevailing circumstances;

c) that the Corporation's quarterly and annual financial statements are accurate and present fairly the Corporation's financial position and performance in accordance with generally accepted accounting principles and together with management's discussion and analysis and the annual information form constitute a fair presentation of the Corporation's financial condition; and

d) that appropriate information concerning the financial position and performance of the Corporation is disseminated to the public in a timely manner.

The Board is of the view that the Financial Reporting Objective cannot be reliably met unless the following activities (the "Fundamental Activities") are conducted effectively:

i) the Corporation's accounting functions are performed in accordance with a system of internal financial controls designed to capture and record properly and accurately all of the Corporation's financial transactions;

ii) the Corporation's internal financial controls are regularly assessed for effectiveness and efficiency;

iii) the Corporation's quarterly and annual financial statements are properly prepared by management;

iv) the Corporation's quarterly and annual financial statements are reported on by an external auditor appointed by the shareholders of the Corporation; and

v) the financial components of the Corporation's Disclosure Policy are complied with by management and the Board.

To assist the Board in its monitoring of the Corporation's financial reporting and disclosure, the Board has established, and hereby continues the existence of, a committee of the Board known as the Audit Committee (the "Committee"). The Committee shall develop and present to the Board for the Board's approval a Charter which, amongst other things, will describe the activities in which the Committee will engage for the purpose of gaining reasonable assurance that the Fundamental Activities are being conducted effectively and that the Financial Reporting Objective is being met.

2. **Composition of Committee**
   a) The Committee shall be appointed annually by the Board and consist of at least five (5) members from among the directors of the Corporation, each of whom shall be an independent director as defined under the applicable requirements of the securities regulatory authorities as adopted or amended and in force from time to time and free from any relationship that, in the opinion of the Board, could interfere with the exercise of his or her independent judgement as a member of the Committee. Officers of the Corporation, including the Chairman of the Board, may not serve as members of the Audit Committee.
   b) All members of the Committee shall be financially literate as described in paragraph 3 of the Operating Principles.
   c) The Board shall designate the Chairman of the Committee.

3. **Reliance on Experts**
   In contributing to the Committee's discharging of its duties under this mandate, each member of the Committee shall be entitled to rely in good faith upon:
   a) financial statements of the Corporation represented to him or her by an officer of the Corporation or in a written report of the external auditors to present fairly the financial position of the Corporation in accordance with generally accepted accounting principles; and
   b) any report of a lawyer, accountant, engineer, appraiser or other person whose profession lends credibility to a statement made by any such person.

4. **Limitations on Committee's Duties**
   In contributing to the Committee's discharging of its duties under this mandate, each member of the Committee shall be obliged only to exercise the care, diligence and skill that a reasonably prudent person would exercise in comparable circumstances. Nothing in this mandate is intended, or may be construed, to impose on any member of the Committee a standard of care or diligence that is in any way more onerous or extensive than the standard to which all Board members are subject. The essence of the Committee's duties is monitoring and reviewing to gain reasonable assurance (but not

to ensure) that the Fundamental Activities are being conducted effectively and that the Financial Reporting Objective is being met and to enable the Committee to report thereon to the Board.

II. AUDIT COMMITTEE CHARTER

The Audit Committee's Charter outlines how the Committee will satisfy the requirements set forth by the Board in its mandate. This Charter comprises:
- Operating Principles;
- Operating Procedures;
- Specific Responsibilities and Duties.

A. *Operating Principles*

The Committee shall fulfill its responsibilities within the context of the following principles:

1. Committee Values

The Committee expects the management of the Corporation to operate in compliance with the Corporation's Code of Conduct and corporate policies; with laws and regulations governing the Corporation; and to maintain strong financial reporting and control processes.

2. Communications

The Chairman and members of the Committee expect to have direct, open and frank communications throughout the year with management, other Committee Chairmen, the external auditors, the Internal Auditor and other key Committee advisors as applicable.

3. Financial Literacy

All Committee members shall have the ability to read and understand a set of financial statements that present a breadth and level of complexity of accounting issues that are generally comparable to the breadth and complexity of the issues that can reasonably be expected to be raised by the Corporation's financial statements.

4. Annual Audit Committee Work Plan

The Committee, in consultation with management and the external auditors, shall develop an annual Audit Committee Work Plan responsive to the Committee's responsibilities as set out in this Charter.

In addition, the Committee, in consultation with management and the external auditors, shall develop and participate in a process for review of important financial topics that have the potential to impact the Corporation's financial disclosure.

5. **Meeting Agenda**

   Committee meeting agendas shall be the responsibility of the Chairman of the Committee in consultation with Committee members, senior management and the external auditors.

6. **Committee Expectations and Information Needs**

   The Committee shall communicate its expectations to management and the external auditors with respect to the nature, timing and extent of its information needs. The Committee expects that written materials will be received from management and the external auditors at least one week in advance of meeting dates.

7. **External Resources**

   To assist the Committee in discharging its responsibilities, the Committee may, in addition to the external auditors, at the expense of the Corporation, retain one or more persons having special expertise.

8. **In Camera Meetings**

   At each meeting of the Committee, the members of the Committee shall meet in private session with the external auditors; with management; and with the Committee members only. The Committee shall meet in private session with the Internal Auditor as often as it deems necessary, but in any event, no less than twice per year.

9. **Reporting to the Board**

   The Committee, through its Chairman, shall report after each Committee meeting to the Board at the Board's next regular meeting.

10. **Committee Self Assessment**

    The Committee shall annually review, discuss and assess its own performance. In addition, the Committee shall periodically review its role and responsibilities.

11. **The External Auditors**

    The Committee expects that, in discharging their responsibilities to the shareholders, the external auditors shall be accountable to the Board through the Audit Committee. The external auditors shall report all material issues or potentially material issues to the Committee.

12. **Approval of Other Engagements**

    The Committee shall approve all engagements for accounting and tax advice provided by an audit firm other than the external auditors.

B. Operating Procedures

1. The Committee shall meet at least four times annually, or more frequently as circumstances dictate. Meetings shall be held at the call of the Chairman, upon the request of two (2) members of the Committee or at the request of the external auditors.
2. A quorum shall be a majority of the members.
3. Unless the Committee otherwise specifies, the Secretary or Assistant Secretary of the Corporation shall act as Secretary of all meetings of the Committee.
4. In the absence of the Chairman of the Committee, the members shall appoint an acting Chairman.
5. A copy of the minutes of each meeting of the Committee shall be provided to each member of the Committee and to each director of the Corporation in a timely fashion.

C. Responsibilities and Duties

To fulfill its responsibilities and duties, the Committee shall:

Financial Reporting

1. Review the Corporation's annual and quarterly financial statements with management and the external auditors to gain reasonable assurance that the statements are accurate, complete, represent fairly the Corporation's financial position and performance and are in accordance with GAAP and together with management's discussion and analysis and the annual information form constitute a fair presentation of the Corporation's financial condition and report thereon to the Board before such financial statements are approved by the Board;
2. Review with management and the external auditors the financial statements of the Corporation's significant subsidiaries and of the Corporation's profit sharing plans;
3. Receive from the external auditors reports on their review of the annual and quarterly financial statements;
4. Receive from management a copy of the representation letter provided to the external auditors and receive from management any additional representations required by the Committee;
5. Review and, if appropriate, recommend approval to the Board of news releases and reports to shareholders issued by the Corporation with respect to the Corporation's annual and quarterly financial statements;
6. Review and, if appropriate, recommend approval to the Board of all public disclosure documents containing material audited or unaudited financial information, including material change disclosures of a financial nature, earnings press releases, prospectuses, management's discussion and analysis, annual information forms, as well as any earnings guidance; and

7. Satisfy itself that adequate procedures are in place for the review of the Corporation's disclosure of financial information extracted or derived from the Corporation's financial statements in order to satisfy itself that such information is fairly presented and periodically assess the adequacy of these procedures.

Accounting Policies

1. Review with management and the external auditors the appropriateness of the Corporation's accounting policies, disclosures, reserves, key estimates and judgements, including changes or variations thereto and obtain reasonable assurance that they are presented fairly in accordance with GAAP; and report thereon to the Board;

2. Review major issues regarding accounting principles and financial statement presentation including any significant changes in the selection or application of accounting principles to be observed in the preparation of the accounts of the Corporation and its subsidiaries;

3. Review with management and the external auditors the degree of conservatism of the Corporation's underlying accounting policies, key estimates and judgements and reserves.

Risk and Uncertainty

1. Acknowledging that it is the responsibility of the Board, in consultation with management, to identify the principal business risks facing the Corporation, determine the Corporation's tolerance for risk and approve risk management policies, the Committee shall focus on financial risk and gain reasonable assurance that financial risk is being effectively managed or controlled by:
   a) reviewing with management the Corporation's tolerance for financial risk;
   b) reviewing with management its assessment of the significant financial risks facing the Corporation;
   c) reviewing with management the Corporation's policies and any proposed changes thereto for managing those significant financial risks;
   d) reviewing with management its plans, processes and programs to manage and control such risks;

2. Discuss with management, at least annually, the guidelines and policies utilized by management with respect to financial risk assessment and management, and the major financial risk exposures and the procedures to monitor and control such exposures in order to assist the Committee to assess the completeness, adequacy and appropriateness of financial risk disclosure in management's discussion and analysis and in the financial statements;

3. Ascertain that policies and procedures are in place to minimize environmental, occupational health and safety and other risks to asset value and mitigate damage to or deterioration of asset value and review such policies and procedures periodically;

4. Review policies and compliance therewith that require significant actual or potential liabilities, contingent or otherwise, to be reported to the Board in a timely fashion;

5. Review foreign currency, interest rate and commodity price risk mitigation strategies, including the use of derivative financial instruments;
6. Review the adequacy of insurance coverages maintained by the Corporation;
7. Review regularly with management, the external auditors and the Corporation's legal counsel, any legal claim or other contingency, including tax assessments, that could have a material effect upon the financial position or operating results of the Corporation and the manner in which these matters have been disclosed in the financial statements.

Financial Controls and Control Deviations

1. Review the plans of the internal and external auditors to gain reasonable assurance that the combined evaluation and testing of internal financial controls is comprehensive, coordinated and cost-effective;
2. Receive regular reports from management, the external auditors and its legal department on all significant deviations or indications/detection of fraud and the corrective activity undertaken in respect thereto.

Compliance with Laws and Regulations

1. Review regular reports from management and others (e.g., internal and external auditors) with respect to the Corporation's compliance with laws and regulations having a material impact on the financial statements including:
   a) tax and financial reporting laws and regulations;
   b) legal withholding requirements;
   c) environmental protection laws and regulations;
   d) other laws and regulations which expose directors to liability;
2. Review reports from the Social Responsibility Committee with respect to Occupational Health and Safety matters having a potential significant financial impact and to gain reasonable assurance annually that the Corporation's reserves with respect to such matters are sufficient and appropriate;
3. Review the status of the Corporation's tax returns and those of its subsidiaries;
4. Discuss with the General Counsel any significant legal, compliance or regulatory matters that may have a material effect on the financial statements or the business of the Corporation, or on the compliance policies of the Corporation.

Relationship with External Auditors

1. Recommend to the Board the nomination of the external auditors;
2. Recommend to the Board the remuneration and the terms of engagement of the external auditors;
3. If necessary, recommend the removal by the shareholders of the current external auditors and replacement with new external auditors;
4. Review the performance of the external auditors annually or more frequently as required;
5. Receive annually from the external auditors an acknowledgement in writing that the shareholders, as represented by the Board and the Committee, are their primary client;

6. Receive a report annually from the external auditors with respect to their independence, such report to include a disclosure of all engagements (and fees related thereto) for non-audit services by the Corporation;

7. Establish a policy under which management shall bring to the attention of the Chairman of the Committee all requests for non-audit services to be performed by the external auditors for the Corporation and its subsidiaries before such work is commenced. The Chairman is authorized to approve all such requests, but if any such service exceeds $100,000 in fees, or the service is of a sensitive or unusual nature, the Chairman shall consult with the Committee before approving the service. The Chairman has the responsibility to inform the Committee of all pre-approved services at its next meeting;

8. Discuss with management and the external auditors the timing and the process for implementing the rotation of the lead audit partner, the concurring partner and any other active audit engagement team partner;

9. Review with the external auditors the scope of the audit, the areas of special emphasis to be addressed in the audit, the extent to which the external audit can be coordinated with internal audit activities and the materiality levels which the external auditors propose to employ;

10. Meet regularly with the external auditors in the absence of management to determine, *inter alia*, that no management restrictions have been placed on the scope and extent of the audit examinations by the external auditors or the reporting of their findings to the Committee;

11. Establish effective communication processes with management and the Corporation's internal and external auditors to assist the Committee to monitor objectively the quality and effectiveness of the relationship among the external auditors, management and the Committee;

12. Oversee the work of the external auditors and the resolution of disagreements between management and the external auditors with respect to financial reporting; and

13. Request that the external auditors provide to the Committee, at least annually, an oral and/or written report describing the external auditors' internal quality assurance policies and procedures as well as any material issues raised in the most recent internal quality assurance reviews, quality reviews conducted by the Canadian Public Accountability Board, or any inquiry or investigation conducted by government or regulatory authorities.

Internal Auditor

1. Review the Internal Auditor's terms of reference;

2. Review the annual plan of the Internal Auditor;

3. Review the reports of the Corporation's Internal Auditor with respect to control and financial risk, and any other matters appropriate to the Committee's duties. The Committee shall review the adequacy and appropriateness of management's response, including the implementation thereof;

4. Review and approve the reporting relationship of the Internal Auditor to ensure that an appropriate segregation of duties is maintained and that the Internal Auditor has an obligation to report directly to the Committee on matters affecting the Committee's duties, irrespective of his or her other reporting relationships;
5. Review and report to the Board on the appointment, replacement, reassignment or dismissal of the Internal Auditor.

Other Responsibilities

1. Periodically review the form, content and level of detail of financial reports to the Board;
2. Approve annually the reasonableness of the expenses of the Chairman of the Board and the Chief Executive Officer;
3. After consultation with the Chief Financial Officer and the external auditors, gain reasonable assurance, at least annually, of the quality and sufficiency of the Corporation's accounting and financial personnel and other resources;
4. Review in advance the appointment of the Corporation's senior financial executives;
5. Investigate any matters that, in the Committee's discretion, fall within the Committee's duties;
6. Review reports from the Internal Auditor, the external auditors, and/or other Committee Chairmen on their review of compliance with the Corporation's Code of Conduct, and the Corporation's policies on political donations and commissions paid to suppliers or others;
7. Review and approve the Corporation's policies with respect to the hiring of partners, employees and former partners and employees of the current and former external auditors;
8. a) Establish procedures for:
    i) the confidential receipt, retention and treatment of complaints received by the Corporation regarding the Corporation's accounting, internal accounting controls or auditing matters; and
    ii) the confidential anonymous submission, retention and treatment of concerns by employees regarding questionable accounting or auditing matters; and
   b) Require that all such matters be reported to the Committee together with a description of the resolution of the complaints or concerns.

Accountability

1. Review and update this Charter on a regular basis for approval by the Board;
2. From time to time, as requested by the Board, disclose its Mandate and this Charter in the Corporation's statement of corporate governance practices and in its annual information form;
3. Review the description of the Committee's activities as set forth in the Corporation's statement of corporate governance practices.

O&Y PROPERTIES CORPORATION
AUDIT COMMITTEE CHARTER

1. Continuation of the Audit Committee

The Board of Directors ("Board") bears responsibility for the stewardship of O&Y Properties Corporation (the "Corporation") and in this regard, the Board supervises and directs management of the Corporation in carrying out the business of the Corporation, in the interest and for the benefit of the Corporation's shareholders.

To assist the Board in its monitoring of the Corporation's financial reporting and disclosure and to assist the Board in the identification and oversight of the management of financial risk, the Board has established, and hereby continues the existence of, a committee of the Board known as the Audit Committee (the "Committee"). The Committee's existing mandate is hereby repealed and replaced by this Charter.

2. Composition of Committee

a) The Committee will be appointed annually by the Board and consist of at least 3 members from among the Directors of the Corporation, each of whom shall be, in the opinion of the Board, both an unrelated director within the meaning of s.472 of the Toronto Stock Exchange Company Manual and an Audit Committee independent director under the Rules of the U.S. Securities Exchange Act of 1934.

b) No member of the Committee may (other than in his or her capacity as a member of the Committee, the Board or another Board committee) accept any consulting, advisory or other compensatory fee from the Corporation or be an affiliated person of the Corporation or any subsidiary.

c) All members of the Committee shall be financially literate (i.e., have the ability to read and understand the Corporation's financial statements and notes). At least one member of the Committee shall have accounting or related financial experience (i.e., the ability to analyze and interpret financial statements and notes in accordance with Canadian generally accepted accounting principles) and shall be an audit committee financial expert under the Rules of the U.S. Securities Exchange Act of 1934.

d) Officers of the Corporation, including the Chairman of the Board unless he or she is an unrelated director, may not serve as members of the Committee.

e) The Board will designate the Chairman of the Committee. The Chairman shall have responsibility for overseeing that the Committee fulfills its mandate and its duties effectively.

3. Responsibilities and Duties of the Committee

The Board mandates the Committee to monitor and be responsible for the supervision of the Corporation's financial reporting and disclosure obligations. To fulfill this role, the Committee shall have the following responsibilities and duties:

a) To oversee compliance by the Corporation with all legal, regulatory and contractual requirements relating to financial reporting and disclosure and to oversee the accounting and financial reporting processes and audits of the financial statements of the Corporation;

b) To review the financial statements and other financial information of the Corporation with management and the external auditors to gain reasonable assurance that they present fairly (in accordance with generally accepted accounting principles in Canada) in all material respects the financial condition, results of operations and cash flows of the Corporation as of, and for, the periods presented, and report thereon to the Board before same are approved by the Board;

c) To review with management and the external auditors the financial statements of any significant subsidiary of the Corporation;

d) To review with management the representation letter provided to the external auditors, to receive from management any additional representations required by the Committee, and to receive from the external auditors reports on their audit of the annual and their review of the quarterly financial statements of the Corporation;

e) To review news releases and reports to shareholders to be issued by the Corporation containing earnings guidance or containing financial information based on the Corporation's financial statements;

f) To review the Corporation's annual and quarterly "management's discussion and analysis" with management and report thereon to the Board before it is approved by the Board;

g) To review the financial information in prospectuses, annual reports, material change disclosures of a financial nature, annual information forms and similar disclosure documents to be issued by the Corporation;

h) To review with management and the external auditors the acceptability, appropriateness and quality of the Corporation's accounting principles;

i) To review an annual report by the external auditors describing: (i) all critical accounting practices and policies to be used; (ii) all alternative treatments of financial information within generally accepted accounting principles that have been discussed with management, the impact of the alternative treatments, and the treatment preferred by the external auditors; and (iii) other material written communications between the external auditors and management, and to meet with the external auditors to discuss the said annual report;

j) To review with management the principal financial risks facing the Corporation and gain reasonable assurance that financial risk is being effectively managed or controlled;

k) To review with management significant contingent liabilities;

l) To review with management and the external auditors the Corporation's internal financial control system for its effectiveness and integrity and to oversee management's reporting on that system;

m) To review with management the Corporation's management information systems for their effectiveness and their integrity;

n) To approve hiring, the remuneration and the terms of engagement of the external auditors as set forth in their engagement letter and, if necessary, their termination, and to review the performance of the external auditors as required. The Committee shall also require that the lead or responsible audit partner of the external auditors in charge of the Corporation's audit, is rotated every 5 years and that other rules relating to the audit partner as enacted by securities regulatory authorities of Canada and the United States are followed;

o) To review regularly with the external auditors their independence, including preapproval of all engagements (and fees related thereto) for non-audit services with the Corporation, and to ensure disclosure of any such non-audit services annually but in no event shall any of the following non-audit services be performed by the external auditors:

   i)   bookkeeping or other services related to the accounting records or financial statements;

   ii)   financial information systems design and implementation;

   iii) appraisal or valuation services, fairness opinions or contribution-in-kind reports;

   iv)   actuarial services;

   v)   internal audit outsourcing services;

   vi)   management functions or human resources;

   vii) broker or dealer, investment advisor or investment banking services;

   viii) legal services and expert services unrelated to the audit; and

   ix)   other services prescribed by legislation;

p) To review with the external auditors the scope of the audit, the areas of special emphasis to be addressed in the audit, the materiality levels which the external auditors propose to employ and other issues which are appropriate in the view of either the Committee or the external auditors;

q) To put in place procedures to receive and handle complaints or concerns received by the Corporation about accounting, internal accounting controls and audit matters including those submitted anonymously by an employee of the Corporation;

r) To review with management periodically the Corporation's code of ethics for senior financial officers;

s) To ensure that an external auditor cannot act as auditor of the Corporation if the Chief Executive Officer, President, Controller, Chief Financial Officer or person serving in an equivalent position was employed by the external auditor and participated in any capacity in the audit of the Corporation during a 1 year period preceding the date of initiation of the audit; and

t) To perform any other matters referred to the Committee or delegated to it by the Directors.

4. Operating Principles

The Committee will fulfill its responsibilities within the context of the following operating principles:

a) Committee Duties

Committee members are required to act honestly and in good faith with a view to the best interests of the Corporation and to exercise the care, diligence and skill that a reasonably prudent person would exercise in comparable circumstances.

b) Committee Values

The Committee expects management of the Corporation to operate in compliance with all corporate policies and codes, and all laws and regulations governing the Corporation and to maintain strong financial reporting and control processes.

c) Communications

The Chairman and all members of the Committee expect to have direct, open and frank communications throughout the year with management, other committee chairmen, the external auditors, the internal auditor, if any, the chairman of the audit committee of any subsidiaries, where applicable, and other key Committee advisors, as applicable.

d) External Resources

To assist the Committee in discharging its responsibilities, the Committee may, in addition to the external auditors, at the expense of the Corporation, retain one or more persons having special expertise. The Corporation shall pay all fees and expenses of the external auditors or other persons retained by the Committee.

e) Reporting to the Board

The Committee, through its Chairman, will report regularly to the Board, and in any event no less frequently than on a quarterly basis.

f) Time Commitment

Members of the Committee are expected to commit whatever time may be necessary to fulfill the mandate of the Committee. Members should prepare for Committee meetings by reviewing the materials sent to them by management for discussion at the meeting, as well as other material they feel is necessary. Members are expected to attend (in person or by telephone) all meetings of the Committee and to participate in those meetings through the asking of relevant questions and the expression of opinions on items being discussed.

g) External Auditors

The external auditors will be accountable to the Board, as representatives of shareholders, through the Committee. The Committee is directly responsible for recommending the appointment of the auditors to the Corporation's shareholders and for the compensation and oversight of the work of the external auditors, including resolution of disagreements between management and the external auditors regarding financial reporting. The external auditors will report all material issues or potentially material issues to the Committee.

h) Reliance on Experts

In contributing to the Committee's discharging of its duties under this mandate, each member of the Committee will be entitled to rely in good faith upon:

i) financial statements of the Corporation represented to him or her by an officer of the Corporation or in a written report of the external auditors to present fairly the financial position of the Corporation in accordance with Canadian generally accepted accounting principles; and

ii) any report of a lawyer, accountant, engineer, appraiser or other person whose profession lends credibility to a statement made by any such person.

5. Operating Procedures

a) Frequency of Meetings

The Committee will meet at least 6 times annually, and more frequently as circumstances dictate. Meetings will be held on at least 4 hours notice at the call of the Chairman, upon the request of any member of the Committee or at the request of the external auditors.

b) Quorum

A quorum will be a majority of the members of the Committee present in person or by telephone.

c) Chairman

In the absence of the Chairman of the Committee, the members will appoint an acting Chairman.

d) Secretary

Unless the Committee otherwise specifies, the Secretary of the Corporation will act as Secretary of all meetings of the Committee.

e) Meeting Agenda

Committee meeting agendas shall be set by the Chairman of the Committee in consultation with Committee members, management if appropriate, and the external auditors if appropriate.

f) In Camera Meetings

The members of the Committee will meet at regularly scheduled sessions with the external auditors, select members of management, and by themselves, without either or both of management and the external auditors present.

g) Background Material for Meetings

Members of the Committee should be provided with an agenda and sufficient background material prepared in a clear and concise manner relating to a forthcoming meeting as will allow them to understand the items to be discussed at the meeting. The material should contain sufficient information, to the extent such information is reasonably available to management, to enable the Committee members to make an informed decision if one is required. The agenda with this material should be received by the Committee members far enough in advance of the meeting as will allow them sufficient time to review the materials.

h) Minutes

Minutes of each meeting of the Committee will be prepared by the Secretary of the meeting and be provided to each member of the Committee for review and approval at a subsequent Committee meeting. After being approved, a copy of the minutes will be provided to each director of the Corporation for information purposes.

6. Limitations on Committee Members' Duties

Nothing in this mandate is intended, or may be construed, to impose on any member of the Committee a standard of care or diligence that is in any way more onerous or extensive than the standard to which all Board members are subject. It is not the duty of the Committee to prepare financial statements, plan or conduct audits, act as auditors or to determine that the Corporation's financial statements and disclosures are complete and accurate and are in accordance with Canadian generally accepted accounting principles and applicable laws. These are the responsibilities of management and the external auditors. The external auditors are accountable to the Board and the Committee, being the representatives of the shareholders of the Corporation.

With regard to financial risk management, the Committee's responsibility is one of oversight only. Management is responsible to ensure proper financial risk management policies are in place and being adhered to.

ROYAL BANK OF CANADA
AUDIT COMMITTEE CHARTER

2.1 Audit Committee

2.1.1 *Establishment of Committee and Procedures*

a) Establishment of Committee

A committee of the directors to be known as the "Audit Committee" (hereinafter the "Committee") is hereby established.

b) Composition of Committee

The Committee shall be composed of not less than five directors. Each member shall be financially literate, as the Board of Directors interprets such qualification in its business judgment, or must become financially literate within a reasonable period of time after appointment to the Committee. At least one member shall have accounting or related financial management expertise, as the Board of Directors interprets such qualification in its business judgment.

c) Independence of Committee Members

As required by the Bank Act, none of the members of the Committee shall be an officer or employee of the Bank or of an affiliate of the Bank. All of the members of the Committee shall be "unaffiliated", as defined in regulations made under the Bank Act. All of the members of the Committee shall be independent, as determined by director independence standards adopted by the Board. None of the members of the Committee shall receive from the Bank any compensation other than directors' fees.

d) Appointment of Committee Members

Members shall be appointed or reappointed at the annual Organizational Meeting of the directors and in the normal course will serve a minimum of three years. Each member shall continue to be a member until a successor is appointed, unless the member resigns, is removed or ceases to be a director. The Board of Directors may fill a vacancy that occurs in the Committee at any time.

e) Committee Chairman and Secretary

The Board of Directors, or, in the event of its failure to do so, the members of the Committee, shall appoint or reappoint, at the annual Organizational Meeting of the directors, a Chairman from among their number. The Chairman shall not be a former employee of the Bank or of an affiliate. The Committee shall also appoint a Secretary who need not be a director.

f) Time and Place of Meetings

Meetings may be called by any member of the Committee, or by the external auditors. The time and place of and the procedure at meetings shall be determined from time to time by the members provided that:

i) A quorum for meeting shall be three members;

ii) The Committee shall meet at least quarterly;

iii) The Committee may request any officer or employee of the Bank or the Bank's outside counsel or external auditors to attend a meeting of the Committee or to meet with any members of, or consultants to, the Committee;

iv) Notice of the time and place of every meeting shall be given in writing or by telephone, facsimile, email or other electronic communication to each member of the Committee and to the external auditors at least 24 hours prior to the time fixed for such meeting, provided, however, that business referred to in paragraph 2.1.3.f)(ii) below may be transacted at any meeting of which at least one hour prior notice is given as aforesaid, and that a member may in any manner waive notice of a meeting; and attendance of a member at a meeting is a waiver of notice of the meeting, except where a member attends a meeting for the express purpose of objecting to the transaction of any business on the grounds that the meeting is not lawfully called; and

v) A resolution in writing signed by all the members entitled to vote on that resolution at a Committee meeting, other than a resolution of the Committee carrying out its duties under subsection 194(3) of the *Bank Act*, shall be as valid as if it had been passed at a meeting of the Committee.

g) Reporting to the Board of Directors

The Committee shall report verbally after each meeting and annually in writing to the Board of Directors with respect to its activities with such recommendations as are to be deemed desirable in the circumstances. Prior to approval by the directors, the Committee will also report to the Board on the annual statement and returns that must be approved by the directors under the Bank Act.

h) Evaluation of Effectiveness and Review of Mandate

The Committee shall annually review and assess the adequacy of its mandate and evaluate its effectiveness in fulfilling its mandate.

2.1.2   *General Scope of Responsibilities and Purpose of the Committee*

Management of the Bank is responsible for the preparation, presentation and integrity of the Bank's financial statements and for maintaining appropriate accounting and financial reporting principles and policies and internal controls and procedures designed to ensure compliance with accounting standards and applicable laws and regulations.

The external auditors are responsible for planning and carrying out, in accordance with professional standards, an audit of the Bank's annual financial statements and reviews of the Bank's quarterly financial information.

The Committee's purpose is to review the adequacy and effectiveness of these activities and to assist the Board in its oversight of:
i)   the integrity of the Bank's financial statements;
ii) the external auditors' qualifications and independence;
iii) the performance of the Bank's internal audit function and external auditors;
iv) the adequacy and effectiveness of internal controls; and
v)   the Bank's compliance with legal and regulatory requirements.

The Committee is also responsible for preparing any report from the Committee that may be required to be included in the Bank's annual proxy statement or that the Board elects to include on a voluntary basis.

The Committee shall meet every fiscal quarter, or more frequently at the discretion of the Committee if circumstances dictate, to discuss with management the annual audited financial statements and quarterly financial statements.

At least quarterly, the Committee shall have separate private meetings with the external auditors, the chief internal auditor and management to discuss any matters that the Committee or these groups believe should be discussed.

In fulfilling its role, the Committee is empowered to investigate any matter with full access to all books, records, facilities and personnel of the Bank and the authority to retain outside counsel or other experts for this purpose.

2.1.3   *Specific Responsibilities*
a) Documents and Reports
The Committee shall review:
i)   the annual statements of the Bank that under the Bank Act must be approved by the Directors and shall report to the directors before such annual statement is approved by the directors;
ii) the quarterly financial statements of the Bank;
iii) the Annual Information Form;
iv) the quarterly and annual Management's Discussion and Analysis;
v)   earnings press releases, and the types of financial information and earnings guidance provided and types of presentations made to analysts and ratings agencies;
vi) such returns and other periodic disclosure documentation as the Bank is required to file pursuant to applicable legislation, or as the Superintendent of Financial Institutions or as other regulators may specify;

vii) such investments and transactions that could adversely affect the well-being of the Bank as the external auditors or any other officer of the Bank may bring to the attention of the Committee;

viii) prospectuses relating to the issuance of securities of the Bank;

ix) an annual report on any litigation matters which could significantly affect the financial statements; and

x) an annual report from the chief compliance officer on regulatory compliance matters.

b) Internal Control

The Committee shall require management of the Bank to implement and maintain appropriate systems of internal control. The Committee shall review, evaluate and approve those procedures and meet with the chief internal auditor of the Bank and with management of the Bank to assess the adequacy and effectiveness of these systems of internal control and to obtain on a regular basis reasonable assurance that the organization is in control.

c) Internal Auditor

The Committee shall:

i) review and concur in the appointment, reassignment or dismissal of the chief internal auditor and review the mandate, annual audit plan, and the resources of the internal audit function;

ii) meet with the chief internal auditor of the Bank to review the results of internal audit activities, including any significant issues reported to management by the internal audit function and management's responses and/or corrective actions;

iii) meet with the chief internal auditor of the Bank to determine whether any significant weaknesses or breakdowns that have been identified are being addressed;

iv) review representations from the chief internal auditor, based on audit work done, on the adequacy and degree of compliance with the Bank's systems of internal control;

v) review the performance, degree of independence and objectivity of the internal audit function and adequacy of the internal audit process; and

v) review with the chief internal auditor any issues that may not be brought forward by the chief internal auditor, including any difficulties encountered by the internal audit function, such as audit scope, information access, or staffing restriction.

d) External Auditor

The Committee, in its capacity as a committee of the Board of Directors, shall have the authority and responsibility to recommend the appointment and recommend the revocation of the appointment of any registered public accounting firm (including the external auditors) engaged for the purpose of preparing or issuing an audit report or performing other audit, review or attestation services, and to fix their remuneration, subject to the powers conferred on the shareholders by the Bank Act. The Committee shall be responsible for the oversight of the work of each such accounting firm, including resolution of disagreements between management and the accounting firm regarding financial reporting, and each such firm shall report directly to the Committee. The Committee shall:

i) meet with the external auditors to review and discuss the annual audit plan, the results of the audit, their report with respect to the annual statement and the returns and transactions referred to in subsection 194(3) of the Bank Act, and the report required to be provided to the Committee by the external auditors pursuant to Rule 2-07 of the U.S. Securities and Exchange Commission's Regulation S-X;

ii) have the sole authority to approve all audit engagement fees and terms, as well as the provision and the terms of any legally permissible non-audit services to be provided by the external auditors to the Bank, with such approval to be given either specifically or pursuant to preapproval policies and procedures adopted by the Committee;

iii) review with the external auditors any issues that may be brought forward by the external auditors including any audit problems or difficulties, such as restrictions on their audit activities or access to requested information, and management's response;

iv) annually review with the external auditors their qualifications, independence and objectivity, including formal written statements delineating all relationships between the external auditors and the Bank that may impact independence and objectivity;

v) discuss with the external auditors and with management of the Bank the annual audited financial statements and quarterly financial statements, including the disclosures contained in "Management's Discussion and Analysis";

vi) review hiring policies concerning employees or former employees of the external auditors;

vii) review and evaluation the qualifications, performance and independence of the lead partner of the external auditors and discuss the timing and process for implementing the rotation of the lead audit partner, the concurring audit partners, and any other active audit engagement team partner; and

viii) take into account the opinions of management and the Bank's internal auditors in assessing the qualifications, performance and independence of the external auditors.

e) CDIC

To ensure compliance with the standards of the Canada Deposit Insurance Corporation ("CDIC") the Committee shall:

i) review on a regular basis the Bank's control environment and internal controls;

ii) review and approve at least once a year the liquidity and funding management policies and capital management policies recommended by the Bank's management;

iii) review on a regular basis the liquidity and funding management processes and the capital management process;

iv) obtain on a regular basis reasonable assurance that the Bank's liquidity and funding management policies and capital management policies are being adhered to;

v) annual review a senior management representation letter concerning adherence to CDIC standards and presented to the Committee; and

vi) review and approve a periodic standards report and any other matters required from time to time by CDIC.

f) Other

i) The Committee shall discuss major issues regarding accounting principles and financial statement presentations, including significant changes in the Bank's selection or application of accounting principles, analyses prepared by management or the external auditor setting forth significant financial reporting issues and judgments made in connection with the preparation of the financial statement, including analyses of the effect on the financial statements of alternative methods of applying Canadian or U.S. generally accepted accounting principles, of regulatory and accounting initiatives and of off-balance sheet structures;

ii) The Committee shall establish procedures for the receipt, retention, treatment and resolution of complaints received by the Bank regarding accounting or auditing matters, as well as procedures for the confidential and anonymous submission by employees of the Bank of concerns regarding accounting or auditing matters;

iii) The Committee shall review and discuss any reports concerning material violations submitted to it by Bank attorneys or outside counsel pursuant to the attorney professional responsibility rules of the U.S. Securities and Exchange Commission, the Bank's attorney reporting policy, or otherwise;

iv) The Committee may designate and authorize the issue of First Preferred Shares as provided in the relevant Standing Resolution of the Board of Directors;

v) The Committee shall, as appropriate, obtain at the expense of the Bank advice and assistance from outside legal, accounting or other advisors;

vi) The Committee shall discuss the major financial risk exposures of the Bank and the steps management has taken to monitor and control such exposures;

vii) In connection with the exercise of the delegated power to authorize and approve issues of subordinated indebtedness of the Bank, the Committee shall review and approve the Draft Securities Disclosure Document as provided in the relevant Standing Resolution of the Board of Directors; and

viii) Subject to the laws applicable to the subsidiary, the Committee may perform for and on behalf of a subsidiary the functions of an audit committee of the subsidiary.

NORTEL NETWORKS CORPORATION
AUDIT COMMITTEE MANDATE

Reporting to the Board of Directors, the Audit Committee shall be responsible for assisting in the Board of Directors' oversight of the reliability and integrity of the accounting principles and practices, financial statements and other financial reporting, and disclosure principles and practices followed by management of the Corporation and its subsidiaries. The Committee shall also assist the Board of Directors in its oversight of (i) the qualifications, independence and performance of the independent auditors of the Corporation, (ii) the establishment by management of an adequate system of internal controls and procedures, (iii) the effectiveness of the internal controls and procedures, and (iv) the compliance by the Corporation with legal and regulatory requirements.

The Committee shall be composed of not less than three Directors of the Corporation, none of whom are officers or employees of the Corporation or any of its affiliates, and all of whom are "independent" as defined under the applicable requirements of all stock exchanges on which the Corporation lists its securities and of securities regulatory authorities, as adopted or amended and in force from time to time. In addition, the Committee composition, including the qualifications of its members, shall comply with the applicable requirements of stock exchanges on which the Corporation lists its securities and of securities regulatory authorities, as adopted or amended and in force from time to time. The Board of Directors will consider the appropriateness of the application of any applicable stock exchange guidelines or recommendations regarding the composition of the Committee.

Regular meetings of the Committee may be held at such time or times as the Board of Directors, the Chairman of the Board, or the Committee Chairman may determine and special meetings of the Committee may be called by, or by the order of, the Chairman of the Board, the Committee Chairman, or any member of the Committee. In accordance with the *Canada Business Corporations Act* (the "Act"), the independent auditors may also call a meeting of the Committee. The independent auditors shall receive notice of every meeting of the Committee and the independent auditors are entitled to attend and participate in such meetings. The Committee shall meet periodically in executive session, without members of management present. The Committee Chairman, or an alternate Committee member, shall provide a report on each Committee meeting to the Board of Directors and minutes of Committee meetings shall be prepared and circulated to the Board of Directors. The Committee's report to the Board of Directors shall include any issues that arise with respect to the quality or integrity of the financial statements, the compliance of the Corporation and its subsidiaries with legal or regulatory requirements, the performance and independence of the independent auditors, or the performance of the internal audit function of the Corporation and its subsidiaries.

The Board of Directors, after consideration of the recommendation of the Committee, shall nominate the independent auditors for appointment by the shareholders of the Corporation or, if appropriate, recommend the removal by the shareholders of the then current independent auditors and replacement with new independent auditors, so recommended, all in accordance with applicable law and applicable stock exchange requirements. The independent auditors shall report directly to the Committee and are ultimately accountable to the Committee and the Board of Directors as the representatives of shareholders of the Corporation.

In carrying out its responsibilities, the Committee shall have the following specific oversight duties:

a) review, at least annually, the performance of the independent auditors, and annually recommend to the Board of Directors, for approval by the shareholders, the appointment of the independent auditors of the Corporation (and, if applicable, the removal of the then current independent auditors) in accordance with the Act, and review and approve the terms of the annual audit engagement;

b) review, and engage in an active dialogue with the independent auditors on, the independent auditors' written statement confirming their relationships with the Corporation and their independence from the Corporation, and either confirm to the Board of Directors that the independent auditors are independent in accordance with applicable regulations or recommend that the Board of Directors take appropriate action in response to the independent auditors' written statement to enable the Board of Directors to satisfy itself of such independence;

c) discuss with management and the independent auditors the timing and process for implementing the rotation of the lead audit partner, the concurring partner and any other active audit engagement team partner;

d) approve and, at least annually, review compliance with the hiring policies for employees and former employees of the independent auditors;

e) at least annually, review a report by the independent auditors describing: the audit firm's internal quality-control procedures; any material issues raised by the most recent quality-control review, or peer review, of the firm, or by any inquiry or investigation by governmental or professional authorities of the firm, within the preceding five years, respecting one or more independent audits carried out by the firm, and any steps taken to deal with any such issues;

f) review and pre-approve, or adopt appropriate procedures or delegations of authority to pre-approve, all audit and non-audit services to be provided by the independent auditors in accordance with the requirements of applicable law, and the requirements of stock exchanges on which the Corporation lists its securities and of securities regulatory authorities, as adopted or amended and in force from time to time, and in view of the policy adopted by the Board of Directors with respect to the provision of services by the independent auditors on April 25, 2002;

g) review and approve, at least annually, the overall scope of the independent auditors' annual audit program and the internal audit annual (and, if applicable, periodic) audit program, including any special audit steps adopted in light of material control deficiencies, if any, existing from time to time;

h) obtain assurances from the independent auditors that their audit was conducted in a manner consistent with the applicable standards for the conduct of an audit in accordance with Canadian and United States generally accepted auditing standards;

i) periodically review the adequacy of internal controls established by management, including receiving reports from management of any significant deficiencies in the design or operation and/or major issues in the adequacy of internal controls and evidence of fraud, whether or not material, that involves management or other employees who have a significant role in the internal controls and, where appropriate, make recommendations or reports thereon to the Board of Directors;

j) periodically review the status and findings of the independent auditors' audit program and the internal audit program;

k) receive and review reports and communications from the internal auditors and the independent auditors (including as required by applicable statements of auditing standards), and review management's response and actions taken to remedy any identified weaknesses or deficiencies identified in such reports and communications, including any audit problems or difficulties encountered in performing the audit and management's response, and resolve disagreements between management and the independent auditors;

l) discuss with management, at least annually, the guidelines and policies utilized by management with respect to risk assessment and risk management and the major financial risk exposures and the steps to monitor and control such exposures;

m) review major issues regarding accounting principles and financial statement presentation, including any significant changes in the selection or application of accounting principles to be observed in the preparation of the accounts of the Corporation and its subsidiaries, or in their application;

n) review a report from the independent auditors, in connection with any audited financial statements, describing all critical accounting policies and practices used, all alternative treatments of financial information within generally accepted accounting principles that have been discussed with management, the ramifications of the use of alternative disclosures and treatments and the treatment preferred by the independent auditors, and any material written communications between the independent auditors and management, such as any management representation or other letter, internal control letter, or schedule of unadjusted differences;

o) review analyses prepared by management and/or the independent auditor setting forth significant financial reporting issues and judgments made in connection with the preparation of the financial statements, including analyses of the effects of alternative generally accepted accounting principles on the financial statements, and the effect of regulatory or accounting initiatives, as well as off balance-sheet structures, on the financial statements of the Corporation;

p) review and discuss the annual and quarterly financial statements with the independent auditors and management, and, following such discussion, recommend to the Board of Directors, approval of audited annual consolidated financial statements of the Corporation and of its pension plans and such other financial statements of the Corporation required to be approved by the Board of Directors;

q) review and monitor practices and procedures adopted by management to assure compliance with applicable laws and the requirements of the applicable stock exchanges, including reporting, disclosure and officer certification requirements under applicable corporate and securities laws and the applicable requirements of stock exchanges on which the Corporation's securities are listed related to financial performance and, where appropriate, make recommendations or reports thereon to the Board of Directors;

r) review with management for recommendation to the Joint Leadership Resources Committee, the appointment of the chief financial officer and other key financial executives involved in the financial reporting processes and procedures of the Corporation and its subsidiaries, including the Controller and the General Auditor;

s) review the annual performance assessment of the General Auditor completed by the Chief Financial Officer and the annual performance self-assessment completed by the General Auditor;

t) periodically, but not less than quarterly, (and at any time in response to a specific request by management, the independent auditors, or the internal auditor), meet separately with management, the independent auditors, and/or the General Auditor, in a manner that facilitates separate independent communication with the Committee, with respect to such matters as the effectiveness of the system of internal controls established by management, the adequacy of the financial reporting processes and procedures, the quality and integrity of the financial statements, the evaluation of the performance of the independent auditors and any other matter that may be appropriate;

u) periodically and not less than annually, receive and review a report on the insurance programs in place for the Corporation and its subsidiaries;

v) review, with the independent auditors where appropriate, public disclosure documents containing material audited or unaudited financial information, including earnings press releases, prospectuses, annual and quarterly reports on Form 10-K and Form 10-Q, financial statements, management's discussion and analyses of financial condition and results of operations, as well as financial information and the earnings guidance provided to analysts and rating agencies generally and, where appropriate, make recommendations or reports thereon to the Board of Directors;

w) prepare such reports of the Committee as may be required by any applicable law or stock exchanges or other securities regulatory authorities to be included in the proxy circular and statement or any other public disclosure document of the Corporation and review the disclosure to be contained in the proxy circular and statement or any other public disclosure document of the Corporation of the services performed and the fees paid to the independent auditor;

x) periodically review the activities and business practices followed by senior management so as to assess compliance with appropriate corporate policies and the Code of Business Conduct and to address any deficiencies in such compliance;

y) discuss with the Chief Legal Officer periodically any significant legal, compliance, or regulatory matters that may have a material effect on the financial statements or the business of the Corporation or on the compliance policies of the Corporation, including material notices to or inquiries received from governmental agencies; and

z) establish and maintain procedures for the receipt, retention and treatment of complaints received by the Corporation regarding accounting, internal accounting controls or auditing matters, and procedures for the confidential, anonymous submission by employees of concerns regarding accounting or auditing matters and receive periodic reports with respect thereto.

In discharging its duties and responsibilities, the Committee may direct that the independent auditors or internal auditors examine or consider a specific matter or area and report to the Committee on the findings of such examination. The Committee may direct the independent auditors or internal auditors to perform supplemental reviews or audits as the Committee deems desirable. The Committee may also conduct such examinations, investigations or inquiries, and engage such special legal, accounting or other advisors on the terms and conditions, including fees, as the Committee considers appropriate, to conduct or assist in the conduct of such examinations, investigations or inquiries. The Corporation shall provide appropriate funding, as determined by the Committee, for payment of compensation and fees to the external auditors, any advisors employed or retained by the Committee and the ordinary administrative expenses of the Committee that are necessary or appropriate for the Committee to carry out its duties. The Committee may request any officer or employee of the Corporation or any of its affiliates or the legal advisors or independent auditors for the Corporation or any of its affiliates to attend a meeting of the Committee or to meet independently with any members of, or advisors to, the Committee.

The Committee shall review and assess the adequacy of the Committee mandate annually, report to the Board of Directors on the results of such assessment, and recommend any proposed changes to the Board of Directors for approval. The Committee shall also conduct an annual evaluation of the performance by the Committee of its responsibilities in accordance with the Committee mandate, and such evaluation shall be conducted in such manner as the Committee deems appropriate. The Committee shall report the results of its performance evaluation to the Board of Directors and such report may be an oral report by the Committee Chairman or by any other member of the Committee designated by the Committee to make the report.

While the Committee has the responsibilities and powers set forth in this mandate, it is not the duty of the Committee to plan or conduct audits, to prepare or audit financial statements, to determine that the Corporation's financial statements are complete and accurate and are in accordance with generally accepted accounting principles, or to design or implement an effective system of internal controls. Such matters are the responsibility of management, the internal auditors and the independent auditors, as the case may be. Nor is it the duty of the Committee to conduct investigations or to assure compliance with applicable accounting standards, laws and regulations and the Code of Business Conduct.

Effective February 26, 2004

GENERAL ELECTRIC COMPANY (U.S. ISSUER)
AUDIT COMMITTEE CHARTER

The Audit Committee of the board of directors of General Electric Company shall consist of a minimum of four directors. Members of the committee shall be appointed by the board of directors upon the recommendation of the Nominating and Corporate Governance Committee and may be removed by the board of directors in its discretion. All members of the committee shall be independent directors under the New York Stock Exchange's listing requirements and GE's independence guidelines, and shall also satisfy the Securities and Exchange Commission's more rigorous independence requirement for members of the audit committee. All members shall have sufficient financial experience and ability to enable them to discharge their responsibilities and at least one member shall be a financial expert.

The purpose of the committee shall be to assist the board in its oversight of the integrity of the financial statements of the company, of the company's compliance with legal and regulatory requirements, of the independence and qualifications of the independent auditor, and of the performance of the company's internal audit function and independent auditors.

In furtherance of this purpose, the committee shall have the following authority and responsibilities:
1. To discuss with management and the independent auditor the annual audited financial statements and quarterly financial statements, including matters required to be reviewed under applicable legal, regulatory or New York Stock Exchange requirements.
2. To discuss with management and the independent auditor, as appropriate, earnings press releases and financial information and earnings guidance provided to analysts and to rating agencies.
3. To select the independent auditor to examine the company's accounts, controls and financial statements. The committee shall have the sole authority and responsibility to select, evaluate, compensate and oversee the work of any registered public accounting firm engaged for the purpose of preparing or issuing an audit report or performing other audit, review or attest services for the company (including resolution of disagreements between management and the auditor regarding financial reporting). The independent auditor and each such registered public accounting firm will report directly to the committee. The committee shall have the sole authority to approve all audit engagement fees and terms and the committee, or a member of the committee, must pre-approve any audit and non-audit service provided to the company by the company's independent auditor.
4. To discuss with management and the independent auditor, as appropriate, any audit problems or difficulties and management's response, and the company's risk assessment and risk management policies, including the company's major financial risk exposure and steps taken by management to monitor and mitigate such exposure.

5. To review the company's financial reporting and accounting standards and principles, significant changes in such standards or principles or in their application and the key accounting decisions affecting the company's financial statements, including alternatives to, and the rationale for, the decisions made.

6. To review and approve the internal corporate audit staff functions, including: (i) purpose, authority and organizational reporting lines; (ii) annual audit plan, budget and staffing; and (iii) concurrence in the appointment, compensation and rotation of the vice president-corporate audit staff.

7. To review, with the senior vice president-finance, the vice president-corporate audit staff, or such others as the committee deems appropriate, the company's internal system of audit and financial controls and the results of internal audits.

8. To obtain and review at least annually a formal written report from the independent auditor delineating: the auditing firm's internal quality-control procedures; any material issues raised within the preceding five years by the auditing firm's internal quality-control reviews, by peer reviews of the firm, or by any governmental or other inquiry or investigation relating to any audit conducted by the firm. The committee will also review steps taken by the auditing firm to address any findings in any of the foregoing reviews. Also, in order to assess auditor independence, the committee will review at least annually all relationships between the independent auditor and the company.

9. To prepare and publish an annual committee report in the company's proxy statement.

10. To set policies for the hiring of employees or former employees of the company's independent auditor.

11. To review and investigate any matters pertaining to the integrity of management, including conflicts of interest, or adherence to standards of business conduct as required in the policies of the company. This should include regular reviews of the compliance processes in general and the corporate ombudsman process in particular. In connection with these reviews, the committee will meet, as deemed appropriate, with the general counsel and other company officers or employees.

The committee shall meet separately at least quarterly with management, with the corporate audit staff and also with the company's independent auditors.

The committee shall have authority to retain such outside counsel, experts and other advisors as the committee may deem appropriate in its sole discretion. The committee shall have sole authority to approve related fees and retention terms.

The committee shall report its recommendations to the board after each committee meeting and shall conduct and present to the board an annual performance evaluation of the committee. The committee shall review at least annually the adequacy of this charter and recommend any proposed changes to the board for approval.

12. To establish procedures for the receipt, retention and treatment of complaints on accounting, internal accounting controls or auditing matters, as well as for confidential, anonymous submissions by company employees of concerns regarding questionable accounting or auditing matters.

Audit Committee: Key Practices

The Audit Committee has adopted the following key practices to assist it in undertaking the functions and responsibilities set forth in its charter:

1. *Meetings.* The committee will meet at least 7 times a year, generally on a day different than the regularly scheduled board meeting to allow time for in-depth discussion.

2. *Review of Financial Statements.* The committee will review the company's 10-K in detail with the CEO, the CFO and the full board at an extended February board meeting. The committee will meet to review the company's 10-Qs with the CFO. The head of the corporate audit staff and the company's independent auditor will be present at these meetings.

3. *Quarterly Review of CEO and CFO Certification Process.* In conjunction with its reviews of the 10-Ks and 10-Qs, the committee will also review the process for the CEO and CFO quarterly certifications required by the SEC with respect to the financial statements and the company's disclosure and internal controls, including any material changes or deficiencies in such controls. The committee shall also meet twice a year with the corporate disclosure committee responsible for reviewing the company's disclosure controls and procedures.

4. *Review of Earnings Releases and Information Provided to Analysts and Rating Agencies.* The CFO shall review earnings releases with the chair of the committee prior to their release to the public. Prior to the event, the CEO or the CFO shall review with the committee, or the full board, the substance of any presentations to analysts or rating agencies which constitute a shift in company strategy or outlook. In addition, the CEO or CFO shall review subsequently with the committee, or the full board, a summary of major presentations that have been given to analysts or rating agencies that do not constitute a shift in strategy or outlook.

5. *Approval of Audit and Non-audit Services.* To minimize relationships which could appear to impair the objectivity of the independent auditor, it is the committee's practice to restrict the non-audit services that may be provided to the company by the company's independent auditor primarily to tax services and merger and acquisition due diligence and integration services. The company will obtain such limited non-audit services from the company's independent auditor only when the services offered by the auditor's firm are more effective or economical than services available from other providers, and, to the extent possible, only following competitive bidding for such services. The committee

has also adopted policies and procedures for pre-approving all non-audit work performed by the company's independent auditor. Specifically, the committee shall pre-approve the use of the company's independent auditor for detailed, specific types of services within the following categories of non-audit services: merger and acquisition due diligence and audit services; internal control reviews; tax compliance services; tax consulting services; employee benefit plan audits; and reviews and procedures that the company requests the independent auditor to undertake to provide assurances on matters not required by laws or regulations. For each category of non-audit service listed in the preceding sentence, the committee shall also set a specific annual limit on the amount of such services which the company may obtain from the company's independent auditor, and shall require management to report the specific engagements to the committee on a quarterly basis, and also to obtain pre-approval from the committee for any single engagement over $500,000.

6. **Hiring Guidelines for Independent Auditor Employees.** The committee has adopted the following practices regarding the hiring by the company of any partner, director, manager, staff, advising member of the department of professional practice, reviewing actuary, reviewing tax professional and any other persons having responsibility for providing audit assurance to the company's independent auditor on any aspect of their certification of the company's financial statements. "Audit assurance" includes all work that results in the expression of an opinion on financial statements, including audits of statutory accounts.

   a) No member of the audit team that is auditing a GE business can be hired into that GE business or into a position to which that business reports for a period of 2 years following association with that audit.

   b) No former employee of the independent auditor may sign a GE or GE affiliate's SEC filing for 5 years following employment with the independent auditor.

   c) No former employee of the independent auditor may be named a GE or major affiliate officer for 3 years following employment by the independent auditor.

   d) GE's CFO must approve all executive-band and higher hires from the independent auditor.

   e) GE's CFO shall report annually to the audit committee the profile of the preceding year's hires from the independent auditor.

7. *Process for Handling Complaints About Accounting Matters.* As part of the board's procedure for receiving and handling complaints or concerns about the company's conduct, the committee has established the following procedures for: (i) the receipt, retention, and treatment of complaints received by the company regarding accounting, internal accounting controls, or auditing matters; and (ii) the confidential, anonymous submission by GE employees of concerns regarding questionable accounting or auditing matters.

a) GE has established and published on its Web site special mail and e-mail addresses and a toll-free telephone number for receiving complaints regarding accounting, internal accounting controls, or auditing matters.

b) All such complaints will be sent to the presiding director and to the chair of the Audit Committee.

c) All complaints will be tracked on a separate board of directors' ombuds docket, but handled by the company's ombuds, finance and legal staffs in the normal manner, except as the Audit Committee may request.

d) The status of the specially docketed complaints will be reported on a quarterly basis to the presiding director and the chair of the Audit Committee and, if they so direct, to the committee or the full board.

e) The presiding director or Audit Committee chair may request special treatment, including the retention of outside counsel or other advisors, for any complaint addressed to them.

The company's integrity manual prohibits any employee from retaliating or taking any adverse action against anyone for raising or helping to resolve an integrity concern.

8. **Audit Committee Memberships.** The committee has determined that in view of the increasing demands and responsibilities of the Audit Committee, members of the committee should not serve on more than two additional Audit Committees of other public companies, and the chair of the committee should not serve on more than one other Audit Committee of a public company. Existing relationships exceeding these limits may continue in place provided that the full board of directors determines that such relationships do not impair the member's ability to serve effectively on the committee.

9. **Code of Ethics for CEO and Senior Financial Officers.** GE's integrity manual, *Integrity: The Spirit & the Letter of Our Commitment*, applies to all of the company's directors, officers and employees, including the CEO and all financial professionals. GE's policy 30.5, *Conflicts of Interest*, and policy 30.7, *Controllership*, require all employees, including the CEO and senior financial officers, to resolve ethically any actual or apparent conflicts of interest, and to comply with all generally accepted accounting principles, laws and regulations designed to produce full, fair, accurate, timely and understandable disclosure in the company's periodic reports filed with the SEC. Annual acknowledgment of the *Spirit & Letter* is required of all salaried employees, including the company's CEO and financial professionals.

10. **Conflict of Interest Review.** The committee will review twice a year the corporate audit staff's audit of the application of GE policy 30.5, *Conflicts of Interest*, to the company's officers.

11. **Financial Expertise.** Each member of the committee will be financially literate, as determined by the board in its business judgment. At least one member of the committee will qualify as an "audit committee financial expert," as defined by the SEC. The board has

determined that Robert J. Swieringa, dean of the S. C. Johnson Graduate School of Management and professor of accounting at Cornell University, and a member of the audit committee, is an audit committee financial expert.

12. **Audit Partner Rotation.** The committee shall ensure that the lead audit partners assigned by the company's independent auditor to the company, and to each of its subsidiaries that have securities registered with the SEC, as well as the audit partner responsible for reviewing the company's audit shall be changed at least every five years.

13. **Share Owner Ratification of Independent Auditor.** Although the committee has the sole authority to appoint the independent auditor, the committee will recommend that the board ask the share owners, at their annual meeting, to ratify the committee's selection of the independent auditor.

Audit Committee Effectiveness

Self-Assessment

Deloitte Generic Audit Committee Evaluation Questionnaire

The following questionnaire is intended to assist audit committees in completing a thorough self-assessment of their effectiveness. The questions were derived from various sources, including the "Call to Action" items in the January 2002 document entitled, *Impact of the Current Economic and Business Environment on Financial Reporting* prepared by the Big Five accounting firms and the AICPA. The responses should represent the committee's collective view. It is not critical that audit committees follow the format or rating mechanism set forth below, but that they consider each point carefully in determining strengths and areas in need of improvement.

Note: *Disclaimer for the Effectiveness Self-assessment*
This questionnaire is limited in nature and does not encompass all matters relating to audit committee effectiveness that may be pertinent to a specific audit committee's self-assessment. No representation is made as to the sufficiency of this questionnaire for a company's purposes, and by means of this questionnaire, the authors are not rendering professional advice or services. The questionnaire should not be used as a basis for any decision that may affect the company's business. No responsibility is assumed as a result of a company's use of this questionnaire.

RATE EFFECTIVENESS **1 = Less Effective** **5 = Highly Effective**		Comments
Risk Management		
1. The audit committee has assessed the effectiveness of the risk management processes used by management.	1 2 3 4 5	
2. The audit committee meets periodically with the chief risk officer or his or her equivalent to understand relevant risks facing the organization and how those risks are monitored for possible financial reporting implications.	1 2 3 4 5	
3. The audit committee periodically meets with key members of management such as general counsel, the chief information officer, the director of environmental compliance, the tax director, and others to assist in identifying significant risks.	1 2 3 4 5	
4. The audit committee reviews and understands the processes used by management, the external auditor, and the internal auditor to identify and respond to risks related to critical third-party interdependencies (suppliers, customers, outsourced operations, counterparties) that influence the organization's operations.	1 2 3 4 5	
5. The audit committee questions management and the external auditor about how they assess the risk of material misstatement, what the major risk areas are, and how they respond to identified risks.	1 2 3 4 5	
6. The audit committee reviews and obtains an understanding of the processes used by management, the external auditor, and the internal auditor to identify and respond to risks related to subsidiary locations, joint ventures, equity affiliates, off-balance-sheet transactions, and related entities.	1 2 3 4 5	

RATE EFFECTIVENESS **1 = Less Effective** **5 = Highly Effective**		**Comments**
Risk Management (cont'd)		
7. The audit committee has an understanding of the company's critical business continuity risks and management's plans to address such risks.	1 2 3 4 5	
8. The audit committee discusses with management the guidelines and policies utilized with respect to financial risk assessment and management, the major financial risk exposures and the procedures to monitor and control such exposures in order to assist the committee to assess the completeness, adequacy and appropriateness of financial risk disclosure in management MD&A and in the financial statements.	1 2 3 4 5	
9. The audit committee ascertains that policies and procedures are in place to minimize environmental, occupational health and safety and other risks to asset value and mitigate damage to or deterioration of asset value and reviews such policies and procedures periodically.	1 2 3 4 5	
10. The audit committee reviews foreign currency, interest rate and commodity price risk mitigation strategies, including the use of derivative financial instruments.	1 2 3 4 5	
11. The audit committee reviews insurance programs in place and evaluates their appropriateness.	1 2 3 4 5	

RATE EFFECTIVENESS **1 = Less Effective** **5 = Highly Effective**		**Comments**
Financial Reporting and Compliance		
1. The audit committee requests and obtains sufficient information related to important financial reporting issues, such as the use of complex financial instruments, areas of judgment or high subjectivity, unusual transactions, and changes in accounting policies.	1 2 3 4 5	
2. The audit committee reads the company's annual report, financial statements, and MD&A to determine if anything is inconsistent with its own knowledge, including areas such as liquidity, unusual transactions, and off-balance-sheet arrangements.	1 2 3 4 5	
3. The audit committee understands why critical accounting principles were chosen and how they were applied, and considers the quality, not just the acceptability, of financial accounting and reporting, including the transparency of disclosures.	1 2 3 4 5	
4. The audit committee understands the process used by management to identify related parties and considers the transparency of the related-party disclosures.	1 2 3 4 5	
5. The audit committee obtains from management and the external auditors an understanding of significant transactions and how they were accounted for, such as acquisitions, dispositions, and special-purpose entities.	1 2 3 4 5	
6. The audit committee reviews all unrecorded audit adjustments with management and the external auditor and obtains an understanding as to why they were not recorded.	1 2 3 4 5	
7. The audit committee asks the external auditor about pressures on management that may have an impact on the quality of financial reporting, such as earnings targets and performance measures.	1 2 3 4 5	

RATE EFFECTIVENESS 1 = Less Effective 5 = Highly Effective		Comments
Financial Reporting and Compliance (cont'd)		
8. The audit committee makes inquiries of management and the external auditor on the experience and sufficiency of the audit team assigned to the engagement.	1 2 3 4 5	
9. The audit committee reviews and pre-approves, in accordance with an established pre-approval policy, all services (audit and non-audit) to be provided to the company or its subsidiary entities by the external auditor. In performing such a review, the committee ensures that none of the services to be provided would breach the external auditor's independence.	1 2 3 4 5	
10. The audit committee reviews the external auditor's scope and audit plan to its satisfaction prior to commencement of the audit.	1 2 3 4 5	
11. The audit committee chairman meets with the external and internal auditors outside of the regularly scheduled meetings to encourage open and frank dialogue.	1 2 3 4 5	
12. The audit committee chairman communicates to the external auditor the expectation that the external auditor will contact the committee when necessary.	1 2 3 4 5	
13. The audit committee is satisfied that management exhibits the proper "tone at the top" and is committed to promoting high-quality financial reporting and strong internal controls.	1 2 3 4 5	
14. The audit committee reviews business practices followed by senior management to assess compliance with appropriate Corporate Policies and the code of Business Conduct and to address deficiencies in such compliance.	1 2 3 4 5	

RATE EFFECTIVENESS 1 = Less Effective 5 = Highly Effective		Comments
Financial Reporting and Compliance (cont'd)		
15. The audit committee satisfies itself that adequate procedures are in place for the review of the company's public disclosure of financial information extracted or derived from the financial statements, and periodically assesses the adequacy of those procedures.	1 2 3 4 5	
16. The audit committee reviews the CEO/CFO certifications. The committee inquires as to practices and procedures adopted to permit managements' assurance on the underlying controls.	1 2 3 4 5	
17. The audit committee reviews fraud prevention policies and programs, and monitors their implementation.	1 2 3 4 5	
18. The audit committee reviews and approves the company's hiring policies regarding partners, employees and former partners and employees of the current and former external auditor.	1 2 3 4 5	
19. The audit committee discusses with the external auditor the rotation plan for all audit partners active on the engagement.	1 2 3 4 5	
20. At least annually, the audit committee reviews and discusses with the external auditor, the policies and procedures followed to ensure the maintenance of the external auditors' independence.	1 2 3 4 5	
21. The audit committee has ensured there are direct channels of communication between itself, and (i) management, (ii) the internal auditor and (iii) the external auditor to allow the discussion of and review of specific issues as required.	1 2 3 4 5	

RATE EFFECTIVENESS 1 = Less Effective 5 = Highly Effective		Comments
Internal Control Environment		
1. The audit committee receives enough information to review, understand, and assess the organization's system of internal controls, including information technology controls.	1 2 3 4 5	
2. Along with having the sole authority to recommend the hiring and firing and compensation of the external auditor to the board, the committee reviews the terms of engagement of the external auditor, including their qualifications, professional competence, experience and performance. If required, the committee reviews management's plans for an orderly transition to a new external auditor. The external auditor reports directly to the audit committee.	1 2 3 4 5	
3. The audit committee is directly responsible for overseeing the work of the external auditor, and is effective at resolving any disagreements between management and the external auditor regarding financial reporting.	1 2 3 4 5	
4. The audit committee makes inquiries of the external auditor and management on the depth of experience and sufficiency of staff in the finance and internal audit organizations.	1 2 3 4 5	
5. The audit committee reviews the internal audit plan annually.	1 2 3 4 5	
6. The audit committee reviews the management recommendation letters, written by the internal and external auditors, to ensure that all significant matters are properly addressed.	1 2 3 4 5	
7. The audit committee assesses both the compliance effectiveness and the value of service of the internal audit department.	1 2 3 4 5	

RATE EFFECTIVENESS 1 = Less Effective 5 = Highly Effective		Comments
Corporate Governance		
1. The board of directors or audit committee assesses the financial literacy of audit committee members in accordance with the applicable accounting rules and regulatory procedures.	1 2 3 4 5	
2. The audit committee has an orientation program to educate new members on their responsibilities.	1 2 3 4 5	
3. The audit committee participates in a continuing education program to enhance audit committee members' understanding of relevant accounting and reporting areas.	1 2 3 4 5	
4. Management, the external auditor, and the board of directors provide input on the audit committee charter and meeting agendas.	1 2 3 4 5	
5. Audit committee meetings are scheduled with sufficient time to cover all agenda items.	1 2 3 4 5	
6. The audit committee and/or its chairman have a process in place to review significant issues with management and the external auditor prior to quarterly and annual earnings releases.	1 2 3 4 5	
7. The audit committee is authorized to retain independent counsel, accountants, or other advisors to assist in investigating any matters within the committee's scope, as appropriate.	1 2 3 4 5	
8. The audit committee is informed of communications received from governmental or regulatory agencies, or similar parties, relating to areas of alleged violations or noncompliance.	1 2 3 4 5	
9. The audit committee establishes procedures for the receipt, retention and treatment of complaints received by the issuer regarding accounting, internal accounting controls or auditing matters, as well as the confidential, anonymous submission by employees of the issuer of concerns regarding questionable accounting or auditing matters.	1 2 3 4 5	

RATE EFFECTIVENESS 1 = Less Effective 5 = Highly Effective		Comments
Corporate Governance (cont'd)		
10. The audit committee has a written charter that sets out its mandate and responsibilities. In consultation with management and the external auditor, an annual audit committee work plan is developed to ensure all responsibilities as set out in the charter are adequately met. The audit committee performs an evaluation of its performance in relation to the mandate annually. The audit committee reviews and assesses such mandate annually.	1 2 3 4 5	

Canadian Tire Corporation Audit Committee Evaluation Questionnaire

The audit committee has agreed to evaluate its performance against the operating principles and procedures set out in its charter (see Part I and Part II). In addition, the Committee has agreed to answer some additional questions set out in Part III of the Evaluation Form.

With respect to Parts I and II, you should indicate how well you believe the committee has adhered to its operating principles and how well it has discharged each of the responsibilities.

Please use the following scoring system.

1. *Addressed Appropriately*
2. *Requires Improvement*

The form also provides space for comments which cannot be properly expressed or reflected by numerical assessment. Given the objective of this process, constructive comments are essential.

Part III requires answers to the questions.

Part I — Operating Principles

	Score	Comments
Committee Values		
The Committee expects the management of the Corporation to operate in compliance with the Corporation's Code of Conduct and corporate policies; with laws and regulations governing the Corporation; and to maintain strong financial reporting and control processes.		
Communications		
The Chairman (and others on the Committee) expects to have direct, open and frank communications throughout the year with management, other Committee Chairmen, the external auditor, the Internal Auditor and other key Committee advisors as applicable.		
Financial Literacy		
All Audit Committee Members should be sufficiently versed in financial matters to understand the Corporation's accounting practices and policies and the major judgments involved in preparing the financial statements.		
Annual Audit Committee Work Plan		
The Committee, in consultation with management and the external auditor, shall develop an annual Audit Committee Work Plan responsive to the Committee's responsibilities as set out in this Charter. In addition, the Committee, in consultation with management and the external auditor, shall develop and participate in a process for review of important financial topics that have the potential to impact the Corporation's financial disclosure.		
Meeting Agenda		
Committee meeting agendas shall be the responsibility of the Chairman of the Committee in consultation with Committee members, senior management and the external auditor.		

	Score	Comments
Committee Expectations and Information Needs		
The Committee shall communicate its expectations to management and the external auditor with respect to the nature, timing and extent of its information needs. The Committee expects that written materials will be received from management and the external auditor at least one week in advance of meeting dates.		
External Resources		
To assist the Committee in discharging its responsibilities, the Committee may, in addition to the external auditor, at the expense of the Corporation, retain one or more persons having special expertise.		
In Camera Meetings		
At each meeting of the Committee, the members of the Committee shall meet in private session with the external auditors; with management; and with the Committee members only.		
Reporting to the Board		
The Committee, through its Chairman, shall report after each Committee meeting to the Board at the Board's next regular meeting.		
Committee Self Assessment		
The Committee shall annually review, discuss and assess its own performance. In addition, the Committee shall periodically review its role and responsibilities.		
The External Auditor		
The Committee expects that, in discharging their responsibilities to the shareholders, the external auditor shall be accountable to the Board through the Audit Committee. The external auditor shall report all material issues or potentially material issues to the Committee.		

Part II — Operating Procedures — Responsibilities and Duties

Financial Reporting	Score	Comments
Review the Corporation's annual and quarterly financial statements with management and the external auditor to gain reasonable assurance that the statements are accurate, complete, represent fairly the Corporation's financial position and performance and are in accordance with GAAP and report thereon to the Board before such financial statements are approved by the Board.		
Review with management and the external auditor the financial statements of the Corporation's significant subsidiaries and of the Corporation's profit sharing plans.		
Receive from the external auditor reports on their review of the annual and quarterly financial statements.		
Receive from management a copy of the representation letter provided to the external auditors and receive from management any additional representations required by the Committee.		
Review and, if appropriate, recommend approval to the Board of news releases and reports to shareholders issued by the Corporation with respect to the Corporation's annual and quarterly financial statements.		
Review and, if appropriate, recommend approval to the Board of prospectuses, material change disclosures of a financial nature, management discussion and analysis, annual information forms and similar disclosure documents to be issued by the Corporation.		

Accounting Policies	Score	Comments
Review with management and the external auditor the appropriateness of the Corporation's accounting policies, disclosures, reserves, key estimates and judgements, including changes or variations thereto and to obtain reasonable assurance that they are in compliance with GAAP; and report thereon to the Board.		
Review with management and the external auditor the degree of conservatism of the Corporation's underlying accounting policies, key estimates and judgments and reserves.		

Risk and Uncertainty	Score	Comments
Acknowledging that it is the responsibility of the Board, in consultation with management, to identify the principal business risks facing the Corporation, determine the Corporation's tolerance for risk and approve risk management policies, the Committee shall focus on financial risk and gain reasonable assurance that financial risk is being effectively managed or controlled by: a) reviewing with management the Corporation's tolerance for financial risks; b) reviewing with management its assessment of the significant financial risks facing the Corporation; c) reviewing with management the Corporation's policies and any proposed changes thereto for managing those significant financial risks; d) reviewing with management its plans, processes and programs to manage and control such risks.		
Ascertain that policies and procedures are in place to minimize environmental, occupational health and safety and other risks to asset value and mitigate damage to or deterioration of asset value and review such policies and procedures periodically.		
Review policies and compliance therewith that require significant actual or potential liabilities, contingent or otherwise, to be reported to the Board in a timely fashion.		
Review foreign currency, interest rate and commodity price risk mitigation strategies, including the use of derivative financial instruments.		
Review the adequacy of insurance coverages maintained by the Corporation.		
Review regularly with management, the external auditor and the Corporation's legal counsel, any legal claim or other contingency, including tax assessments, that could have a material effect upon the financial position or operating results of the Corporation and the manner in which these matters have been disclosed in the financial statements.		

Financial Controls and Control Deviations	Score	Comments
Review the plans of the internal and external auditors to gain reasonable assurance that the combined evaluation and testing of internal financial controls is comprehensive, coordinated and cost-effective.		
Receive regular reports from management, the external auditors and its legal department on all significant deviations or indications/detection of fraud and the corrective activity undertaken in respect thereto.		

Compliance with Laws and Regulations	Score	Comments
Review regular reports from management and others (e.g. internal and external auditors) with respect to the Corporation's compliance with laws and regulations having a material impact on the financial statements including: a) tax and financial reporting laws and regulations b) legal withholding requirements c) environmental protection laws and regulations d) other laws and regulations which expose directors to liability.		
Review reports from the Social Responsibility Committee with respect to Occupational Health and Safety matters having a potential significant financial impact and to gain reasonable assurance annually that the Corporation's reserves with respect to such matters are sufficient and appropriate.		
Review the status of the Corporation's tax returns and those of its subsidiaries.		

Relationship with External Auditors	Score	Comments
Recommend to the Board the nomination of the external auditor.		
Approve the remuneration and the terms of engagement of the external auditors as set forth in the Engagement Letter.		
Review the performance of the external auditor annually or more frequently as required.		
Receive annually from the external auditor an acknowledgement in writing that the shareholders, as represented by the Board and the Committee, are their primary client.		
Receive a report annually from the external auditor with respect to their independence, such report to include a disclosure of all engagements (and fees related thereto) for non-audit services by the Corporation.		
Review with the external auditor the scope of the audit, the areas of special emphasis to be addressed in the audit, the extent to which the external audit can be coordinated with internal audit activities and the materiality levels which the external auditors propose to employ.		
Meet regularly with the external auditor in the absence of management to determine, inter alia, that no management restrictions have been placed on the scope and extent of the audit examinations by the external auditor or the reporting of their findings to the Committee.		
Establish effective communication processes with management and the Corporation's internal and external auditors to assist the Committee to monitor objectively the quality and effectiveness of the relationship among the external auditor, management and the Committee.		

Internal Auditor	Score	Comments
Review the Internal Auditor's terms of reference.		
Review the annual plan of the Internal Auditor.		
Review the reports of the Corporation's Internal Auditor with respect to control and financial risk, and any other matters appropriate to the Committee's duties. The Committee shall review the adequacy and appropriateness of management's response, including the implementation thereof.		
Review and approve the reporting relationship of the Internal Auditor to ensure that an appropriate segregation of duties is maintained and that the Internal Auditor has an obligation to report directly to the Committee on matters affecting the Committee's duties, irrespective of his or her other reporting relationships.		
Review and report to the Board on the appointment, replacement, reassignment or dismissal of the Internal Auditor.		

Other Responsibilities	Score	Comments
Periodically review the form, content and level of detail of financial reports to the Board.		
Approve annually the reasonableness of the expenses of the Chairman of the Board and the Chief Executive Officer.		
After consultation with the Chief Financial Officer and the external auditor, gain reasonable assurance, at least annually, of the quality and sufficiency of the Corporation's accounting and financial personnel and other resources.		
Review in advance the appointment of the Corporation's senior financial executives.		
Investigate any matters that, in the Committee's discretion, fall within the Committee's duties.		
Review reports from the Internal Auditor, the external auditor, and/or other Committee Chairmen on their review of compliance with the Corporation's Code of Conduct, and the Corporation's policies on political donations and commissions paid to suppliers or others.		
Perform such other functions as may from time to time be assigned to the Committee by the Board.		

Accountability	Score	Comments
Review and update this Charter on a regular basis for approval by the Board.		
From time to time, as requested by the Board, disclose its Mandate and this Charter in the Corporation's statement of corporate governance practices.		
Review the description of the Committee's activities as set forth in the Corporation's statement of corporate governance practices.		

Part III — Additional Questions

	Comments
Are you satisfied with the quality and timeliness of the material in your briefing books? a) Do you have any suggestions for improvement? b) Is the level of detail appropriate?	
Are you satisfied with the quality of the presentations made a) by management b) by the External Auditor?	
Has sufficient time been set aside at each meeting for discussion and for answering your questions? Are you satisfied with the answers you receive?	
Are there any issues that you feel are not being addressed by the Committee?	
Given the matters which come before the Committee at each meeting, are the meetings: a) too long? b) too short? c) an appropriate length?	
Are there an appropriate number of Audit Committee meetings?	
Do you believe the Committee is taking full advantage of the in-camera sessions?	
Are there sufficient educational opportunities covering both the external and internal environments?	
Are you aware of any Audit Committee best practices which you believe the Committee should adopt?	
Are you satisfied that the Committee has effectively discharged its responsibilities and duties?	
Are all members of the Committee contributing effectively?	
How would you evaluate the Chairman's performance?	
What are your suggestions for improvement?	

Additional Comments:

_____

_____

_____

_____

_____

_____

_____

_____

_____

_____

_____

_____

_____

_____

_____

_____

_____

_____

_____

TSX Listing Requirements and Guidelines

This appendix presents the amended TSX corporate governance disclosure requirements and guidelines and the amendments and practice notes related to guideline 13, which deals with audit committees.

TSX COMPANY MANUAL
M. CORPORATE GOVERNANCE

Introduction
Sec. 472
For the purposes of sections 472 and 473:

"company" includes a corporation, trust, partnership or other form of business organization;

"corporation" means a company incorporated under a business corporation act or similar legislation;

"inside director" means a director who is a member of management;

"outside director" means a director who is not a member of management;

"related director" means a director who is not an unrelated director or is a member of management;

"significant shareholder" means a shareholder with the ability to exercise a majority of the votes for the election of the board of directors; and "unrelated director" means a director who is independent of management and is free from any interest and any business or other relationship which could, or could reasonably be perceived to, materially interfere with the director 's ability to act with a view to the best interests of the company, other than interests and relationships arising from shareholding.

Every listed corporation incorporated in Canada or a province of Canada shall make full and complete disclosure of its system of corporate governance on an annual basis in its annual report or information circular. The disclosure shall be made with reference to each of the guidelines set out in Section 473 and where the corporation's system is different from any of the guidelines, each difference and the reason for the difference shall be clearly disclosed. Every listed company which is not a corporation shall also make full and complete disclosure of its system of governance on an annual basis in its annual filing. The disclosure shall be appropriate to the listed company's form of business organization and shall, to the extent applicable, refer to the established guidelines set out in Section 473.

In addition to disclosures of its system of governance, every listed company shall disclose, in general terms, the operation of its system of governance.

Guidelines
Sec. 473
The following are the guidelines for effective corporate governance:
1. The board of directors of every corporation should explicitly assume responsibility for the stewardship of the corporation[1.1] and, as part of the overall stewardship responsibility, should assume responsibility for the following matters:
   a) adoption of a strategic planning process and approval of a strategic plan which takes into account, among other things, the opportunities and risks of the business;
   b) the identification of the principal risks of the corporation's business and ensuring the implementation of appropriate systems to manage these risks;
   c) succession planning , including appointing , training and monitoring senior management;
   d) a communication policy for the corporation[1.2]; and
   e) the integrity of the corporation's internal control and management information systems.

[1.1] **Practice Note:** *In order to help boards discharge appropriately their stewardship responsibility, boards should adopt a formal mandate setting out their responsibilities. Such mandates can also be used in conducting regular assessments of board effectiveness referred to in Guideline 5. In describing the responsibilities of the board, it would be appropriate for the corporation to describe:*
   • *the decisions requiring prior approval of the board;*

- *measures for receiving shareholder feedback; and*
- *the board's expectations of management.*

1.2 **Practice Note:** *In assuming responsibility for the communication policy of the corporation, the board should ensure that the policy: (i) addresses how the corporation interacts with analysts and the public; (ii) contains measures for the corporation to avoid selective disclosure; and (iii) is reviewed annually.*

2. The board of directors of every corporation should be constituted with a majority of individuals who qualify as unrelated directors. If the corporation has a significant shareholder, in addition to a majority of unrelated directors, the board should include a number of directors who do not have interests in or relationships with either the corporation or the significant shareholder and which fairly reflects the investment in the corporation by shareholders other than the significant shareholder.
3. The application of the definition of "unrelated director" to the circumstances of each individual director should be the responsibility of the board which will be required to disclose on an annual basis whether the board has a majority of unrelated directors or, in the case of a corporation with a significant shareholder, whether the board is constituted with the appropriate number of directors which are not related to either the corporation or the significant shareholder. Management directors are related directors. The board will also be required to disclose on an annual basis the analysis of the application of the principles supporting this conclusion.[3.1]

   3.1 **Practice Note:** *Relevant points of discussion in making this analysis include:*
   - *composition of the board;*
   - *whether the board has a majority of unrelated directors and the basis of this analysis; and*
   - *if the corporation has a significant shareholder, whether the corporation satisfies the requirement for fairly reflecting the investment of minority shareholders in the corporation and the basis for this analysis.*

4. The board of directors of every corporation should appoint a committee of directors composed exclusively of outside, directors, a majority of whom are unrelated directors, with the responsibility for proposing to the full board new nominees to the board[4.1] and for assessing directors on an ongoing basis.

   4.1 **Practice Note:** *The full board should engage in a disciplined process to determine, in light of the opportunities and risks facing the corporation, what competencies, skills and personal qualities it should seek in new board members in order to add value to the corporation. The results of such a discussion provide a framework for the work of those directors charged with developing lists of candidates. Prospective candidates, once identified, can be approached by* *the chair of the board, the chair of the nominating committee or another director appointed by the board to be responsible for recruiting directors, with or without the CEO, to explore their interest in joining the board.*

5. Every board of directors should implement a process to be carried out by the nominating committee or other appropriate committee for assessing the effectiveness of the board as a whole, the committees of the board and the contribution of individual directors.[5.1]

   [5.1] **Practice Note:** *In describing the process for assessing board, committee and director effectiveness, identify which director or committee of the board has responsibility for these assessments and how frequently these assessments are made.*

6. Every corporation, as an integral element of the process for appointing new directors, should provide an orientation and education program for new recruits to the board.[6.1]

   [6.1] **Practice Note:** *Boards should ensure that prospective candidates fully understand the role of the board, the role of the committees of the board and the contribution individual directors are expected to make, including in particular, the commitment of time and energy that the corporation expects of its directors.*

7. Every board of directors should examine its size and, undertake, where appropriate, a program to establish a board size which facilitates effective decision-making.
8. The board of directors should review the adequacy and form of the compensation of directors and ensure the compensation realistically reflects the responsibilities and risk involved in being an effective director.
9. Subject to guideline 13, committees of the board of directors should generally be composed of outside directors, a majority of whom are unrelated directors, although some board committees, may include one or more inside directors.
10. Every board of directors should expressly assume responsibility for, or assign to a committee of directors the general responsibility for, developing the corporation's approach to governance issues. This committee would, among other things, be responsible for the corporation's response to these governance guidelines.
11. The board of directors, together with the CEO, should develop position descriptions for the board and for the CEO, including the definition of the limits to management's responsibilities. In addition, the board should approve or develop the corporate objectives which the CEO is responsible for meeting and assess the CEO against these objectives.[11.1]

    [11.1] **Practice Note:** *The board or a committee of the board should assess the CEO, and if a committee conducts the assessment, the results should be reported to the board.*

12. Every board of directors should implement structures and procedures which ensure that the board can function independently of management. An appropriate structure would be to (i) appoint a chair of the board who is not a member of management with responsibility to ensure the board discharges its responsibilities or (ii) assign this responsibility to an outside director, sometimes referred to as the "lead director". The chair or lead director should ensure that the board carries out its responsibilities effectively which will involve the board meeting on a regular basis without management present and may involve assigning the responsibility for administering the board's relationship to management to a committee of the board.[12.1]

> [12.1] **Practice Note:** *Discuss board effectiveness, management of the board and liaison between the board and management in describing the mandates of the board, committees of the board and of the chair of the board. If the board does not have a chair separate from management, it is essential that the corporation discuss the structures and processes that are in place to facilitate the functioning of the board independently of management. In addition, to ensure the board carries out its responsibilities:*
> - *the chair or lead director should ensure the board understands the boundaries between board and management responsibilities;*
> - *prospective candidates should fully understand the role of the board and the contribution they are expected to make; and*
> - *the board should address its responsibilities under the governance system.*

13. The audit committee of every board of directors should be composed only of unrelated directors. All of the members of the audit committee should be financially literate and at least one member should have accounting or related financial expertise. Each board shall determine the definition of and criteria for "financial literacy" and "accounting or related financial expertise".[13.1] The board should adopt a charter for the audit committee which sets out the roles and responsibilities of the audit committee which should be specifically defined so as to provide appropriate guidance to audit committee members as to their duties.[13.2] The audit committee should have direct communication channels with the internal and external auditors to discuss and review specific issues as appropriate.[13.3] The audit committee duties should include oversight responsibility for management reporting on internal control. While it is management's responsibility to design and implement an effective system of internal control, it is the responsibility of the audit committee to ensure that management has done so.

> [13.1] **Practice Note:** *An acceptable definition of "financial literacy" is the ability to read and understand a balance sheet, an income statement and a cash flow statement. An acceptable definition of "accounting or related financial expertise" is the ability to analyze and interpret a full set of financial statements, including the notes attached thereto, in accordance with Canadian generally accepted accounting principles.*

13.2 **Practice Note:** *The audit committee charter should set out explicitly the role and responsibility of the audit committee with respect to:*

- *its relationship with and expectation of the external auditors including the establishment of the independence of the external auditor;*
- *its relationship with and expectation of the internal auditor function;*
- *its oversight of internal control;*
- *disclosure of financial and related information; and*
- *any other matters that the audit committee feels are important to its mandate or that the board chooses to delegate to it.*

The audit committee charter should specify that the external auditor is ultimately accountable to the board of directors and the audit committee as representatives of shareholders.

The board of directors should review and reassess the adequacy of the audit committee charter on an annual basis.

13.3 **Practice Note:** *The audit committee should discuss with the auditor the quality and not just the accept ability of the corporation's accounting principles. The audit committee should implement structures and procedures to ensure that it meets the auditors on a regular basis in the absence of management.*

14. The board of directors should implement a system which enables an individual director to engage an outside adviser at the expense of the company in appropriate circumstances. The engagement of the outside advisor should be subject to the approval of an appropriate committee of the board.

NYSE

Corporate Governance Standards

What follows are the final corporate governance rules of the New York Stock Exchange approved by the SEC on November 4, 2003, other than Section 303A.08, which was filed separately and approved by the SEC on June 30, 2003. These final rules will be codified in Section 303A of the NYSE's Listed Company Manual.

303A

General Application

Companies listed on the Exchange must comply with certain standards regarding corporate governance as codified in this Section 303A. Consistent with the NYSE's traditional approach, as well as the requirements of the Sarbanes-Oxley Act of 2002, certain provisions of Section 303A are applicable to some listed companies but not to others.

Equity Listings

Section 303A applies in full to all companies listing common equity securities, with the following exceptions:

Controlled Companies

A company of which more than 50% of the voting power is held by an individual, a group or another company need not comply with the requirements of Sections 303A.01, .04 or .05. A controlled company that chooses to take advantage of any or all of these exemptions must disclose that choice, that it is a controlled company and the basis for the determination in its annual proxy statement or, if the company does not file an annual proxy statement, in the company's annual report on Form 10-K filed with the SEC. Controlled companies must comply with the remaining provisions of Section 303A.

Limited Partnerships and Companies in Bankruptcy

Due to their unique attributes, limited partnerships and companies in bankruptcy proceedings need not comply with the requirements of Sections 303A.01, .04 or .05. However, all limited partnerships (at the general partner level) and companies in bankruptcy proceedings must comply with the remaining provisions of Section 303A.

Closed-end and Open-end Funds

The Exchange considers the significantly expanded standards and requirements provided for in Section 303A to be unnecessary for closed-end and open-end management investment companies that are registered under the Investment Company Act of 1940, given the pervasive federal regulation applicable to them. However, closed-end funds must comply with the requirements of Sections 303A.06, .07(a) and (c), and .12. Note, however, that in view of the common practice to utilize the same directors for boards in the same fund complex, closed-end funds will not be required to comply with the disclosure requirement in the second paragraph of the Commentary to 303A.07(a), which calls for disclosure of a board's determination with respect to simultaneous service on more than three public company audit committees. However, the other provisions of that paragraph will apply.

Business development companies, which are a type of closed-end management investment company defined in Section 2(a)(48) of the Investment Company Act of 1940 that are not registered under that Act, are required to comply with all of the provisions of Section 303A applicable to domestic issuers other than Sections 303A.02 and .07(b). For purposes of Sections 303A.01, .03, .04, .05, and .09, a director of a business development company shall be considered to be independent if he or she is not an "interested person" of the company, as defined in Section 2(a)(19) of the Investment Company Act of 1940.

As required by Rule 10A-3 under the Exchange Act, open-end funds (which can be listed as Investment Company Units, more commonly known as Exchange Traded Funds or ETFs) are required to comply with the requirements of Sections 303A.06 and .12(b).

Rule 10A-3(b)(3)(ii) under the Exchange Act requires that each audit committee must establish procedures for the confidential, anonymous submission by employees of the listed issuer of concerns regarding questionable accounting or auditing matters. In view of the external management structure often employed by closed-end and open-end funds, the Exchange also requires the audit committees of such companies to establish such procedures for the confidential, anonymous submission by employees of the investment adviser, administrator, principal underwriter, or any other provider of accounting related services for the management company, as well as employees of the management company. This responsibility must be addressed in the audit committee charter.

Other Entities

Except as otherwise required by Rule 10A-3 under the Exchange Act (for example, with respect to open-end funds), Section 303A does not apply to passive business organizations in the form of trusts (such as royalty trusts) or to derivatives and special purpose securities (such as those described in Sections 703.16, 703.19, 703.20 and 703.21). To the extent that Rule 10A-3 applies to a passive business organization, listed derivative or special purpose security, such entities are required to comply with Sections 303A.06 and .12(b).

Foreign Private Issuers

Listed companies that are foreign private issuers (as such term is defined in Rule 3b-4 under the Exchange Act) are permitted to follow home country practice in lieu of the provisions of this Section 303A, except that such companies are required to comply with the requirements of Sections 303A.06, .11 and .12(b).

Preferred and Debt Listings

Section 303A does not generally apply to companies listing only preferred or debt securities on the Exchange. To the extent required by Rule 10A-3 under the Exchange Act, all companies listing only preferred or debt securities on the NYSE are required to comply with the requirements of Sections 303A.06 and .12(b).

Effective Dates/Transition Periods

Except for Section 303A.08, which became effective June 30, 2003, listed companies will have until the earlier of their first annual meeting after January 15, 2004, or October 31, 2004, to comply with the new standards contained in Section 303A, although if a company with a classified board would be required (other than by virtue of a requirement under Section 303A.06) to change a director who would not normally stand for election in such annual meeting, the company may continue such director in office until the second annual meeting after such date, but no later than December 31, 2005. In addition, foreign private issuers will have until July 31, 2005, to comply with the new audit committee standards set out in Section 303A.06. As a general matter, the existing audit committee requirements provided for in Section 303 continue to apply to listed companies pending the transition to the new rules.

Companies listing in conjunction with their initial public offering will be permitted to phase in their independent nomination and compensation committees on the same schedule as is permitted pursuant to Rule 10A-3 under the Exchange Act for audit committees, that is, one independent member at the time of listing, a majority of independent members within 90 days of listing and fully independent committees within one year. Such companies will be required to meet the majority independent board requirement within 12 months of listing. For purposes of Section 303A other than Sections 303A.06 and .12(b), a company will be considered to be listing in conjunction with an initial public offering if, immediately prior to listing, it does not have a class of common stock registered under the Exchange Act. The

Exchange will also permit companies that are emerging from bankruptcy or have ceased to be controlled companies within the meaning of Section 303A to phase in independent nomination and compensation committees and majority independent boards on the same schedule as companies listing in conjunction with an initial public offering. However, for purposes of Sections 303A.06 and .12(b), a company will be considered to be listing in conjunction with an initial public offering only if it meets the conditions of Rule 10A-3(b)(1)(iv)(A) under the Exchange Act, namely, that the company was not, immediately prior to the effective date of a registration statement, required to file reports with the SEC pursuant to Section 13(a) or 15(d) of the Exchange Act.

Companies listing upon transfer from another market have 12 months from the date of transfer in which to comply with any requirement to the extent the market on which they were listed did not have the same requirement. To the extent the other market has a substantially similar requirement but also had a transition period from the effective date of that market's rule, which period had not yet expired, the company will have the same transition period as would have been available to it on the other market. This transition period for companies transferring from another market will not apply to the requirements of Section 303A.06 unless a transition period is available pursuant to Rule 10A-3 under the Exchange Act.

References to Form 10-K

There are provisions in this Section 303A that call for disclosure in a company's Form 10-K under certain circumstances. If a company subject to such a provision is not a company required to file a Form 10-K, then the provision shall be interpreted to mean the annual periodic disclosure form that the company does file with the SEC. For example, for a closed-end fund, the appropriate form would be the annual Form N-CSR. If a company is not required to file either an annual proxy statement or an annual periodic report with the SEC, the disclosure shall be made in the annual report required under Section 203.01 of the NYSE Listed Company Manual.

1. Listed companies must have a majority of independent directors.

Commentary: Effective boards of directors exercise independent judgment in carrying out their responsibilities. Requiring a majority of independent directors will increase the quality of board oversight and lessen the possibility of damaging conflicts of interest.

2. **In order to tighten the definition of "independent director" for purposes of these standards:**

   a) **No director qualifies as "independent" unless the board of directors affirmatively determines that the director has no material relationship with the listed company (either directly or as a partner, shareholder or officer of an organization that has a relationship with the company). Companies must disclose these determinations.**

Commentary: It is not possible to anticipate, or explicitly to provide for, all circumstances that might signal potential conflicts of interest, or that might bear on the materiality of a director's relationship to a listed company (references to "company" would include any parent or subsidiary in a consolidated group with the company). Accordingly, it is best that boards making "independence" determinations broadly consider all relevant facts and circumstances. In particular, when assessing the materiality of a director's relationship with the company, the board should consider the issue not merely from the standpoint of the director, but also from that of persons or organizations with which the director has an affiliation. Material relationships can include commercial, industrial, banking, consulting, legal, accounting, charitable and familial relationships, (among others). However, as the concern is independence from management, the Exchange does not view ownership of even a significant amount of stock, by itself, as a bar to an independence finding.

The basis for a board determination that a relationship is not material must be disclosed in the company's annual proxy statement or, if the company does not file an annual proxy statement, in the company's annual report on Form 10-K filed with the SEC. In this regard, a board may adopt and disclose categorical standards to assist it in making determinations of independence and may make a general disclosure if a director meets these standards. Any determination of independence for a director who does not meet these standards must be specifically explained. A company must disclose any standard it adopts. It may then make the general statement that the independent directors meet the standards set by the board without detailing particular aspects of the immaterial relationships between individual directors and the company. In the event that a director with a business or other relationship that does not fit within the disclosed standards is determined to be independent, a board must disclose the basis for its determination in the manner described above. This approach provides investors with an adequate means of assessing the quality of a board's independence and its independence determinations while avoiding excessive disclosure of immaterial relationships.

b) In addition:

i) A director who is an employee, or whose immediate family member is an executive officer, of the company is not independent until three years after the end of such employment relationship.

Commentary: Employment as an interim Chairman or CEO shall not disqualify a director from being considered independent following that employment.

ii) A director who receives, or whose immediate family member receives, more than $100,000 per year in direct compensation from the listed company, other than director and committee fees and pension or other forms of deferred compensation for prior service (provided such compensation is not contingent in any way on continued service), is not independent until three years after he or she ceases to receive more than $100,000 per year in such compensation.

Commentary: Compensation received by a director for former service as an interim Chairman or CEO need not be considered in determining independence under this test. Compensation received by an immediate family member for service as a non-executive employee of the listed company need not be considered in determining independence under this test.

iii) A director who is affiliated with or employed by, or whose immediate family member is affiliated with or employed in a professional capacity by, a present or former internal or external auditor of the company is not "independent" until three years after the end of the affiliation or the employment or auditing relationship.

iv) A director who is employed, or whose immediate family member is employed, as an executive officer of another company where any of the listed company's present executives serve on that company's compensation committee is not "independent" until three years after the end of such service or the employment relationship.

v) A director who is an executive officer or an employee, or whose immediate family member is an executive officer, of a company that makes payments to, or receives payments from, the listed company for property or services in an amount which, in any single fiscal year, exceeds the greater of $1 million, or 2% of such other company's consolidated gross revenues, is not "independent" until three years after falling below such threshold.

Commentary: In applying the test in Section 303A.02(b)(v), both the payments and the consolidated gross revenues to be measured shall be those reported in the last completed fiscal year. The look-back provision for this test applies solely to the financial relationship between the listed company and the director or immediate family member's current employer; a listed company need not consider former employment of the director or immediate family member.

Charitable organizations shall not be considered "companies" for purposes of Section 303A.02(b)(v), provided however that a listed company shall disclose in its annual proxy statement, or if the listed company does not file an annual proxy statement, in the company's annual report on Form 10-K filed with the SEC, any charitable contributions made by the listed company to any charitable organization in which a director serves as an executive officer if, within the preceding three years, contributions in any single fiscal year exceeded the greater of $1 million, or 2% of such charitable organization's consolidated gross revenues. Listed company boards are reminded of their obligations to consider the materiality of any such relationship in accordance with Section 303A.02(a) above.

General Commentary to Section 303A.02(b): An "immediate family member" includes a person's spouse, parents, children, siblings, mothers and fathers-in-law, sons and daughters-in-law, brothers and sisters-in-law, and anyone (other than domestic employees) who shares such person's home. When applying the lookback provisions in Section 303A.02(b), listed companies need not consider individuals who are no longer immediate family members as a result of legal separation or divorce, or those who have died or become incapacitated. In addition, references to the "company" would include any parent or subsidiary in a consolidated group with the company.

Transition Rule. Each of the above standards contains a three-year "look-back" provision. In order to facilitate a smooth transition to the new independence standards, the Exchange will phase in the "look-back" provisions by applying only a one-year look-back for the first year after adoption of these new standards. The three-year look-backs provided for in Section 303A.02(b) will begin to apply only from and after November 4, 2004.

As an example, until November 3, 2004, a company need look back only one year when testing compensation under Section 303A.02(b)(ii). Beginning November 4, 2004, however, the company would need to look back the full three years provided in Section 303A.02(b)(ii).

3. **To empower non-management directors to serve as a more effective check on management, the non-management directors of each company must meet at regularly scheduled executive sessions without management.**

Commentary: To promote open discussion among the non-management directors, companies must schedule regular executive sessions in which those directors meet without management participation. ("Non-management" directors are all those who are not company officers (as that term is defined in Rule 16a-1(f) under the Securities Act of 1933), and includes such directors who are not independent by virtue of a material relationship, former status or family membership, or for any other reason).

Regular scheduling of such meetings is important not only to foster better communication among non-management directors, but also to prevent any negative inference from attaching to the calling of executive sessions. There need not be a single presiding director at all executive sessions of the non-management directors. If one director is chosen to preside at these meetings, his or her name must be disclosed in the company's annual proxy statement or, if the company does not file an annual proxy statement, in the company's annual report on Form 10-K filed with the SEC. Alternatively, a company may disclose the procedure by which a presiding director is selected for each executive session. For example, a company may wish to rotate the presiding position among the chairs of board committees.

In order that interested parties may be able to make their concerns known to the non-management directors, a company must disclose a method for such parties to communicate directly with the presiding director or with the non-management directors as a group. Companies may, if they wish, utilize for this purpose the same procedures they have established to comply with the requirement of Rule 10A-3 (b)(3) under the Exchange Act, as applied to listed companies through Section 303A.06.

While this Section 303A.03 refers to meetings of non-management directors, if that group includes directors who are not independent under this Section 303A, listed companies should at least once a year schedule an executive session including only independent directors.

4. a) **Listed companies must have a nominating/corporate governance committee composed entirely of independent directors.**
   b) **The nominating/corporate governance committee must have a written charter that addresses:**
      i) **the committee's purpose and responsibilities — which, at minimum, must be to: identify individuals qualified to become board members, consistent with criteria approved by the board, and to select, or to recommend that the board select, the director nominees for the next annual meeting of shareholders; develop and recommend to the board a set of corporate governance principles applicable to the corporation; and oversee the evaluation of the board and management; and**
      ii) **an annual performance evaluation of the committee.**

Commentary: A nominating/corporate governance committee is central to the effective functioning of the board. New director and board committee nominations are among a board's most important functions. Placing this responsibility in the hands of an independent nominating/corporate governance committee can enhance the independence and quality of nominees. The committee is also responsible for taking a leadership role in shaping the corporate governance of a corporation.

If a company is legally required by contract or otherwise to provide third parties with the ability to nominate directors (for example, preferred stock rights to elect directors upon a dividend default, shareholder agreements, and management agreements), the selection and nomination of such directors need not be subject to the nominating committee process.

The nominating/corporate governance committee charter should also address the following items: committee member qualifications; committee member appointment and removal; committee structure and operations (including authority to delegate to subcommittees); and committee reporting to the board. In addition, the charter should give the nominating/corporate governance committee sole authority to retain and terminate any search firm to be used to identify director candidates, including sole authority to approve the search firm's fees and other retention terms.

Boards may allocate the responsibilities of the nominating/corporate governance committee, to committees of their own denomination, provided that the committees are composed entirely of independent directors. Any such committee must have a published committee charter.

5. a) **Listed companies must have a compensation committee composed entirely of independent directors.**
    b) **The compensation committee must have a written charter that addresses:**
       i) **the committee's purpose and responsibilities — which, at minimum, must be to have direct responsibility to:**
          A) **review and approve corporate goals and objectives relevant to CEO compensation, evaluate the CEO's performance in light of those goals and objectives, and either as a committee or together with the other independent directors (as directed by the board), determine and approve the CEO's compensation level based on this evaluation; and**
          B) **make recommendations to the board with respect to non-CEO compensation, incentive-compensation plans and equity-based plans; and**
          C) **produce a compensation committee report on executive compensation as required by the SEC to be included in the company's annual proxy statement or annual report on Form 10-K filed with the SEC;**
       ii) **an annual performance evaluation of the compensation committee.**

Commentary: In determining the long-term incentive component of CEO compensation, the committee should consider the company's performance and relative shareholder return, the value of similar incentive awards to CEOs at comparable companies, and the awards given to the listed company's CEO in past years. To avoid confusion, note that the compensation committee is not precluded from approving awards (with or without ratification of the board) as may be required to comply with applicable tax laws (i.e., Rule 162(m)).

The compensation committee charter should also address the following items: committee member qualifications; committee member appointment and removal; committee structure and operations (including authority to delegate to subcommittees); and committee reporting to the board.

Additionally, if a compensation consultant is to assist in the evaluation of director, CEO or senior executive compensation, the compensation committee charter should give that committee sole authority to retain and terminate the consulting firm, including sole authority to approve the firm's fees and other retention terms.

Boards may allocate the responsibilities of the compensation committee to committees of their own denomination, provided that the committees are composed entirely of independent directors. Any such committee must have a published committee charter.

Nothing in this provision should be construed as precluding discussion of CEO compensation with the board generally, as it is not the intent of this standard to impair communication among members of the board.

6. Listed companies must have an audit committee that satisfies the requirements of Rule 10A-3 under the Exchange Act.

Commentary: The Exchange will apply the requirements of Rule 10A-3 in a manner consistent with the guidance provided by the Securities and Exchange Commission in SEC Release No. 34-47654 (April 1, 2003). Without limiting the generality of the foregoing, the Exchange will provide companies the opportunity to cure defects provided in Rule 10A-3(a)(3) under the Exchange Act.

7. a) The audit committee must have a minimum of three members.

Commentary: Each member of the audit committee must be financially literate, as such qualification is interpreted by the company's board in its business judgment, or must become financially literate within a reasonable period of time after his or her appointment to the audit committee. In addition, at least one member of the audit committee must have accounting or related financial management expertise, as the company's board interprets such qualification in its business judgment. While the Exchange does not require that a listed company's audit committee include a person who satisfies the definition of audit committee financial expert set out in Item 401(e) of Regulation S-K, a board may presume that such a person has accounting or related financial management expertise.

Because of the audit committee's demanding role and responsibilities, and the time commitment attendant to committee membership, each prospective audit committee member should evaluate carefully the existing demands on his or her time before accepting this important assignment. Additionally, if an audit committee member simultaneously serves on the audit committees of more than three public companies, and the listed company does not limit the number of audit committees on which its audit committee members serve, then in each case, the board must determine that such simultaneous service would not impair the ability of such member to effectively serve on the listed company's audit committee and disclose such determination in the company's annual proxy statement or, if the company does not file an annual proxy statement, in the company's annual report on Form 10-K filed with the SEC.

    b) In addition to any requirement of Rule 10A-3(b)(1), all audit committee members must satisfy the requirements for independence set out in Section 303A.02.

    c) The audit committee must have a written charter that addresses:

        i) the committee's purpose — which, at minimum, must be to:

            A) assist board oversight of (1) the integrity of the company's financial statements, (2) the company's compliance with legal and regulatory requirements, (3) the independent auditor's qualifications and independence, and (4) the performance of the company's internal audit function and independent auditors; and

            B) prepare an audit committee report as required by the SEC to be included in the company's annual proxy statement;

        ii) an annual performance evaluation of the audit committee; and

        iii) the duties and responsibilities of the audit committee — which, at a minimum, must include those set out in Rule 10A-3(b)(2), (3), (4) and (5) of the Exchange Act, as well as to:

            A) at least annually, obtain and review a report by the independent auditor describing: the firm's internal quality-control procedures; any material issues raised by the most recent internal quality-control review, or peer review, of the firm, or by any inquiry or investigation by governmental or professional authorities, within the preceding five years, respecting one or more independent audits carried out by the firm, and any steps taken to deal with any such issues; and (to assess the auditor's independence) all relationships between the independent auditor and the company; (note — this was B in original set of rules)

Commentary: After reviewing the foregoing report and the independent auditor's work throughout the year, the audit committee will be in a position to evaluate the auditor's qualifications, performance and independence. This evaluation should include the review and evaluation of the lead partner of the independent auditor. In making its evaluation, the audit committee should take into account the opinions of management and the company's internal auditors (or other personnel responsible for the internal audit function). In addition to assuring the regular rotation of the lead audit partner as required by law, the audit committee should further consider whether, in order to assure continuing auditor independence, there should be regular rotation of the audit firm itself. The audit committee should present its conclusions with respect to the independent auditor to the full board.

> **B) discuss the company's annual audited financial statements and quarterly financial statements with management and the independent auditor, including the company's disclosures under "Management's Discussion and Analysis of Financial Condition and Results of Operations";**
> **C) discuss the company's earnings press releases, as well as financial information and earnings guidance provided to analysts and rating agencies;**

Commentary: The audit committee's responsibility to discuss earnings releases, as well as financial information and earnings guidance, may be done generally (i.e., discussion of the types of information to be disclosed and the type of presentation to be made). The audit committee need not discuss in advance each earnings release or each instance in which a company may provide earnings guidance.

> **D) discuss policies with respect to risk assessment and risk management;**

Commentary: While it is the job of the CEO and senior management to assess and manage the company's exposure to risk, the audit committee must discuss guidelines and policies to govern the process by which this is handled. The audit committee should discuss the company's major financial risk exposures and the steps management has taken to monitor and control such exposures. The audit committee is not required to be the sole body responsible for risk assessment and management, but, as stated above, the committee must discuss guidelines and policies to govern the process by which risk assessment and management is undertaken. Many companies, particularly financial companies, manage and assess their risk through mechanisms other than the audit committee. The processes these companies have in place should be reviewed in a general manner by the audit committee, but they need not be replaced by the audit committee.

> **E) meet separately, periodically, with management, with internal auditors (or other personnel responsible for the internal audit function) and with independent auditors;**

Commentary: To perform its oversight functions most effectively, the audit committee must have the benefit of separate sessions with management, the independent auditors and those responsible for the internal audit function. As noted herein, all listed companies must have an internal audit function. These separate sessions may be more productive than joint sessions in surfacing issues warranting committee attention.

F) review with the independent auditor any audit problems or difficulties and management's response;

Commentary: The audit committee must regularly review with the independent auditor any difficulties the auditor encountered in the course of the audit work, including any restrictions on the scope of the independent auditor's activities or on access to requested information, and any significant disagreements with management. Among the items the audit committee may want to review with the auditor are: any accounting adjustments that were noted or proposed by the auditor but were "passed" (as immaterial or otherwise); any communications between the audit team and the audit firm's national office respecting auditing or accounting issues presented by the engagement; and any "management" or "internal control" letter issued, or proposed to be issued, by the audit firm to the company. The review should also include discussion of the responsibilities, budget and staffing of the company's internal audit function.

G) set clear hiring policies for employees or former employees of the independent auditors; and

Commentary: Employees or former employees of the independent auditor are often valuable additions to corporate management. Such individuals' familiarity with the business, and personal rapport with the employees, may be attractive qualities when filling a key opening. However, the audit committee should set hiring policies taking into account the pressures that may exist for auditors consciously or subconsciously seeking a job with the company they audit.

H) report regularly to the board of directors.

Commentary: The audit committee should review with the full board any issues that arise with respect to the quality or integrity of the company's financial statements, the company's compliance with legal or regulatory requirements, the performance and independence of the company's independent auditors, or the performance of the internal audit function.

General Commentary to Section 303A.07(c): While the fundamental responsibility for the company's financial statements and disclosures rests with management and the independent auditor, the audit committee must review: (A) major issues regarding accounting principles and financial statement presentations, including any significant changes in the company's selection or application of accounting principles, and major issues as to the adequacy of the company's internal controls and any special audit steps adopted in light of material control deficiencies; (B) analyses prepared by management and/or the independent auditor setting forth significant financial reporting issues and judgments made in connection with the preparation of the financial statements, including analyses of the effects of alternative GAAP methods on the financial statements; (C) the effect of regulatory and accounting initiatives, as well as off-balance-sheet structures, on the financial statements of the company; and (D) the type and presentation of information to be included in earnings press releases (paying particular attention to any use of "pro forma," or "adjusted" non-GAAP, information), as well as review any financial information and earnings guidance provided to analysts and rating agencies.

d) Each listed company must have an internal audit function.

Commentary: Listed companies must maintain an internal audit function to provide management and the audit committee with ongoing assessments of the company's risk management processes and system of internal control. A company may choose to outsource this function to a third party service provider other than its independent auditor.

General Commentary to Section 303A.07: To avoid any confusion, note that the audit committee functions specified in Section 303A.07 are the sole responsibility of the audit committee and may not be allocated to a different committee.

8. Reserved.

9. Listed companies must adopt and disclose corporate governance guidelines.

Commentary: No single set of guidelines would be appropriate for every company, but certain key areas of universal importance include director qualifications and responsibilities, responsibilities of key board committees, and director compensation. Given the importance of corporate governance, each listed company's website must include its corporate governance guidelines and the charters of its most important committees (including at least the audit, and if applicable, compensation and nominating committees). Each company's annual report on Form 10-K filed with the SEC must state that the foregoing information is available on its website, and that the information is available in print to any shareholder who requests it. Making this information publicly available should promote better investor understanding of the company's policies and procedures, as well as more conscientious adherence to them by directors and management.

The following subjects must be addressed in the corporate governance guidelines:

- *Director qualification standards.* These standards should, at minimum, reflect the independence requirements set forth in this Section 303A.01 and .02. Companies may also address other substantive qualification requirements, including policies limiting the number of boards on which a director may sit, and director tenure, retirement and succession.
- *Director responsibilities.* These responsibilities should clearly articulate what is expected from a director, including basic duties and responsibilities with respect to attendance at board meetings and advance review of meeting materials.
- *Director access to management and, as necessary and appropriate, independent advisors.*
- *Director compensation.* Director compensation guidelines should include general principles for determining the form and amount of director compensation (and for reviewing those principles, as appropriate). The board should be aware that questions as to directors' independence may be raised when directors' fees and emoluments exceed what is customary. Similar concerns may be raised when the company makes substantial charitable contributions to organizations in which a director is affiliated, or enters into consulting contracts with (or provides other indirect forms of compensation to) a director. The board should critically evaluate each of these matters when determining the form and amount of director compensation, and the independence of a director.
- *Director orientation and continuing education.*
- *Management succession.* Succession planning should include policies and principles for CEO selection and performance review, as well as policies regarding succession in the event of an emergency or the retirement of the CEO.
- *Annual performance evaluation of the board.* The board should conduct a self-evaluation at least annually to determine whether it and its committees are functioning effectively.

10. Listed companies must adopt and disclose a code of business conduct and ethics for directors, officers and employees, and promptly disclose any waivers of the code for directors or executive officers.

Commentary: No code of business conduct and ethics can replace the thoughtful behavior of an ethical director, officer or employee. However, such a code can focus the board and management on areas of ethical risk, provide guidance to personnel to help them recognize and deal with ethical issues, provide mechanisms to report unethical conduct, and help to foster a culture of honesty and accountability.

Each code of business conduct and ethics must require that any waiver of the code for executive officers or directors may be made only by the board or a board committee and must be promptly disclosed to shareholders. This disclosure requirement should inhibit casual and perhaps questionable waivers, and should help assure that, when warranted, a waiver is accompanied by appropriate controls designed to protect the company. It will also give shareholders the opportunity to evaluate the board's performance in granting waivers.

Each code of business conduct and ethics must also contain compliance standards and procedures that will facilitate the effective operation of the code. These standards should ensure the prompt and consistent action against violations of the code. Each listed company's website must include its code of business conduct and ethics. Each company's annual report on Form 10-K filed with the SEC must state that the foregoing information is available on its website and that the information is available in print to any shareholder who requests it.

Each company may determine its own policies, but all listed companies should address the most important topics, including the following:

- *Conflicts of interest.* A "conflict of interest" occurs when an individual's private interest interferes in any way — or even appears to interfere — with the interests of the corporation as a whole. A conflict situation can arise when an employee, officer or director takes actions or has interests that may make it difficult to perform his or her company work objectively and effectively. Conflicts of interest also arise when an employee, officer or director, or a member of his or her family, receives improper personal benefits as a result of his or her position in the company. Loans to, or guarantees of obligations of, such persons are of special concern. The company should have a policy prohibiting such conflicts of interest, and providing a means for employees, officers and directors to communicate potential conflicts to the company.
- *Corporate opportunities.* Employees, officers and directors should be prohibited from (a) taking for themselves personally opportunities that are discovered through the use of corporate property, information or position; (b) using corporate property, information, or position for personal gain; and (c) competing with the company. Employees, officers and directors owe a duty to the company to advance its legitimate interests when the opportunity to do so arises.
- *Confidentiality.* Employees, officers and directors should maintain the confidentiality of information entrusted to them by the company or its customers, except when disclosure is authorized or legally mandated. Confidential information includes all non-public information that might be of use to competitors, or harmful to the company or its customers, if disclosed.

- *Fair dealing.* Each employee, officer and director should endeavor to deal fairly with the company's customers, suppliers, competitors and employees. None should take unfair advantage of anyone through manipulation, concealment, abuse of privileged information, misrepresentation of material facts, or any other unfair-dealing practice. Companies may write their codes in a manner that does not alter existing legal rights and obligations of companies and their employees, such as "at will" employment arrangements.
- *Protection and proper use of company assets.* All employees, officers and directors should protect the company's assets and ensure their efficient use. Theft, carelessness and waste have a direct impact on the company's profitability. All company assets should be used for legitimate business purposes.
- *Compliance with laws, rules and regulations (including insider trading laws).* The company should proactively promote compliance with laws, rules and regulations, including insider trading laws. Insider trading is both unethical and illegal, and should be dealt with decisively.
- *Encouraging the reporting of any illegal or unethical behavior.* The company should proactively promote ethical behavior. The company should encourage employees to talk to supervisors, managers or other appropriate personnel when in doubt about the best course of action in a particular situation. Additionally, employees should report violations of laws, rules, regulations or the code of business conduct to appropriate personnel. To encourage employees to report such violations, the company must ensure that employees know that the company will not allow retaliation for reports made in good faith.

11. Listed foreign private issuers must disclose any significant ways in which their corporate governance practices differ from those followed by domestic companies under NYSE listing standards.

Commentary: Foreign private issuers must make their U.S. investors aware of the significant ways in which their home-country practices differ from those followed by domestic companies under NYSE listing standards. However, foreign private issuers are not required to present a detailed, item-by-item analysis of these differences. Such a disclosure would be long and unnecessarily complicated. Moreover, this requirement is not intended to suggest that one country's corporate governance practices are better or more effective than another. The Exchange believes that U.S. shareholders should be aware of the significant ways that the governance of a listed foreign private issuer differs from that of a U.S. listed company. The Exchange underscores that what is required is a brief, general summary of the significant differences, not a cumbersome analysis.

Listed foreign private issuers may provide this disclosure either on their web site (provided it is in the English language and accessible from the United States) and/or in their annual report as distributed to shareholders in the United States in accordance with Sections 103.00 and 203.01 of the Listed Company Manual (again, in the English language). If the disclosure is only made available on the web site, the annual report shall so state and provide the web address at which the information may be obtained.

12. a) Each listed company CEO must certify to the NYSE each year that he or she is not aware of any violation by the company of NYSE corporate governance listing standards.

Commentary: The CEO's annual certification to the NYSE that, as of the date of certification, he or she is unaware of any violation by the company of the NYSE's corporate governance listing standards will focus the CEO and senior management on the company's compliance with the listing standards. Both this certification to the NYSE, and any CEO/CFO certifications required to be filed with the SEC regarding the quality of the company's public disclosure, must be disclosed in the company's annual report to shareholders or, if the company does not prepare an annual report to shareholders, in the companies annual report on Form 10-K filed with the SEC.

b) Each listed company CEO must promptly notify the NYSE in writing after any executive officer of the listed company becomes aware of any material non-compliance with any applicable provisions of this Section 303A.

13. The NYSE may issue a public reprimand letter to any listed company that violates a NYSE listing standard.

Commentary: Suspending trading in or delisting a company can be harmful to the very shareholders that the NYSE listing standards seek to protect; the NYSE must therefore use these measures sparingly and judiciously. For this reason it is appropriate for the NYSE to have the ability to apply a lesser sanction to deter companies from violating its corporate governance (or other) listing standards. Accordingly, the NYSE may issue a public reprimand letter to any listed company, regardless of type of security listed or country of incorporation, that it determines has violated a NYSE listing standard. For companies that repeatedly or flagrantly violate NYSE listing standards, suspension and delisting remain the ultimate penalties. For clarification, this lesser sanction is not intended for use in the case of companies that fall below the financial and other continued listing standards provided in Chapter 8 of the Listed Company Manual or that fail to comply with the audit committee standards set out in Section 303A.06. The processes and procedures provided for in Chapter 8 govern the treatment of companies falling below those standards.

Sarbanes-Oxley Act of 2002

(Excerpts)

TITLE II — AUDITOR INDEPENDENCE

SEC. 201. SERVICES OUTSIDE THE SCOPE OF PRACTICE OF AUDITORS.

(a) PROHIBITED ACTIVITIES—Section 10A of the Securities Exchange Act of 1934 (15 U.S.C. 78j-1) is amended by adding at the end the following:

"(g) PROHIBITED ACTIVITIES—Except as provided in subsection (h), it shall be unlawful for a registered public accounting firm (and any associated person of that firm, to the extent determined appropriate by the Commission) that performs for any issuer any audit required by this title or the rules of the Commission under this title or, beginning 180 days after the date of commencement of the operations of the Public Company Accounting Oversight Board established under section 101 of the *Sarbanes-Oxley Act of* 2002 (in this section referred to as the 'Board'), the rules of the Board, to provide to that issuer, contemporaneously with the audit, any non-audit service, including—

"(1) bookkeeping or other services related to the accounting records or financial statements of the audit client;

"(2) financial information systems design and implementation; H. R. 3763-28

"(3) appraisal or valuation services, fairness opinions, or contribution-in-kind reports;

"(4) actuarial services;

"(5) internal audit outsourcing services;

"(6) management functions or human resources;

"(7) broker or dealer, investment adviser, or investment banking services;

"(8) legal services and expert services unrelated to the audit; and

"(9) any other service that the Board determines, by regulation, is impermissible.

"(h) PREAPPROVAL REQUIRED FOR NON-AUDIT SERVICES—A registered public accounting firm may engage in any non-audit service, including tax services, that is not described in any of paragraphs (1) through (9) of subsection (g) for an audit client, only if the activity is approved in advance by the audit committee of the issuer, in accordance with subsection (i).".

(b) EXEMPTION AUTHORITY—The Board may, on a case by case basis, exempt any person, issuer, public accounting firm, or transaction from the prohibition on the provision of services under section 10A(g) of the Securities Exchange Act of 1934 (as added by this section), to the extent that such exemption is necessary or appropriate in the public interest and is consistent with the protection of investors, and subject to review by the Commission in the same manner as for rules of the Board under section 107.

SEC. 202. PREAPPROVAL REQUIREMENTS.

Section 10A of the Securities Exchange Act of 1934 (15 U.S.C. 78j-1), as amended by this Act, is amended by adding at the end the following:

"(i) PREAPPROVAL REQUIREMENTS—

"(1) IN GENERAL—

"(A) AUDIT COMMITTEE ACTION—All auditing services (which may entail providing comfort letters in connection with securities underwritings or statutory audits required for insurance companies for purposes of State law) and non-audit services, other than as provided in subparagraph (B), provided to an issuer by the auditor of the issuer shall be preapproved by the audit committee of the issuer.

"(B) DE MINIMUS EXCEPTION—The preapproval requirement under subparagraph (A) is waived with respect to the provision of non-audit services for an issuer, if—

"(i) the aggregate amount of all such non-audit services provided to the issuer constitutes not more than 5 percent of the total amount of revenues paid by the issuer to its auditor during the fiscal year in which the nonaudit services are provided;

"(ii) such services were not recognized by the issuer at the time of the engagement to be non-audit services; and

"(iii) such services are promptly brought to the attention of the audit committee of the issuer and approved prior to the completion of the audit by the audit committee or by 1 or more members of the audit committee who are members of the board of directors to whom authority to grant such approvals has been delegated by the audit committee.

"(2) DISCLOSURE TO INVESTORS—Approval by an audit committee of an issuer under this subsection of a non-audit service to be performed by the auditor of the issuer shall be disclosed to investors in periodic reports required by section 13(a).

"(3) DELEGATION AUTHORITY—The audit committee of an issuer may delegate to 1 or more designated members of the audit committee who are independent directors of the board of directors, the authority to grant preapprovals required by this subsection.

The decisions of any member to whom authority is delegated under this paragraph to preapprove an activity under this subsection shall be presented to the full audit committee at each of its scheduled meetings.

"(4) APPROVAL OF AUDIT SERVICES FOR OTHER PURPOSES— In carrying out its duties under subsection (m)(2), if the audit committee of an issuer approves an audit service within the scope of the engagement of the auditor, such audit service shall be deemed to have been preapproved for purposes of this subsection.".

SEC. 203. AUDIT PARTNER ROTATION.

Section 10A of the Securities Exchange Act of 1934 (15 U.S.C. 78j-1), as amended by this Act, is amended by adding at the end the following:

"(j) AUDIT PARTNER ROTATION—It shall be unlawful for a registered public accounting firm to provide audit services to an issuer if the lead (or coordinating) audit partner (having primary responsibility for the audit), or the audit partner responsible for reviewing the audit, has performed audit services for that issuer in each of the 5 previous fiscal years of that issuer.".

SEC. 204. AUDITOR REPORTS TO AUDIT COMMITTEES.

Section 10A of the Securities Exchange Act of 1934 (15 U.S.C. 78j-1), as amended by this Act, is amended by adding at the end the following:

"(k) REPORTS TO AUDIT COMMITTEES—Each registered public accounting firm that performs for any issuer any audit required by this title shall timely report to the audit committee of the issuer—

"(1) all critical accounting policies and practices to be used;

"(2) all alternative treatments of financial information within generally accepted accounting principles that have been discussed with management officials of the issuer, ramifications of the use of such alternative disclosures and treatments, and the treatment preferred by the registered public accounting firm; and

"(3) other material written communications between the registered public accounting firm and the management of the issuer, such as any management letter or schedule of unadjusted differences.".

SEC. 205. CONFORMING AMENDMENTS.

(a) DEFINITIONS—Section 3(a) of the Securities Exchange Act of 1934 (15 U.S.C. 78c(a)) is amended by adding at the end the following:

"(58) AUDIT COMMITTEE—The term 'audit committee' means—

"(A) a committee (or equivalent body) established by and amongst the board of directors of an issuer for the purpose of overseeing the accounting and financial reporting processes of the issuer and audits of the financial statements of the issuer; and

"(B) if no such committee exists with respect to an issuer, the entire board of directors of the issuer.

"(59) REGISTERED PUBLIC ACCOUNTING FIRM—The term 'registered public accounting firm' has the same meaning as in section 2 of the *Sarbanes-Oxley Act of 2002*.".

(b) AUDITOR REQUIREMENTS—Section 10A of the Securities Exchange Act of 1934 (15 U.S.C. 78j-1) is amended—

(1) by striking "an independent public accountant" each place that term appears and inserting "a registered public accounting firm";

(2) by striking "the independent public accountant" each place that term appears and inserting "the registered public accounting firm";

(3) in subsection (c), by striking "No independent public accountant" and inserting "No registered public accounting firm"; and

(4) in subsection (b)—

(A) by striking "the accountant" each place that term appears and inserting "the firm";

(B) by striking "such accountant" each place that term appears and inserting "such firm"; and

(C) in paragraph (4), by striking "the accountant's report" and inserting "the report of the firm".

(c) OTHER REFERENCES—The Securities Exchange Act of 1934 (15 U.S.C. 78a et seq.) is amended—

(1) in section 12(b)(1) (15 U.S.C. 78l(b)(1)), by striking "independent public accountants" each place that term appears and inserting "a registered public accounting firm"; and

(2) in subsections (e) and (i) of section 17 (15 U.S.C. 78q), by striking "an independent public accountant" each place that term appears and inserting "a registered public accounting firm".

(d) CONFORMING AMENDMENT—Section 10A(f) of the Securities Exchange Act of 1934 (15 U.S.C. 78k(f)) is amended—

(1) by striking "DEFINITION" and inserting "DEFINITIONS"; and

(2) by adding at the end the following: "As used in this section, the term 'issuer' means an issuer (as defined in section 3), the securities of which are registered under section 12, or that is required to file reports pursuant to section 15(d), or that files or has filed a registration statement that has not yet become effective under the Securities Act of 1933 (15 U.S.C. 77a et seq.), and that it has not withdrawn.".

SEC. 206. CONFLICTS OF INTEREST.

Section 10A of the Securities Exchange Act of 1934 (15 U.S.C. 78j-1), as amended by this Act, is amended by adding at the end the following:

"(l) CONFLICTS OF INTEREST—It shall be unlawful for a registered public accounting firm to perform for an issuer any audit service required by this title, if a chief executive officer, controller, chief financial officer, chief accounting officer, or any person serving in an equivalent position for the issuer, was employed by that registered independent public accounting firm and participated in any capacity in the audit of that issuer during the 1-year period preceding the date of the initiation of the audit.".

SEC. 207. STUDY OF MANDATORY ROTATION OF REGISTERED PUBLIC ACCOUNTING FIRMS.

(a) STUDY AND REVIEW REQUIRED—The Comptroller General of the United States shall conduct a study and review of the potential effects of requiring the mandatory rotation of registered public accounting firms.

(b) REPORT REQUIRED—Not later than 1 year after the date of enactment of this Act, the Comptroller General shall submit a report to the Committee on Banking, Housing, and Urban Affairs of the Senate and the Committee on Financial Services of the House of Representatives on the results of the study and review required by this section.

(c) DEFINITION—For purposes of this section, the term "mandatory rotation" refers to the imposition of a limit on the period of years in which a particular registered public accounting firm may be the auditor of record for a particular issuer.

SEC. 208. COMMISSION AUTHORITY.

(a) COMMISSION REGULATIONS—Not later than 180 days after the date of enactment of this Act, the Commission shall issue final regulations to carry out each of subsections (g) through (l) of section 10A of the Securities Exchange Act of 1934, as added by this title.

(b) AUDITOR INDEPENDENCE—It shall be unlawful for any registered public accounting firm (or an associated person thereof, as applicable) to prepare or issue any audit report with respect to any issuer, if the firm or associated person engages in any activity with respect to that issuer prohibited by any of subsections (g) through (l) of section 10A of the Securities Exchange Act of 1934, as added by this title, or any rule or regulation of the Commission or of the Board issued thereunder.

SEC. 209. CONSIDERATIONS BY APPROPRIATE STATE REGULATORY AUTHORITIES.

In supervising nonregistered public accounting firms and their associated persons, appropriate State regulatory authorities should make an independent determination of the proper standards applicable, particularly taking into consideration the size and nature of the business of the accounting firms they supervise and the size and nature of the business of the clients of those firms. The standards applied by the Board under this Act should not be presumed to be applicable for purposes of this section for small and medium sized nonregistered public accounting firms.

TITLE III — CORPORATE RESPONSIBILITY

SEC. 301. PUBLIC COMPANY AUDIT COMMITTEES.

Section 10A of the Securities Exchange Act of 1934 (15 U.S.C. 78f) is amended by adding at the end the following:

"(m) STANDARDS RELATING TO AUDIT COMMITTEES—

"(1) COMMISSION RULES—

"(A) IN GENERAL—Effective not later than 270 days after the date of enactment of this subsection, the Commission shall, by rule, direct the national securities exchanges and national securities associations to prohibit the listing of any security of an issuer that is not in compliance with the requirements of any portion of paragraphs (2) through (6).

"(B) OPPORTUNITY TO CURE DEFECTS—The rules of the Commission under subparagraph (A) shall provide for appropriate procedures for an issuer to have an opportunity to cure any defects that would be the basis for a prohibition under subparagraph (A), before the imposition of such prohibition.

"(2) RESPONSIBILITIES RELATING TO REGISTERED PUBLIC ACCOUNTING FIRMS—The audit committee of each issuer, in its capacity as a committee of the board of directors, shall be directly responsible for the appointment, compensation, and oversight of the work of any registered public accounting firm employed by that issuer (including resolution of disagreements between management and the auditor regarding financial reporting) for the purpose of preparing or issuing an audit report or related work, and each such registered public accounting firm shall report directly to the audit committee.

"(3) INDEPENDENCE—

"(A) IN GENERAL—Each member of the audit committee of the issuer shall be a member of the board of directors of the issuer, and shall otherwise be independent.

"(B) CRITERIA—In order to be considered to be independent for purposes of this paragraph, a member of an audit committee of an issuer may not, other than in his or her capacity as a member of the audit committee, the board of directors, or any other board committee—

"(i) accept any consulting, advisory, or other compensatory fee from the issuer; or

"(ii) be an affiliated person of the issuer or any subsidiary thereof.

"(C) EXEMPTION AUTHORITY—The Commission may exempt from the requirements of subparagraph (B) a particular relationship with respect to audit committee members, as the Commission determines appropriate in light of the circumstances.

"(4) COMPLAINTS—Each audit committee shall establish procedures for—

"(A) the receipt, retention, and treatment of complaints received by the issuer regarding accounting, internal accounting controls, or auditing matters; and

"(B) the confidential, anonymous submission by employees of the issuer of concerns regarding questionable accounting or auditing matters.

"(5) AUTHORITY TO ENGAGE ADVISERS—Each audit committee shall have the authority to engage independent counsel and other advisers, as it determines necessary to carry out its duties.

"(6) FUNDING—Each issuer shall provide for appropriate funding, as determined by the audit committee, in its capacity as a committee of the board of directors, for payment of compensation—

"(A) to the registered public accounting firm employed by the issuer for the purpose of rendering or issuing an audit report; and

"(B) to any advisers employed by the audit committee under paragraph (5).".

SEC. 302. CORPORATE RESPONSIBILITY FOR FINANCIAL REPORTS.

(a) REGULATIONS REQUIRED—The Commission shall, by rule, require, for each company filing periodic reports under section 13(a) or 15(d) of the Securities Exchange Act of 1934 (15 U.S.C. 78m, 78o(d)), that the principal executive officer or officers and the principal financial officer or officers, or persons performing similar functions, certify in each annual or quarterly report filed or submitted under either such section of such Act that—

(1) the signing officer has reviewed the report;

(2) based on the officer's knowledge, the report does not contain any untrue statement of a material fact or omit to state a material fact necessary in order to make the statements made, in light of the circumstances under which such statements were made, not misleading;

(3) based on such officer's knowledge, the financial statements, and other financial information included in the report, fairly present in all material respects the financial condition and results of operations of the issuer as of, and for, the periods presented in the report;

(4) the signing officers—

(A) are responsible for establishing and maintaining internal controls;

(B) have designed such internal controls to ensure that material information relating to the issuer and its consolidated subsidiaries is made known to such officers by others within those entities, particularly during the period in which the periodic reports are being prepared;

(C) have evaluated the effectiveness of the issuer's internal controls as of a date within 90 days prior to the report; and

(D) have presented in the report their conclusions about the effectiveness of their internal controls based on their evaluation as of that date;

(5) the signing officers have disclosed to the issuer's auditors and the audit committee of the board of directors (or persons fulfilling the equivalent function)—

(A) all significant deficiencies in the design or operation of internal controls which could adversely affect the issuer's ability to record, process, summarize, and report financial data and have identified for the issuer's auditors any material weaknesses in internal controls; and

(B) any fraud, whether or not material, that involves management or other employees who have a significant role in the issuer's internal controls; and

(6) the signing officers have indicated in the report whether or not there were significant changes in internal controls or in other factors that could significantly affect internal controls subsequent to the date of their evaluation, including any corrective actions with regard to significant deficiencies and material weaknesses.

(b) FOREIGN REINCORPORATIONS HAVE NO EFFECT—Nothing in this section 302 shall be interpreted or applied in any way to allow any issuer to lessen the legal force of the statement required under this section 302, by an issuer having reincorporated or having engaged in any other transaction that resulted in the transfer of the corporate domicile or offices of the issuer from inside the United States to outside of the United States.

(c) DEADLINE—The rules required by subsection (a) shall be effective not later than 30 days after the date of enactment of this Act.

SEC. 303. IMPROPER INFLUENCE ON CONDUCT OF AUDITS.

(a) RULES TO PROHIBIT—It shall be unlawful, in contravention of such rules or regulations as the Commission shall prescribe as necessary and appropriate in the public interest or for the protection of investors, for any officer or director of an issuer, or any other person acting under the direction thereof, to take any action to fraudulently influence, coerce, manipulate, or mislead any independent public or certified accountant engaged in the performance of an audit of the financial statements of that issuer for the purpose of rendering such financial statements materially misleading.

(b) ENFORCEMENT—In any civil proceeding, the Commission shall have exclusive authority to enforce this section and any rule or regulation issued under this section.

(c) NO PREEMPTION OF OTHER LAW—The provisions of subsection (a) shall be in addition to, and shall not supersede or preempt, any other provision of law or any rule or regulation issued thereunder.

(d) DEADLINE FOR RULEMAKING—The Commission shall—

(1) propose the rules or regulations required by this section, not later than 90 days after the date of enactment of this Act; and

(2) issue final rules or regulations required by this section, not later than 270 days after that date of enactment.

SEC. 304. FORFEITURE OF CERTAIN BONUSES AND PROFITS.

(a) ADDITIONAL COMPENSATION PRIOR TO NONCOMPLIANCE WITH COMMISSION FINANCIAL REPORTING REQUIREMENTS—If an issuer is required to prepare an accounting restatement due to the material noncompliance of the issuer, as a result of misconduct, with any financial reporting requirement under the securities laws, the chief executive officer and chief financial officer of the issuer shall reimburse the issuer for—

   (1) any bonus or other incentive—based or equity-based compensation received by that person from the issuer during the 12-month period following the first public issuance or filing with the Commission (whichever first occurs) of the financial document embodying such financial reporting requirement; and

   (2) any profits realized from the sale of securities of the issuer during that 12-month period.

(b) COMMISSION EXEMPTION AUTHORITY—The Commission may exempt any person from the application of subsection (a), as it deems necessary and appropriate.

SEC. 305. OFFICER AND DIRECTOR BARS AND PENALTIES.

(a) UNFITNESS STANDARD—

   (1) SECURITIES EXCHANGE ACT OF 1934—Section 21(d)(2) of the Securities Exchange Act of 1934 (15 U.S.C. 78u(d)(2)) is amended by striking "substantial unfitness" and inserting "unfitness".

   (2) SECURITIES ACT OF 1933—Section 20(e) of the Securities Act of 1933 (15 U.S.C. 77t(e)) is amended by striking "substantial unfitness" and inserting "unfitness".

(b) EQUITABLE RELIEF—Section 21(d) of the Securities Exchange Act of 1934 (15 U.S.C. 78u(d)) is amended by adding at the end the following:

   "(5) EQUITABLE RELIEF—In any action or proceeding brought or instituted by the Commission under any provision of the securities laws, the Commission may seek, and any Federal court may grant, any equitable relief that may be appropriate or necessary for the benefit of investors.".

SEC. 306. INSIDER TRADES DURING PENSION FUND BLACKOUT PERIODS.

(a) PROHIBITION OF INSIDER TRADING DURING PENSION FUND BLACKOUT PERIODS—

   (1) IN GENERAL—Except to the extent otherwise provided by rule of the Commission pursuant to paragraph (3), it shall be unlawful for any director or executive officer of an issuer of any equity security (other than an exempted security), directly or indirectly, to purchase, sell, or otherwise acquire or transfer any equity security of the issuer (other than an exempted security) during any blackout period with respect to such equity security if such director or officer acquires such equity security in connection with his or her service or employment as a director or executive officer.

(2) REMEDY—

    (A) IN GENERAL—Any profit realized by a director or executive officer referred to in paragraph (1) from any purchase, sale, or other acquisition or transfer in violation of this subsection shall inure to and be recoverable by the issuer, irrespective of any intention on the part of such director or executive officer in entering into the transaction.

    (B) ACTIONS TO RECOVER PROFITS—An action to recover profits in accordance with this subsection may be instituted at law or in equity in any court of competent jurisdiction by the issuer, or by the owner of any security of the issuer in the name and in behalf of the issuer if the issuer fails or refuses to bring such action within 60 days after the date of request, or fails diligently to prosecute the action thereafter, except that no such suit shall be brought more than 2 years after the date on which such profit was realized.

(3) RULEMAKING AUTHORIZED—The Commission shall, in consultation with the Secretary of Labor, issue rules to clarify the application of this subsection and to prevent evasion thereof. Such rules shall provide for the application of the requirements of paragraph (1) with respect to entities treated as a single employer with respect to an issuer under section 414(b), (c), (m), or (o) of the Internal Revenue Code of 1986 to the extent necessary to clarify the application of such requirements and to prevent evasion thereof. Such rules may also provide for appropriate exceptions from the requirements of this subsection, including exceptions for purchases pursuant to an automatic dividend reinvestment program or purchases or sales made pursuant to an advance election.

(4) BLACKOUT PERIOD—For purposes of this subsection, the term "blackout period", with respect to the equity securities of any issuer—

    (A) means any period of more than 3 consecutive business days during which the ability of not fewer than 50 percent of the participants or beneficiaries under all individual account plans maintained by the issuer to purchase, sell, or otherwise acquire or transfer an interest in any equity of such issuer held in such an individual account plan is temporarily suspended by the issuer or by a fiduciary of the plan; and

    (B) does not include, under regulations which shall be prescribed by the Commission—

        (i) a regularly scheduled period in which the participants and beneficiaries may not purchase, sell, or otherwise acquire or transfer an interest in any equity of such issuer, if such period is—

            (I) incorporated into the individual account plan; and

            (II) timely disclosed to employees before becoming participants under the individual account plan or as a subsequent amendment to the plan; or

        (ii) any suspension described in subparagraph (A) that is imposed solely in connection with persons becoming participants or beneficiaries, or ceasing to be participants or beneficiaries, in an individual account plan by reason of a corporate merger, acquisition, divestiture, or similar transaction involving the plan or plan sponsor.

(5) INDIVIDUAL ACCOUNT PLAN—For purposes of this subsection, the term "individual account plan" has the meaning provided in section 3(34) of the Employee Retirement Income Security Act of 1974 (29 U.S.C. 1002(34), except that such term shall not include a one-participant retirement plan (within the meaning of section 101(i)(8)(B) of such Act (29 U.S.C. 1021(i)(8)(B))).

(6) NOTICE TO DIRECTORS, EXECUTIVE OFFICERS, AND THE COMMISSION—In any case in which a director or executive officer is subject to the requirements of this subsection in connection with a blackout period (as defined in paragraph (4)) with respect to any equity securities, the issuer of such equity securities shall timely notify such director or officer and the Securities and Exchange Commission of such blackout period.

(b) NOTICE REQUIREMENTS TO PARTICIPANTS AND BENEFICIARIES UNDER ERISA—

(1) IN GENERAL—Section 101 of the Employee Retirement Income Security Act of 1974 (29 U.S.C. 1021) is amended by redesignating the second subsection (h) as subsection (j), and by inserting after the first subsection (h) the following new subsection:

"(i) NOTICE OF BLACKOUT PERIODS TO PARTICIPANT OR BENEFICIARY UNDER INDIVIDUAL ACCOUNT PLAN—

"(1) DUTIES OF PLAN ADMINISTRATOR—In advance of the commencement of any blackout period with respect to an individual account plan, the plan administrator shall notify the plan participants and beneficiaries who are affected by such action in accordance with this subsection.

"(2) NOTICE REQUIREMENTS—

"(A) IN GENERAL—The notices described in paragraph (1) shall be written in a manner calculated to be understood by the average plan participant and shall include—

"(i) the reasons for the blackout period,

"(ii) an identification of the investments and other rights affected,

"(iii) the expected beginning date and length of the blackout period,

"(iv) in the case of investments affected, a statement that the participant or beneficiary should evaluate the appropriateness of their current investment decisions in light of their inability to direct or diversify assets credited to their accounts during the blackout period, and

"(v) such other matters as the Secretary may require by regulation.

"(B) NOTICE TO PARTICIPANTS AND BENEFICIARIES— Except as otherwise provided in this subsection, notices described in paragraph (1) shall be furnished to all participants and beneficiaries under the plan to whom the blackout period applies at least 30 days in advance of the blackout period.

"(C) EXCEPTION TO 30-DAY NOTICE REQUIREMENT—In any case in which—

"(i) a deferral of the blackout period would violate the requirements of subparagraph (A) or (B) of section 404(a)(1), and a fiduciary of the plan reasonably so determines in writing, or "(ii) the inability to provide the 30-day advance notice is due to events that were unforeseeable or circumstances beyond the reasonable control of the plan administrator, and a fiduciary of the plan reasonably so determines in writing, subparagraph (B) shall not apply, and the notice shall be furnished to all participants and beneficiaries under the plan to whom the blackout period applies as soon as reasonably possible under the circumstances unless such a notice in advance of the termination of the blackout period is impracticable.

"(D) WRITTEN NOTICE—The notice required to be provided under this subsection shall be in writing, except that such notice may be in electronic or other form to the extent that such form is reasonably accessible to the recipient.

"(E) NOTICE TO ISSUERS OF EMPLOYER SECURITIES SUBJECT TO BLACKOUT PERIOD—In the case of any blackout period in connection with an individual account plan, the plan administrator shall provide timely notice of such blackout period to the issuer of any employer securities subject to such blackout period.

"(3) EXCEPTION FOR BLACKOUT PERIODS WITH LIMITED APPLICABILITY—In any case in which the blackout period applies only to 1 or more participants or beneficiaries in connection with a merger, acquisition, divestiture, or similar transaction involving the plan or plan sponsor and occurs solely in connection with becoming or ceasing to be a participant or beneficiary under the plan by reason of such merger, acquisition, divestiture, or transaction, the requirement of this subsection that the notice be provided to all participants and beneficiaries shall be treated as met if the notice required under paragraph (1) is provided to such participants or beneficiaries to whom the blackout period applies as soon as reasonably practicable.

"(4) CHANGES IN LENGTH OF BLACKOUT PERIOD—If, following the furnishing of the notice pursuant to this subsection, there is a change in the beginning date or length of the blackout period (specified in such notice pursuant to paragraph (2)(A)(iii)), the administrator shall provide affected participants and beneficiaries notice of the change as soon as reasonably practicable. In relation to the extended blackout period, such notice shall meet the requirements of paragraph (2)(D) and shall specify any material change in the matters referred to in clauses (i) through (v) of paragraph (2)(A).

"(5) REGULATORY EXCEPTIONS—The Secretary may provide by regulation for additional exceptions to the requirements of this subsection which the Secretary determines are in the interests of participants and beneficiaries.

"(6) GUIDANCE AND MODEL NOTICES—The Secretary shall issue guidance and model notices which meet the requirements of this subsection.

"(7) BLACKOUT PERIOD—For purposes of this subsection—

"(A) IN GENERAL—The term 'blackout period' means, in connection with an individual account plan, any period for which any ability of participants or beneficiaries under the plan, which is otherwise available under the terms of such plan, to direct or diversify assets credited to their accounts, to obtain loans from the plan, or to obtain distributions from the plan is temporarily suspended, limited, or restricted, if such suspension, limitation, or restriction is for any period of more than 3 consecutive business days.

"(B) EXCLUSIONS—The term 'blackout period' does not include a suspension, limitation, or restriction—

"(i) which occurs by reason of the application of the securities laws (as defined in section 3(a)(47) of the Securities Exchange Act of 1934),

"(ii) which is a change to the plan which provides for a regularly scheduled suspension, limitation, or restriction which is disclosed to participants or beneficiaries through any summary of material modifications, any materials describing specific investment alternatives under the plan, or any changes thereto, or

"(iii) which applies only to 1 or more individuals, each of whom is the participant, an alternate payee (as defined in section 206(d)(3)(K)), or any other beneficiary pursuant to a qualified domestic relations order (as defined in section 206(d)(3)(B)(i)).

"(8) INDIVIDUAL ACCOUNT PLAN—

"(A) IN GENERAL—For purposes of this subsection, the term 'individual account plan' shall have the meaning provided such term in section 3(34), except that such term shall not include a one-participant retirement plan.

"(B) ONE-PARTICIPANT RETIREMENT PLAN—For purposes of subparagraph (A), the term 'one-participant retirement plan' means a retirement plan that—

"(i) on the first day of the plan year—

"(I) covered only the employer (and the employer's spouse) and the employer owned the entire business (whether or not incorporated), or

"(II) covered only one or more partners (and their spouses) in a business partnership (including partners in an S or C corporation (as defined in section 1361(a) of the Internal Revenue Code of 1986)),

"(ii) meets the minimum coverage requirements of section 410(b) of the Internal Revenue Code of 1986 (as in effect on the date of the enactment of this paragraph) without being combined with any other plan of the business that covers the employees of the business,

"(iii) does not provide benefits to anyone except the employer (and the employer's spouse) or the partners (and their spouses),

"(iv) does not cover a business that is a member of an affiliated service group, a controlled group of corporations, or a group of businesses under common control, and

"(v) does not cover a business that leases employees.".

(2) ISSUANCE OF INITIAL GUIDANCE AND MODEL NOTICE— The Secretary of Labor shall issue initial guidance and a model notice pursuant to section 101(i)(6) of the Employee Retirement Income Security Act of 1974 (as added by this subsection) not later than January 1, 2003. Not later than 75 days after the date of the enactment of this Act, the Secretary shall promulgate interim final rules necessary to carry out the amendments made by this subsection.

(3) CIVIL PENALTIES FOR FAILURE TO PROVIDE NOTICE— Section 502 of such Act (29 U.S.C. 1132) is amended—

(A) in subsection (a)(6), by striking "(5), or (6)" and inserting "(5), (6), or (7)";

(B) by redesignating paragraph (7) of subsection (c) as paragraph (8); and

(C) by inserting after paragraph (6) of subsection (c) the following new paragraph:

"(7) The Secretary may assess a civil penalty against a plan administrator of up to $100 a day from the date of the plan administrator's failure or refusal to provide notice to participants and beneficiaries in accordance with section 101(i). For purposes of this paragraph, each violation with respect to any single participant or beneficiary shall be treated as a separate violation.".

(3) PLAN AMENDMENTS—If any amendment made by this subsection requires an amendment to any plan, such plan amendment shall not be required to be made before the first plan year beginning on or after the effective date of this section, if—

(A) during the period after such amendment made by this subsection takes effect and before such first plan year, the plan is operated in good faith compliance with the requirements of such amendment made by this subsection, and

(B) such plan amendment applies retroactively to the period after such amendment made by this subsection takes effect and before such first plan year.

(c) EFFECTIVE DATE—The provisions of this section (including the amendments made thereby) shall take effect 180 days after the date of the enactment of this Act. Good faith compliance with the requirements of such provisions in advance of the issuance of applicable regulations thereunder shall be treated as compliance with such provisions.

SEC. 307. RULES OF PROFESSIONAL RESPONSIBILITY FOR ATTORNEYS.

Not later than 180 days after the date of enactment of this Act, the Commission shall issue rules, in the public interest and for the protection of investors, setting forth minimum standards of professional conduct for attorneys appearing and practicing before the Commission in any way in the representation of issuers, including a rule—

(1) requiring an attorney to report evidence of a material violation of securities law or breach of fiduciary duty or similar violation by the company or any agent thereof, to the chief legal counsel or the chief executive officer of the company (or the equivalent thereof); and

(2) if the counsel or officer does not appropriately respond to the evidence (adopting, as necessary, appropriate remedial measures or sanctions with respect to the violation), requiring the attorney to report the evidence to the audit committee of the board of directors of the issuer or to another committee of the board of directors comprised solely of directors not employed directly or indirectly by the issuer, or to the board of directors.

SEC. 308. FAIR FUNDS FOR INVESTORS.

(a) CIVIL PENALTIES ADDED TO DISGORGEMENT FUNDS FOR THE RELIEF OF VICTIMS—If in any judicial or administrative action brought by the Commission under the securities laws (as such term is defined in section 3(a)(47) of the Securities Exchange Act of 1934 (15 U.S.C. 78c(a)(47)) the Commission obtains an order requiring disgorgement against any person for a violation of such laws or the rules or regulations thereunder, or such person agrees in settlement of any such action to such disgorgement, and the Commission also obtains pursuant to such laws a civil penalty against such person, the amount of such civil penalty shall, on the motion or at the direction of the Commission, be added to and become part of the disgorgement fund for the benefit of the victims of such violation.

(b) ACCEPTANCE OF ADDITIONAL DONATIONS—The Commission is authorized to accept, hold, administer, and utilize gifts, bequests and devises of property, both real and personal, to the United States for a disgorgement fund described in subsection (a). Such gifts, bequests, and devises of money and proceeds from sales of other property received as gifts, bequests, or devises shall be deposited in the disgorgement fund and shall be available for allocation in accordance with subsection (a).

(c) STUDY REQUIRED—

(1) SUBJECT OF STUDY—The Commission shall review and analyze—

(A) enforcement actions by the Commission over the five years preceding the date of the enactment of this Act that have included proceedings to obtain civil penalties or disgorgements to identify areas where such proceedings may be utilized to efficiently, effectively, and fairly provide restitution for injured investors; and

(B) other methods to more efficiently, effectively, and fairly provide restitution to injured investors, including methods to improve the collection rates for civil penalties and disgorgements.

(2) REPORT REQUIRED—The Commission shall report its findings to the Committee on Financial Services of the House of Representatives and the Committee on Banking, Housing, and Urban Affairs of the Senate within 180 days after of the date of the enactment of this Act, and shall use such findings to revise its rules and regulations as necessary. The report shall include a discussion of regulatory or legislative actions that are recommended or that may be necessary to address concerns identified in the study.

(d) CONFORMING AMENDMENTS—Each of the following provisions is amended by inserting ", except as otherwise provided in section 308 of the *Sarbanes-Oxley Act of* 2002" after "Treasury of the United States":

(1) Section 21(d)(3)(C)(i) of the Securities Exchange Act of 1934 (15 U.S.C. 78u(d)(3)(C)(i)).

(2) Section 21A(d)(1) of such Act (15 U.S.C. 78u-1(d)(1)).

(3) Section 20(d)(3)(A) of the Securities Act of 1933 (15 U.S.C. 77t(d)(3)(A)).

(4) Section 42(e)(3)(A) of the Investment Company Act of 1940 (15 U.S.C. 80a-41(e)(3)(A)).

(5) Section 209(e)(3)(A) of the Investment Advisers Act of 1940 (15 U.S.C. 80b-9(e)(3)(A)).

(e) DEFINITION—As used in this section, the term "disgorgement fund" means a fund established in any administrative or judicial proceeding described in subsection (a).

TITLE IV — ENHANCED FINANCIAL DISCLOSURES

SEC. 401. DISCLOSURES IN PERIODIC REPORTS.

(a) DISCLOSURES REQUIRED—Section 13 of the Securities Exchange Act of 1934 (15 U.S.C. 78m) is amended by adding at the end the following:

"(i) ACCURACY OF FINANCIAL REPORTS—Each financial report that contains financial statements, and that is required to be prepared in accordance with (or reconciled to) generally accepted accounting principles under this title and filed with the Commission shall reflect all material correcting adjustments that have been identified by a registered public accounting firm in accordance with generally accepted accounting principles and the rules and regulations of the Commission.

"(j) OFF-BALANCE SHEET TRANSACTIONS—Not later than 180 days after the date of enactment of the *Sarbanes-Oxley Act of* 2002, the Commission shall issue final rules providing that each annual and quarterly financial report required to be filed with the Commission shall disclose all material off-balance sheet transactions, arrangements, obligations (including contingent obligations), and other relationships of the issuer with unconsolidated entities or other persons, that may have a material current or future effect on financial condition, changes in financial condition, results of operations, liquidity, capital expenditures, capital resources, or significant components of revenues or expenses.".

(b) COMMISSION RULES ON PRO FORMA FIGURES—Not later than 180 days after the date of enactment of the *Sarbanes-Oxley Act of* 2002, the Commission shall issue final rules providing that pro forma financial information included in any periodic or other report filed with the Commission pursuant to the securities laws, or in any public disclosure or press or other release, shall be presented in a manner that—

(1) does not contain an untrue statement of a material fact or omit to state a material fact necessary in order to make the pro forma financial information, in light of the circumstances under which it is presented, not misleading; and

(2) reconciles it with the financial condition and results of operations of the issuer under generally accepted accounting principles.

(c) STUDY AND REPORT ON SPECIAL PURPOSE ENTITIES—

(1) STUDY REQUIRED—The Commission shall, not later than 1 year after the effective date of adoption of off-balance sheet disclosure rules required by section 13(j) of the Securities Exchange Act of 1934, as added by this section, complete a study of filings by issuers and their disclosures to determine—

(A) the extent of off-balance sheet transactions, including assets, liabilities, leases, losses, and the use of special purpose entities; and

(B) whether generally accepted accounting rules result in financial statements of issuers reflecting the economics of such off-balance sheet transactions to investors in a transparent fashion.

(2) REPORT AND RECOMMENDATIONS—Not later than 6 months after the date of completion of the study required by paragraph (1), the Commission shall submit a report to the President, the Committee on Banking, Housing, and Urban Affairs of the Senate, and the Committee on Financial Services of the House of Representatives, setting forth—

(A) the amount or an estimate of the amount of offbalance sheet transactions, including assets, liabilities, leases, and losses of, and the use of special purpose entities by, issuers filing periodic reports pursuant to section 13 or 15 of the Securities Exchange Act of 1934;

(B) the extent to which special purpose entities are used to facilitate off-balance sheet transactions;

(C) whether generally accepted accounting principles or the rules of the Commission result in financial statements of issuers reflecting the economics of such transactions to investors in a transparent fashion;

(D) whether generally accepted accounting principles specifically result in the consolidation of special purpose entities sponsored by an issuer in cases in which the issuer has the majority of the risks and rewards of the special purpose entity; and

(E) any recommendations of the Commission for improving the transparency and quality of reporting offbalance sheet transactions in the financial statements and disclosures required to be filed by an issuer with the Commission.

SEC. 402. ENHANCED CONFLICT OF INTEREST PROVISIONS.

(a) PROHIBITION ON PERSONAL LOANS TO EXECUTIVES—Section 13 of the Securities Exchange Act of 1934 (15 U.S.C. 78m), as amended by this Act, is amended by adding at the end the following:

"(k) PROHIBITION ON PERSONAL LOANS TO EXECUTIVES—

"(1) IN GENERAL—It shall be unlawful for any issuer (as defined in section 2 of the *Sarbanes-Oxley Act of* 2002), directly or indirectly, including through any subsidiary, to extend or maintain credit, to arrange for the extension of credit, or to renew an extension of credit, in the form of a personal loan to or for any director or executive officer (or equivalent thereof) of that issuer. An extension of credit maintained by the issuer on the date of enactment of this subsection shall not be subject to the provisions of this subsection, provided that there is no material modification to any term of any such extension of credit or any renewal of any such extension of credit on or after that date of enactment.

"(2) LIMITATION—Paragraph (1) does not preclude any home improvement and manufactured home loans (as that term is defined in section 5 of the Home Owners' Loan Act (12 U.S.C. 1464)), consumer credit (as defined in section 103 of the Truth in Lending Act (15 U.S.C. 1602)), or any extension of credit under an open end credit plan (as defined in section 103 of the Truth in Lending Act (15 U.S.C. 1602)), or a charge card (as defined in section 127(c)(4)(e) of the Truth in Lending Act (15 U.S.C. 1637(c)(4)(e)), or any extension of credit by a broker or dealer registered under section 15 of this title to an employee of that broker or dealer to buy, trade, or carry securities, that is permitted under rules or regulations of the Board of Governors of the Federal Reserve System pursuant to section 7 of this title (other than an extension of credit that would be used to purchase the stock of that issuer), that is—

"(A) made or provided in the ordinary course of the consumer credit business of such issuer;

"(B) of a type that is generally made available by such issuer to the public; and

"(C) made by such issuer on market terms, or terms that are no more favorable than those offered by the issuer to the general public for such extensions of credit.

"(3) RULE OF CONSTRUCTION FOR CERTAIN LOANS—Paragraph (1) does not apply to any loan made or maintained by an insured depository institution (as defined in section 3 of the Federal Deposit Insurance Act (12 U.S.C. 1813)), if the loan is subject to the insider lending restrictions of section 22(h) of the Federal Reserve Act (12 U.S.C. 375b).".

SEC. 403. DISCLOSURES OF TRANSACTIONS INVOLVING MANAGEMENT AND PRINCIPAL STOCKHOLDERS.

(a) AMENDMENT—Section 16 of the Securities Exchange Act of 1934 (15 U.S.C. 78p) is amended by striking the heading of such section and subsection (a) and inserting the following:

"SEC. 16. DIRECTORS, OFFICERS, AND PRINCIPAL STOCKHOLDERS.

"(a) DISCLOSURES REQUIRED—

"(1) DIRECTORS, OFFICERS, AND PRINCIPAL STOCKHOLDERS REQUIRED TO FILE— Every person who is directly or indirectly the beneficial owner of more than 10 percent of any class of any equity security (other than an exempted security) which is registered pursuant to section 12, or who is a director or an officer of the issuer of such security, shall file the statements required by this subsection with the Commission (and, if such security is registered on a national securities exchange, also with the exchange).

"(2) TIME OF FILING—The statements required by this subsection shall be filed—

"(A) at the time of the registration of such security on a national securities exchange or by the effective date of a registration statement filed pursuant to section 12(g);

"(B) within 10 days after he or she becomes such beneficial owner, director, or officer;

"(C) if there has been a change in such ownership, or if such person shall have purchased or sold a security based swap agreement (as defined in section 206(b) of the Gramm-Leach-Bliley Act (15 U.S.C. 78c note)) involving such equity security, before the end of the second business day following the day on which the subject transaction has been executed, or at such other time as the Commission shall establish, by rule, in any case in which the Commission determines that such 2-day period is not feasible.

"(3) CONTENTS OF STATEMENTS—A statement filed—

"(A) under subparagraph (A) or (B) of paragraph (2) shall contain a statement of the amount of all equity securities of such issuer of which the filing person is the beneficial owner; and

"(B) under subparagraph (C) of such paragraph shall indicate ownership by the filing person at the date of filing, any such changes in such ownership, and such purchases and sales of the security-based swap agreements as have occurred since the most recent such filing under such subparagraph.

"(4) ELECTRONIC FILING AND AVAILABILITY—Beginning not later than 1 year after the date of enactment of the *Sarbanes-Oxley Act of 2002*—

"(A) a statement filed under subparagraph (C) of paragraph (2) shall be filed electronically;

"(B) the Commission shall provide each such statement on a publicly accessible Internet site not later than the end of the business day following that filing; and

"(C) the issuer (if the issuer maintains a corporate website) shall provide that statement on that corporate website, not later than the end of the business day following that filing.".

(b) EFFECTIVE DATE—The amendment made by this section shall be effective 30 days after the date of the enactment of this Act.

SEC. 404. MANAGEMENT ASSESSMENT OF INTERNAL CONTROLS.

(a) RULES REQUIRED—The Commission shall prescribe rules requiring each annual report required by section 13(a) or 15(d) of the Securities Exchange Act of 1934 (15 U.S.C. 78m or 78o(d)) to contain an internal control report, which shall—

(1) state the responsibility of management for establishing and maintaining an adequate internal control structure and procedures for financial reporting; and

(2) contain an assessment, as of the end of the most recent fiscal year of the issuer, of the effectiveness of the internal control structure and procedures of the issuer for financial reporting.

(b) INTERNAL CONTROL EVALUATION AND REPORTING—With respect to the internal control assessment required by subsection (a), each registered public accounting firm that prepares or issues the audit report for the issuer shall attest to, and report on, the assessment made by the management of the issuer. An attestation made under this subsection shall be made in accordance with standards for attestation engagements issued or adopted by the Board. Any such attestation shall not be the subject of a separate engagement.

SEC. 405. EXEMPTION.

Nothing in section 401, 402, or 404, the amendments made by those sections, or the rules of the Commission under those sections shall apply to any investment company registered under section 8 of the Investment Company Act of 1940 (15 U.S.C. 80a-8).

SEC. 406. CODE OF ETHICS FOR SENIOR FINANCIAL OFFICERS.

(a) CODE OF ETHICS DISCLOSURE—The Commission shall issue rules to require each issuer, together with periodic reports required pursuant to section 13(a) or 15(d) of the Securities Exchange Act of 1934, to disclose whether or not, and if not, the reason therefor, such issuer has adopted a code of ethics for senior financial officers, applicable to its principal financial officer and comptroller or principal accounting officer, or persons performing similar functions.

(b) CHANGES IN CODES OF ETHICS—The Commission shall revise its regulations concerning matters requiring prompt disclosure on Form 8-K (or any successor thereto) to require the immediate disclosure, by means of the filing of such form, dissemination by the Internet or by other electronic means, by any issuer of any change in or waiver of the code of ethics for senior financial officers.

(c) DEFINITION—In this section, the term "code of ethics" means such standards as are reasonably necessary to promote—

  (1) honest and ethical conduct, including the ethical handling of actual or apparent conflicts of interest between personal and professional relationships;

  (2) full, fair, accurate, timely, and understandable disclosure in the periodic reports required to be filed by the issuer; and

  (3) compliance with applicable governmental rules and regulations.

(d) DEADLINE FOR RULEMAKING—The Commission shall—

  (1) propose rules to implement this section, not later than 90 days after the date of enactment of this Act; and

  (2) issue final rules to implement this section, not later than 180 days after that date of enactment.

SEC. 407. DISCLOSURE OF AUDIT COMMITTEE FINANCIAL EXPERT.

(a) RULES DEFINING "FINANCIAL EXPERT"—The Commission shall issue rules, as necessary or appropriate in the public interest and consistent with the protection of investors, to require each issuer, together with periodic reports required pursuant to sections 13(a) and 15(d) of the Securities Exchange Act of 1934, to disclose whether or not, and if not, the reasons therefor, the audit committee of that issuer is comprised of at least 1 member who is a financial expert, as such term is defined by the Commission.

(b) CONSIDERATIONS—In defining the term "financial expert" for purposes of subsection (a), the Commission shall consider whether a person has, through education and experience as a public accountant or auditor or a principal financial officer, comptroller, or principal account-ing officer of an issuer, or from a position involving the performance of similar functions—

(1) an understanding of generally accepted accounting principles and financial statements;

(2) experience in—

(A) the preparation or auditing of financial statements of generally comparable issuers; and

(B) the application of such principles in connection with the accounting for estimates, accruals, and reserves;

(3) experience with internal accounting controls; and

(4) an understanding of audit committee functions.

(c) DEADLINE FOR RULEMAKING—The Commission shall—

(1) propose rules to implement this section, not later than 90 days after the date of enact-ment of this Act; and

(2) issue final rules to implement this section, not later than 180 days after that date of enact-ment.

SEC. 408. ENHANCED REVIEW OF PERIODIC DISCLOSURES BY ISSUERS.

(a) REGULAR AND SYSTEMATIC REVIEW—The Commission shall review disclosures made by issuers reporting under section 13(a) of the Securities Exchange Act of 1934 (including reports filed on Form 10-K), and which have a class of securities listed on a national securities exchange or traded on an automated quotation facility of a national securities association, on a regular and systematic basis for the protection of investors. Such review shall include a review of an issuer's financial statement.

(b) REVIEW CRITERIA—For purposes of scheduling the reviews required by subsection (a), the Commission shall consider, among other factors—

(1) issuers that have issued material restatements of financial results;

(2) issuers that experience significant volatility in their stock price as compared to other issuers;

(3) issuers with the largest market capitalization;

(4) emerging companies with disparities in price to earning ratios;

(5) issuers whose operations significantly affect any material sector of the economy; and

(6) any other factors that the Commission may consider relevant.

(c) MINIMUM REVIEW PERIOD—In no event shall an issuer required to file reports under section 13(a) or 15(d) of the Securities Exchange Act of 1934 be reviewed under this section less frequently than once every 3 years.

SEC. 409. REAL TIME ISSUER DISCLOSURES.

Section 13 of the Securities Exchange Act of 1934 (15 U.S.C. 78m), as amended by this Act, is amended by adding at the end the following:

"(l) REAL TIME ISSUER DISCLOSURES—Each issuer reporting under section 13(a) or 15(d) shall disclose to the public on a rapid and current basis such additional information concerning material changes in the financial condition or operations of the issuer, in plain English, which may include trend and qualitative information and graphic presentations, as the Commission determines, by rule, is necessary or useful for the protection of investors and in the public interest.".

TITLE IX — WHITE-COLLAR CRIME PENALTY ENHANCEMENTS

SEC. 906. CORPORATE RESPONSIBILITY FOR FINANCIAL REPORTS.

(a) IN GENERAL.-Chapter 63 of title 18, United States Code, is amended by inserting after section 1349, as created by this Act, the following:

"§ 1350. Failure of corporate officers to certify financial reports

(a) CERTIFICATION OF PERIODIC FINANCIAL REPORTS.—Each periodic report containing financial statements filed by an issuer with the Securities Exchange Commission pursuant to section 13(a) or 15(d) of the Securities Exchange Act of 1934 (15 U.S.C. 78m(a) or 78o(d)) shall be accompanied by a written statement by the chief executive officer and chief financial officer (or equivalent thereof) of the issuer.

"(b) CONTENT.—The statement required under subsection (a) shall certify that the periodic report containing the financial statements fully complies with the requirements of section 13(a) or 15(d) of the Securities Exchange Act pf 1934 (15 U.S.C. 78m or 78o(d)) and that information contained in the periodic report fairly presents, in all material respects, the financial condition and results of operations of the issuer.

"(c) CRIMINAL PENALTIES.—Whoever—

"(1) certifies any statement as set forth in subsections (a) and (b) of this section knowing that the periodic report accompanying the statement does not comport with all the requirements set forth in this section shall be fined not more than $1,000,000 or imprisoned not more than 10 years, or both; or

"(2) willfully certifies any statement as set forth in subsections (a) and (b) of this section knowing that the periodic report accompanying the statement does not comport with all the requirements set forth in this section shall be fined not more than $5,000,000, or imprisoned not more than 20 years, or both.".

(b) CLERICAL AMENDMENT—The table of sections at the beginning of chapter 63 of title 18, United States Code, is amended by adding at the end the following:

"1350. Failure of corporate officers to certify financial reports.".

J

The Impact of Sarbanes-Oxley on Foreign Private Issuers

Section	Provision	Effective Date	Applicability
201	Prohibited services.	Effective May 6, 2003. (Engagements existing on May 6, 2003 can be completed through May 6, 2004.)	Yes.
202	Pre-approval of audit and non-audit services.	Effective May 6, 2003.	Yes.
203	Audit partner rotation.	Effective May 6, 2003. (Service period starts for fiscal years beginning after the effective date, therefore for calendar year end company that is January 1, 2004.)	Yes.
204	Reporting certain items to the audit committee.	Effective May 6, 2003.	Yes.
206	Prohibition on audit services when audit firm previously employed senior executive.	Effective May 6, 2003.	Yes.

Section	Provision	Effective Date	Applicability
301	Independence of audit committee members. Direct responsibility for appointing/compensating/retaining/overseeing work of the independent auditor. Establish procedures for receipt, retention, and treatment of complaints relating to accounting, auditing and internal control matters.	July 31, 2005.	Yes, with accommodations.
	Authority to engage advisors, and to be given appropriate funding for same, as determined by the audit committee. Disclosure of fees for audit and non-audit services.	Years ending after December 15, 2003.	Yes.
302	Certification of periodic financial reports filed under Section 13(a) or 15(d) of the Securities Exchange Act of 1934.	August 29, 2002 except for certifications related to disclosure controls and procedures, which are effective for periods ending after August 29, 2002.	Yes. Applicable for annual reports on Form 20-F, 40-F and financial statements filed on Form 6-K.
303	Prohibition on officers of an issuer from improperly influencing an audit.	June 27, 2003.	Yes.
304	Forfeiture of certain bonuses and profits by CEO and CFO.	Upon enactment, although SEC may provide exemptions as deemed necessary and appropriate.	Yes.

Section	Provision	Effective Date	Applicability
306	Prohibition of insider trades during pension fund blackout periods.	January 26, 2003.	No exemption is provided for, although this would appear to apply to pension plans subject to ERISA.
401	Disclosure of off-balance sheet transactions in periodic reports.	Disclosure required in filings with the SEC that include financial statements for fiscal years ending on or after June 15, 2003.	Yes.
	Disclosures relating to pro-forma information in periodic reports or any other public disclosure, including news releases.	Disclosure required in filings with the SEC that include financial statements for fiscal years ending on or after December 15, 2003.	
402	Prohibition on loans to directors or officers.	Upon enactment.	Yes.
403	Disclosures of transactions involving management and principal stockholders.	June 30, 2003.	No exemption is provided, although foreign private issuers are exempt from the insider reporting provisions of Section 16 of the Securities Exchange Act of 1934.
404	Management assessment of internal control and auditor reporting.	Fiscal year ending on or after July 15, 2005.	Yes.
406	Code of ethics for senior financial officers.	Effective March 1, 2003 with new disclosures required in annual reports for fiscal years ending on or after July 15, 2003.	Yes.
407	Disclosure of audit committee financial expert.	Effective March 1, 2003 with disclosure required in annual reports for fiscal years ending on or after July 15, 2003.	Yes.

Section	Provision	Effective Date	Applicability
409	Real time disclosure of material changes in financial condition or operation.	Upon enactment.	Yes.
906	Certification of periodic financial reports filed under Section 13(a) or 15(d) of the Securities Exchange Act of 1934. Note: This provision amends the U.S. Code for penalties related to non-compliance with the certification requirements of the Act (see Section 302) but appears to be effective immediately versus 30 days from enactment.	Upon enactment.	Yes. Applicable for annual reports on Form 20-F, 40-F and financial statements filed on Form 6-K.

Deloitte Audit Committee Checklist for New Sarbanes-Oxley and NYSE and NASDAQ Listing Requirements

This checklist was compiled based on the incremental audit committee requirements set forth in the Sarbanes-Oxley Act of 2002 and the new corporate governance listing standards of the NYSE and NASDAQ. The latter were approved by the SEC on November 4, 2003. The italicized notations following each requirement indicate which *Sarbanes-Oxley Act* section or listing standards include and discuss that requirement. The middle column indicates the effectiveness/compliance timeframe for each requirement. Many of the new responsibilities require modification of the audit committee charter to reflect the new responsibility by the specified date, while other new requirements must be performed by the specified date. Unless noted that the charter requires modification by the specified date, the requirement must be performed or in place by the date specified.

This checklist is designed for the general SEC issuer; certain issuers, including investment companies, small business issuers, and foreign private issuers, are granted some exceptions or accommodations. Many of the items presented here are not applicable to voluntary filers.

Because many of the new NYSE requirements are common or emerging practices, NASDAQ-listed companies may want to consider implementing certain of those requirements. Similarly, NYSE companies may consider implementing the NASDAQ requirement relating to review and approval of related-party transactions. This checklist only includes duties that are required of the audit committee; it does not include duties that might commonly be assigned to the audit committee by the board outside of those required by rules and regulations (e.g., maintenance of a code of business conduct and ethics, interactions with internal audit, etc.).

Note: This checklist contains general information only and does not constitute, and should not be regarded as, legal or similar professional advice or service. This checklist is not a substitute for such professional advice or services, nor should it be used as a basis for any decision or action that may affect you or your business. Any such decision or action should be taken only upon the advice of a qualified professional advisor. This checklist was prepared based on information available as of March 1, 2004, and is subject to change as interpretive guidance is issued by the SEC, NYSE, or NASDAQ. Neither Deloitte & Touche LLP, Deloitte Touche Tohmatsu, nor any of their affiliates or related entities shall have any liability or responsibility to any person or entity with respect to the use of or reliance on this checklist. All companies should consult with legal counsel regarding the applicability and implementation of the various requirements presented.

REQUIREMENT	EFFECTIVENESS/COMPLIANCE TIMEFRAME	ACTIONS TO COMPLY[1]
General		
The audit committee comprises at least three directors, all of whom meet the independence requirements, including compensation-related provisions, of Sarbanes-Oxley and the applicable SRO rules.[2] *[Sarbanes-Oxley Act Section 301; NYSE Corporate Governance Rules 6 and 7(a) and (b); and NASDAQ Corporate Governance Rule 4350(d)(2)]*	**Sarbanes-Oxley, NYSE, and NASDAQ:** First annual shareholders' meeting occurring after January 15, 2004, but not later than October 31, 2004	
The audit committee has a formal, written charter that is reviewed annually and addresses the items required by applicable rules. *[NYSE Corporate Governance Rule 7(c) and NASDAQ Corporate Governance Rule 4350(d)(1)]*	**NYSE and NASDAQ:** First annual shareholders' meeting occurring after January 15, 2004, but not later than October 31, 2004; previous NYSE and NASDAQ charter requirements are still applicable to the extent they were not superseded by new listing standards	
Disclose whether at least one member of the audit committee qualifies as an "audit committee financial expert." If the board determines that at least one member fulfills the SEC criteria, disclose the name of that individual and whether he or she is independent of management. If the board determines there is no audit committee financial expert, disclose why the company does not have a qualifying individual. *[Sarbanes-Oxley Act Section 407]*	**Sarbanes-Oxley:** Disclosure is required for fiscal years ending on or after July 15, 2003	

(1) This column is intended to permit each company to document actions necessary to comply with the requirement or to enhance the benefits resulting from compliance with the requirement.

(2) If the board of a NASDAQ company determines, under an "exceptional and limited circumstances" test, that membership on the committee by a single individual who does not meet all of the independence standards is warranted, a limited exception to this rule may be available [NASDAQ *Corporate Governance Rule 4350(d)(2)(B)*]. For both the NYSE and NASDAQ, if an audit committee member is no longer independent for reasons outside the member's reasonable control, transition accommodations may be available [*Exchange Act Rule 10A-3(a)(3)*; NASDAQ *Corporate Governance Rule 4350(d)(4)*; NYSE *Corporate Governance Rule 6 and related commentary*].

REQUIREMENT	EFFECTIVENESS/COMPLIANCE TIMEFRAME	ACTIONS TO COMPLY[1]
General (cont'd)		
All audit committee members are able to read and understand financial statements at the time of their appointment (rather than within a reasonable period of time after appointment, as was the case under pre-existing requirements). *[NASDAQ Corporate Governance Rule 4350(d)(2)]*	**NASDAQ:** First annual shareholders' meeting occurring after January 15, 2004, but not later than October 31, 2004	
The audit committee meets periodically with management, the internal auditor, and the independent auditor in separate executive sessions. *[NYSE Corporate Governance Rule 7(c)(iii)(E)]*	**NYSE:** The audit committee charter must include this provision by the first annual shareholders' meeting occurring after January 15, 2004, but not later than October 31, 2004	
The audit committee has the authority to engage independent counsel and other advisors as it deems appropriate. *[Sarbanes-Oxley Act Section 301; NYSE Corporate Governance Rule 6; and NASDAQ Corporate Governance Rule 4350(d)(3)]*	**Sarbanes-Oxley, NYSE, and NASDAQ:** First annual shareholders' meeting occurring after January 15, 2004, but not later than October 31, 2004	
The audit committee has the authority to determine funding for the appropriate compensation of the independent auditors, other advisors that the audit committee chooses to engage, and ordinary administrative expenses of the audit committee. *[Sarbanes-Oxley Act Section 301; NYSE Corporate Governance Rule 6; and NASDAQ Corporate Governance Rule 4350(d)(3)]*	**Sarbanes-Oxley, NYSE, and NASDAQ:** First annual shareholders' meeting occurring after January 15, 2004, but not later than October 31, 2004	
The audit committee reports regularly to the board of directors. *[NYSE Corporate Governance Rule 7(c)(iii)(H)]*	**NYSE:** The audit committee charter must include this provision by the first annual shareholders' meeting occurring after January 15, 2004, but not later than October 31, 2004	

REQUIREMENT	EFFECTIVENESS/COMPLIANCE TIMEFRAME	ACTIONS TO COMPLY[1]
General (cont'd)		
An annual performance assessment of the audit committee is performed. *[NYSE Corporate Governance Rule 7(c)(ii)]*	**NYSE:** The audit committee charter must include this provision by the first annual shareholders' meeting occurring after January 15, 2004, but not later than October 31, 2004	
An internal audit function is maintained. [NYSE Corporate Governance Rule 7(d)]	**NYSE:** First annual shareholders' meeting occurring after January 15, 2004, but not later than October 31, 2004	
Independent Auditors		
The audit committee is directly responsible for the following regarding the independent auditor: • Appointment • Compensation • Retention • Oversight • Resolution of any disagreements with management regarding financial reporting. *[Sarbanes-Oxley Act Section 301; NYSE Corporate Governance Rule 6; and NASDAQ Corporate Governance Rule 4350(d)(3)]*	**Sarbanes-Oxley, NYSE, and NASDAQ:** First annual shareholders' meeting occurring after January 15, 2004, but not later than October 31, 2004	
The audit committee reviews with the independent auditor any audit problems or difficulties and management's response. Such reviews should include a discussion concerning the responsibilities, budget, and staffing of the internal audit function. *[NYSE Corporate Governance Rule 7(c)(iii)(F)]*	**NYSE:** The audit committee charter must include this provision by the first annual shareholders' meeting occurring after January 15, 2004, but not later than October 31, 2004	
The audit committee establishes clear hiring policies, compliant with governing laws and regulations, for employees or former employees of the independent auditor. *[NYSE Corporate Governance Rule 7(c)(iii)(G)]*	**NYSE:** The audit committee charter must include this provision by the first annual shareholders' meeting occurring after January 15, 2004, but not later than October 31, 2004	

REQUIREMENT	EFFECTIVENESS/COMPLIANCE TIMEFRAME	ACTIONS TO COMPLY[1]
Independent Auditors (cont'd)		
The audit committee holds timely discussions with the independent auditor regarding: • All critical accounting policies and practices • All alternative treatments of financial information within GAAP that have been discussed with management, ramifications of the use of such alternative disclosure and treatments, and the treatment preferred by the independent auditor • Other material written communications between the independent auditor and management, including, but not limited to, the management letter and schedule of unadjusted differences. *[Sarbanes-Oxley Act Section 204]*	**Sarbanes-Oxley:** Effective May 6, 2003	
To assist in evaluating the auditor's performance, qualification, and independence, the audit committee obtains and reviews (at least annually) a report by the independent auditor describing: • The firm's internal quality-control procedures • Any material issues raised by the most recent internal quality-control review or peer review, or by any inquiry or investigation conducted by governmental or professional authorities during the preceding five years with respect to independent audits carried out by the firm, and any steps taken to deal with any such issues	**NYSE:** The audit committee charter must include this provision by the first annual shareholders' meeting occurring after January 15, 2004, but not later than October 31, 2004	

REQUIREMENT	EFFECTIVENESS/COMPLIANCE TIMEFRAME	ACTIONS TO COMPLY[1]
Independent Auditors (cont'd)		
• To assess the auditor's independence, all relationships between the independent auditor and the company. The report is used in evaluating the independent auditor and the lead audit partner, in ensuring the regular rotation of the lead audit partner, and in considering rotation of the audit firm. *[NYSE Corporate Governance Rule 7(c)(iii)(A) and related commentary]*		
The audit committee (or the appropriate designated member(s) of the audit committee, whose decisions shall be presented to the full audit committee at its next scheduled session), pre-approves (which may be pursuant to pre-approval policies and procedures) all services provided by the independent auditor. *[Sarbanes-Oxley Act Section 202]*	**Sarbanes-Oxley:** Effective May 6, 2003	

REQUIREMENT	EFFECTIVENESS/COMPLIANCE TIMEFRAME	ACTIONS TO COMPLY[1]
Financial Reporting and Compliance		
The audit committee meets with management and the independent auditor to discuss the annual audited financial statements and quarterly financial statements, including the company's disclosures under "Management's Discussion and Analysis of Financial Condition and Results of Operations." *[NYSE Corporate Governance Rule 7(c)(iii)(B)]*	**NYSE:** The audit committee charter must include this provision by the first annual shareholders' meeting occurring after January 15, 2004, but not later than October 31, 2004	
The audit committee reviews and discusses with management all Section 302 and 906 certifications required by Sarbanes-Oxley.	The timing of effectiveness for certification requirements varied; all management certification requirements mandated by Sections 302 and 906 of the Sarbanes-Oxley Act are now effective	
The audit committee reviews management's report on internal control and the independent auditor's attestation on management's assertion as required by Section 404 of Sarbanes-Oxley.	The internal control reporting and attestation requirements of Section 404 are effective for fiscal years ending on or after June 15, 2004	
The audit committee reviews and discusses earnings press releases, including the type and presentation of information, paying particular attention to any pro forma or adjusted non-GAAP information, as well as financial information and earnings guidance provided to analysts and ratings agencies. *[NYSE Corporate Governance Rule 7(c)(iii)(C) and general commentary to Rule 7(c)]*	**NYSE:** The audit committee charter must include this provision by the first annual shareholders' meeting occurring after January 15, 2004, but not later than October 31, 2004	

REQUIREMENT	EFFECTIVENESS/COMPLIANCE TIMEFRAME	ACTIONS TO COMPLY[1]
Financial Reporting Processes, Accounting Policies, and Internal Control Structure		
The audit committee reviews major issues regarding accounting principles and the presentation of financial statements, including any significant changes in the company's selection or application of accounting principles, major issues regarding the adequacy of the company's internal controls, and any special audit steps adopted in light of material control deficiencies. *[General commentary to NYSE Corporate Governance Rule 7(c)]*	**NYSE:** The audit committee charter must include this provision by the first annual shareholders' meeting occurring after January 15, 2004, but not later than October 31, 2004	
The audit committee reviews analyses prepared by management and/or the independent auditor setting forth significant financial reporting issues and judgments made in connection with the preparation of the financial statements, including analyses of the effects of alternative GAAP methods on the financial statements. *[General commentary to NYSE Corporate Governance Rule 7(c)]*	**NYSE:** The audit committee charter must include this provision by the first annual shareholders' meeting occurring after January 15, 2004, but not later than October 31, 2004	
The audit committee reviews the effect of regulatory and accounting initiatives, as well as off-balance-sheet structures, on the financial statements. *[General commentary to NYSE Corporate Governance Rule 7(c)]*	**NYSE:** The audit committee charter must include this provision by the first annual shareholders' meeting occurring after January 15, 2004, but not later than October 31, 2004	

REQUIREMENT	EFFECTIVENESS/COMPLIANCE TIMEFRAME	ACTIONS TO COMPLY[1]
Financial Reporting Processes, Accounting Policies, and Internal Control Structure (cont'd)		
The audit committee, or another independent body of the board, reviews and approves all related-party transactions. *[NASDAQ Corporate Governance Rule 4350(h)]*	**NASDAQ:** Effective January 15, 2004	
The audit committee discusses the company's policies with respect to risk assessment and risk management, including appropriate guidelines and policies to govern the process, as well as the company's major financial risk exposures and the steps management has undertaken to control them. *[NYSE Corporate Governance Rule 7(c)(iii)(D)]*	**NYSE:** The audit committee charter must include this provision by the first annual shareholders' meeting occurring after January 15, 2004, but not later than October 31, 2004	
The audit committee establishes procedures for the receipt, retention, and treatment of complaints regarding accounting, internal accounting controls, or auditing matters. *[Sarbanes-Oxley Act Section 301; NYSE Corporate Governance Rule 6; and NASDAQ Corporate Governance Rule 4350(d)(3)]*	**Sarbanes-Oxley, NYSE, and NASDAQ:** First annual shareholders' meeting occurring after January 15, 2004, but not later than October 31, 2004	
The audit committee establishes procedures for confidential, anonymous submissions by company employees regarding questionable accounting or auditing matters. *[Sarbanes-Oxley Act Section 301; NYSE Corporate Governance Rule 6; and NASDAQ Corporate Governance Rule 4350(d)(3)]*	**Sarbanes-Oxley, NYSE, and NASDAQ:** First annual shareholders' meeting occurring after January 15, 2004, but not later than October 31, 2004	

L

Executive Summary of the CICA Discussion Brief "CEO and CFO Certification: Improving Transparency and Accountability"

Note: This summary is provided to help orient readers to the way in which this paper is organized. Readers are urged to read the full paper to obtain a fuller understanding of the themes discussed in the summary. The objective of this paper is to provide information that will assist CEOs and CFOs in better understanding the certification requirement, the objectives of transparency and accountability, and to enable them to develop their own practical approaches to the certification process. The information contained in this paper does not constitute legal advice. Before making any interpretation of the regulators' intent or the actions required of reporting issuers, readers should refer to MI 52-109.

Beginning in 2004, CEOs and CFOs of Canadian pubic companies are required to certify that the financial statements, together with other financial information included in their company's filings "fairly present" in all material respects the financial condition, results of operations and cash flows of the issuer.

The CEO and CFO must also certify that the annual filings do not contain any untrue statement of a material fact or omit to state a material fact required to be stated or that is necessary to make a statement not misleading. This statement is not limited to financial information — it applies to *everything* in the filings. Therefore, this paragraph in the certificate can have a much broader reach than the "fairly present" assessment.

The certification requirement is being introduced in phases so companies will need to develop multi-year implementation plans.

The certificates are prescribed and cannot be altered. Because separate personal certificates are required from the CEO *and* the CFO, both executives must lead and actively participate in the process. While CFOs may "quarterback" the process, the CEO must assume overall leadership, make his or her own assessment, and take responsibility for setting the proper "tone at the top."

Transparency and Accountability

The CPR Board[1] believes that two fundamental principles, which are central to the new regulations and to the functioning of our capital markets, can serve as a guide to CEOs and CFOs in the certification process:

- *Transparency* refers to the degree to which the information contained in the filings being certified by the CEO and CFO enables a reader to reliably assess and interpret the results of operations, financial condition and cash flows of the issuer. For the CEO and CFO certification, the "fairly present" assessment and the attestation that the filings do not contain any untrue statement of a material fact or omit to state a material fact is the mechanism used to achieve transparency.
- *Accountability* refers to the public acknowledgement by the CEO and CFO of their responsibility for the completeness, accuracy, timeliness and reliability of the information contained in the filings being certified.

The "Fairly Present" Assessment

In the first phase, which beings in 2004, CEOs and CFOs are required to assess whether the financial information contained in financial statements and MD&A in the interim and annual filings, as well as the annual information form in the annual filing, "fairly present" in all material respects the financial condition, results of operations and cash flows of the issuer. This "fairly present" assessment is a judgment of all the financial information contained in the filings and is not restricted to the financial statements' compliance with generally accepted accounting principles (GAAP). The assessment of "financial condition" (a different and more dynamic concept than "financial position" as reflected in the balance sheet) requires consideration of the company's ability to achieve results in the future.

[1] The Canadian Public Reporting Board of the Canadian Institute of Chartered Accountants.

Appendix L: *Executive Summary of the CICA Discussion Brief*
"CEO and CFO Certification: Improving Transparency and Accountability"

447

In making their "fairly present" assessment, CEOs and CFOs should consider the disclosure of the non-financial and non-GAAP financial performance measures that they consider critical to understanding their business, comparing their company's performance with others in their industry, and assessing the company's financial condition. It is also essential that any non-financial or non-GAAP financial performance measures be carefully explained and, where appropriate, reconciled to GAAP.

Importance of the MD&A

The MD&A is central to the "fairly present" assessment of results and financial condition. For example, if the CEO and CFO conclude that the financial statements do not by themselves "fairly present" the results of operations, they may decide to provide the appropriate disclosure in the MD&A so the two documents, together, constitute a fair presentation. Similarly, the assessment of financial condition may require enhanced disclosure in the MD&A. Therefore, CEOs and CFOs may need to reassess the way in which the MD&A is prepared and organized, and the nature of the disclosures provided in it.

Disclosure Controls and Procedures

In phase two, which begins with financial years ending on or after March 31, 2005, CEOs and CFOs will be required to certify that they have designed disclosure controls and procedures (or caused them to be designed under their supervision) to provide reasonable assurance that material information relating to the issuer and its consolidated subsidiaries, is made known to them. They will also be required to certify that they have evaluated the effectiveness of these disclosure controls and procedures as of the end of the period covered by the annual filings, and to disclose their conclusions of that evaluation in the annual MD&A.

Disclosure controls and procedures are those that cover all information required to be disclosed in the interim and annual filings as well as continuous disclosure and other reports required to be filed under provincial and territorial securities legislation or regulation. They also include disclosure policies, disclosure committees (where justified by a company's size and complexity) and procedures put in place to ensure that information is brought to management's attention in a timely fashion to enable management to decide if disclosure is required.

Internal Control Over Financial Reporting

Also in phase two, beginning with financial years ending on or after March 31, 2005, CEOs and CFOs will be required to certify that they have designed internal control over financial reporting, or caused it to be designed under their supervision. Under the certification requirement, internal control over financial reporting addresses the reliability of financial reporting and the preparation of financial statements in accordance with the issuer's GAAP. Unlike the certification for disclosure controls and procedures, CEOs and CFOs are not required to certify that they have evaluated the effectiveness of internal control over financial reporting. Nevertheless, such ongoing evaluations would be necessary to conclude on the accuracy and reliability of the financial statements and to identify any need for changes to internal control over financial reporting, which are required to be disclosed under the full certification.

A third phase is expected to require the provision of a formal report on the internal control over financial reporting. This requirement is not included in MI 52-109. However, the Canadian Securities Administrators (CSA) is studying the U.S. rules implementing Section 404 of the *Sarbanes-Oxley Act* and is reported to be developing a proposed instrument to require a report on management's assessment of an issuer's internal control over financial reporting. It is expected that this instrument will likely require some form of auditor attestation.

Supporting Processes

CEOs and CFOs will need to put supporting processes into place, appropriate to the size and complexity of their company, to give them the information and assurance they need to make the statements required in the certificates, and to provide appropriate documentation.

While not required, many larger companies are establishing sub-certification processes, whereby the direct reports to the CEO and CFO provide formal certifications to them on the completeness and accuracy of the financial information pertaining to their area of responsibility, and the effectiveness of disclosure controls and procedures and internal control over financial reporting.

The new requirements also present opportunities for companies to strengthen and align their risk management programs and to ensure that internal management responsibilities and accountability for financial reporting includes the leaders of business units as well as the finance function.

While supporting processes and documentation are important, the "fairly present" assessment of the financial information contained in the filings and the certification that the annual filings do not contain any untrue statement of a material fact or omit to state a material fact are separate and distinct exercises based on the personal knowledge and judgment of both the CEO and CFO. Meeting these requirements involves much more than just ensuring that subordinates complete a prescribed sub-certification process.

The Audit Committee and External Auditor

The CEO and CFO certification requirements are directed at management, and do not make reference to either the audit committee or the external auditor. However, given the audit committee's responsibility for reviewing the annual and interim financial statements, MD&A and earnings news releases, the audit committee will likely want reports from the CEO and CFO on their overall approach to the certification process, the issues that were raised, the results of the control evaluations and the conclusions that were reached. Similarly, the external auditor will likely want to understand the conclusions reached by the CEO and CFO and how the certification process, including the control design and evaluation activities, impacts their assessment of internal control and their audit approach.

Critical Success Factors

The CPR Board believes that companies should not approach the certification requirement as being yet another regulatory compliance exercise. Instead, they should view it as an opportunity to regularly assess and continually improve their processes for public disclosures, and control and risk management. In taking this approach, management can use the certification process to continually strengthen internal accountabilities and run their business better. By contrast, companies that take a mechanistic, compliance-type approach to meeting the certification requirements will not only fail to achieve these additional positive business benefits, but may also end up providing the CEO and CFO with a false sense of security.

How successfully a company achieves these objectives will depend on many factors, including:
- the quality of the leadership provided by the CEO and CFO
- the extent to which other senior operating executives are involved in the process, and
- the commitment to learning from experience, and striving for continual improvement.

CEO *and* CFO *Certification:*
The Required Certificates

Form 52-109F1 — Certification of Annual Filings

I, *<identify the certifying officer, the issuer, and his or her position at the issuer>*, certify that:

1. I have reviewed the annual filings (as this term is defined in Multilateral Instrument 52-109 *Certification of Disclosure in Issuers' Annual and Interim Filings*) of *‹identify issuer›* (the issuer) for the period ending *‹state the relevant date›*;
2. Based on my knowledge, the annual filings do not contain any untrue statement of a material fact or omit to state a material fact required to be stated or that is necessary to make a statement not misleading in light of the circumstances under which it was made, with respect to the period covered by the annual filings;
3. Based on my knowledge, the annual financial statements together with the other financial information included in the annual filings fairly present in all material respects the financial condition, results of operations and cash flows of the issuer, as of the date and for the periods presented in the annual filings;
4. The issuer's other certifying officers and I are responsible for establishing and maintaining disclosure controls and procedures and internal control over financial reporting for the issuer, and we have:
    a) designed such disclosure controls and procedures, or caused them to be designed under our supervision, to provide reasonable assurance that material information relating to the issuer, including its consolidated subsidiaries, is made known to us by others within those entities, particularly during the period in which the annual filings are being prepared;

b) designed such internal control over financial reporting, or caused it to be designed under our supervision, to provide reasonable assurance regarding the reliability of financial reporting and the preparation of financial statements for external purposes in accordance with the issuer's GAAP; and

c) evaluated the effectiveness of the issuer's disclosure controls and procedures as of the end of the period covered by the annual filings and have caused the issuer to disclose in the annual MD&A our conclusions about the effectiveness of the disclosure controls and procedures as of the end of the period covered by the annual filings based on such evaluation; and

5. I have caused the issuer to disclose in the annual MD&A any change in the issuer's internal control over financial reporting that occurred during the issuer's most recent interim period that has materially affected, or is reasonably likely to materially affect, the issuer's internal control over financial reporting.

Date: _____

_____[Signature] [Title]

Form 52-109FT1 — Certification of Annual Filings during Transition Period

I, *<identify the certifying officer, the issuer, and his or her position at the issuer>*, certify that:

1. I have reviewed the annual filings (as this term is defined in Multilateral Instrument 52-109 *Certification of Disclosure in Issuers' Annual and Interim Filings*) of ‹*identify issuer*› (the issuer) for the period ending ‹*state the relevant date*›;
2. Based on my knowledge, the annual filings do not contain any untrue statement of a material fact or omit to state a material fact required to be stated or that is necessary to make a statement not misleading in light of the circumstances under which it was made, with respect to the period covered by the annual filings; and
3. Based on my knowledge, the annual financial statements together with the other financial information included in the annual filings fairly present in all material respects the financial condition, results of operations and cash flows of the issuer, as of the date and for the periods presented in the annual filings;

Date:_____

_____[Signature] [Title]

Form 52-109F2 — Certification of Interim Filings

I, <*identify the certifying officer, the issuer, and his or her position at the issuer*>, certify that:

1. I have reviewed the interim filings (as this term is defined in Multilateral Instrument 52-109 *Certification of Disclosure in Issuers' Annual and Interim Filings*) of <*identify the issuer*> (the issuer) for the interim period ending <*state the relevant date*>;
2. Based on my knowledge, the interim filings do not contain any untrue statement of a material fact or omit to state a material fact required to be stated or that is necessary to make a statement not misleading in light of the circumstances under which it was made, with respect to the period covered by the interim filings;
3. Based on my knowledge, the interim financial statements together with the other financial information included in the interim filings fairly present in all material respects the financial condition, results of operations and cash flows of the issuer, as of the date and for the periods presented in the interim filings;
4. The issuer's other certifying officers and I are responsible for establishing and maintaining disclosure controls and procedures and internal control over financial reporting for the issuer, and we have:
   a) designed such disclosure controls and procedures, or caused them to be designed under our supervision, to provide reasonable assurance that material information relating to the issuer, including its consolidated subsidiaries, is made known to us by others within those entities, particularly during the period in which the interim filings are being prepared;
   b) designed such internal control over financial reporting, or caused it to be designed under our supervision, to provide reasonable assurance regarding the reliability of financial reporting and the preparation of financial statements for external purposes in accordance with the issuer's GAAP; and
   c) I have caused the issuer to disclose in the interim MD&A any change in the issuer's internal control over financial reporting that occurred during the issuer's most recent interim period that has materially affected, or is reasonably likely to materially affect, the issuer's internal control over financial reporting.

Date:_____

_____[Signature] [Title]

Form 52-109FT2 — Certification of Interim Filings during Transition Period

I, <identify the certifying officer, the issuer, and his or her position at the issuer>, certify that:

1. I have reviewed the interim filings (as this term is defined in Multilateral Instrument 52-109 *Certification of Disclosure in Issuers' Annual and Interim Filings*) of <identify the issuer> (the issuer) for the interim period ending <state the relevant date>;
2. Based on my knowledge, the interim filings do not contain any untrue statement of a material fact or omit to state a material fact required to be stated or that is necessary to make a statement not misleading in light of the circumstances under which it was made, with respect to the period covered by the interim filings; and
3. Based on my knowledge, the interim financial statements together with the other financial information included in the interim filings fairly present in all material respects the financial condition, results of operations and cash flows of the issuer, as of the date and for the periods presented in the interim filings.

Date:_____

_____[Signature] [Title]

Multilateral Instrument 52-109

Certification of Disclosure in Issuers' Annual and Interim Filings

Part 1 — Definitions and Application

1.1 Definitions — In this Instrument,

"AIF" has the meaning ascribed to it in NI 51-102;

"annual certificate" means the certificate required to be filed pursuant to Part 2;

"annual filings" means the issuer's AIF, if any, and annual financial statements and annual MD&A filed under provincial and territorial securities legislation for the most recently completed financial year, including for greater certainty all documents and information that are incorporated by reference in the AIF;

"annual financial statements" means the annual financial statements required to be filed under NI 51-102;

"disclosure controls and procedures" means controls and other procedures of an issuer that are designed to provide reasonable assurance that information required to be disclosed by the issuer in its annual filings, interim filings or other reports filed or submitted by it under provincial and territorial securities legislation is recorded, processed, summarized and reported within the time periods specified in the provincial and territorial securities legislation and include, without limitation, controls and procedures designed to ensure that information required to be disclosed by an issuer in its annual filings, interim filings or other reports filed or submitted under provincial and territorial securities legislation is accumulated and communicated to the issuer's management, including its chief executive officers and chief financial officers (or persons who perform similar functions to a chief executive officer or a chief financial officer), as appropriate to allow timely decisions regarding required disclosure;

"interim certificate" means the certificate required to be filed pursuant to Part 3;

"interim filings" means the issuer's interim financial statements and interim MD&A filed under provincial and territorial securities legislation for the most recently completed interim period;

"interim financial statements" means the interim financial statements required to be filed under NI 51-102;

"interim period" has the meaning ascribed to it in NI 51-102;

"internal control over financial reporting" means a process designed by, or under the supervision of, the issuer's chief executive officers and chief financial officers, or persons performing similar functions, and effected by the issuer's board of directors, management and other personnel, to provide reasonable assurance regarding the reliability of financial reporting and the preparation of financial statements for external purposes in accordance with the issuer's GAAP and includes those policies and procedures that:

a) pertain to the maintenance of records that in reasonable detail accurately and fairly reflect the transactions and dispositions of the assets of the issuer,

b) provide reasonable assurance that transactions are recorded as necessary to permit preparation of financial statements in accordance with the issuer's GAAP, and that receipts and expenditures of the issuer are being made only in accordance with authorizations of management and directors of the issuer, and

c) provide reasonable assurance regarding prevention or timely detection of unauthorized acquisition, use or disposition of the issuer's assets that could have a material effect on the annual financial statements or interim financial statements;

"investment fund" has the meaning ascribed to it in NI 51-102;

"issuer's GAAP" has the meaning ascribed to it in NI 52-107;

"MD&A" has the meaning ascribed to it in NI 51-102;

"NI 51-102" means National Instrument 51-102 *Continuous Disclosure Obligations*;

"NI 52-107" means National Instrument 52-107 *Acceptable Accounting Principles, Auditing Standards and Reporting Currency*;

"Sarbanes-Oxley Act" means the Sarbanes-Oxley Act of 2002, Pub.L. 107-204, 116 Stat. 745 (2002);

"SEDAR" means the computer system for the transmission, receipt, acceptance, review and dissemination of documents filed in electronic format known as the System for Electronic Document Analysis and Retrieval;

"subsidiary" has the meaning ascribed to it in Section 1590 of the CICA *Handbook*; and

"US GAAP" has the meaning ascribed to it in NI 52-107.

1.2 Application – This Instrument applies to all reporting issuers other than investment funds.

Part 2 — Certification of Annual Filings

2.1 Every issuer must file a separate annual certificate, in Form 52-109F1, in respect of and personally signed by each person who, at the time of filing the annual certificate:
1.   is a chief executive officer;
2.   is a chief financial officer; and
3.   in the case of an issuer that does not have a chief executive officer or chief financial officer, performs similar functions to a chief executive officer or a chief financial officer, as the case may be.

2.2 The annual certificates must be filed by the issuer separately but concurrently with the latest of the following:
1.   if it files an AIF, the filing of its AIF; and
2.   the filing of its annual financial statements and annual MD&A.

Part 3 — Certification of Interim Filings

3.1 Every issuer must file for each interim period a separate interim certificate, in Form 52-109F2, in respect of and personally signed by each person who, at the time of the filing of the interim certificate:
1.   is a chief executive officer;
2.   is a chief financial officer; and
3.   in the case of an issuer that does not have a chief executive officer or chief financial officer, performs similar functions to a chief executive officer or a chief financial officer, as the case may be.

3.2 The interim certificates must be filed by the issuer separately but concurrently with the filing of its interim filings.

Part 4 — Exemptions

4.1 Exemption for Issuers that Comply with U.S. Laws —

1) Subject to subsection (4), an issuer is exempt from Part 2 with respect to the most recently completed financial year if:

    a) the issuer is in compliance with U.S. federal securities laws implementing the annual report certification requirements in section 302(a) of the Sarbanes-Oxley Act; and

    b) the issuer's signed certificates relating to its annual report for its most recently completed financial year are filed through SEDAR as soon as reasonably practicable after they are filed with the SEC.

2) Subject to subsection (5), an issuer is exempt from Part 3 with respect to the most recently completed interim period if:

    a) the issuer is in compliance with U.S. federal securities laws implementing the quarterly report certification requirements in section 302(a) of the Sarbanes-Oxley Act; and

    b) the issuer's signed certificates relating to its quarterly report for its most recently completed quarter are filed through SEDAR as soon as reasonably practicable after they are filed with the SEC.

3) An issuer is exempt from Part 3 with respect to the most recently completed interim period if:

    a) the issuer furnishes to the SEC a current report on Form 6-K containing the issuer's quarterly financial statements and MD&A;

    b) the Form 6-K is accompanied by signed certificates that are furnished to the SEC in the same form required by U.S. federal securities laws implementing the quarterly report certification requirements in section 302(a) of the Sarbanes-Oxley Act; and

    c) the signed certificates relating to the quarterly report filed under cover of the Form 6-K are filed through SEDAR as soon as reasonably practicable after they are furnished to the SEC.

4) Notwithstanding subsection 4.1(1), Part 2 of this Instrument applies to an issuer with respect to the most recently completed financial year if the issuer files annual financial statements prepared in accordance with Canadian GAAP, unless the issuer files those statements with the SEC in compliance with U.S. federal securities laws implementing the annual report certification requirements in section 302(a) of the Sarbanes-Oxley Act.

5) Notwithstanding subsection 4.1(2), Part 3 of this Instrument applies to an issuer with respect to the most recently completed interim period if the issuer files interim financial statements prepared in accordance with Canadian GAAP, unless the

issuer files those statements with the SEC in compliance with U.S. federal securities laws implementing the quarterly report certification requirements in section 302(a) of the Sarbanes-Oxley Act.

4.2 Exemption for Foreign Issuers – An issuer is exempt from the requirements in this Instrument so long as it qualifies for the relief contemplated by, and is in compliance with the requirements and conditions set out in, sections 5.4 and 5.5 of National Instrument 71-102 *Continuous Disclosure and Other Exemptions Relating to Foreign Issuers.*

4.3 Exemption for Certain Exchangeable Security Issuers – An issuer is exempt from the requirements in this Instrument so long as it qualifies for the relief contemplated by, and is in compliance with the requirements and conditions set out in, section 13.3 of NI 51-102.

4.4 Exemption for Certain Credit Support Issuers – An issuer is exempt from the requirements in this Instrument so long as it qualifies for the relief contemplated by, and is in compliance with the requirements and conditions set out in, section 13.4 of NI 51-102.

4.5 General Exemption –
1) The regulator or securities regulatory authority may grant an exemption from this Instrument, in whole or in part, subject to such conditions or restrictions as may be imposed in the exemption.
2) Despite subsection (1), in Ontario only the regulator may grant such an exemption.

Part 5 — Effective Date and Transition

5.1 Effective Date — This Instrument comes into force on March 30, 2004.

5.2 Transition –
1) Annual Certificates —
   a) Subject to paragraph (1)(b), the provisions of this Instrument concerning annual certificates apply for financial years beginning on or after January 1, 2004.
   b) Notwithstanding Part 2 or paragraph (1)(a), an issuer may file annual certificates in Form 52-109FT1 in respect of any financial year ending on or before March 30, 2005.
2) Interim Certificates —
   a) Subject to paragraph (2)(b), the provisions of this Instrument concerning interim certificates apply for interim periods beginning on or after January 1, 2004.
   b) Notwithstanding Part 3 or paragraph (2)(a), an issuer may file interim certificates in Form 52-109FT2 in respect of any interim period that occurs prior to the end of the first financial year in respect of which the issuer is required to file an annual certificate in Form 52-109F1.

Companion Policy 52-109CP —

To Multilateral Instrument 52-109

Certification of Disclosure in Issuers'

Annual and Interim Filings

Part 1 — General

This Companion Policy provides information about how the provincial and territorial securities regulatory authorities interpret Multilateral Instrument 52-109, and should be read in conjunction with it.

Part 2 — Form and Filing of Certificates

The annual certificates and interim certificates must be filed in the exact language prescribed in Forms 52-109F1 and 52-109F2 (subject to Part 3 — Form of Certificates during Transition Period). Each certificate must be separately filed through SEDAR under the issuer's profile in the appropriate annual certificate or interim certificate filing type:

> Category of Filing — Continuous Disclosure
> Folder for Filing Type — General
>
> Filing Type — Annual Certificates
> Document Type:
> Form 52-109F1 — Certification of Annual Filings — CEO
> Form 52-109F1 — Certification of Annual Filings — CFO
> Form 52-109FT1 — Certification of Annual Filings — CEO
> Form 52-109FT1 — Certification of Annual Filings — CFO
>
> or

Filing Type — Interim Certificates
Document Type:
Form 52-109F2 — Certification of Interim Filings — CEO
Form 52-109F2 — Certification of Interim Filings — CFO
Form 52-109FT2 — Certification of Interim Filings — CEO
Form 52-109FT2 — Certification of Interim Filings — CFO

As indicated in Part 11, an issuer that is in compliance with U.S. federal securities laws imple-menting the certification requirements in section 302(a) of the Sarbanes-Oxley Act, may be able to rely upon the exemptions from the annual certificate and interim certificate require-ments under section 4.1. To avail itself of these exemptions, an issuer must file through SEDAR the certificates of the chief executive officer and chief financial officer that the issuer filed with SEC as exhibits to the annual or quarterly reports with respect to the relevant reporting period. These certificates should be filed in the appropriate filing type described above.

An issuer relying on the exemptions in section 4.1 of the Instrument need not file the paper copies of the signed certificates that it filed with, or furnished to, the SEC.

Part 3 — Certificates during Transition Period

Section 5.2 provides for a transition period for the filing of both annual certificates and interim certificates.

Pursuant to section 2.1, an issuer is required to file its annual certificates in Form 52-109F1. Under subsection 5.2(1)(b), however, an issuer may file annual certificates in Form 52-109FT1 in respect of any financial year ending on or before March 30, 2005. Form 52-109FT1 does not require the certifying officers to make the representations set out in paragraphs 4 and 5 of Form 52-109F1 regarding the design of disclosure controls and procedures and internal control over financial reporting, the evaluation of the effectiveness of disclosure controls and procedures and any changes in the issuer's internal control over financial reporting.

Pursuant to section 3.1, an issuer is required to file its interim certificates in Form 52-109F2. Under subsection 5.2(2)(b), however, an issuer may file interim certificates in Form 52-109FT2 in respect of any interim period that occurs prior to the end of the first financial year in respect of which the issuer is required to file an annual certificate in Form 52-109F1. The representations set out in paragraphs 4 and 5 of Form 52-109F1 will serve as the basis for the corresponding representations set out in paragraphs 4 and 5 of Form 52-109F2.

Upon completion of the transition period, issuers must file annual certificates and interim certificates in Forms 52-109F1 and 52-109F2, respectively, which will include the representations in paragraph 4 of these forms. For further clarification, we do not expect the representations in paragraph 4 to extend to the prior period comparative information included in the annual filings or interim filings if:

a) the prior period comparative information was previously the subject of certificates in Forms 52-109FT1 or 52-109FT2; or

b) the Instrument did not require an annual certificate or interim certificate in respect of the prior period to be filed.

For illustration purposes only, the table in Appendix A sets out the filing requirements for annual certificates and interim certificates of issuers with financial years beginning on the first day of a month.

Part 4 — Persons Performing Functions Similar to a Chief Executive Officer and Chief Financial Officer

Where an issuer does not have a chief executive officer or chief financial officer, each person who performs similar functions to a chief executive officer or chief financial officer must certify the annual filings and interim filings. It is left to the issuer's discretion to determine who those persons are. In the case of an income trust reporting issuer (as described in proposed National Policy 41-201 *Income Trusts and Other Indirect Offerings*) where executive management resides at the underlying business entity level or in an external management company, we would generally consider the chief executive officer or chief financial officer of the underlying business entity or the external management company to be persons performing functions in respect of the income trust similar to a chief executive officer or chief financial officer. In the case of a limited partnership reporting issuer with no chief executive officer or chief financial officer, we would generally consider the chief executive officer or chief financial officer of its general partner to be persons performing functions in respect of the limited partnership reporting issuer similar to a chief executive officer or chief financial officer.

Part 5 — "New" Chief Executive Officers and Chief Financial Officers

Chief executive officers and chief financial officers (or persons performing functions similar to a chief executive officer or chief financial officer) holding such offices at the time that annual certificates and interim certificates are required to be filed are the persons who must sign those certificates. Certifying officers are required to file annual certificates and interim certificates in the specified form (without any amendment) and failure to do so will be a breach of the Instrument.

Pursuant to paragraphs 4(a) and (b) of Forms 52-109F1 and 52-109F2, the certifying officers are required to represent that they have designed (or caused to be designed under their supervision) disclosure controls and procedures and internal control over financial reporting. There may be situations where an issuer's disclosure controls and procedures and internal control over financial reporting have been designed and implemented prior to the certifying officers assuming their respective offices. We recognize that in these situations the certifying officers may have difficulty in representing that they have designed or caused to be designed these controls and procedures. In our view, where:

a)   disclosure controls and procedures and internal control over financial reporting have been designed and implemented prior to the certifying officers assuming their respective offices;

b)   the certifying officers have reviewed the existing controls and procedures upon assuming their respective offices; and

c)   the certifying officers have designed (or caused to be designed under their supervision) any modifications or enhancements to the existing controls and procedures determined to be necessary following their review,

the certifying officers will have designed (or caused to be designed under their supervision) these controls and procedures for the purposes of paragraphs 4(a) and (b) of Forms 52-109F1 and 52-109F2.

Part 6 — Internal Control over Financial Reporting and Disclosure Controls and Procedures

We believe that chief executive officers and chief financial officers should be required to certify that their issuers have adequate internal control over financial reporting and disclosure controls and procedures. We believe that this is an important factor in maintaining integrity in our capital markets and thereby enhancing investor confidence in our capital markets. The Instrument defines "disclosure controls and procedures" and "internal control over financial reporting". The Instrument does not, however, prescribe the degree of complexity or any specific policies or procedures that must make up those controls and procedures. This is intentional. In our view, these considerations are best left to management's judgement based on various factors that may be particular to an issuer, including its size, the nature of its business and the complexity of its operations.

While there is a substantial overlap between the definition of disclosure controls and procedures and internal control over financial reporting, there are both some elements of disclosure controls and procedures that are not subsumed within the definition of internal control over financial reporting and some elements of internal control over financial reporting that are not subsumed within the definition of disclosure controls and procedures. For example, disclosure controls and procedures may include those components of internal control over financial reporting that provide reasonable assurances that transactions are recorded as necessary to permit the preparation of financial statements in accordance with the issuer's GAAP. However, some issuers may design their disclosure controls and procedures so that certain components of internal control over financial reporting pertaining to the accurate recording of transactions and disposition of assets or to the safeguarding of assets are not included.

Part 7 — Evaluation of Effectiveness of Disclosure Controls and Procedures

Paragraph 4(c) of Form 52-109F1 requires the certifying officers to represent that they have evaluated the effectiveness of the issuer's disclosure controls and procedures and have caused the issuer to disclose in the annual MD&A their conclusions about the effectiveness of the disclosure controls and procedures based on such evaluation. The Instrument does not specify the contents of the certifying officers' report on its evaluation of disclosure controls and procedures; however, given that disclosure controls and procedures should be designed to provide, at a minimum, reasonable assurance of achieving their objectives, the report should set forth, at a minimum, the conclusions of the certifying officers as to whether the controls and procedures are, in fact, effective at the "reasonable assurance" level.

Part 8 — Fair Presentation

Pursuant to the third paragraph in each of the annual certificates and interim certificates, the chief executive officer and chief financial officer must each certify that their issuer's financial statements and other financial information "fairly present" the financial condition of the issuer for the relevant time period. Those representations are not qualified by the phrase "in accordance with generally accepted accounting principles" which Canadian auditors typically include in their financial statement audit reports. This qualification has been specifically excluded from the Instrument to prevent management from relying entirely upon compliance with the issuer's GAAP in this representation, particularly where the issuer's GAAP financial statements may not reflect the financial condition of an issuer (since the issuer's GAAP does not always define all the components of an overall fair presentation).

The Instrument requires the certifying officers to certify that the financial statements (including prior period comparative financial information) *and the other financial information* included in the annual filings and interim filings fairly present the issuer's financial condition, results of operation and cash flows. The certification statement regarding the fair presentation of financial statements and other information is not limited to a representation that the financial statements and other financial information have been presented in accordance with the issuer's GAAP. We believe that this is appropriate as the certification is intended to provide assurances that the financial information disclosed in the annual filings and interim filings, viewed in their entirety, meets a standard of overall material accuracy and completeness that is broader than financial reporting requirements under GAAP. As a result, issuers are not entitled to limit the representation to Canadian GAAP, US GAAP or any other source of generally accepted accounting principles.

We do not believe that a formal definition of fair presentation is appropriate as it encompasses a number of qualitative and quantitative factors that may not be applicable to all issuers. In our view, fair presentation includes but is not necessarily limited to:
- selection of appropriate accounting policies
- proper application of appropriate accounting policies
- disclosure of financial information that is informative and reasonably reflects the underlying transactions
- inclusion of additional disclosure necessary to provide investors with a materially accurate and complete picture of financial condition, results of operations and cash flows.

The concept of fair presentation as used in the annual certificates and interim certificates is not limited to compliance with the issuer's GAAP; however, it is not intended to permit an issuer to depart from the issuer's GAAP recognition and measurement principles in the preparation of its financial statements. In the event that an issuer is of the view that there are limitations to the issuer's GAAP based financial statements as an indicator of the issuer's financial condition, the issuer should provide additional disclosure in its MD&A necessary to provide a materially accurate and complete picture of the issuer's financial condition, results of operations and cash flows.

For additional commentary on what constitutes fair presentation we refer you to case law in this area. The leading U.S. case in this area is U.S. *v. Simon* (425 F.2d 796); the leading Canadian case in this area is the B.C. Court of Appeal decision in *Kripps v. Touche Ross and Co.* [1997] B.C.J. No. 968.

Part 9 — Financial Condition

Pursuant to the third paragraph in each of the annual certificates and interim certificates, the chief executive officer and chief financial officer must each certify that their issuer's financial statements fairly present the financial condition of the issuer for the relevant time period. The Instrument does not formally define financial condition. The term "financial condition" in the annual certificates and interim certificates is intended to be used in the same manner as the term "financial condition" is used in The Canadian Institute of Chartered Accountants' MD&A Guidelines and NI 51-102. In our view, financial condition encompasses a number of qualitative and quantitative factors which would be difficult to enumerate in a comprehensive list applicable to all issuers. Financial condition of an issuer includes, without limitation, considerations such as:

- liquidity
- solvency
- capital resources
- overall financial health of the issuer's business
- current and future considerations, events, risks or uncertainties that might impact the financial health of the issuer's business.

Part 10 — Consolidation

Issuers are required to prepare their financial statements on a consolidated basis under the issuer's GAAP. As a result the representations in paragraphs 2 and 3 of the certification will extend to consolidated financial statements. In addition, when the certifying officers provide these two representations, we expect that these representations will indicate that their issuers' disclosure controls and procedures provide reasonable assurance that material information relating to their issuers *and their consolidated subsidiaries* is made known to them.

We are of the view that regardless of the level of control that an issuer has over a consolidated subsidiary, management of the issuer has an obligation to present consolidated disclosure that includes a fair presentation of the financial condition of the subsidiary. An issuer needs to maintain adequate internal control over financial reporting and disclosure controls and procedures to accomplish this. In the event that a chief executive officer or chief financial officer is not satisfied with his or her issuer's controls and procedures insofar as they relate to consolidated subsidiaries, the chief executive officer or chief financial officer should cause the issuer to disclose in its MD&A his or her concerns regarding such controls and procedures.

An issuer's financial results and MD&A may consolidate those of a subsidiary which is also a reporting issuer. In those circumstances, it is left to the business judgment of the certifying officers of the issuer to determine the level of due diligence required in respect of the consolidated subsidiary in order to provide the issuer's certification.

Part 11 — Exemptions

The exemptions in section 4.1 of the Instrument are based on our view that the investor confidence aims of the Instrument do not justify requiring issuers to comply with the certification requirements in the Instrument if such issuers already comply with substantially similar requirements in the U.S.

As a condition to being exempt from the annual certificate and interim certificate requirements under subsections 4.1(1) and (2) respectively, issuers must file through SEDAR the certificates of the chief executive officer and chief financial officer that they filed with the SEC in compliance with its rules implementing the certification requirements prescribed in section 302(a) of the Sarbanes-Oxley Act.

Pursuant to NI 52-107 certain Canadian issuers are able to satisfy their requirements to file financial statements prepared in accordance with Canadian GAAP by filing statements prepared in accordance with US GAAP. However, it is possible that some Canadian issuers may still continue to prepare two sets of financial statements and continue to file their Canadian GAAP statements in the applicable jurisdictions. In order to ensure that the Canadian GAAP financial statements are certified (pursuant to either the Sarbanes-Oxley Act or the Instrument) those issuers will not have recourse to the exemptions in subsections 4.1(1) and(2).

Part 12 — Liability for False Certification

An officer providing a false certification potentially could be subject to quasi-criminal, administrative or civil proceedings under securities law.

Officers providing a false certification could also potentially be subject to private actions for damages either at common law or, in Québec, under civil law, or under the *Securities Act* (Ontario) when amendments which create statutory civil liability for misrepresentations in continuous disclosure are proclaimed in force. The liability standard applicable to a document required to be filed with the Ontario Securities Commission, including an annual certificate or interim certificate, will depend on whether the document is a "core" document as defined under Part XXIII.1 of the *Securities Act* (Ontario). Annual certificates and interim certificates are currently not included in the definition of "core document" but would be caught by the definition of "document".

In any action commenced under Part XXIII.1 of the *Securities Act* (Ontario) a court has the discretion to treat multiple misrepresentations having common subject matter or content as a single misrepresentation. This provision could permit a court in appropriate cases to treat a misrepresentation in an issuer's financial statements and a misrepresentation made by an officer in an annual certificate or interim certificate that relate to the underlying financial statements as a single misrepresentation.

APPENDIX A —
ANNUAL CERTIFICATE AND INTERIM
CERTIFICATE FILING REQUIREMENTS

For illustration purposes only, the following table sets out the filing requirements for annual certificates and interim certificates for issuers with financial years beginning on the first day of a month.

Financial Year Beginning On	Financial Period	Annual Certificate Required	Interim Certificate Required	Form of Certificate
January 1 (i.e. year end of December 31)	Financial year January 1, 2003 to December 31, 2003	No	Not Applicable	The Instrument does not apply to financial years beginning before January 1, 2004.
	Interim period January 1, 2004 to March 31, 2004	Not Applicable	Yes	"Bare" Interim Certificate[2]
	Interim period April 1, 2004 to June 30, 2004	Not Applicable	Yes	"Bare" Interim Certificate
	Interim period July 1, 2004 to September 30, 2004	Not Applicable	Yes	"Bare" Interim Certificate
	Financial year January 1, 2004 to December 31, 2004	Yes	Not Applicable	"Bare" Annual Certificate[3]
	Interim period January 1, 2005 to March 31, 2005	Not Applicable	Yes	"Bare" Interim Certificate (If an issuer voluntarily filed its annual certificate for financial year January 1, 2004 to December 31, 2004 as a "Full" Annual Certificate[4], the issuer should file its interim certificate as a "Full" Interim Certificate.[5])

[1] Where the form requirement specified is a "bare" annual certificate, issuers may voluntarily choose to file a "full" annual certificate. Where the form reqirement specified is a "bare" interim certificate, issuers may voluntarily choose to file a "full" interim certificate.

[2] For the purposes of Appendix A, "bare" interim certificate" means a certificate in Form 52-109FT2.

[3] Fro the purposes of Appendix A, "bare" annual certificate" means a certificate in Form 52-109FT1.

[4] For the purposes of Appendix A, "full" annual certificate" means a certificate in Form 52-109I.

[5] For the purposes of Appendix A, "full" interim certificate" means a certificate in Form 52-109F2.

Financial Year Beginning On	Financial Period	Annual Certificate Required	Interim Certificate Required	Form of Certificate
January 1 (i.e. year end of December 31)	Interim period April 1, 2005 to June 30, 2005	Not Applicable	Yes	"Bare" Interim Certificate (If an issuer voluntarily filed its annual certificate for financial year January 1, 2004 to December 31, 2004 as a "Full" Annual Certificate, the issuer should file its interim certificate as a "Full" Interim Certificate.)
	Interim period July 1, 2005 to September 30, 2005	Not Applicable	Yes	"Bare" Interim Certificate (If an issuer voluntarily filed its annual certificate for financial year January 1, 2004 to December 31, 2004 as a "Full" Annual Certificate, the issuer should file its interim certificate as a "Full" Interim Certificate.)
	Financial year January 1, 2005 to December 31, 2005 and each successive financial year	Yes	Not Applicable	"Full" Annual Certificate
	Interim period January 1, 2006 to March 31, 2006 and each successive interim period	Not Applicable	Yes	"Full" Interim Certificate

Financial Year Beginning On	Financial Period	Annual Certificate Required	Interim Certificate Required	Form of Certificate
February 1 (i.e. year end of January 31)	Financial year February 1, 2003 to January 31, 2004	No	Not Applicable	The Instrument does not apply to financial years beginning before January 1, 2004.
	Interim period February 1, 2004 to April 30, 2004	Not Applicable	Yes	"Bare" Interim Certificate
	Interim period May 1, 2004 to July 31, 2004	Not Applicable	Yes	"Bare" Interim Certificate
	Interim period August 1, 2004 to October 31, 2004	Not Applicable	Yes	"Bare" Interim Certificate
	Financial year February 1, 2004 to January 31, 2005	Yes	Not Applicable	"Bare" Annual Certificate
	Interim period February 1, 2005 to April 30, 2005	Not Applicable	Yes	"Bare" Interim Certificate (If an issuer voluntarily filed its annual certificate for financial year February 1, 2004 to January 31, 2005 as a "Full" Annual Certificate, the issuer should file its interim certificate as a "Full" Interim Certificate.)
	Interim period May 1, 2005 to July 31, 2005	Not Applicable	Yes	"Bare" Interim Certificate (If an issuer voluntarily filed its annual certificate for financial year February 1, 2004 to January 31, 2005 as a "Full" Annual Certificate, the issuer should file its interim certificate as a "Full" Interim Certificate.)
	Interim period August 1, 2005 to October 31, 2005	Not Applicable	Yes	"Bare" Interim Certificate (If an issuer voluntarily filed its annual certificate for financial year February 1, 2004 to January 31, 2005 as a "Full" Annual Certificate, the issuer should file its interim certificate as a "Full" Interim Certificate.)

Financial Year Beginning On	Financial Period	Annual Certificate Required	Interim Certificate Required	Form of Certificate
February 1 (i.e. year end of January 31)	Financial year February 1, 2005 to January 31, 2006 and each successive financial year	Yes	Not Applicable	"Full" Annual Certificate
	Interim period February 1, 2006 to April 30, 2006 and each successive interim period	Not Applicable	Yes	"Full" Interim Certificate

Financial Year Beginning On	Financial Period	Annual Certificate Required	Interim Certificate Required	Form of Certificate
March 1 (i.e. year end of February 28/29)	Interim period September 1, 2003 to November 30, 2003	Not applicable	No	The Instrument does not apply to interim periods beginning before January 1, 2004.
	Financial year March 1, 2003 to February 29, 2004	No	Not Applicable	The Instrument does not apply to financial years beginning before January 1, 2004.
	Interim period March 1, 2004 to May 31, 2004	Not Applicable	Yes	"Bare" Interim Certificate
	Interim period June 1, 2004 to August 31, 2004	Not Applicable	Yes	"Bare" Interim Certificate
	Interim period September 1, 2004 to November 30, 2004	Not Applicable	Yes	"Bare" Interim Certificate
	Financial year March 1, 2004 to February 28, 2005	Yes	Not Applicable	"Bare" Annual Certificate
	Interim period March 1, 2005 to May 31, 2005	Not Applicable	Yes	"Bare" Interim Certificate (If an issuer voluntarily filed its annual certificate for financial year March 1, 2004 to February 28, 2005 as a "Full" Annual Certificate, the issuer should file its interim certificate as a "Full" Interim Certificate.)
	Interim period June 1, 2005 to August 31, 2005	Not Applicable	Yes	"Bare" Interim Certificate (If an issuer voluntarily filed its annual certificate for financial year March 1, 2004 to February 28, 2005 as a "Full" Annual Certificate, the issuer should file its interim certificate as a "Full" Interim Certificate.)

Financial Year Beginning On	Financial Period	Annual Certificate Required	Interim Certificate Required	Form of Certificate
March 1 (i.e. year end of February 28/29)	Interim period September 1, 2005 to November 30, 2005	Not Applicable	Yes	"Bare" Interim Certificate (If an issuer voluntarily filed its annual certificate for financial year March 1, 2004 to February 28, 2005 as a "Full" Annual Certificate, the issuer should file its interim certificate as a "Full" Interim Certificate.)
	Financial year March 1, 2005 to February 28, 2006 and each successive financial year	Yes	Not Applicable	"Full" Annual Certificate
	Interim period March 1, 2006 to May 31, 2006 and each successive interim period	Not Applicable	Yes	"Full" Interim Certificate

Financial Year Beginning On	Financial Period	Annual Certificate Required	Interim Certificate Required	Form of Certificate
April 1 (i.e. year end of March 31)	Interim period October 1, 2003 to December 31, 2003	Not Applicable	No	The Instrument does not apply to interim periods beginning before January 1, 2004.
	Financial year April 1, 2003 to March 31, 2004	No	Not Applicable	The Instrument does not apply to financial years beginning before January 1, 2004.
	Interim period April 1, 2004 to June 30, 2004	Not Applicable	Yes	"Bare" Interim Certificate
	Interim period July 1, 2004 to September 30, 2004	Not Applicable	Yes	"Bare" Interim Certificate
	Interim period October 1, 2004 to December 31, 2004	Not Applicable	Yes	"Bare" Interim Certificate
	Financial year April 1, 2004 to March 31, 2005 and each successive financial year	Yes	Not Applicable	"Full" Annual Certificate
	Interim period April 1, 2005 to June 30, 2005 and each successive interim period	Not Applicable	Yes	"Full" Interim Certificate

Financial Year Beginning On	Financial Period	Annual Certificate Required	Interim Certificate Required	Form of Certificate
May 1 (i.e. year end of April 30)	Interim period November 1, 2003 to January 31, 2004	Not Applicable	No	The Instrument does not apply to interim periods beginning before January 1, 2004.
	Financial year May 1, 2003 to April 30, 2004	No	Not Applicable	The Instrument does not apply to financial years beginning before January 1, 2004.
	Interim period May 1, 2004 to July 31, 2004	Not Applicable	Yes	"Bare" Interim Certificate
	Interim period August 1, 2004 to October 31, 2004	Not Applicable	Yes	"Bare" Interim Certificate
	Interim period November 1, 2004 to January 31, 2005	Not Applicable	Yes	"Bare" Interim Certificate
	Financial year May 1, 2004 to April 30, 2005 and each successive financial year	Yes	Not Applicable	"Full" Annual Certificate
	Interim period May 1, 2005 to July 31, 2005 and each successive interim period	Not Applicable	Yes	"Full" Interim Certificate

Financial Year Beginning On	Financial Period	Annual Certificate Required	Interim Certificate Required	Form of Certificate
June 1 (i.e. year end of May 31)	Interim period September 1, 2003 to November 30, 2003	Not Applicable	No	The Instrument does not apply to interim periods beginning before January 1, 2004.
	Interim period December 1, 2003 to February 29, 2004	Not Applicable	No	The Instrument does not apply to interim periods beginning before January 1, 2004.
	Financial year June 1, 2003 to May 31, 2004	No	Not Applicable	The Instrument does not apply to financial years beginning before January 1, 2004.
	Interim period June 1, 2004 to August 31, 2004	Not Applicable	Yes	"Bare" Interim Certificate
	Interim period September 1, 2004 to November 30, 2004	Not Applicable	Yes	"Bare" Interim Certificate
	Interim period December 1, 2004 to February 28, 2005	Not Applicable	Yes	"Bare" Interim Certificate
	Financial year June 1, 2004 to May 31, 2005 and each successive financial year	Yes	Not Applicable	"Full" Annual Certificate
	Interim period June 1, 2005 to August 31, 2005 and each successive interim period	Not Applicable	Yes	"Full" Interim Certificate

Financial Year Beginning On	Financial Period	Annual Certificate Required	Interim Certificate Required	Form of Certificate
July 1 (i.e. year end of June 30)	Interim period October 1, 2003 to December 31, 2003	No	Not Applicable	The Instrument does not apply to interim periods beginning before January 1, 2004.
	Interim period January 1, 2004 to March 31, 2004	Not Applicable	Yes	"Bare" Interim Certificate
	Financial year July 1, 2003 to June 30, 2004	No	Not Applicable	The Instrument does not apply to financial years beginning before January 1, 2004.
	Interim period July 1, 2004 to September 30, 2004	Not Applicable	Yes	"Bare" Interim Certificate
	Interim period October 1, 2004 to December 31, 2004	Not Applicable	Yes	"Bare" Interim Certificate
	Interim period January 1, 2005 to March 31, 2005	Not Applicable	Yes	"Bare" Interim Certificate
	Financial year July 1, 2004 to June 30, 2005 and each successive financial year	Yes	Not Applicable	"Full" Annual Certificate
	Interim period July 1, 2005 to September 30, 2005 and each successive interim period	Not Applicable	Yes	"Full" Interim Certificate

Financial Year Beginning On	Financial Period	Annual Certificate Required	Interim Certificate Required	Form of Certificate
August 1 (i.e. year end of July 31)	Interim period November 1, 2003 to January 31, 2004	Not Applicable	No	The Instrument does not apply to interim periods beginning before January 1, 2004.
	Interim period February 1, 2004 to April 30, 2004	Not Applicable	Yes	"Bare" Interim Certificate
	Financial year August 1, 2003 to July 31, 2004	No	Not Applicable	The Instrument does not apply to financial years beginning before January 1, 2004.
	Interim period August 1, 2004 to October 31, 2004	Not Applicable	Yes	"Bare" Interim Certificate
	Interim period November 1, 2004 to January 31, 2005	Not Applicable	Yes	"Bare" Interim Certificate
	Interim period February 1, 2005 to April 30, 2005	Not Applicable	Yes	"Bare" Interim Certificate
	Financial year August 1, 2004 to July 31, 2005 and each successive financial year	Yes	Not Applicable	"Full" Annual Certificate
	Interim period August 1, 2005 to October 31, 2005 and each successive interim period	Not Applicable	Yes	"Full" Interim Certificate

Financial Year Beginning On	Financial Period	Annual Certificate Required	Interim Certificate Required	Form of Certificate
September 1 (i.e. year end of August 31)	Interim period September 1, 2003 to November 30, 2003	Not Applicable	No	The Instrument does not apply to interim periods beginning before January 1, 2004.
	Interim period December 1, 2003 to February 29, 2004	Not Applicable	No	The Instrument does not apply to interim periods beginning before January 1, 2004.
	Interim period March 1, 2004 to May 31, 2004	Not Applicable	Yes	"Bare" Interim Certificate
	Financial year September 1, 2003 to August 31, 2004	No	Not Applicable	The Instrument does not apply to financial years beginning before January 1, 2004.
	Interim period September 1, 2004 to November 30, 2004	Not Applicable	Yes	"Bare" Interim Certificate
	Interim period December 1, 2004 to February 28, 2005	Not Applicable	Yes	"Bare" Interim Certificate
	Interim period March 1, 2005 to May 31, 2005	Not Applicable	Yes	"Bare" Interim Certificate
	Financial year September 1, 2004 to August 31, 2005 and each successive financial year	Yes	Not Applicable	"Full" Annual Certificate
	Interim period September 1, 2005 to November 30, 2005 and each successive interim period	Not Applicable	Yes	"Full" Interim Certificate

Financial Year Beginning On	Financial Period	Annual Certificate Required	Interim Certificate Required	Form of Certificate
October 1 (i.e. year end of September 30)	Interim period October 1, 2003 to December 31, 2003	Not Applicable	No	The Instrument does not apply to interim periods beginning before January 1, 2004.
	Interim period January 1, 2004 to March 31, 2004	Not Applicable	Yes	"Bare" Interim Certificate
	Interim period April 1, 2004 to June 30, 2004	Not Applicable	Yes	"Bare" Interim Certificate
	Financial year October 1, 2003 to September 30, 2004	No	Not Applicable	The Instrument does not apply to financial years beginning before January 1, 2004.
	Interim period October 1, 2004 to December 31, 2004	Not Applicable	Yes	"Bare" Interim Certificate
	Interim period January 1, 2005 to March 31, 2005	Not Applicable	Yes	"Bare" Interim Certificate
	Interim period April 1, 2005 to June 30, 2005	Not Applicable	Yes	"Bare" Interim Certificate
	Financial year October 1, 2004 to September 30, 2005 and each successive financial year	Yes	Not Applicable	"Full" Annual Certificate
	Interim period October 1, 2005 to December 31, 2005 and each successive interim period	Not Applicable	Yes	"Full" Interim Certificate

Financial Year Beginning On	Financial Period	Annual Certificate Required	Interim Certificate Required	Form of Certificate
November 1 (i.e. year end of October 31)	Financial year November 1, 2002 to October 31, 2003	No	Not Applicable	The Instrument does not apply to financial years beginning before January 1, 2004.
	Interim period November 1, 2003 to January 31, 2004	Not Applicable	No	The Instrument does not apply to interim periods beginning before January 1, 2004.
	Interim period February 1, 2004 to April 30, 2004	Not Applicable	Yes	"Bare" Interim Certificate
	Interim period May 1, 2004 to July 31, 2004	Not Applicable	Yes	"Bare" Interim Certificate
	Financial year November 1, 2003 to October 31, 2004	No	Not Applicable	The Instrument does not apply to financial years beginning before January 1, 2004.
	Interim period November 1, 2004 to January 31, 2005	Not Applicable	Yes	"Bare" Interim Certificate
	Interim period February 1, 2005 to April 30, 2005	Not Applicable	Yes	"Bare" Interim Certificate
	Interim period May 1, 2005 to July 31, 2005	Not Applicable	Yes	"Bare" Interim Certificate
	Financial year November 1, 2004 to October 31, 2005 and each successive financial year	Yes	Not Applicable	"Full" Annual Certificate
	Interim period November 1, 2005 to January 31, 2006 and each successive interim period	Not Applicable	Yes	"Full" Interim Certificate

Financial Year Beginning On	Financial Period	Annual Certificate Required	Interim Certificate Required	Form of Certificate
December 1 (i.e. year end of November 30)	Financial year December 1, 2002 to November 30, 2003	No	Not Applicable	The Instrument does not apply to financial years beginning before January 1, 2004.
	Interim period December 1, 2003 to February 29, 2004	Not Applicable	No	The Instrument does not apply to interim periods beginning before January 1, 2004.
	Interim period March 1, 2004 to May 31, 2004	Not Applicable	Yes	"Bare" Interim Certificate
	Interim period June 1, 2004 to August 31, 2004	Not Applicable	Yes	"Bare" Interim Certificate
	Financial year December 1, 2003 to November 30, 2004	No	Not Applicable	The Instrument does not apply to financial years beginning before January 1, 2004.
	Interim period December 1, 2004 to February 28, 2005	Not Applicable	Yes	"Bare" Interim Certificate
	Interim period March 1, 2005 to May 31, 2005	Not Applicable	Yes	"Bare" Interim Certificate
	Interim period June 1, 2005 to August 31, 2005	Not Applicable	Yes	"Bare" Interim Certificate
	Financial year December 1, 2004 to November 30, 2005 and each successive financial year	Yes	Not Applicable	"Full" Annual Certificate
	Interim period December 1, 2005 to February 28, 2006 and each successive interim period	Not Applicable	Yes	"Full" Interim Certificate

National Policy 58-201

Corporate Governance Guidelines

PART 1 — PURPOSE AND APPLICATION

1.1 **Purpose of this Policy** – This Policy provides guidance on corporate governance practices which have been formulated to:
- achieve a balance between providing protection to investors and fostering fair and efficient capital markets and confidence in capital markets;
- be sensitive to the realities of the greater numbers of small companies and controlled companies in the Canadian corporate landscape;
- take into account the impact of corporate governance developments in the U.S. and around the world; and
- recognize that corporate governance is evolving.

The guidelines in this Policy are not intended to be prescriptive. We encourage issuers to consider the guidelines in developing their own corporate governance practices.

1.2 **Application** – This Policy applies to all reporting issuers, other than investment funds. Consequently, it applies to both corporate and non-corporate entities. Reference to a particular corporate characteristic, such as a board of directors (the board), includes any equivalent characteristic of a non-corporate entity. For example, in the case of a limited partnership, we recommend that a majority of the directors of the general partner should be independent of the limited partnership (including the general partner).

Income trust issuers should, in applying these guidelines, recognize that certain functions of a corporate issuer, its board and its management may be performed by any or all of the trustees, the board or management of a subsidiary of the trust, or the board, management or employees of a management company. For this purpose, references to "the issuer" refer to both the trust and any underlying entities, including the operating entity.

PART 2 — MEANING OF INDEPENDENCE

2.1 **Meaning of Independence** – For the purposes of this Policy, a director is independent if he or she would be independent for the purposes of National Instrument 58-101 *Disclosure of Corporate Governance Practices*.

PART 3 — CORPORATE GOVERNANCE GUIDELINES

Composition of the Board

3.1 The board should have a majority of independent directors.

3.2 The chair of the board should be an independent director. Where this is not appropriate, an independent director should be appointed to act as "lead director". However, either an independent chair or an independent lead director should act as the effective leader of the board and ensure that the board's agenda will enable it to successfully carry out its duties.

Meetings of Independent Directors

3.3 The independent directors should hold regularly scheduled meetings at which members of management are not in attendance.

Board Mandate

3.4 The board should adopt a written mandate in which it explicitly acknowledges responsibility for the stewardship of the issuer, including responsibility for:

  a) to the extent feasible, satisfying itself as to the integrity of the chief executive officer (the CEO) and other executive officers and that the CEO and other executive officers create a culture of integrity throughout the organization;

  b) adopting a strategic planning process and approving, on at least an annual basis, a strategic plan which takes into account, among other things, the opportunities and risks of the business;

  c) the identification of the principal risks of the issuer's business, and ensuring the implementation of appropriate systems to manage these risks;

  d) succession planning (including appointing, training and monitoring senior management);

  e) adopting a communication policy for the issuer;

  f) the issuer's internal control and management information systems; and

g) developing the issuer's approach to corporate governance, including developing a set of corporate governance principles and guidelines that are specifically applicable to the issuer.[1]

The written mandate of the board should also set out:

i) measures for receiving feedback from security holders (e.g., the board may wish to establish a process to permit security holders to directly contact the independent directors), and

ii) expectations and responsibilities of directors, including basic duties and responsibilities with respect to attendance at board meetings and advance review of meeting materials.

In developing an effective communication policy for the issuer, issuers should refer to the guidance set out in National Policy 51-201 *Disclosure Standards*.

For purposes of this Policy, "executive officer" has the same meaning as in National Instrument 51-102 *Continuous Disclosure Obligations*.

Position Descriptions

3.5 The board should develop clear position descriptions for the chair of the board and the chair of each board committee. In addition, the board, together with the CEO, should develop a clear position description for the CEO, which includes delineating management's responsibilities. The board should also develop or approve the corporate goals and objectives that the CEO is responsible for meeting.

Orientation and Continuing Education

3.6 The board should ensure that all new directors receive a comprehensive orientation. All new directors should fully understand the role of the board and its committees, as well as the contribution individual directors are expected to make (including, in particular, the commitment of time and energy that the issuer expects from its directors).[2] All new directors should also understand the nature and operation of the issuer's business.

3.7 The board should provide continuing education opportunities for all directors, so that individuals may maintain or enhance their skills and abilities as directors, as well as to ensure their knowledge and understanding of the issuer's business remains current.

---

[1] Issuers may consider appointing a corporate governance committee to consider these issues. A corporate governance committee should have a majority of independent directors, with the remaining members being "non-management" directors.

[2] Issuers should only recruit individuals who have sufficient time and energy to devote to the task.

Code of Business Conduct and Ethics

3.8 The board should adopt a written code of business conduct and ethics (a code). The code should be applicable to directors, officers and employees of the issuer. The code should constitute written standards that are reasonably designed to promote integrity and to deter wrongdoing. In particular, it should address the following issues:

a) conflicts of interest, including transactions and agreements in respect of which a director or executive officer has a material interest;

b) protection and proper use of corporate assets and opportunities;

c) confidentiality of corporate information;

d) fair dealing with the issuer's security holders, customers, suppliers, competitors and employees;

e) compliance with laws, rules and regulations; and

f) reporting of any illegal or unethical behavior.

3.9 The board should be responsible for monitoring compliance with the code. Any waivers from the code that are granted for the benefit of the issuer's directors or executive officers should be granted by the board (or a board committee) only.

Although issuers must exercise their own judgement in making materiality determinations, the Canadian securities regulatory authorities consider that conduct by a director or executive officer which constitutes a material departure from the code will likely constitute a "material change" within the meaning of National Instrument 51-102 *Continuous Disclosure Obligations*. National Instrument 51-102 requires every material change report to include a full description of the material change. Where a material departure from the code constitutes a material change to the issuer, we expect that the material change report will disclose, among other things:

- the date of the departure(s),
- the party(ies) involved in the departure(s),
- the reason why the board has or has not sanctioned the departure(s), and
- any measures the board has taken to address or remedy the departure(s).

Nomination of Directors

3.10 The board should appoint a nominating committee composed entirely of independent directors.

3.11 The nominating committee should have a written charter that clearly establishes the committee's purpose, responsibilities, member qualifications, member appointment and removal, structure and operations (including any authority to delegate to individual members and subcommittees), and manner of reporting to the board. In addition, the nominating committee should be given authority to engage and compensate any outside advisor that it determines to be necessary to permit it to carry out its duties. If an issuer is legally required by contract or otherwise to provide third parties with the right to nominate directors, the selection and nomination of those directors need not involve the approval of an independent nominating committee.

3.12 Prior to nominating or appointing individuals as directors, the board should adopt a process involving the following steps:

A) Consider what competencies and skills the board, as a whole, should possess. In doing so, the board should recognize that the particular competencies and skills required for one issuer may not be the same as those required for another.

B) Assess what competencies and skills each existing director possesses. It is unlikely that any one director will have all the competencies and skills required by the board. Instead, the board should be considered as a group, with each individual making his or her own contribution. Attention should also be paid to the personality and other qualities of each director, as these may ultimately determine the boardroom dynamic.

The board should also consider the appropriate size of the board, with a view to facilitating effective decision-making. In carrying out each of these functions, the board should consider the advice and input of the nominating committee.

3.13 The nominating committee should be responsible for identifying individuals qualified to become new board members and recommending to the board the new director nominees for the next annual meeting of shareholders.

3.14 In making its recommendations, the nominating committee should consider:

a) the competencies and skills that the board considers to be necessary for the board, as a whole, to possess;

b) the competencies and skills that the board considers each existing director to possess; and

c) the competencies and skills each new nominee will bring to the boardroom.

Compensation

3.15 The board should appoint a compensation committee composed entirely of independent directors.

3.16 The compensation committee should have a written charter that establishes the committee's purpose, responsibilities, member qualifications, member appointment and removal, structure and operations (including any authority to delegate to individual members or subcommittees), and the manner of reporting to the board. In addition, the compensation committee should be given authority to engage and compensate any outside advisor that it determines to be necessary to permit it to carry out its duties.

3.17 The compensation committee should be responsible for:

a) reviewing and approving corporate goals and objectives relevant to CEO compensation, evaluating the CEO's performance in light of those corporate goals and objectives, and determining (or making recommendations to the board with respect to) the CEO's compensation level based on this evaluation;

b) making recommendations to the board with respect to non-CEO officer and director compensation, incentive-compensation plans and equity-based plans; and

c) reviewing executive compensation disclosure before the issuer publicly discloses this information.

Regular Board Assessments

3.18 The board, its committees and each individual director should be regularly assessed regarding his, her or its effectiveness and contribution. An assessment should consider:

a) in the case of the board or a board committee, its mandate or charter, and

b) in the case of an individual director, the applicable position description(s), as well as the competencies and skills each individual director is expected to bring to the board.

National Instrument 58-101

Disclosure of Corporate Governance

Practices

PART 1 — DEFINITIONS AND APPLICATION

1.1 **Definitions** — In this Instrument,

"AIF" has the same meaning as in National Instrument 51-102 *Continuous Disclosure Obligations*;

"CEO" means a chief executive officer;

"code" means a code of business conduct and ethics;

"executive officer" has the same meaning as in National Instrument 51-102 *Continuous Disclosure Obligations*;

"marketplace" has the same meaning as in National Instrument 21-101 *Marketplace Operation*;

"MD&A" has the same meaning as in National Instrument 51-102 *Continuous Disclosure Obligations*;

"SEDAR" has the same meaning as in National Instrument 13-101 *System for Electronic Document Analysis and Retrieval* (SEDAR);

"U.S. marketplace" means an exchange registered as a 'national securities exchange' under section 6 of the 1934 Act, or the Nasdaq Stock Market;

"venture issuer" means an issuer that does not have any of its securities listed or quoted on any of the Toronto Stock Exchange, a U.S. marketplace, or a marketplace outside of Canada and the United States of America.

1.2 **Meaning of Independence —**
1) Except in British Columbia, a director is independent if he or she would be independent within the meaning of section 1.4 of Multilateral Instrument 52-110 *Audit Committees.*
2) In British Columbia, a director is independent
   a) unless a reasonable person with knowledge of all the relevant circumstances would conclude that the director is in fact not independent of management or of any significant shareholder, or
   b) if the issuer is a reporting issuer in a jurisdiction other than British Columbia, and the director is independent under subsection (1).

1.3 **Application —** This Instrument applies to a reporting issuer other than:
   a) an investment fund or issuer of asset-backed securities, as defined in National Instrument 51-102;
   b) a designated foreign issuer or SEC foreign issuer, as defined in National Instrument 71-102 *Continuous Disclosure and Other Exemptions Relating to Foreign Issuers;*
   c) a credit support issuer or exchangeable security issuer that is exempt under Part 13 of National Instrument 51-102; and
   d) an issuer that is a wholly-owned subsidiary of another entity, if:
      i) the issuer does not have equity securities (other than non-convertible, non-participating preferred securities) trading on a marketplace, and
      ii) the entity that owns the issuer is:
         A) subject to the requirements of this Instrument, or
         B) an issuer that (1) has securities listed or quoted on a U.S. marketplace and (2) is in compliance with the corporate governance requirements of that U.S. marketplace.

PART 2 — DISCLOSURE AND FILING REQUIREMENTS

2.1 **Required Disclosure —**
1) If management of an issuer, other than a venture issuer, solicits proxies from the security holders of the issuer for the purpose of electing directors to the issuer's board of directors, the issuer must include in its management information circular the disclosure required by Form 58-101F1.
2) An issuer, other than a venture issuer, that is not required to send a management information circular to its security holders must provide the disclosure required by Form 58-101F1 in its AIF.

2.2 **Venture Issuers —**
1) If management of a venture issuer solicits proxies from the security holders of the venture issuer for the purpose of electing directors to the issuer's board of directors, the venture issuer must include in its management information circular the disclosure required by Form 58-101 F2.
2) A venture issuer that is not required to send a management information circular to its security holders must provide the disclosure required by Form 58-101 F2 in its AIF or annual MD&A.

2.3 **Filing of Code —** If an issuer has adopted or amended a written code, the issuer must file a copy of the code or amendment on SEDAR no later than the date on which the issuer's next financial statements must be filed, unless a copy of the code or amendment has been previously filed.

PART 3 — EXEMPTIONS AND EFFECTIVE DATE

3.1 **Exemptions —**
1) The securities regulatory authority or regulator may grant an exemption from this rule, in whole or in part, subject to any conditions or restrictions imposed in the exemption.
2) Despite subsection (1), in Ontario, only the regulator may grant an exemption.

3.2 **Effective Date —** This Instrument comes into force on •.

FORM 58-101F1
CORPORATE GOVERNANCE DISCLOSURE

1. **Board of Directors —**
   a) Disclose the identity of directors who are independent.
   b) Disclose the identity of directors who are not independent, and describe the basis for that determination.
   c) Disclose whether or not a majority of directors are independent. If a majority of directors are not independent, describe what the board of directors (the board) does to facilitate its exercise of independent judgement in carrying out its responsibilities.
   d) If a director is presently a director of any other issuer that is a reporting issuer (or the equivalent) in a jurisdiction or a foreign jurisdiction, identify both the director and the other issuer.
   e) Disclose whether or not the independent directors hold regularly scheduled meetings at which members of management are not in attendance. If the independent directors hold such meetings, disclose the number of meetings held during the preceding 12 months. If the independent directors do not hold such meetings, describe what the board does to facilitate open and candid discussion among its independent directors.
   f) Disclose whether or not the chair of the board is an independent director. If the board has a chair or lead director who is an independent director, disclose the identity of the independent chair or lead director, and describe his or her role and responsibilities. If the board has neither a chair that is independent nor a lead director that is independent, describe what the board does to provide leadership for its independent directors.

2. **Board Mandate —** Disclose the text of the board's written mandate. If the board does not have a written mandate, describe how the board delineates its role and responsibilities.

3. **Position Descriptions —**
   a) Disclose whether or not the board has developed written position descriptions for the chair and the chair of each board committee. If the board has not developed written position descriptions for the chair and/or the chair of each board committee, briefly describe how the board delineates the role and responsibilities of each such position.

    b) Disclose whether or not the board and CEO have developed a written position description for the CEO. If the board and CEO have not developed such a position description, briefly describe how the board delineates the role and responsibilities of the CEO.

4. **Orientation and Continuing Education —**
   a) Briefly describe what measures the board takes to orient new directors regarding
      i) the role of the board, its committees and its directors, and
      ii) the nature and operation of the issuer's business.
   b) Briefly describe what measures, if any, the board takes to provide continuing education for its directors. If the board does not provide continuing education, describe how the board ensures that its directors maintain the skill and knowledge necessary for them to meet their obligations as directors.

5. **Ethical Business Conduct —**
   a) Disclose whether or not the board has adopted a written code for its directors, officers and employees. If the board has adopted a written code:
      i) disclose how an interested party may obtain a copy of the written code;
      ii) describe how the board monitors compliance with its code, or if the board does not monitor compliance, explain whether and how the board ensures compliance with its code; and
      iii) provide a cross-reference to any material change report(s) filed within the preceding 12 months that pertains to any conduct of a director or executive officer that constitutes a departure from the code.
   b) Describe any steps the board takes to ensure directors exercise independent judgement in considering transactions and agreements in respect of which a director or executive officer has a material interest.
   c) Describe any other steps the board takes to encourage and promote a culture of ethical business conduct.

6. **Nomination of Directors —**
   a) Describe the process by which the board identifies new candidates for board nomination.
   b) Disclose whether or not the board has a nominating committee composed entirely of independent directors. If the board does not have a nominating committee composed entirely of independent directors, describe what steps the board takes to encourage an objective nomination process.
   c) If the board has a nominating committee, describe the responsibilities, powers and operation of the nominating committee.

7. **Compensation —**
   a) Describe the process by which the board determines the compensation for your company's directors and officers.
   b) Disclose whether or not the board has a compensation committee composed entirely of independent directors. If the board does not have a compensation committee composed entirely of independent directors, describe what steps the board takes to ensure an objective process for determining such compensation.
   c) If the board has a compensation committee, describe the responsibilities, powers and operation of the compensation committee.

8. **Other Board Committees —** If the board has standing committees other than the audit, compensation and nominating committees, identify the committees and describe their function.

9. **Assessments —** Disclose whether or not the board, its committees and individual directors are regularly assessed with respect to their effectiveness and contribution. If assessments are regularly conducted, describe the process used for the assessments. If assessments are not regularly conducted, describe how the board satisfies itself that it, its committees, and individual directors are performing effectively.

INSTRUCTION:
1) References to corporate governance practices in this Form are to the guidelines included in National Policy 58-201 *Corporate Governance Guidelines*.
2) This Form applies to both corporate and non-corporate entities. Reference to a particular corporate characteristic, such as a board, includes any equivalent characteristic of a non-corporate entity.

Income trust issuers should provide disclosure in a manner which recognizes that certain functions of a corporate issuer, its board and its management may be performed by any or all of the trustees, the board or management of a subsidiary of the trust, or the board, management or employees of a management company. In the case of an income trust, references to "the issuer" refer to both the trust and any underlying entities, including the operating entity.

FORM 58-101F2
CORPORATE GOVERNANCE DISCLOSURE
(VENTURE ISSUERS)

1. **Board of Directors** — Disclose how the board of directors (the board) facilitates its exercise of independent supervision over management, including:
   i)   the identity of directors that are independent, and
   ii) the identity of directors who are not independent, and the basis for that determination.

2. **Directorships** — If a director is presently a director of any other issuer that is a reporting issuer (or the equivalent) in a jurisdiction or a foreign jurisdiction, identify both the director and the other issuer.

3. **Orientation and Continuing Education** — Describe what steps, if any, the board takes to orient new board members, and describe any measures the board takes to provide continuing education for directors.

4. **Ethical Business Conduct** — Describe what steps, if any, the board takes to encourage and promote a culture of ethical business conduct.

5. **Nomination of Directors** — Disclose what steps, if any, are taken to identify new candidates for board nomination, including:
   i)   who identifies new candidates, and
   ii) the process of identifying new candidates.

6. **Compensation** — Disclose what steps, if any, are taken to determine compensation for the directors and CEO, including:
   i)   who determines compensation, and
   ii) the process of determining compensation.

7. **Other Board Committees** — If the board has standing committees other than the audit, compensation and nominating committees, identify the committees and describe their function.

8. **Assessments** — Disclose whether or not the board, its committees and individual directors are regularly assessed with respect to their effectiveness and contributions. If assessments are regularly conducted, describe the process used for the assessments. If assessments are not regularly conducted, describe how the board satisfies itself that it, its committees, and individual directors are performing effectively.

INSTRUCTION:

1) This form applies to both corporate and non-corporate entities. Reference to a particular corporate characteristic, such as a board, includes any equivalent characteristic of a non-corporate entity.

   Income trust issuers should provide disclosure in a manner which recognizes that certain functions of a corporate issuer, its board and its management may be performed by any or all of the trustees, the board or management of a subsidiary of the trust, or the board, management or employees of a management company. In the case of an income trust, references to "the issuer" refer to both the trust and any underlying entities, including the operating entity.

2) The items referred to in section 3.4 of National Policy 58-201 *Corporate Governance Guidelines* may be considered in disclosure regarding your board made under Item 1 of this Form.

3) The issues referred to in section 3.8 of National Policy 58-201 *Corporate Governance Guidelines* may be considered in disclosure regarding ethical business conduct made under Item 4 of this Form.

4) Disclosure regarding board committees made under Item 7 of this Form may include the existence and summary content of any committee charter.

Amendments to Multilateral Instrument 52-110 Audit Committees

PART 1 — AMENDMENTS

1.1 **Meaning of Control —** Subsection 1.3(4) of Multilateral Instrument 52-110 *Audit Committees* (the "Instrument") is amended by deleting the words "be an affiliated entity of" and substituting the word "control".

1.2 **Meaning of Independence —**

(1) Section 1.4 of the Instrument is deleted and replaced by the following:

"**1.4 Meaning of Independence —**

(1) An audit committee member is independent if he or she has no direct or indirect material relationship with the issuer.

(2) For the purposes of subsection (1), a "material relationship" is a relationship which could, in the view of the issuer's board of directors, be reasonably expected to interfere with the exercise of a member's independent judgement.

(3) Despite subsection (2), the following individuals are considered to have a material relationship with an issuer:

(a) an individual who is, or has been within the last three years, an employee or executive officer of the issuer;

(b) an individual whose immediate family member is, or has been within the last three years, an executive officer of the issuer;

(c) an individual who:

(i) is a partner of a firm that is the issuer's internal or external auditor,

(ii) is an employee of that firm, or

(iii) was within the last three years a partner or employee of that firm and personally worked on the issuer's audit within that time;

(d) an individual whose spouse, minor child or stepchild, or child or stepchild who shares a home with the individual:

  (i) is a partner of a firm that is the issuer's internal or external auditor,

  (ii) is an employee of that firm and participates in its audit, assurance or tax compliance (but not tax planning) practice, or

  (iii) was within the last three years a partner or employee of that firm and personally worked on the issuer's audit within that time;

(e) an individual who, or whose immediate family member, is or has been within the last three years, an executive officer of an entity if any of the issuer's current executive officers serves or served at that same time on the entity's compensation committee; and

(f) an individual who received, or whose immediate family member who is employed as an executive officer of the issuer received, more than $75,000 in direct compensation from the issuer during any 12 month period within the last three years.

(4) Despite subsection (3), an individual will not be considered to have a material relationship with the issuer solely because he or she had a relationship identified in subsection (3) if that relationship ended before March 30, 2004.

(5) For the purposes of clauses (3)(c) and (3)(d), a partner does not include a fixed income partner whose interest in the firm that is the internal or external auditor is limited to the receipt of fixed amounts of compensation (including deferred compensation) for prior service with that firm if the compensation is not contingent in any way on continued service.

(6) For the purposes of clause (3)(f), direct compensation does not include:

(a) remuneration for acting as a member of the board of directors or of any board committee of the issuer, and

(b) the receipt of fixed amounts of compensation under a retirement plan (including deferred compensation) for prior service with the issuer if the compensation is not contingent in any way on continued service.

(7) Despite subsection (3), an individual will not be considered to have a material relationship with the issuer solely because the individual or his or her immediate family member:

(a) has previously acted as an interim chief executive officer of the issuer, or

(b) acts, or has previously acted, as a chair or vice-chair of the board of directors or of any board committee of the issuer on a part-time basis.

(8) For the purpose of section 1.4, an issuer includes a subsidiary entity of the issuer and a parent of the issuer.

1.5 Additional Independence Requirements —

(1) Despite any determination made under section 1.4, an individual who

  (a) has a relationship with the issuer pursuant to which the individual may accept, directly or indirectly, any consulting, advisory or other compensatory fee from the issuer or any subsidiary entity of the issuer, other than as remuneration for acting in his or her capacity as a member of the board of directors or any board committee, or as a part-time chair or vice-chair of the board or any board committee; or

  (b) is an affiliated entity of the issuer or any of its subsidiary entities, is considered to have a material relationship with the issuer.

(2) For the purposes of subsection (1), the indirect acceptance by an individual of any consulting, advisory or other compensatory fee includes acceptance of a fee by:

  (a) an individual's spouse, minor child or stepchild, or a child or stepchild who shares the individual's home; or

  (b) an entity in which such individual is a partner, member, an officer such as a managing director occupying a comparable position or executive officer, or occupies a similar position (except limited partners, non-managing members and those occupying similar positions who, in each case, have no active role in providing services to the entity) and which provides accounting, consulting, legal, investment banking or financial advisory services to the issuer or any subsidiary entity of the issuer.

(3) For the purposes of subsection (1), compensatory fees do not include the receipt of fixed amounts of compensation under a retirement plan (including deferred compensation) for prior service with the issuer if the compensation is not contingent in any way on continued service."

  2. Section 1.5 of the Instrument is re-numbered section 1.6.

1.3 **Controlled Companies —** Paragraph (a) of subsection 3.3(2) is amended by deleting the words "paragraph 1.4(3)(g)" and substituting the words "paragraph 1.5(1)(b)".

1.4 **Temporary Exemption for Limited and Exceptional Circumstances —** Paragraph (a) of section 3.6 is amended by deleting the words "paragraph 1.4(3)(f)(i) or 1.4(3)(g)" and substituting the words "subsection 1.5(1)".

1.5 **U.S. Listed Issuers —** Section 7.1 of the Instrument is amended by

  (i) deleting the word "a" as it appears before the words "issuers, other than foreign private issuers," and

  (ii) deleting the words "paragraph 5 of Form 52-110F1" and substituting the words "paragraph 7 of Form 52-110F1".

1.6 **Replacement of "person" with "individual" —**
(1) Paragraph 1.3(1)(b) is amended by deleting the words "or company" and substituting the words "is an individual who".
(2) Subsection 1.3(4) is amended by deleting the words "a person" and substituting the words "an individual" and by deleting the words "the person" and substituting the words "the individual".

1.7 **Form 52-110F1 —** Paragraph (c) of Item 3 of Form 52-110F1 is amended by deleting the word "persons" and substituting the word "individuals".

1.8 **Form 52-110F2 —**
(1) Form 52-110F2 is amended by re-numbering Items 3 through 7 as Items 4 through 8, respectively, and adding the following as a new Item 3:
"3. Relevant Education and Experience
Describe the education and experience of each audit committee member that is relevant to the performance of his or her responsibilities as an audit committee member and, in particular, disclose any education or experience that would provide the member with:
(a) an understanding of the accounting principles used by the issuer to prepare its financial statements;
(b) the ability to assess the general application of such accounting principles in connection with the accounting for estimates, accruals and reserves;
(c) experience preparing, auditing, analyzing or evaluating financial statements that present a breadth and level of complexity of accounting issues that are generally comparable to the breadth and complexity of issues that can reasonably be expected to be raised by the issuer's financial statements, or experience actively supervising one or more individuals engaged in such activities; and
(d) an understanding of internal controls and procedures for financial reporting."
(2) Form 52-110F2 is amended by deleting the words "this paragraph 5" in the instruction to Item 7 and substituting the words "this paragraph 7".

PART 2 — EFFECTIVE DATE

2.1 **Effective Date —** These amendments come into force on • .

Amendments to Companion Policy 52-110CP *to Multilateral Instrument* 52-110 Audit Committees

1.1 **Application to Non-Corporate Entities.** Section 1.2 of 52-110CP is deleted and replaced by the following:

"**1.2 Application to Non-Corporate Entities.** The Instrument applies to both corporate and non-corporate entities. Where the Instrument or this Policy refers to a particular corporate characteristic, such as a board of directors, the reference should be read to also include any equivalent characteristic of a non-corporate entity. For example, in the case of a limited partnership, the directors of the general partner who are independent of the limited partnership (including the general partner) should form an audit committee which fulfils these responsibilities.

Income trust issuers should apply the Instrument in a manner which recognizes that certain functions of a corporate issuer, its board and its management may be performed by any or all of the trustees, the board or management of a subsidiary of the trust, or the board, management or employees of a management company. For this purpose, references to "the issuer" refer to both the trust and any underlying entities, including the operating entity.

If the structure of an issuer will not permit it to comply with the Instrument, the issuer should seek exemptive relief."

1.2 **Meaning of Independence.** Part Three of 52-110CP is amended by deleting Part Three and replacing it with the following:

"PART THREE
INDEPENDENCE

3.1 Meaning of Independence. The Instrument generally requires every member of an audit committee to be independent. Subsection 1.4(1) of the Instrument defines independence to mean the absence of any direct or indirect material relationship between the director and the issuer. In our view, this may include a commercial, charitable, industrial, banking, consulting, legal, accounting or familial relationship, or any other relationship that the board considers to be material. Although shareholding alone may not interfere with the exercise of a director's independent judgement, we believe that other relationships between an issuer and a shareholder may constitute material relationships with the issuer, and should be considered by the board when determining a director's independence. However, only those relationships which could, in the view of the issuer's board of directors, be reasonably expected to interfere with the exercise of a member's independent judgement should be considered material relationships within the meaning of section 1.4.

Subsection 1.4(3) and section 1.5 of the Instrument describe those individuals that we believe have a relationship with an issuer that would reasonably be expected to interfere with the exercise of the individual's independent judgement. Consequently, these individuals are not considered independent for the purposes of the Instrument and are therefore precluded from serving on the issuer's audit committee. Directors and their counsel should therefore consider the nature of the relationships outlined in subsection 1.4(3) and section 1.5 as guidance in applying the general independence requirement set out in subsection 1.4(1).

3.2 Derivation of Definition. In the United States, listed issuers must comply with the audit committee requirements contained in SEC rules as well as the director independence and audit committee requirements of the applicable securities exchange or market. The definition of independence included in the Instrument has therefore been derived from both the applicable SEC rules and the corporate governance rules issued by the New York Stock Exchange. The portion of the definition of independence that parallels the NYSE rules is found in section 1.4 of the Instrument. Section 1.5 of the Instrument contains additional rules regarding audit committee member independence that were derived from the applicable SEC rules. To be independent for the purposes of the Instrument, a director must satisfy the requirements in both sections 1.4 and 1.5.

3.3 Safe Harbour. Subsection 1.3(1) of the Instrument provides, in part, that a person or company is an affiliated entity of another entity if the person or company controls the other entity. Subsection 1.3(4), however, provides that an individual will not be considered to control an issuer if the individual:

(a) owns, directly or indirectly, ten per cent or less of any class of voting equity securities of the issuer; and

(b) is not an executive officer of the issuer.

Subsection 1.3(4) is intended only to identify those individuals who are not considered to control an issuer. The provision is not intended to suggest that an individual who owns more than ten percent of an issuer's voting equity securities automatically controls an issuer. Instead, an individual who owns more than ten percent of an issuer's voting equity securities should examine all relevant facts and circumstances to determine if he or she controls the issuer and is therefore an affiliated entity within the meaning of subsection 1.3(1)."

1.3 **Replacement of "person" with "individual".** Subsection 4.2(2) of 52-110CP is amended by deleting the word "persons" and substituting the word "individuals", by deleting the words "A person" and substituting the words "An individual", and by deleting the word "person" and substituting the word "individual".

1.4 **Effective Date.** These amendments are effective on ● .

Examples of Fraud and Risk Factors

Many new regulations have been issued throughout North America dealing with isues of fraud and error, including CICA *Handbook* Section 5135, SAS 99, and the PCAOB's Auditing Standard No. 2. An outcome of these regulations is a better definition of the roles of management, the audit committee and the external auditor in terms of the responsibilities of each for detecting and preventing fraud.

Although management has the primary responsibility for an organization's internal control environment, the audit committee has oversight responsibilities for management's efforts to create a strong internal control environment. This includes an oversight responsibility for antifraud programs and control activities. As such, audit committees have a responsibility for ensuring that they have a clear understanding of the fraud risks facing the company. The material in this appendix, excerpted from the CICA *Handbook*, provides some examples of the fraud risk factors, which should be considered:

Examples of Fraud and Risk Factors[1]

The fraud risk factors identified in this Appendix are examples of such factors typically faced by auditors in a broad range of situations. Separately presented are examples relating to the two types of fraud relevant to the auditor's consideration — that is, fraudulent financial reporting and misappropriation of assets. For each of these types of fraud, the risk factors are further classified based on the three conditions generally present when material misstatements due to fraud occur: incentives / pressures, opportunities, and attitudes / rationalizations. Although the risk factors cover a broad range of situations, they are only examples and, accordingly, the auditor may identify additional or different risk factors. They do not necessarily indicate the existence of fraud. However, they are often present when fraud has occurred. Some of these factors will be present in entities in which specific conditions do not present a risk of material misstatement. Therefore, the auditor uses professional judgment when considering fraud risk factors individually or in combination and whether

---

[1] CICA *Handbook*, Section 5135 "The Auditors Responsibility to Consider Fraud and Error", Appendix A: Examples of Fraud and Risk Factors.

there are specific controls or circumstances that mitigate or eliminate the risk. Fraud risk factors are discussed in paragraphs 5135.047-.051. Also, the order of the examples of risk factors provided is not intended to reflect their relative importance or frequency of occurrence.

Risk Factors Relating to Misstatements Arising from Fraudulent Financial Reporting

The following are examples of risk factors relating to misstatements arising from fraudulent financial reporting:

Incentives/Pressures

a) Financial stability or profitability is threatened by economic, industry or entity operating conditions, such as (or as indicated by):
  i) high degree of competition or market saturation, accompanied by declining margins;
  ii) high vulnerability to rapid changes, such as changes in technology, product obsolescence or interest rates;
  iii) significant declines in customer demand and increasing business failures in either the industry or the overall economy;
  iv) operating losses making the threat of bankruptcy, foreclosure or hostile takeover imminent;
  v) recurring negative cash flows from operations or an inability to generate cash flows from operations while reporting earnings and earnings growth;
  vi) rapid growth or unusual profitability, especially compared to that of other companies in the same industry;
  vii) new accounting, statutory or regulatory requirements.
b) Excessive pressure exists for management to meet the requirements or expectations of third parties due to the following:
  i) profitability or trend level expectations of investment analysts, institutional investors, significant creditors or other external parties (particularly expectations that are unduly aggressive or unrealistic), including expectations created by management in, for example, overly optimistic press releases or annual report messages;
  ii) need to obtain additional debt or equity financing to stay competitive (including financing of major research and development or capital expenditures);
  iii) marginal ability to meet exchange listing requirements or debt repayment or other debt covenant requirements;
  iv) perceived or real adverse effects of reporting poor financial results on significant pending transactions, such as business combinations or contract awards.
c) Information available indicates that the personal financial situation of management or those charged with governance is threatened by the entity's financial performance arising from the following:
  i) significant financial interests in the entity;

    ii) significant portions of their compensation (for example, bonuses, stock options and earn-out arrangements) being contingent upon achieving aggressive targets for stock price, operating results, financial position or cash flow;

    iii) personal guarantees of debts of the entity.

d) There is excessive pressure on management or operating personnel to meet financial targets established by those charged with governance, including sales or profitability incentive goals.

Opportunities

a) The nature of the industry or the entity's operations provides opportunities to engage in fraudulent financial reporting that can arise from the following:

    i)   significant related party transactions not in the ordinary course of business or with related entities not audited or audited by another firm;

    ii) a strong financial presence, or ability to dominate a certain industry sector, that allows the entity to dictate terms or conditions to suppliers or customers, which may result in inappropriate or non-arm's length transactions;

    iii) assets, liabilities, revenues or expenses based on significant estimates that involve subjective judgments or uncertainties that are difficult to corroborate;

    iv) significant, unusual or highly complex transactions, especially those close to period end that pose difficult "substance over form" questions;

    v)   significant operations located or conducted across international borders in jurisdictions where differing business environments and cultures exist;

    vi) use of business intermediaries for which there appears to be no clear business justification;

    vii)significant bank accounts or subsidiary or branch operations in tax-haven jurisdictions for which there appears to be no clear business justification.

b) There is ineffective monitoring of management as a result of the following:

    i)   domination of management by a single person or small group (in a non-owner-managed business) without compensating controls;

    ii) ineffective oversight by those charged with governance over the financial reporting process and internal control.

c) There is a complex or unstable organizational structure, as evidenced by the following:

    i)   difficulty in determining the organization or individuals that have controlling interest in the entity;

    ii) overly complex organizational structure involving unusual legal entities or managerial lines of authority;

    iii) high turnover of senior management, legal counsel or those charged with governance.

d) Internal control components are deficient as a result of the following:
   i) inadequate monitoring of controls, including automated controls and controls over interim financial reporting (where external reporting is required);
   ii) high turnover rates or employment of ineffective accounting, internal audit or information technology staff;
   iii) ineffective accounting and information systems, including situations involving significant weaknesses in internal control.

Attitudes/Rationalizations

a) There is ineffective communication, implementation, support or enforcement by management of the entity's values or ethical standards, or communication of inappropriate values or ethical standards.

b) Non-financial management participates excessively in or is preoccupied with the selection of accounting policies or the determination of significant estimates.

c) There is a known history of violations of securities laws or other laws and regulations, or there are claims against the entity, its senior management or those charged with governance alleging fraud or violations of laws and regulations.

d) There is excessive interest by management in maintaining or increasing the entity's stock price or earnings trend.

e) There is a practice by management of committing to analysts, creditors and other third parties to achieve aggressive or unrealistic forecasts.

f) Management fails to correct known significant weaknesses in internal control on a timely basis.

g) There is an interest by management in employing inappropriate means to minimize reported earnings for tax-motivated reasons.

h) There is low morale among senior management.

i) The owner-manager makes no distinction between personal and business transactions.

j) There is a dispute between shareholders in a closely-held entity.

k) There are recurring attempts by management to justify marginal or inappropriate accounting on the basis of materiality.

l) The relationship between management and the current or predecessor auditor is strained, as exhibited by the following:
   i) frequent disputes with the current or predecessor auditor on accounting, auditing or reporting matters;
   ii) unreasonable demands on the auditor, such as unreasonable time constraints regarding the completion of the audit or the issuance of the auditor's report;
   iii) formal or informal restrictions on the auditor that inappropriately limit access to people or information or the ability to communicate effectively with those charged with governance;
   iv) domineering management behaviour in dealing with the auditor, especially involving attempts to influence the scope of the auditor's work or the selection or continuance of personnel assigned to or consulted on the audit engagement.

Risk Factors Relating to Misstatements Arising from Misappropriation of Assets

Risk factors that relate to misstatements arising from misappropriation of assets are also classified according to the three conditions generally present when fraud exists: incentives / pressures, opportunities, and attitudes / rationalization. Some of the risk factors related to misstatements arising from fraudulent financial reporting also may be present when misstatements arising from misappropriation of assets occur. For example, ineffective monitoring of management and weaknesses in internal control may be present when misstatements due to either fraudulent financial reporting or misappropriation of assets exist. The following are examples of risk factors related to misstatements arising from misappropriation of assets.

Incentives/Pressures

a) Personal financial obligations may create pressure on management or employees with access to cash or other assets susceptible to theft to misappropriate those assets.

b) Adverse relationships between the entity and employees with access to cash or other assets susceptible to theft may motivate those employees to misappropriate those assets. For example, adverse relationships may be created by the following:
   i) known or anticipated future employee layoffs;
   ii) recent or anticipated changes to employee compensation or benefit plans;
   iii) promotions, compensation or other rewards inconsistent with expectations.

Opportunities

a) Certain characteristics or circumstances may increase the susceptibility of assets to misappropriation. For example, opportunities to misappropriate assets increase when there are the following:
   i) large amounts of cash on hand or processed;
   ii) inventory items that are small in size, of high value or in high demand;
   iii) easily convertible assets, such as bearer bonds, diamonds or computer chips;
   iv) fixed assets which are small in size, marketable or lacking observable identification of ownership.

b) Inadequate internal control over assets may increase the susceptibility of misappropriation of those assets. For example, misappropriation of assets may occur because there is the following:
   i) inadequate segregation of duties or independent checks;
   ii) inadequate management oversight of employees responsible for assets (for example, inadequate supervision or monitoring of remote locations);
   iii) inadequate oversight of senior management expenditures, such as travel and other reimbursements;
   iv) inadequate job applicant screening of employees with access to assets;
   v) inadequate record keeping with respect to assets;
   vi) an inadequate system of authorization and approval of transactions (for example, in purchasing);

vii) inadequate physical safeguarding of cash, investments, inventory or fixed assets;
viii) a lack of complete and timely reconciliations of assets;
ix) a lack of timely and appropriate documentation of transactions, for example, credits for merchandise returns;
x) a lack of mandatory vacations for employees performing key control functions;
xi) inadequate management understanding of information technology, which enables information technology employees to perpetrate a misappropriation;
xii) inadequate access controls over automated records, including controls over and review of computer systems event logs.

Attitudes/Rationalizations

a) There is a disregard for the need for monitoring or reducing risks related to misappropriation of assets.
b) There is a disregard for internal control over misappropriation of assets by overriding existing controls or by failing to correct known internal control deficiencies.
c) Behaviour indicates displeasure or dissatisfaction with the entity or its treatment of the employee.
d) There are changes in behaviour or lifestyle that may indicate assets have been misappropriated.
e) There is tolerance of petty theft.